Prehistoric and Roman Sites in East Devon: The A30 Honiton to Exeter Improvement DBFO, 1996–9

by A.P. Fitzpatrick, C.A. Butterworth, and J. Grove

Volume 1: Prehistoric Sites

Prehistoric and Roman Sites in East Devon: The A30 Honiton to Exeter Improvement DBFO, 1996–9

by A.P. Fitzpatrick, C.A. Butterworth, and J. Grove

Volume 1: Prehistoric Sites

with contributions from

Michael J. Allen, Phil Andrews, Peter S. Bellamy, Alan J. Clapham, Hayley F. Clark, Nicholas Cooke, R.A. Davis, Brenda Dickinson, Rowena Gale, F.M. Griffith, P.A. Harding, M. Laidlaw, Emma Loader, Lorraine Mepham, J.M. Mills, Mark Robinson, Robert G. Scaife, Rachael Seager Smith, C.J. Stevens, R.S.O. Tomlin, David F. Williams and Sarah F. Wyles

Principal illustrator K.M. Nichols,
with Rob Goller

Wessex Archaeology Report No. 16
Wessex Archaeology 1999

Published 1999 by the Trust for Wessex Archaeology Ltd
Portway House, Old Sarum Park, Salisbury, England SP4 6EB

British Library Cataloguing in Publication Data
A catalogue record for this book is available from the British Library

ISBN 1–874350–31–0
ISSN 0965 5778

Series editor: Julie Gardiner

Produced by Wessex Archaeology
Printed by Redwood Books Ltd, Trowbridge

Front cover: The south-eastern arm of the enclosure ditch of the Iron Age settlement at Blackhorse under excavation, looking north towards the old A30 (photograph by Elaine A. Wakefield).

Back cover: (left to right) recording a post-hole at the Bronze Age settlement at Hayne Lane (photograph by Elaine A. Wakefield); air photograph with the Middle Bronze Age enclosure at Castle Hill visible in the foreground and road building works leading away to the east and crossing the River Otter. The old A30 is at the top right of the photograph (slide of 29 October 1997) by Bill Horner, Devon County Council. Copyright reserved; recording a gully at the Iron Age settlement of Blackhorse, looking south (photograph by Elaine A. Wakefield).

Contents

List of Figures

List of Tables

List of Plates

Contributors

Michael J. Allen
Wessex Archaeology, Portway House, Old Sarum Park, Salisbury SP4 6EB

Phil Andrews
Wessex Archaeology

Peter S. Bellamy
Terrain Archaeology, 10 Monmouth Street, Dorchester DT1 2DG

C.A. Butterworth
The Cottage, Great Durnford, Salisbury SP4 6AX

Alan J. Clapham
18 Thorpe Way, Cambridge CB5 8UB/ McDonald Institute, University of Cambridge, Downing Street, Cambridge CB2 3ER

Hayley F. Clark
Wessex Archaeology

Nicholas Cooke
Wessex Archaeology

R.A. Davis
Wessex Archaeology

Brenda Dickinson
Department of Classics, University of Leeds, Leeds LS2 9JT

A.P. Fitzpatrick
Wessex Archaeology

Rowena Gale
Folly Cottage, Chute Hadley, Andover SP11 9EB

Rob Goller
Wessex Archaeology

F.M. Griffith
Archaeology Group, Environment Department, Lucombe House, County Hall, Topsham Road, Exeter EX2 4QW

J.Grove
Wessex Archaeology

P.A. Harding
Wessex Archaeology

Moira Laidlaw
Wessex Archaeology

Emma Loader
Wessex Archaeology

Lorraine Mepham
Wessex Archaeology

J.M. Mills
Archaeological Finds Services, 1 Prospect Place, Dark Lane, Seavington St Mary, Ilminster TA19 0QW

K.M. Nichols
Wessex Archaeology

Mark Robinson
Oxford University Museum of Natural History, Parks Road, Oxford OX1 3PW

Robert G. Scaife
Palaeopol, 'Heyside', Dodpits Corner, Newbridge, Isle of Wight PO41 0YR/Department of Geography, University of Southampton. Southampton, SO17 1BJ

Rachael Seager Smith
Wessex Archaeology

C.J. Stevens
McDonald Institute, University of Cambridge, Downing Street, Cambridge CB2 3ER

R.S.O. Tomlin
Wolfson College, Oxford OX2 6UD

David F. Williams
Department of Archaeology, University of Southampton. Southampton, SO17 1BJ

Sarah F. Wyles
Wessex Archaeology

Abbreviations

ON   Object Number
PRN   Pottery Record Number
PH   Post-hole

Acknowledgments

The BBTA Joint Construction Venture on behalf of Connect A30/35 Limited, a Connect Group company consisting of BICC plc, Philip Holzmann AG and W.S. Atkins plc, commissioned the archaeological works reported upon here. The Joint Construction Venture comprises Balfour Beatty Civil Engineering Ltd, Tilbury Douglas Construction Ltd and Deutsche Asphalt GmbH. The work has been undertaken on behalf of the Highways Agency, through whose good offices additional funds were forthcoming to examine the Roman site at Pomeroy Wood whose existence was unknown before the building programme began.

The excavations reported here were undertaken over a period of 19 months from November 1996 to May 1998 and ran in parallel with a major building programme. The Watching Brief was concluded in September 1999. Particular thanks are due to Anne Brogden, Nigel Roberts and Ian Rowley of BBTA for their work in integrating the engineering and archaeological programmes. Dave Walker (Project director), Mike Agg, Geoff Tilling, Adrian Izod, Sean Jeffries, Chris Malone, Dave Neal, and Phil Williams also of BBTA helped in a variety of ways. Paul Luft the Connect A30/35 Ltd Construction Site Manager, Clive Park the Highways Agency Construction Manager, Mick Farey, Project Manager, and Cliff Stringer, both of Hyder Consulting, the Department's Agents for the Highways Agency, also provided invaluable assistance.

The archaeological works were monitored by: the Department's Agent's Agent, Peter Weddell of Exeter Archaeology (for Hyder Consulting); the Project Archaeologist, George Lambrick and his Deputy, Brian Durham, of Oxford Archaeological Unit (for Connect A30/35 Ltd and BBTA Construction Joint Venture) and by Frances Griffith, the Devon County Council County Archaeological Officer, and they have also commented critically on the drafts of this report. John Allen of the Royal Albert Memorial Museum, Exeter, and Bill Horner of Devon County Council have also provided assistance.

Many staff of Wessex Archaeology have been part of the project team. The principal Project Officers were Christine Butterworth and Jan Grove, while Rod Brook, Phil Harding, Paul Pearce and John Taylor also supervised excavations. The Project Supervisors during the fieldwork were Paul Cafe, Bob Davis, Dave Murdie, and Rob Symmons. The Watching Brief monitoring and associated fieldwork was carried out by Rod Brook, Richard Connolly, Bob Davis, Mark Dunkley, Dave Farwell, Andrew Fitzpatrick, Jan Grove, Guy Hopkinson, Moira Laidlaw, Jenni Morrison, Dave Murdie, Kate O'Farrell, Paul Pearce, Kevin Ritchie, Jim Stedman, and Kit Watson.

The fieldwork team also included Caroline Barker, Dom Barker, John Bendicks, Joanna Best, Tom Bradley-Lovekin, Fraser Brown, Gary Burgess, Gary Calland, Steve Campbell-Curtis, Angela Cave, Ben Chan, Katie Chapman, Alistair Clark, Hayley Clark, Niels Dagless, Dan Dodds, Marie-Claire Ferguson, Susan Fielding, Paul Gajos, Pippa Gilbert, Candice Hatherley, Barry Hennessy, Richard Hewitt, Phil Jefferson, Jane Liddle, Darren Limbert, John Martin, Paul Masser, Ben Middleton, Bill Moffat, Doug Murphy, Nick Plunkett, Jon Privett, Tobyn Rayner, Ailidh Ross, Stuart Selwood, Anthony Sibthorpe, Gemma Smith, Hilary Valler, Kim Watkins, Nick Wells, Gary Wickenden, Tom Williams, and Matt Wright.

The finds were processed and recorded by Rachel Every, Natasha Hutcheson and Richard May and the work on the finds was coordinated by Lorraine Mepham. The environmental samples were processed, assessed and extracted by Hayley Clark and Sarah F. Wyles and the work on the environmental materials was coordinated by Michael J. Allen.

Dr Gordon Cook of the Scottish Universities Research and Reactor Centre provided the radiocarbon determinations and Sarah Stanley, Wiltshire County Council Conservation Centre, Salisbury undertook the conservation of the objects of metal, shale and wood. The project was established by Carrie Hearne and Kit Watson and managed successively by Carrie Hearne, Dave Farwell, and from September 1997 by Andrew Fitzpatrick.

This report has been prepared in a timely manner and owes much to the spirit of the *Managment of Archaeological Projects II*. I am grateful to all the contributors and to Dr Julie Gardiner for her editorial work for helping make such a rapid publication possible. Barbara Hird produced the index promptly, and Karen E. Walker assisted with the reading of the proofs. A number of colleagues have helped by commenting on sections of the draft reports: Dr Denise Allen, Dr Alex Bayliss (English Heritage), Paul Bidwell (Arbeia Roman Fort and Museum), Professor Richard Bradley (University of Reading), Gill Campbell (English Heritage), Dr Rosamund Cleal (Alexander Keiller Museum), Dr Caroline Earwood, Professor Andrew Fleming (University College Lampeter, University of Wales), Neil Holbrook (Cotswold Archaeological Trust), Professor Lawrence Keppie (University of Glasgow), Dr Valerie Maxfield (University of Exeter), Henrietta Quinnell (University of Exeter), and Vanessa Straker (English Heritage).

With the exception of Figures 94–6, 145–6, 148–72, 174, and 177, which are by Rob Goller, all the line drawings are by Karen Nichols. Plates 2, 8, 13, 17 and 41 by Bill Horner, and 11 and 16 by Frances Griffith are reproduced by kind permission of Devon County Council, copyright reserved. Plates 1, 3–6, 23, 33, and 40 are by Elaine A. Wakefield of Wessex Archaeology.

A.P. Fitzpatrick
June 1999

Abstract

Eight excavations on sites of prehistoric and Roman date were undertaken during 1996–8 in advance of the A30 road improvement between Honiton and Exeter in Devon in south-west England.

At Castle Hill, two rectilinear enclosures of Neolithic date and part of a Middle Bronze Age farm and a co-axial field system were excavated. One of the Neolithic enclosures is a 'Long Mortuary Enclosure' and although the full extent of the other is not known it is likely to fall within the 'cursus continuum.' It is likely that there was Beaker period activity in the immediate vicinity of the sites. Only a part of the farm compound could be excavated but it yielded a relatively large assemblage of Trevisker/Deverel-Rimbury pottery and well-preserved charred plant remains.

At Patteson's Cross a single round-house dating to early in the Middle Bronze Age was found. After several centuries a small Middle Bronze Age enclosure containing a single round-house was built nearby. These buildings yielded few finds and little evidence for the cultivation of cereals. At Hayne Lane an enclosed farmstead of Middle/Late Bronze Age date was almost completely excavated. There appear to have been two main buildings, a larger, double-post ring round-house which was the dwelling, and a smaller, single-post ring round-house which may have been used for textile working and for food preparation. A number of three- and four-post structures were scattered around the compound and it is likely that some of these structures represent buildings for storing crops. The charred plant remains from this settlement were abundant.

At Langland Lane a single Middle Iron Age round-house, and a few field boundaries, which may be contemporaneous, were recorded. This site is very close to the Bronze Age round-houses at Patteson's Cross and again there was little evidence for the cultivation of crops. Part of a more extensive Mid–Late Iron Age settlement was examined at Long Range. The settlement was unenclosed and a number of round-houses and three- and four-post structures were recorded. Only a single round-house need have been in use at any time. An isolated Early Neolithic pit was also excavated at Long Range.

Occupation at Blackhorse started in the Early–Middle Iron Age and is represented by a single post-built round-house with which some field boundaries may be contemporary. Two later round-houses and some four-post buildings may belong to another phase of open settlement before a square enclosure was built. All of this enclosure was excavated showing that it contained only a single large round-house and a small number of four-post structures. The majority of the finds were found in the southern half of the site.

At Pomeroy Wood a 1st century AD military base with a possible outwork or annexe was superseded by an extensive Romano-British settlement occupied until the 4th century. The base has commanding views along the valley of the River Otter. Much of the base had been destroyed before the excavations recorded here – without any finds being reported – by the building of the existing A30 in the 1960s. Accordingly only a limited area of the interior of the base, which was occupied c. AD 65–85 was available for examination, but two sub-phases of occupation may be distinguished. On the basis of the waterlogged plant remains from one well it is possible that the garrison in one of the sub-phases was a cavalry unit.

It is likely that the Roman road between Dorchester and Exeter ran next to the base and that the succeeding civil settlement was a roadside one. In the 2nd century AD a series of round-houses was built on the site of the military base and a number of compounds laid out alongside the presumed course of the Roman road. In the 3rd century the focus of the settlement appears to have shifted away from the excavated area. A field system or series of compounds associated with the roadside settlement was also examined at Gittisham Forge 300 m to the east. It is possible that this previously unknown road-side settlement is *Moridunum*, which is mentioned in several Roman literary sources.

As a whole the excavations yielded large finds assemblages and well-preserved charred plant remains and charcoals. Two waterlogged Roman wells also provide valuable categories of data that do not survive at the sites of later prehistoric date. The environmental evidence shows the gradual clearance of the landscape but, in general, after the Middle Bronze Age there appears to have been little change in the crops cultivated over several millennia and oak woodland appears to have remained a significant part of the landscape.

The sites of later prehistoric date are concentrated in the valley of the River Otter, which appears to have been used intensively in this period. The sites are particularly important as they form the first major series of sites of this date to have been systematically excavated and sampled in east Devon. The series of 28 radiocarbon determinations from them also helps to provide a framework for the absolute chronology of the period in the area.

Résumé

Huit fouilles de sauvetage furent entreprises, entre 1996 et 1998, sur des sites datant de la préhistoire et de l'époque romaine avant le début des travaux d'amélioration de la route A30 entre Honiton et Exeter, dans le comté de Devon, dans le sud-ouest de l'Angleterre.

A Castle Hill, deux enceintes rectilignes datant du néolithique, une partie d'une ferme de l'âge du bronze moyen et des traces de champs coaxiales ont été mis au jour. Une des enceintes néolithiques est une 'longue enceinte mortuaire' et bien qu'on ne connaisse pas toute l'étendue de l'autre, il est probable qu'elle appartienne à la catégorie *cursus continuum*. Il est probable qu'il y ait eu des activités à proximité immédiate de ces sites pendant l'âge du bronze ancien. Seule une partie de l'ensemble de la ferme a pu être mise au jour mais elle a révélé une collection relativement importante de céramique du type Trevisker/Deverel-Rimbury et des restes végétaux carbonisés bien conservés.

A Patteson's Cross on a découvert une seule maison ronde datant du début de l'âge du bronze moyen. Plusieurs siècles plus tard on a construit près de là un petit enclos, aussi de l'âge du bronze moyen, contenant une seule maison ronde. Ces bâtiments ne recelaient que peu de trouvailles et n'ont révélé que peu de témoignages de culture de céréales. A Hayne Lane une ferme avec enclos datant du milieu ou de la fin de l'âge de bronze fut presque complètement fouillée. Elle semble avoir consisté en deux bâtiments principaux, le plus grand, une maison ronde à double rangée de poteaux servait d'habitation, et le plus petit, une maison ronde à une seule rangée de poteaux était peut-être utilisée pour le travail du textile ou la préparation de la nourriture. Un certain nombre de structures à trois et quatre poteaux étaient éparpillés de ci de là dans l'enceinte et il se peut que certaines de ces structures aient consisté en bâtiments de stockage pour les récoltes. Les restes végétaux carbonisés de cette occupation étaient abondants.

A Langland Lane, une seule maison ronde datant du milieu de l'âge du fer, et quelques délimitations de champs, peut-être contemporaines, ont été relevées. Ce site se trouve tout près des maisons rondes de l'âge du bronze de Patterson's Cross et, à nouveau, on n'a que peu de preuves de culture de céréales. Une partie d'une occupation plus importante datant du milieu ou de la fin de l'âge du fer a été étudiée à Long Range. L'occupation ne comportait pas d'enceinte et on y a relevé un certain nombre de maisons rondes et de structures à trois et quatre poteaux. Il est tout à fait possible qu'une seule de ces maisons rondes ait été en usage à un moment donné. Une fosse isolée du début du néolithique a également été fouillée à Long Range.

L'occupation à Blackhorse a commencé au début ou au milieu de l'âge du fer et est représentée par une seule maison ronde avec poteaux ; certaines limites de champs lui sont peut-être contemporaines. Deux maisons rondes plus tardives et des bâtiments à quatre poteaux appartiennent à une autre phase d'occupation sans enclos qui aurait précédé la construction d'une enceinte carrée. La totalité de cette enceinte a été fouillée, il est apparu qu'elle ne contenait qu'une seule grande maison ronde et un petit nombre de structures à quatre poteaux. La majorité des trouvailles se situaient dans la moitié sud du site.

A Pomeroy Wood, une base militaire du Ier siècle après J.-C. avec peut-être un ouvrage avancé ou une annexe, a été remplacée par une importante occupation romano-britannique qui est restée active jusqu'au IVème siècle. La base domine toute la vallée de la rivière Otter. Une grande partie de la base avait été détruite avant les fouilles décrites ici - sans qu'on ait enregistré aucune trouvaille - dans les années soixante, au cours de la construction de l'actuelle route A30. De ce fait, seule une aire limitée à l'intérieur de la base, occupée vers 65-85 après J.-C., a pu être étudiée ; on a cependant pu identifier deux sous-phases d'occupation. Au vu des restes végétaux saturés d'eau retrouvés dans un puits, il se pourrait que la garnison en poste au cours d'une des sous-phases ait été une unité de cavalerie.

Il est probable que la voie romaine entre Dorchester et Exeter ait longé la base et que l'occupation civile qui lui a succédé ait été du type bordure de route. Au IIème siècle après J.-C. on construisit une série de maisons rondes sur le site de la base militaire et on établit un certain nombre d'enceintes le long du tracé présumé de la voie romaine. Au IIIème siècle le noyau de l'occupation semble s'être éloigné de la région fouillée. Des délimitations de champs ou une série d'enclos associés à l'occupation en bordure de la route ont également été examinées à Githsham Forge à 300 m à l'est. Il se pourrait que cette occupation en bordure de route jusqu'ici inconnue soit *Moridunum*, nom mentionné dans plusieurs sources littéraires romaines.

Dans l'ensemble, les fouilles ont rélévé d'importantes collections de trouvailles, des restes végétaux carbonisés bien préservés et des charbons de bois. Deux puits romains envahis par les eaux ont aussi fourni de précieuses catégories de données qui n'ont pas survécu sur les sites datant de la fin de la préhistoire. Les témoignages relatifs à l'environnement montrent que le paysage a été peu à peu défriché mais, en général, à partir du milieu de l'âge de bronze, il semble y avoir eu peu de changements dans les plantes cultivées pendant plusieurs millénaires et selon toute apparence les forêts de chênes ont continué à représenter une part significative du paysage.

Les sites datant de la fin de la préhistoire sont concentrés dans la vallée de la rivière Otter, qui semble avoir été utilisée intensivement à cette époque. Ces sites sont particulièrement importants car ils constituent la première série majeure de sites de cette date à avoir été systématiquement fouillés et étudiés dans l'est du Devon. La série de 28 déterminations au radiocarbone élaborée à partir de ceux-ci facilite aussi l'établissement d'une fourchette pour la chronologie finale de cette période dans la région.

Annie Pritchard

Zusammenfassung

Zwischen 1996 und 1998 wurden im Vorfeld des Ausbaus der A30 zwischen Honiton und Exeter in Devon in Südwestengland Ausgrabungen an acht prähistorischen und römischen Fundplätzen durchgeführt.

In Castle Hill wurden zwei rechteckige Umfassungen aus dem Neolithikum, ein Teil eines mittelbronzezeitlichen Bauernhofs und ein konzentrisches Feldsystem ausgegraben. Eine der neolithischen Umfassungen ist eine 'lange Grabeinfassung' (sog. Long Mortuary Enclosure), und obwohl die volle Ausdehnung der anderen nicht bekannt ist, fällt sie wahrscheinlich in das Spektrum der 'Kursusmonumente'. Es ist wahrscheinlich, daß es während der Glockenbecherperiode zu Aktivitäten in der unmittelbaren Nachbarschaft der Fundplätze kam. Nur ein Teil des umzäunten Bauernhofareals konnte ausgegraben werden, aber er erbrachte eine relativ große Kollektion von Trevisker/Deverel-Rimbury Keramik und gut erhaltenen verkohlten Pflanzenresten.

In Patteson's Cross wurde ein einzelnes mittelbronzezeitliche Rundhaus gefunden. Mehrere Jahrhunderte später wurde in der Nähe eine andere mittelbronzezeitliche Umfassung gebaut, die ein einzelnes Rundhaus enthielt. Diese Gebäude erbrachten wenige Funde und kaum Anhaltspunkte für Getreideanbau. In Hayne Lane wurde ein befestigtes Gehöft der Mittel-/Spätbronzezeit fast vollständig ausgegraben. Es scheint sich um zwei Hauptgebäude gehandelt zu haben, und zwar ein größeres Rundhaus mit doppeltem Pfostenkreis, das als Wohnhaus diente, und ein kleineres Rundhaus mit einfachem Pfostenkreis, das für Textilarbeiten und zur Essenszubereitung benutzt worden sein mag. Eine Anzahl von auf drei oder vier Pfosten errichteten Anlagen lagen verstreut über das Areal und es ist wahrscheinlich, daß einige davon Gebäude darstellen, in denen die Ernte gelagert wurde. In dieser Siedlung wurden reichlich verkohlte Pflanzenreste gefunden.

In Langland Lane wurden ein einzelnes Rundhaus der mittleren Eisenzeit und einige möglicherweise gleichzeitige Feldbegrenzungen aufgenommen. Der Fundplatz liegt sehr dicht an den bronzezeitlichen Rundhäusern von Patteson's Cross und auch hier gab es wenige Anhaltspunkte für Getreideanbau. Ein Teil einer ausgedehnteren mittel- bis späteisenzeitlichen Siedlung wurde in Long Range untersucht. Die Siedlung war unbefestigt, und eine Reihe von Rundhäusern und Strukturen mit drei bzw. vier Pfosten wurden dokumentiert. Es braucht jeweils nur ein einziges Rundhaus gleichzeitig in Benutzung gewesen zu sein. In Long Range wurde ferner eine für sich stehende frühneolithische Grube ausgegraben.

In Blackhorse begann die Besiedlung in der frühen bis mittleren Eisenzeit, aus der ein Rundhaus mit einfachem Pfostenkreis stammt, zu dem einige der Feldbegrenzungen gehört haben mögen. Zwei spätere Rundhäuser und einige Gebäude mit vier Pfosten mögen zu einer weiteren Phase offener Besiedlung gehört haben, bevor eine rechtwinklige Einfassung gebaut wurde. Der gesamte Innenbereich der Einfassung wurde ausgegraben, wodurch gezeigt wurde, daß sie lediglich ein einziges großes Rundhaus und eine kleine Anzahl von Strukturen mit vier Pfosten enthielt. Die Mehrzahl der Funde wurde in der südlichen Hälfte des Fundplatzes gefunden.

In Pomeroy Wood wurde ein militärischer Stützpunkt des ersten Jahrhunderts n. Chr. mit einem möglichen Außenwerk oder Anbau von einer ausgedehnten romano-britischen Siedlung abgelöst, die bis zum vierten Jahrhundert bestand. Der Stützpunkt bietet beherrschende Ausblicke über das Ottertal. Ein großer Teil des Stützpunktes war bereits vor den hier dokumentierten Ausgrabungen durch den Bau der bestehenden A 30 in den 1960er Jahren zerstört worden – ohne daß irgendwelche Funde gemeldet worden wären. Dementsprechend stand nur ein begrenztes Gebiet des Stützpunktinneren zur Untersuchung zur Verfügung. Dennoch konnten zwei Unterphasen innerhalb der von 65 bis 85 n. Chr. dauernden Belegungszeit unterschieden werden. Auf der Grundlage von in Wasser erhaltenen Pflanzenresten aus dem einen Brunnen ist es möglich zu vermuten, daß die Garnison während einer der Unterphasen aus einer Kavallerieeinheit bestand.

Es ist wahrscheinlich, daß die römische Straße zwischen Dorchester und Exeter neben dem Stützpunkt verlief und daß die auf sie folgende Zivilsiedlung eine Straßensiedlung war. Im zweiten Jahrhundert n. Chr. wurden an der Stelle des Militärstützpunktes eine Reihe von Rundhäusern gebaut und entlang des vermuteten Verlaufs des römischen Straße wurde eine Anzahl von umzäunten Arealen angelegt. Im dritten Jahrhundert scheint sich das Zentrum der Siedlung von der ausgegrabenen Fläche weg verlagert zu haben. 300 m weiter östlich wurde in Gittisham Forge ferner ein weiteres zu der Straßensiedlung gehörendes Feldsystem oder eine zu ihr gehörende Reihe von umzäunten Arealen untersucht. Es ist möglich, daß es sich bei dieser zuvor unbekannten Straßensiedlung um Moridunum handelt, das in mehreren römischen Schriftquellen erwähnt wird.

Im ganzen gesehen erbrachten die Ausgrabungen umfangreiche Fundkollektionen und gut erhaltene verkohlte Pflanzenreste und Holzkohlefragmente. Zwei mit Wasser gefüllte römische Brunnen stellen außerdem wertvolle Quellengattungen zur Verfügung, die an später vorgeschichtlichen Fundstellen nicht erhalten bleiben. Die umweltgeschichtlich relevanten Funde zeigen eine schrittweise Auflichtung der Landschaft, aber im allgemeinen scheint es nach der Mittelbronzezeit für mehrere Jahrtausende kaum einen Wandel in den kultivierten Feldfruchtarten gegeben zu haben, und Eichenwald scheint ein bestimmender Teil der Landschaft geblieben zu sein.

Die Fundplätze der späteren Vorgeschichte sind im Ottertal konzentriert, das während dieser Periode intensiv genutzt worden zu sein scheint. Die Fundplätze sind insofern besonders wichtig als sie die erste größere Reihe von Fundplätzen dieser Zeit in Ostdevon darstellen, die systematisch ausgegraben und mit Hilfe naturwissenschaftlicher Proben untersucht wurden. Die Serie von 28 Radiokarbonbestimmungen von diesen Fundplätzen hilft uns ferner einen Rahmen für die absolute Chronologie der Periode in diesem Gebiet zu erstellen.

Cornelius Holtorf

1. Introduction

by A.P. Fitzpatrick

Introduction

The archaeology of east Devon lies in the long shadow cast by the well-preserved prehistoric antiquities of Dartmoor. It comes as something of a surprise to discover that the pioneering work of the Devon Exploration Society and the Archaeological Section of the Devonshire Association in the 1930s at the Neolithic causewayed enclosure and Iron Age hillfort of Hembury close to Honiton remains the most sustained campaign of excavations in the area. Although excavations at Hembury were renewed in the 1980s, there has been comparatively little fieldwork on the prehistoric and Roman periods in east Devon in recent years.

The pattern of land-use, largely as pasture, and the essentially rural pattern of modern settlement contrive to frustrate efforts at fieldwalking and aerial photography alike (Griffith 1994), and to restrict the opportunities for evaluation work in advance of development. While the work that has taken place has been of high quality, it has often been on a small scale and there is a certain irony that one of the larger pieces of recent work in east Devon, the excavations at Hayes Farm, Clyst Honiton, was partly undertaken as a response to the anticipated realignment of the A30 (Simpson *et al.* 1989).

Indeed the archaeological background to the excavations reported here can be sketched with a deceptive rapidity. The earliest archaeological evidence in the lowlands of east Devon is usually flaked stone, either flint or chert, found in fieldwalking and some scatters of these materials are known from around Honiton (Miles 1976). Neolithic and Bronze Age types usually dominate scatters of these materials but a small Mesolithic element is often present. It is suggestive that, at one of the few excavated sites in the area (the Bronze Age, Romano-British, and post-Roman site at Hayes Farm, Clyst Honiton), a single microlith was found and one of the radiocarbon determinations indicated activity in this period.

The Neolithic causewayed enclosure, Iron Age hillfort, and Roman base at Hembury is perhaps the most important group of monuments in the area (Todd 1984) but in many regards it stands – or stood – in splendid isolation. Apart from finds of flaked stone, evidence for Neolithic activity remains elusive and much of the Bronze Age is represented by finds of metalwork or by ring ditches recorded by aerial photography and presumed to be the ploughed-out remains of round barrows. Some of the enclosed farms also known only from aerial photography may date to the Bronze Age, like the settlement at Hayne Lane reported on below. However, on the evidence presently available (Griffith 1994) such enclosures are as likely to date to the Iron Age – like the Blackhorse settlement also reported below – or the Romano-British or post-Roman periods like the enclosures at Hayes Farm.

While a number of the hillforts in the area have been sampled by excavation; Dumpdon, Hembury, and Woodbury Castle, only Hembury has seen excavation on any scale but it has yielded little evidence for features of Iron Age date within the area enclosed by the ramparts. Other types of site of this date are virtually unknown. The Roman army garrisoned Hembury itself in the Conquest period but apart from a few isolated finds of pottery, and increasing signs of the exploitation of the iron ores of the Blackdown Hills, few sites are known. The long running speculation concerning the exact location of *Moridunum*, known to be sited somewhere between Dorchester and Exeter is many ways symptomatic of the lack of available evidence (Chapter 13, below).

The scale of the A30 Honiton to Exeter improvement (Fig. 2), essentially 21 km of new dual carriageway road, therefore provided the opportunity to examine a swathe across a landscape which is relatively poorly known in archaeological terms, but long suspected to be rich in archaeological remains.

The route runs west from Honiton along the valley of the River Otter (Fig. 2) before rising to *c.* 160 m at an escarpment, and then descending into the valley of the River Clyst and thence onwards towards Exeter and the broad and low-lying valley of the Exe. The river valleys are generally wide and slope gently, and the landscape is undulating. Much of the countryside is set to pasture but the soils over the river gravels in the valley of the River Otter are suitable for cultivation, as are the light sandy soils of the Bridgnorth Series close to Exeter. The Blackdown Hills rise to the north of the route, while to the south-east, the eastern valley side of the River Otter rises to a Greensand plateau.

The Nature of the Project

It is helpful to continue by outlining something of the history of the road improvement and the organisation of the archaeological works in relation to it, before turning to review briefly the contribution of the pre-project evaluations and to explain the organisation of the present report.

The Pre-project Evaluations

An archaeological assessment of the Preferred Route for improving the A30 road between Honiton and Exeter was undertaken by the Exeter Museums Archaeological Field Unit (now Exeter Archaeology) on behalf of the then Department of Transport in 1989 (Weddell 1989). A detailed assessment of the Published Route was subsequently also carried out by the Exeter Museums Archaeological Field Unit (Weddell 1991). That assessment included a desk-based study that included

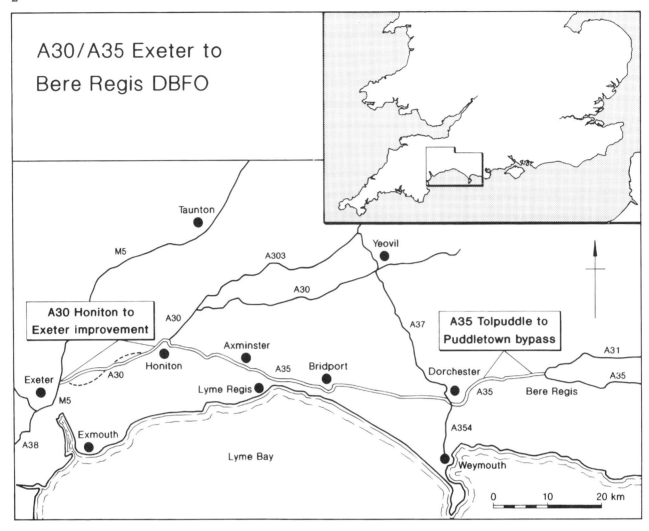

Figure 1   Location of the A30/A35 Exeter to Bere Regis Design, Build, Finance and Operate scheme

the examination of cartographic and documentary sources and of the Devon County Sites and Monuments Register. Fieldwalking of all available arable land and a walkover survey of non-arable land was also undertaken.

After a Public Inquiry, a third phase of work was instigated in April 1994, when geophysical survey was carried out by Oxford Archaeotechnics, and field evaluation undertaken by the Exeter Museums Archaeological Field Unit. Seventeen areas amounting to some 85 ha were surveyed using Topsoil Magnetic Susceptibility Survey followed by detailed Magnetometer (Gradiometer) Survey of areas of higher potential. Ten areas were investigated by excavation using trial trenching and test pits, including those identified by the geophysical survey, which ran concurrently. As crops were growing in a number of areas an exhaustive evaluation of the entire Published Route was not possible (Reed and Manning 1994a–d; 1995; Johnson 1995). On the basis of these results a Brief which included site-specific mitigation strategies was prepared on behalf of the Highways Agency by Exeter Archaeology. The mitigation strategies were (i) excavation, (ii) strip and record, or (iii) watching brief. The principal results of the pre-project evaluations and

the mitigation strategies are summarised at the beginning of the relevant individual excavation reports in the succeeding chapters.

The Design, Build, Finance and Operate Scheme

The A30 Honiton to Exeter improvement itself represents a new way of funding the improvement of existing roads and the building of new ones. As part of a Government Private Finance Initiative to introduce private funding into public services, in 1995 the improvement between Honiton and Exeter was integrated with a bypass scheme for the A35 between Tolpuddle and Puddletown in Dorset (Hearne and Birbeck 1999). The enlarged project became the A30/A35 Exeter to Bere Regis, Design, Build, Finance and Operate scheme that incorporated 102 km of road (Fig. 1). It is one of the first such schemes to be completed.

The essence of the scheme is that private companies are contracted by the Government to design and build roads, in this case 21 km of new dual carriageway road between Honiton and Exeter, and a further 9 km between Tolpuddle and Puddletown. As well as building the lengths of new road, the Design Build, Finance and Operate Company is also responsible for operating and maintaining the whole 102 km of road until the year 2026.

In 1995 the Government awarded the contract for the scheme to Connect A30/A35 Limited, which comprises three major construction companies, BICC plc, Philipp Holzmann AG and WS Atkins plc. In turn, Connect A30/A35 Limited appointed a Construction Joint Venture called BBTA to build the road, the acronym being coined from the three companies involved; Balfour Beatty, Tilbury Douglas, and Deutsche Asphalt. Oxford Archaeological Unit and Wessex Archaeology were respectively appointed as the Project Archaeologist and the Archaeological Contractor in the August of 1996.

One of the results of such Private Finance Initiatives has been to see archaeological works firmly bound within the overall contract of such schemes. Hence the objectives of the archaeological works thought necessary at the time that the contract was to be let, and the methods by which they were to be undertaken, form part of the Construction and Handback Requirements of the Highways Agency. For the A30 Honiton to Exeter improvement the *Brief and Specifications for Archaeological Mitigation* forms schedule 4 of the Construction and Handback Requirements, Part 1: Archaeology (Honiton to Exeter), Annex 4A: Archaeological Requirements.

Types of Archaeological Fieldwork

Three categories of archaeological fieldwork or 'mitigation action' were defined in the Brief as follows;

'(1) *Excavation*: to be undertaken in areas of high importance where there is no scope within the scheme for the preservation of deposits.

(2) *Strip and record*: to be undertaken where areas of medium importance are to be destroyed; on the fringes of high importance where excavation of the core has already taken place; and in areas where evaluation was not carried out but where evidence suggests archaeological remains may be present. The technique is defined by topsoil stripping (under archaeological supervision) over a given area; a clean machine finish of the exposed areas will generally suffice except where hand-cleaning would substantially benefit understanding of the archaeological deposits. Less intensive hand-sampling than in (1) would generally then be employed. Intercutting features would be hand-sampled at points where the stratigraphic relationships could be established, and where artefactual of palaeo-environmental evidence was likely to be recovered; thereafter machine sampling of bulk fills could be conducted to supplement the artefactual record if necessary. Where complex archaeological deposits of high importance are revealed during the strip these must be identified

at an early stage in order to formulate and alternative (i.e. excavation) strategy.

(3) *Watching brief*: to be carried out over all areas not covered by excavation or strip and record, with the aim of compiling a record of low-medium importance archaeological deposits not predicted by the evaluation and providing a safety check in areas which were not, or could not, be evaluated. The watching brief must identify at an early stage any areas of high archaeological importance, in order that an appropriate mitigation strategy can be formulated.'

At the time that the contract was agreed it was understood that, apart from the areas of the archaeological excavations, the whole of route would be stripped of topsoil in one operation and that there would not be any opportunity for further archaeological evaluation. For this reason areas which were suspected to have a higher archaeological potential but where evaluation work had not been possible were designated as areas of Strip and Record. Here the topsoil stripping would be monitored more closely by archaeologists.

In practice it proved possible to examine a number of the Strip and Record sites using an array of mechanically excavated evaluation trenches in advance of the topsoil stripping. At those sites the area sampled by trial trenching was relatively high in relation to most contemporary archaeological evaluations (e.g. Patteson's Cross, Fig. 28, below). However, the need to complete pieces of work in advance of the road building programme along the whole route meant that it was not possible to strip, excavate, and record all of the archaeological sites in one stage if more work than the original sample was considered necessary by the monitoring meeting. Two sites in particular, Patteson's Cross and Long Range, were returned to on a number of occasions for additional work.

Monitoring and Certification

The Highways Agency appointed, on behalf of the then Department of Transport, an Agent known as the Department's Archaeologist (in this case Peter Weddell of Exeter Archaeology) to monitor the archaeological works and to report to the Department's Agent (in this case Hyder Consulting). The Design Build, Finance and Operate company appointed a Project Archaeologist (in this case George Lambrick of Oxford Archaeological Unit, and his Deputy for the A30, Brian Durham) to represent them and to monitor the Archaeological Contractor. The Project Archaeologist was also responsible for preparing the certification documentation. The Department's Archaeologist and the Project Archaeologist liased with English Heritage, the Government's statutory archaeological advisor, and with Devon County Council. Frances Griffith, the County Archaeological Officer also took an active part in the weekly or more frequent monitoring meetings.

The purpose of certification was to formally agree that pieces of work have been completed to the agreed standard. Four certificates were established for the

A30/A35. All project designs, including the method statement for the Watching Brief and the assessment reports received a Certificate 1 on their agreement by the Department's Agent. All excavations received a Certificate 2 on completion, while all areas of topsoil stripping observed by the watching brief which did not require further archaeological work received a Certificate 3. The Certificate 4 is reserved for the publication of this report and the deposition of the project archive with Exeter City Museums.

The Principal Archaeological Sites

Three sites were initially selected for excavation (Fig. 2), Castle Hill, Hayne Lane, and Blackhorse (Chapters 3, 5, and 8 below respectively). The recommended mitigation strategy for a further six sites was Strip and Record, at Sowton Lane (adjacent to Blackhorse), Pound Corner (SX 9928 9319), Brickyard Copse (SY 0506 9526), Laurel Copse (SY 0598 9538), Long Range, and Patteson's Cross. In the case of Patteson's Cross, further geophysical survey of that land which had been under crop in 1994 and so unavailable for survey at that time, was undertaken shortly before the Strip and Record works started (Johnson 1996).

In addition to these nine sites, three other sites identified during the Watching Brief were subject to further excavation; Langland Lane, Pomeroy Wood, and Gittisham Forge. In addition to this, trial trenching was also undertaken along 1 km of the route west of Pomeroy Wood to Iron Bridge where it ran parallel to the suspected route of the Roman road between Dorchester and Exeter (Fig. 2). Further recording and/or trial trenching was undertaken at three locations; River Otter Bridge, Brinor, and Fairmile and the results of that work are summarised in Chapter 2 and Appendix 8. Other additional archaeological works included (i) a Watching Brief over a water pipeline needed to supply the concrete-making plant for the road scheme at Lily Cottage as it was thought that the pipeline might cross the Roman road (Chapter 12, below), (ii) an evaluation by geophysical survey (Johnson 1997a) and trial trenching during the Watching Brief at the Lily Cottage site, (iii) recording of the turnpike road at the River Clyst bridge, and (iv) geophysical survey and trial trenching were also undertaken on the possible site for a borrow pit (a temporary quarry to supply aggregates for the road building) at Northfield (SY 0040 9260) (Johnson 1997b; Wessex Archaeology 1997). As the Northfield site lay outside the scope of the DBFO scheme, that evaluation was requested by the County Archaeological Officer under the Town and Country Planning Act following *PPG 16: archaeology and planning*.

The Evaluation in Retrospect

A brief review of the pre-project evaluation works is appropriate. As we have seen, the evaluation reports identified nine sites as meriting further work, three were recommended for open area excavation, and six for Strip and Record. Two of the sites recommended for excavation (Hayne Lane and Blackhorse) were

enclosures identified through aerial photography, while the third, Castle Hill, was identified through a combination of the suggestive place name, fieldwalking and trial trenching which was followed by geophysical survey. Strip and Record areas were specified either side of the open excavation area at Castle Hill.

Of the sites recommended for Strip and Record, two proved to contain significant archaeological remains. The presence of the prehistoric site at Patteson's Cross was first suggested by fieldwalking finds made by a local amateur archaeologist, and geophysical survey in the pre-project evaluation endorsed this. However, as we have seen, due to difficulties of access it was not possible to examine the site further until the start of the road building programme. The site at Long Range was identified by geophysical survey and the subsequent 10 x 10 m evaluation trench confirmed the presence of features of prehistoric date. These two sites, and also the Strip and Record areas either side of the original excavation area at Castle Hill, were retrospectively reclassified as open area excavation sites after the completion of the fieldwork.

In contrast, four of the sites recommended for Strip and Record failed to yield significant archaeological results. In view of the limited pre-project evaluation works that were possible at these sites, such a result should not occasion surprise. At Laurel Copse (SY 0598 9538), geophysical survey had indicated magnetically enhanced soils and the possible presence of linear features. An evaluation trench did not reveal any ancient finds or features but four pieces of flaked stone were recovered 'from on the ground surface in the general area of the excavation' (Reed and Manning 1995, 2). Twenty evaluation trenches were subsequently excavated as part of the Strip and Record works reported here, but no ancient finds or features were discovered.

At Brickyard Copse (SY 0565 9526) no evaluation work was possible as the site was under woodland. The Strip and Record works were requested on the basis of a single sherd of prehistoric pottery found in the roots of an upturned tree; such is the rarity of prehistoric pottery in east Devon. Although quarries and dumps associated with the nearby brickyard site were found, no features or any further pottery of prehistoric date were found. At Sowton Lane, the geophysical survey suggested the possible presence of linear features adjacent to the enclosure at Blackhorse, but these were not confirmed by the trenching undertaken in either the pre-project evaluation or the Strip and Record works. At Pound Corner (SX 9928 9319) geophysical survey also indicated a possible enclosure. This was not tested by invasive fieldwork in the evaluation and no evidence for an enclosure was found subsequently during the Strip and Record works. At the conclusion of the Assessment Stage of that part of the project it was recommended that no analyses should be undertaken on these sites and further details are presented in the relevant Assessment Report (Wessex Archaeology 1998a).

Expressed in another way (Table 1), aerial photography initially located two sites, Hayne Lane and Blackhorse, both of which are enclosed settlements. Fieldwalking directly identified one site Patteson's Cross (and the discovery of a sherd of Roman pottery at

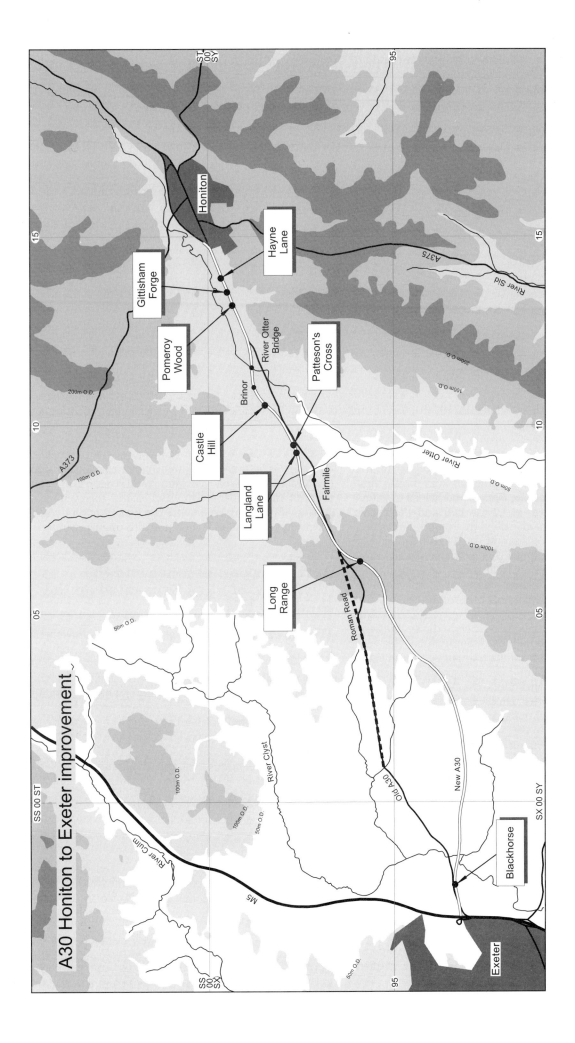

Figure 2   Location of the A30 Honiton to Exeter improvement

Table 1: Major methods of discovery of principal sites

Site code	Site name	Aerial reconnaissance	Fieldwalking	Trial trenching	Geophysical survey	Watching Brief
W2414.8	Castle Hill		*	*	*	
W2414.12	Patteson's Cross		*		*	
W2414.10	Hayne Lane	*		*		
W2414.15	Langland Lane					*
W2414.6	Long Range			*	*	
W2414.1	Blackhorse	*		*		
W2414.15	Pomeroy Wood					*
W2414.13	Gittisham Forge					*
W2414.5	Laurel Copse				*	
W2414.4	Brickyard Copse		*			
W2414.2	Sowton Lane				*	
W2414.11	Pound Corner				*	

More than one method may be indicated where different methods contributed significantly to the understanding of the extent and dates of individual sites

Castle Hill was a significant factor leading to the trenching at that site). Geophysical survey also first identified one site, at Long Range, and helped to define the extent of the sites at Castle Hill and Patteson's Cross. Trial trenching identified the Neolithic sites and the Bronze Age field system at Castle Hill, though not the presence of the Bronze Age settlement enclosure, and confirmed the geophysical survey at Long Range. The trenching also helped characterise the sites at Hayne Lane and Blackhorse as being of Bronze Age and Iron Age dates respectively. Of these sites, Castle Hill and Long Range were unknown before the evaluation.

The importance of the Geophysical Survey, especially magnetic susceptibility, is perhaps understated by this simple comparison of methods. As well as helping to further define the extent of individual sites and confirming those known from aerial reconnaissance, it did not identify any new sites along the western part of the route, providing valuable negative evidence. The lack of finds made during the Watching Brief in this part of the route echoes this distribution. In areas that are predominantly pastoral magnetic susceptibility may be a particularly valuable evaluation method. The fact that the enclosures at Blackhorse and Hayne Lane were only observed once by aerial reconnaissance in a year of drought serves to emphasise this point.

Three sites were identified during the Watching Brief. Despite the proximity of the Middle Iron Age round-house at Langland Lane to the Early and Middle Bronze Age examples at Patteson's Cross, the two phases of activity may well be completely unrelated. The sites at Gittisham Forge and Pomeroy Wood could not be evaluated due to difficulties of access, but it must be considered likely that they would have been identified by Geophysical Survey and trial trenching. The

discovery of an extensive Roman settlement either side of a major Roman road astride a small stream is in some regards unsurprising. In view of the topographical setting of Pomeroy Wood, and the benefit of hindsight, the siting of a Roman fort on it is also unsurprising.

Aerial Reconnaissance and the 'Visibility' of Sites Excavated on the Route, by F.M. Griffith

The line of the A30 Honiton to Exeter improvement passes through a range of different soil types, and this is reflected in the varying ways in which the principal excavated sites were, or were not, identified prior to the start of work. This is a factor not only of the susceptibility of the different soil types to cropmark production, but also of the diversity of land use and vegetation cover resulting from this variety. Thus, the site at Long Range offered no chance of discovery through aerial reconnaissance because of the woodland cover. The principal sites (Fig. 2) are examined below in chronological order.

Castle Hill

The area south of the railway line (Fig. 5) has shown few archaeological features as cropmarks since the inception of the Devon Aerial Reconnaissance Project in 1983, nor can any be seen on vertical photography held by Devon County Council. The underlying geology here is Permian–Triassic sandstones, and the soil type is given by the Soil Survey as reddish loamy soils of the Newnham Series. However, the field immediately to the north of the railway, centred on SY106 987, lying on the same soils, has yielded information to the aerial observer. This field has manifested, in different years from 1985 onward, both a number (two in 1985 (DAP/FN11–2, 30 July 1985) but different in each year recorded) of ring ditches and also the ditches of a field system that appears to be a continuation of that excavated during the present work. In photography of 1992 (DAP/VP 14–6, 21 July 1992), a minimum of three ring ditches is visible, while the field system can be seen continuing into the excavated area, and shows two of the ditches sampled in excavation. In 1994, only one ring ditch and a very short length of ditch could be seen, albeit with great clarity (DAP/XE 6–8, 25 July 1994; Pl. 22). The features at Castle Hill, on either side of the railway line, are not visible on any of the vertical photography held by Devon County Council. Aerial photography cannot at present identify the bounds of the prehistoric field system, although it seems probable that additional gradiometer survey (Johnson 1995, fig. 43) could elucidate this further. Given the good visibility of the features north of the railway line, which were recorded in 1985, 1992 and 1994, it is perhaps surprising that the area excavated in the present project showed so little.

Patteson's Cross / Langland Lane

At no point have the sites of Langland Lane and Patteson's Cross been visible from the air or on aerial photographs. These sites lie on valley gravels with very thin Newnham Series brownearth soils, and there might be some expectation that such soils should yield cropmarks, as they did at Castle Hill. However, the very slight nature of the archaeological features here, and the nature of their fills, makes their identification from the air in other than exceptional circumstances fairly improbable.

Hayne Lane

This site was recognised through aerial reconnaissance prior to the A30 proposals. It was discovered in 1984 (DAP/BW12; BX1, 12 July 1984) (Pl. 11), but not seen subsequently, despite the fact that the field is believed to have been in fairly regular arable cultivation since that time. It is possible that the explanation lies in the fact that the ditch deposits survived beneath some 0.55 m of topsoil and subsoil. Given the nature of the underlying material this would mean that even massive features would only be visible in extreme drought such as 1984 – when we were probably lucky to see it. The site lies on valley gravels overlying Keuper marls. (The Soil Survey 1:250,000 mapping gives the soil as Newnham Series, but the soil here has few characteristics in common with that at, for example, Langland Lane.) In the reconnaissance photographs (admittedly fairly distant) only the enclosure ditch itself can be seen, which was subsequently demonstrated in excavation to be a very substantial feature. No cropmarks of internal features are visible, and only faint evidence of these was recorded in the geophysical surveys. The evidence from this site suggests that, on the valley gravels and floodplain-edge deposits here, it

would be unwise to assume visibility of surviving archaeological sites either through aerial reconnaissance, geophysical survey or fieldwalking.

Blackhorse

The enclosure at Blackhorse was also first recognised in aerial reconnaissance by the writer, on 27 June 1984 (DAP/AG 2–3). The site lies on sandy soils of the Bridgnorth Series, overlying Permian and Triassic sandstones. It was visible as a square enclosure, faint but clear, in crop (Pl. 16). No other features were visible in the field with the exception of two separate phases of linear features: one north–south ditch and two curving north-west to south-east ones that crossed the enclosure. The enclosure has not been visible in subsequent years, and the penannular gullies and the post-settings seen in excavation were not visible from the air.

It was significant that this site, though providing very positive responses to magnetic susceptibility survey (Johnson 1995, figs 5–6), proved almost invisible in gradiometer survey (*ibid.*, fig. 37) despite enhancement endeavours, reflecting its weak signature as a cropmark. The excavation provided a clear explanation of this: the fills of the cut features were very hard to distinguish from the surroundings. In the case of the enclosure ditch, the tendency of the excavated area to backfill with the surrounding sandy material as soon as it rained was very marked (p. 173), and a similar process may be envisaged in antiquity, resulting in the ditch having been open for a very limited time, and being backfilled with material barely dissimilar from that into which it was cut.

This thus provided a very poor differential to be picked up by either geophysical or aerial survey, and apparently needed the exceptional drought conditions of 1984 to be visible at all as a cropmark. The depth of the overburden (up to 0.75 m) on this site proved surprising during excavation, and this must be a further factor in the low visibility of the ditch.

Pomeroy Wood

At no time has any trace of this site, on either the north or south side of the A30, been observed from the air, and nor can it be seen in retrospect on any existing vertical photography. This is surprising, given the scale of the features and the nature of the soil in the excavated area.

Sowton Lane and Pound Corner

East of the main enclosure at Blackhorse, on the same soils, a further possible enclosure at Sowton Lane, centred SX 980 933, was recorded very faintly in 1994 (DAP/WI 1–4, 23 June 1994; DAP/XI 9–14, 1 August 1994). The site was not tested by gradiometer, but produced no noticeable response to topsoil magnetic susceptibility testing. Only one linear feature was recognised in the subsequent excavation. However, the marks observed in 1994, though faint, and though possibly not representing a complete 'enclosure' in the classic sense, appear to be real, and persistent, if faint, and it is disconcerting that more light was not shed on their genesis in excavation.

Aerial photographs showed no trace of the possible enclosure suggested by geophysical survey at Pound Corner. Excavation did not elucidate this site further.

Comments

This brief review of the air photographic evidence for archaeological sites along the line of the A30 Honiton–Exeter improvement brings out a few points. Unsurprisingly, although soils information deriving from Soil Survey publications and Institute of Geological Sciences 1 inch mapping is given here, the level of discrimination at mapped scales is not close enough always to distinguish between soils which in terms both of the characteristics identified in excavation and of their productivity of cropmarks are manifestly different. A good example of this is provided by comparison between the Blackhorse enclosure and another of comparable scale at Hayes Farm (SX 992 945). The latter, partially excavated in 1987 (Simpson *et al.* 1989) has not only been far more regularly visible from the air, despite a range of sub-optimal crops for cropmarks, but has over the years shown a major complex of associated enclosures, field systems etc.

Indeed, the extent of the site as now known, in the light of reconnaissance in the 1990s, is considerably greater than that known at the time of the evaluation excavations. In terms of Soil Survey 1 inch mapping (Clayden 1971), the field at Hayes Farm closer to the A30, centred at SX 994 944, is shown as identical to the fields to the west, where many new features have been identified in cropmark form, but in fact it exhibits both shallower topsoil cover and much harder gravel soils when compared with the sand on which lies the enclosure excavated in 1987. Few cropmarks have ever been recognised in the eastern field, although geophysical survey and evaluation excavations have demonstrated the survival of slight but important prehistoric features here.

Systematic, regular, aerial reconnaissance in Devon has only been carried out since 1983. The results of this work have produced evidence of substantially more enclosed settlement in the lowlands of Devon than had formerly been believed to be the case (Griffith 1994), and indeed may be said to have transformed the perceived level of archaeological activity. However, since this only started some 15 years ago, relatively few enclosures known from aerial reconnaissance have yet been excavated, compared with the numbers in other parts of southern Britain, and for this reason the date distribution of the newly recognised sites is still largely uncertain. The excavations on the line of the A30 Honiton to Exeter improvement have therefore provided valuable additional information to contribute to the interpretation of the results of aerial recon-naissance. In particular, the survival of substantial internal features within and outside enclosures whose ditches were the only features identifiable in cropmark form reinforces the view that, on Devon soils, the non-visibility of such features cannot be interpreted as necessarily implying poor survival (Griffith 1994). Equally, the interestingly wide variety of dates for the excavated enclosures demonstrates once again that attempts to date these essentially simple enclosures on the basis of their morphological characteristics alone is generally unwise.

An interesting point arising from this work is the importance of single sorties in the Devon aerial reconnaissance programme. The value of work in 1984 (Griffith 1984a) is emphasised by the fact that two of the sites, Blackhorse and Hayne Lane, have never been seen in 15 subsequent years of routine reconnaissance (indeed, this area has been subject to particular attention, in view of the proposed developments here). In Devon, and much of western Britain as a whole, the other outstanding year for the identification of sites in cropmark forms was 1989 (Griffith 1990). For some parts of Devon that year was certainly of immense importance, but this brief review has shown that no useful information on any of the sites discussed here was found in it, while the less dramatically dry summers of the early 1990s were more productive. This reinforces our perception of the formation of cropmarks, certainly in the west of Britain, as highly localised, and once again the case for consistent, regular and well-informed local reconnaissance (*ibid.*, 30) is emphasised.

The Initial Project Design

After the setting of the Brief and the mitigation strategies, a *General Project Design for Archaeological Mitigation Works* was prepared as part of the tender competition. This set out a consistent set of methods and also an overarching research framework for all the works on the A30/A35 project. In section 3.3 a number of 'key archaeological themes' were isolated;

'Landscape archaeology is concerned with the ways in which people perceived, used and inhabited their own particular landscapes, and with the changing nature of those relationships through time as other factors or influences – external pressures, economic base, environmental change etc – impact on them. The road scheme offers an opportunity to examine transects across the landscape with evidence of human activity since at least the later Neolithic, and some general themes emerge for both the Devon and Dorset sections. Such themes concur broadly with those identified by English Heritage in *Exploring our Past: strategies for the archaeology of England* (1991).

The themes may be defined as follows:

A the ritual/monumental (funerary) landscape of the later Neolithic/Earlier Bronze Age, and its associated settlements

B the settled agricultural landscape of the late 2nd and 1st millennia BC

C the urban hinterland – impact of urbanisation on rural settlement in the Roman and later periods

D the nature of medieval and post-medieval land management and allotment

Within each of those main themes run a series of sub-themes:

E   the nature of the local environment at any given time
F   the nature of the economic or subsistence base, both at a local level and a wider scale
G   the form, date, organisation and function of specific landscape features, such as enclosures, field systems and communication routes or burial features, and their inter-relationship.'
(Wessex Archaeology, with Lambrick 1996)

Site-specific Project Designs were subsequently prepared by Wessex Archaeology in consultation with the Project Archaeologist for each site defined as requiring archaeological mitigation before the start of the road building. In view of the time which had elapsed between the completion of the detailed assessment in 1991 and the start of the excavations reported here (in 1996) a rapid review of the Devon County Council Sites and Monuments Register was undertaken by Oxford Archaeological Unit early in 1997. Where sites discovered during the course of the Watching Brief required further work, the site-specific Project Designs were prepared by the Project Archaeologist.

A further two themes were added to the Revised Research Design during the Assessment of the Potential for Analysis phase of the project;

H   the Roman conquest of the region
I   the sub-Roman settlement of the region.
(Wessex Archaeology 1998b, 34)

The Current Report

The excavations reported here were undertaken between December 1996 and May 1998 in advance of the building of the road, while a watching brief over the building works was concluded in September 1999.

As has been seen, it transpired that the amount of archaeological work necessary along the route was considerably greater than that originally anticipated and specified. However, as the publication of this archaeological report has been deemed to form part of the contract between Connect Ltd and the Government, it was not possible to accommodate any increase in the amount of time available for the analysis and dissemination stages of the archaeological project. Accordingly, the assessment and analysis stages were split into two parts. The first part dealing with the sites of prehistoric date (Wessex Archaeology 1998a), the second with sites of Roman date (Wessex Archaeology 1998b) and the results of the watching brief. The part 1 assessment and analysis stages ran concurrently with the fieldwork on the sites of Roman date and the continuing Watching Brief. The report was drafted by June 1999.

Of the 'key archaeological themes' defined in the *General Project Design*, the data recovered may be related to themes A and B, accompanied by sub-themes E, F, G, and also to the theme H which was identified in the Revised Research Design in the second Assessment

Report. Theme C, 'the urban hinterland' cannot be addressed meaningfully within the scope of this report due to the nature of the sites recorded. The opportunities to record medieval and later land boundaries during the Watching Brief were limited (see Chapter 2), making it difficult to contribute usefully to the theme. Theme I, introduced lest any of the round-houses at Pomeroy Wood should prove to be sub-Roman in date, cannot be addressed as those buildings have subsequently been firmly dated to the Romano-British period.

Although presented thematically as a landscape archaeology, the key themes are essentially sequential and instead a chronological approach to the organisation of the present report was proposed in the Assessment Reports. Following a summary of the principal results of the Watching Brief, which are largely of earlier prehistoric date (Chapters 3–8), the excavation reports are presented in the chronological order of the principal results from the areas in a series of site-specific reports, starting with the Neolithic monuments at Castle Hill through to the Roman sites at Pomeroy Wood and Gittisham Forge (Chapters 10–11).

It is accepted that this site-specific approach introduces some repetition to the report, but it is considered that the advantages of presenting the data from each site, many of which are the first of their kind to be excavated in east Devon, in a simple and consistent manner outweighs the disadvantages. For this reason the methods statements are presented in a series of appendices (1–8). The tension between overarching research schemes which encompass sites over 100 km apart and the detailed contextual analyses (encompassed within sub-theme G) necessary to interpret some of the sites excavated, such as Hayne Lane, should also be recognised. The constraints of the data pertaining to sub-themes E and F are sketched out below. However, of the categories of data recovered in the project, the environmental data provides the most scope for comparison between sites and between periods and these are explored for the sites of prehistoric date in Chapter 9.

Environmental Strategy and Programme

While older excavations, 'stray finds', upstanding monuments, and the contribution of aerial photography inform us of the morphology and date of individual sites, in the absence of major excavations, there have naturally been relatively few large-scale programmes of palaeo-environmental analysis in lowland Devon.

The current project therefore provided one of the first opportunities to retrieve samples for environmental data from sites covering a wide chronological range, and from a wide range of contexts. Approximately 1300 bulk samples were taken, processed, and assessed and it is the data from these materials which provides the most significant contribution in the form of abundant charred plant remains and charcoals.

However, at the outset it was evident that the recovery of some categories of palaeo-environmental evidence would be extremely limited. And so it proved, animal bones, marine shell, and land snails were – predictably – very poorly preserved, limiting the interpretation of animal husbandry and the utilisation of marine resources and, to a lesser extent, the nature of the land-use and landscape development. Of these absences, the lack of information about animal husbandry is the one felt most keenly.

The presumption was initially made, perhaps incorrectly, that pollen would be poorly preserved and the obtaining of suitable samples was not regarded as a priority. In general, few contexts suitable for sampling for pollen were in fact excavated and where pollen was assessed (e.g. Castle Hill and at Pomeroy Wood), preservation was generally poor apart from in two wells of Roman date at Pomeroy Wood in which material was preserved by waterlogging.

The methods employed in the analyses are given in Appendix 7.

Radiocarbon Dates, by Michael J. Allen

Throughout this report the radiocarbon results are expressed in radiocarbon years BP (Before Present – AD 1950). The results are calibrated using the maximum intercept method (Stuiver and Reimer 1986; *pace* Bowman 1994) with the data sets from Stuiver and Pearson (1986) and Pearson and Stuiver (1986). All calibrated date ranges are quoted at two standard deviations (95% confidence), with the end points rounded outwards to 10 years (Mook 1986). The probability distributions for the results have been prepared using OxCal 2.15.

The Project Archive, by Sarah F. Wyles

The project archive and that from the pre-project evaluation by Exeter Museums Archaeological Field Unit has been deposited with Exeter City Museums, Queen Street, Exeter EX4 3RX. Microfilm copies of the archive are held by Devon County Council, Exeter City Museums, the National Monuments Record (Kemble Drive, Swindon, Wiltshire SN2 2GZ), and Wessex Archaeology.

2. The Watching Brief

by R.A. Davis and A.P. Fitzpatrick

Introduction

Large-scale topsoil stripping of the route was carried out using box-scrapers and bulldozers, while smaller scale works were undertaken with a self-loading elevated scraper, or with 360° excavators, which frequently used toothed buckets. As with the site-specific Project Designs, a method statement was also prepared for the Watching Brief, however, the health and safety implications of working in close proximity to large plant of this kind (Pl. 1) meant that inspections were integrated with planned topsoil stripping. It was, however, possible to monitor other types of ground works such as trenching or the excavation of roadside drainage ditches (called 'V ' ditches after their profile) for which smaller machines were used, more closely, and in safety.

At the outset it was hoped that particular attention could be paid to hedgebanks and the areas adjoining and under them as many of these boundaries could originate in the medieval period and might encapsulate evidence about the development of parish boundaries. In practice it was not possible for the archaeologists to examine these, or other alignments, in any detail during the Watching Brief. On the rare occasions where it was possible to examine boundaries (at Laurel Copse for example), it yielded little information.

Results

One hundred and thirty-two individual find spots were recorded during the Watching Brief, and the principle results are summarised here. In contrast, relatively few archaeological features were recorded and it must be regarded as likely that many of the seemingly isolated finds derive from archaeological features which could not be seen during the course of a Watching Brief. Even where the new line of the road passed very close to known sites of post-medieval date, such as a tenement at Spain Lane, Fair Oak (SY 0012 9308), only cobbling was seen during the Watching Brief. While three sites which went on to be excavated further were identified during the Watching Brief, and which may be held to demonstrate the utility of the method, it is possible that some small sites or groups of archaeological features may simply have been destroyed unseen in the first pass by the box-scrapers. The fact that the Roman road between Dorchester and Exeter was identified only once during the Watching Brief is noteworthy, though it is

Plate 1   Topsoil stripping at Long Range

12

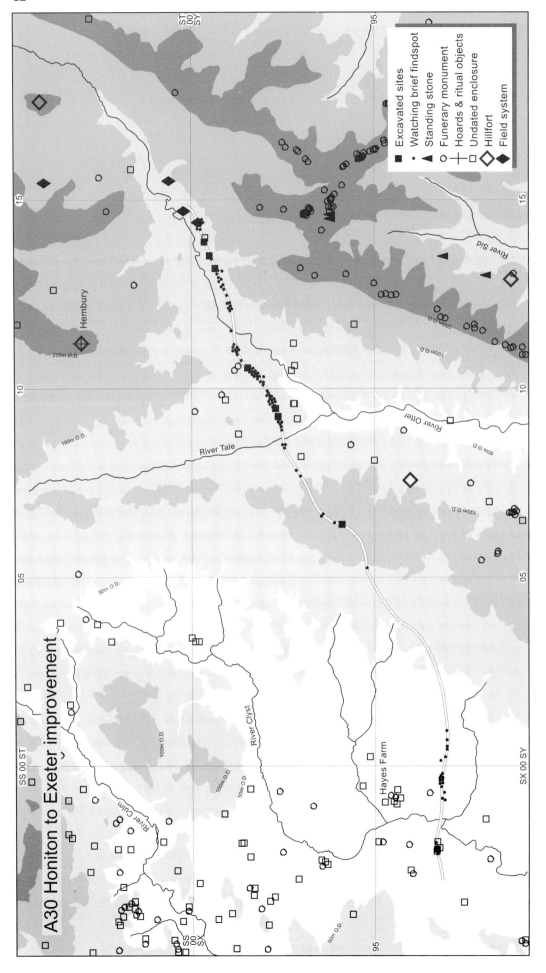

Figure 3   Distribution of finds of prehistoric date in the environs of the road improvement (source: Devon County Council Sites and Monuments Register)

Scale 2:3

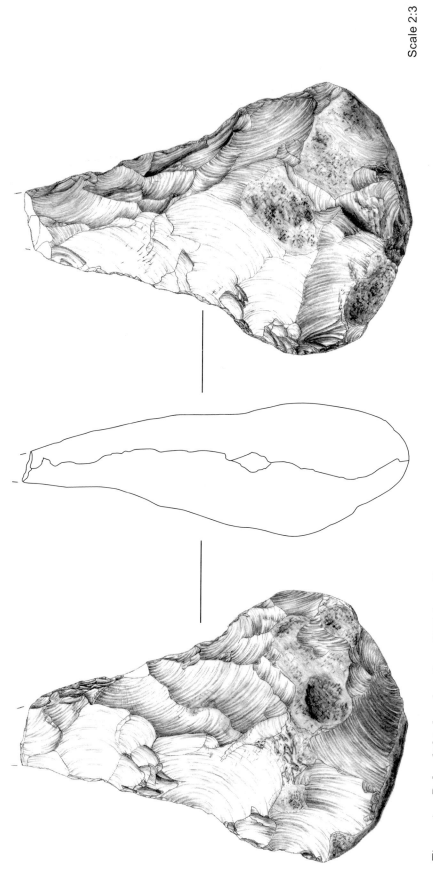

Figure 4   Palaeolithic handaxe from Gittisham Forge

possible that at the eastern part of the route the building of the existing A30 had already removed all trace of it.

The majority of the finds that were recovered were either of post-medieval date or single pieces or small groups of flaked stone of prehistoric date. Identifiable and datable prehistoric pottery was observed and recovered on only two occasions. In view of the poor survival of prehistoric pottery once it has become incorporated within the ploughsoil in Devon it can hardly be fortuitous that both these find spots were in close proximity to known sites; at Patteson's Cross and Hayne Lane. An extensive scatter of flaked stone, some of which may be of Mesolithic date, however, was found at Hayne Farm, c. 600 m to the north-east of the Hayne Lane settlement (Pearce and Reed 1993, 3–4, fig. 5, pls 6–7).

While, for obvious reasons (Pl. 1), it could not be claimed that every piece of flaked stone or pottery was recovered during the Watching Brief, there is a clear concentration in the distribution of the flaked stone in the valley of the River Otter (Fig. 3). By comparison Roman finds were rarer (Chapter 12), and it is noteworthy that apart from at Birdcage Lane, there was no trace of the Roman road. The distribution of Roman finds is clearly related to the course of Dorchester–Exeter Roman road with which the eastern end of the A30 improvements is parallel, but thereafter the two roads take different routes and the quantity of Roman finds decreases (Fig. 104). In contrast to these distributions, medieval, and post-medieval pottery is generally found evenly along the course of the route, particularly where the improvement runs close to the old Honiton–Exeter road, which will, again, have influenced the patterns of settlement during those periods.

In addition to these finds, further works whether as evaluation, mitigation, or detailed recording were undertaken under the rubric of the Watching Brief at 13 places. Where these works required mechanical excavation a toothless ditching bucket was used and the machining was undertaken under constant archaeological supervision.

In three instances, at Gittisham Forge, Langland Lane, and Pomeroy Wood, the sites discovered became the subject of excavations and they are reported on in Chapters 11, 6, and 10 respectively. The results of the work at Castle Hill, where pits of prehistoric date were recorded, are incorporated within Chapter 3. The results of the work at Birdcage Lane, (where the Roman road was identified), Brinor, Dart Lane to Iron Bridge, and the Nag's Head Culvert are all largely of Roman date and so are presented with Roman sites in Chapters 11 and 12. Trial trenching or other mitigation works were carried out at three locations where groups of flaked stone of prehistoric date were recovered; at Marwood Cross (called Site 51 during the fieldwork), Fairmile (Site 54), and Brinor (Site 55). Trial trenching was also undertaken under the rubric of the Watching Brief at Lily Cottage, the site for the concrete-making plant for the road scheme, following on from a geophysical survey (Johnson 1997a) but as no archaeological finds or features were recorded, that work is not considered further here. Lastly, a group of post-medieval timbers recorded at the River Otter bridge are presented as Appendix 8.

Summaries of the finds, any archaeological features and their locations have been transferred to the Devon Sites and Monuments Register.

Finds from the Watching Brief of Prehistoric Date

All the prehistoric flaked stone found during the Watching Brief was scanned during the assessment stage. In a great majority of instances the quantity and quality of the material recovered mean that it is impossible to say more than flaked stone of prehistoric date was present. In three cases, though, larger groups or finds of intrinsic interest were recovered, a Lower Palaeolithic handaxe from Gittisham Forge, and two small groups of flaked stone from Fairmile and Brinor, and they are reported on below in chronological order.

Lower Palaeolithic Handaxe from Gittisham Forge, by P.A. Harding

A Lower Palaeolithic handaxe was found on weathered spoil from trench 6 during the evaluation of the Romano-British site at Gittisham Forge (SY 13630 99500) (Figs 4 and 176). The Romano-British site lies 80 m to the west and the only remains found in trench 6 were of a post-medieval cobbled surface, perhaps for a yard.

The handaxe is made of Upper Greensand chert and is a ficron of Wymer's (1968, 59) Type M. These handaxes are defined as large, elegant tools with symmetrical concave edges. The Gittisham Forge handaxe measures 157 mm long and is 108 mm wide and 50 mm thick at the butt. Patches of cortex remain around the butt, which has been flaked sparingly, however, the point has been shaped into a narrow tapering tip, which is absent. It is in a slightly rolled condition (ibid., pl. x1) individual flake ridges having been dulled by river transport. There is a localised patch of battering on one side of the handaxe near the butt. Wymer (ibid., fig. 32) suggested that this feature which has been seen on other handaxes may represent use as an anvil but its formation is otherwise unexplained.

The findspot lies 300 m to the south of the River Otter at the edge of an eroded patch of valley gravel (BGS Sheet 326/340) which is probably the source of the handaxe. This gravel, which lies 50 m above the present course of the River Otter, forms part of a series of valley gravel remnants that lie on the south bank of the upper Otter valley. The base of the evaluation trench confirmed that only isolated patches of flint and chert remained in the natural clay. Remnants of five terraces have been mapped in the lower reaches of the river (Selwood *et multi alii* 1984) although these terraces have not been correlated with deposits further up the valley at Gittisham.

Eight handaxes (Wessex Archaeology 1993; Pearce and Reed 1993) have been found previously in the Otter valley, of which only one, from Tidwell Mount, Budleigh Salterton, has been assigned to a designated terrace. The remainder were found on unclassified valley gravel,

Table 2: Flaked stone (no./wt(g)) from Fairmile and Brinor

	Cores	Broken cores	Flakes	Broken flakes	Burnt flakes	Blades	Broken blades	Tools	Broken tools	Chips	Broken chips	Burnt chips	Misc. debitage	Total	Tool types
Fairmile															
Chert	1/31	–	5/139	3/21	–	–	–	–	–	–	–	–	–	9/191	
Flint	6/272	1/19	9/140	21/168	2/17	1/25	3/12	7/166	–	5/6	1/1	1/1	3/54	59/880	6 scrapers; 1 scraper/notch
Total Fairmile	7/303	1/19	14/279	24/189	2/17	1/25	3/12	7/166	0	5/6	1/1	1/1	3/54	68/1071	
Brinor															
Chert															
SY 11035 98783	1/83	–	2/36	1/6	–	–	–	–	–	–	–	–	1/19	5/144	
SY 11035 98783	1/194	–	5/72	4/14	–	–	–	–	–	–	–	–	–	10/280	
SY11175 98820	–	–	7/180	2/101	–	–	–	–	–	–	–	–	–	9/281	
Sub-total	2/277	0	14/288	7/121	0	0	0	0	0	0	0	0	1/19	24/705	
Flint															
SY11030 98780	–	–	4/39	5/36	–	1/2	1/4	–	–	1/0	–	–	–	12/81	
SY 11035 98783	–	–	4/16	3/7	–	–	–	–	1/2	–	–	–	–	8/25	?ret. flake
SY 11127 98810	–	–	3/33	1/2	–	–	–	–	1/7	–	–	–	–	5/42	scraper
SY 11175 98820	–	–	18/223	12/82	1/15	1/3	2/2	1/7	–	2/4	–	–	3/61	40/397	scraper
Sub-total	0	0	29/311	21/127	1/15	2/5	3/6	1/7	2/9	3/4	0	0	3/61	65/545	
Total Brinor	2/277	0	43/599	28/248	1/15	2/5	3/6	1/7	2/9	3/4	0	0	4/80	89/1250	

head gravel, alluvium, or Permian deposits. A pointed Greensand chert handaxe of Wymer's (1968, 52) Type F was found 700 m east of Gittisham Forge at Hayne Farm (Pearce and Reed 1993). This handaxe, which has a broken tip, was also found in a similar topographical location within the area of terrace gravel remnants. The Gittisham Forge and Hayne Farm handaxes are the most northerly handaxes yet found in the Otter valley and demonstrate that Lower Palaeolithic hunters had penetrated into the foothills of the Blackdown Hills.

Neolithic Flaked Stone from Fairmile

During the monitoring of topsoil stripping for the base of an embankment for the B 3176 Ottery St Mary to Talaton road at Fairmile (SY 0851 9743), a quantity of flaked stone was recovered (Fig. 2). At the time that the flaked stone was discovered it was difficult to determine if any subsoil features were present due to the disturbance which the heavy plant operating was causing to the surface of the very soft alluvial silts of the area. To try and establish if there were indeed any subsoil archaeological features at the location, five evaluation trenches were mechanically excavated using a toothless ditching bucket under constant archaeological supervision. Although no archaeological features were found, and the additional quantity of flaked stone recovered was small, the group is nonetheless of some interest. The site lies just above the River Tale, on the first terrace of the western valley side.

The flaked stone, by Peter S. Bellamy
A total of 68 pieces (1071 g) of worked flint and chert was recovered (Table 2). All were unstratified and in a slightly rolled condition with frequent edge damage and no patination. A number of pieces have been burnt. Flint is the predominant raw material forming 87% of the assemblage. Where it can be identified, 34% is chalk flint and 19% gravel flint, though caution must be exercised in interpreting this as nodules of gravel flint with a number of relatively fresh cortical surfaces are found in this area and, therefore, some, if not all, of the 'chalk flint' may be derived from local gravel flint. The flint is predominantly mottled grey or glossy dark brown in colour. The chert is all from the Upper Greensand.

A large number of cores are present in comparison with the sites investigated by excavation. The cores include an opposed platform narrow blade core, four small multi-directional flake cores, and a core on a large flake. Four of the cores showed signs of platform abrasion. The flakes mainly comprise undiagnostic core preparation flakes and a smaller number of broad thin flakes, some removed by a soft hammer, and occasionally with signs of platform abrasion. A small number of large blades were present also. There was a comparatively high proportion of tools in this collection, although this may well be due to the circumstances of recovery; mostly during the Watching Brief. A total of six scrapers and one scraper with a notch on the left distal side was recovered. These scrapers included two with abrupt retouch round the distal end and down both

sides to form a regular convex edge – a type common in Late Neolithic/Early Bronze Age assemblages.

This assemblage exhibits characteristics that probably relate most closely to Late Neolithic flintworking. However, the large proportion of undiagnostic material means that there may be material of more than one period present, but unrecognised, in this group. The single small narrow blade may hint at the presence of earlier activity, which may be of note in view of the location of the site above the River Tale.

Neolithic / Early Bronze Age Flaked Stone from Brinor

Following the discovery of a quantity of flaked stone from a number of locations during groundworks at Brinor (SY 1103 9878 – 1117 9882) to the south of the new road bridge over the London to Exeter railway (Fig. 2), ten evaluation trenches were excavated using a mechanical excavator. These trenches did not reveal any features of prehistoric date, though a small number of features of Roman date were identified and they are considered in Chapter 12. The flaked stone is reported here and locations of the individual groups of material are given in Table 2.

The flaked stone, by Peter S. Bellamy
This assemblage was recovered from a c. 150 m long area of the easement for the new road only 500 m to the east of the Neolithic and Bronze Age site at Castle Hill (Chapter 3). A total of 89 pieces (1250 g) was recovered, 73% flint and 27% chert (Table 2), all of which are in a slightly rolled condition with frequent edge damage and no patination. Where it can be identified, the flint comprises 21% chalk flint and 25% gravel flint, though caution must again be exercised in interpreting this. The chert is, again, all derived from the Upper Greensand.

The assemblage comprises undiagnostic trimming flakes, generally with fairly thick butts and removed by a hard hammer. A small number of thin broad flint flakes, some with signs of platform abrasion, are also present as is a very small quantity of narrow flint blades. Two chert cores were recovered – one is a small multi-directional flake core and the other a pebble with a few small removals, possibly the result of testing the raw material. The tools are all made from flint. The two scrapers are both small with regular abrupt retouch round the distal end. The retouched flake has abrupt retouch on the distal end but it is not clear whether this was deliberate or the result of accidental damage.

Overall, this assemblage perhaps fits best into the pattern of Late Neolithic/Early Bronze Age flint-working, although the small narrow blades could be evidence of Early Neolithic or Mesolithic activity. No distinctive patterning could be discerned in the spread of the material, and although there is a slight suggestion that the earlier material came from the eastern end of the spread, in view the circumstances of recovery, little emphasis should be placed on this. This evidence suggests that there is widespread prehistory activity in the vicinity of Castle Hill.

Summary

As we have seen, even after allowing for the difficulties of recovering material and identifying previously unknown archaeological sites during a Watching Brief, it is clear that the majority of the finds of prehistoric date recovered during the Watching Brief come from the eastern half of the A30 improvement, in particular from the valley of the River Otter. This echoes the distribution of the sites excavated in the course of the project and confirms what may have been suspected from existing data (Miles 1975), that the valley of the River Otter was more intensively occupied during the prehistoric period than the areas to the west (Fig. 3). The mixture of material from different periods suggests activity throughout this period.

The assemblages from Fairmile and Brinor were of a broadly similar, Late Neolithic, date and were found on river valley slopes. Neither assemblage could be characterised in terms of the range of activities taking place, though both sites suggested some procurement and working of raw lithic materials, probably collected from the river valley gravels. The quantity of tools and a number of burnt artefacts from Fairmile may suggest some settlement activity also.

3. Castle Hill

by C.A. Butterworth

Introduction

Following the preliminary assessment of the published route, which identified the site as being of archaeological interest, an evaluation undertaken in October–November 1994 recorded linear features and prehistoric pottery and flaked stone. The following summary was provided in *Schedule 4: Construction and Handback Requirements, Part 1, Annex 4A, Appendix 1, section 2.4.1*:

> The site is situated on the lower slopes of Castle Hill, north-west of Skinner's Ash Farm. It was identified as being of archaeological interest in the preliminary assessment of the published route [Weddell 1991]. This was based on the following: fieldwalking finds (flint and chert artefacts, and Roman pottery); the nearby presence of buried prehistoric features (seen as cropmarks on aerial photographs);

place-name evidence and cartographic evidence. The latter suggested that the Roman road (A30) cut across earlier field boundaries.

An evaluation excavation was undertaken by Exeter Museums Archaeological Field Unit in October/November 1994. Three trenches, aligned along the route corridor, were excavated near the railway cutting.

In Trench 1 (OS Field 5651) a number of broadly parallel north–south linear features in the form of ditches, banks and gullies were revealed. One ditch contained Bronze Age pottery and fragments of a late Neolithic or early Bronze Age collared urn. The lower fill of another ditch contained charcoal which was radiocarbon dated to the Neolithic period. Two sets of stakeholes were identified.

In Trench 2 (OS Field 7361) was a shallow ditch containing one flint implement. A

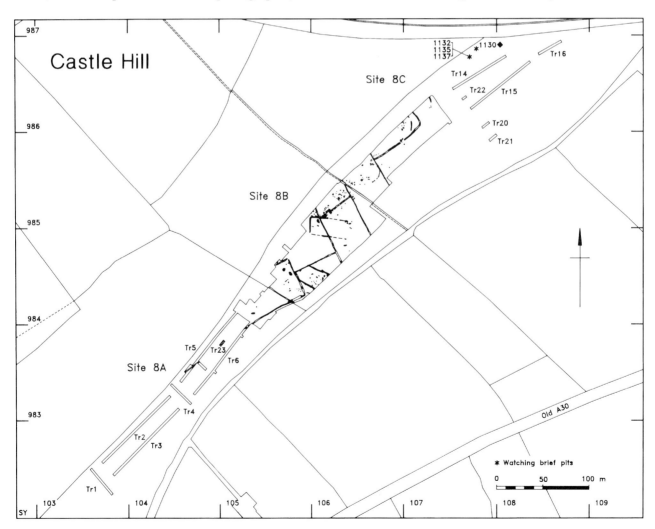

Figure 5   Castle Hill: location and general plan of excavations. The London–Exeter railway is at the top

Plate 2   Castle Hill: Neolithic enclosures 218 and 219 and the overlying Bronze Age field system from the air in the early stages of the excavation. North is to the left. Photograph: DAP/AB7 (2 July 1997) by Bill Horner, Devon County Council. Copyright reserved

further 48 flint and chert artefacts were recovered from the topsoil and lower soil horizon in the immediate vicinity. Three sherds of Roman pottery were also recovered.

Geophysical survey was undertaken by Oxford Archaeotechnics in 1994 as part of the evaluation. Numerous linear and curvilinear features and pits were identified in OS Field 5651 extending across and beyond the survey area in the vicinity of Trench 1. High magnetic susceptibility readings in OS Field 7361 indicated substantial activity, but the nature of any underlying archaeological deposits were not explained by subsequent magnetometer survey. Former banks and ditches were indicated in the field to the west of the site (OS Fields 3830/4640).

One of the ditches yielded a radiocarbon determination of 2920–2600 cal. BC (Beta-78183; 4220±60 BP), indicating Neolithic activity. The undated ring ditches known from air photographs lie *c.* 200 m to the north-east, beyond the London–Exeter railway line (Griffith, Chapter 1; Pl. 22). What may be a continuation

of the Bronze Age field system examined in the excavation is also visible in on the same aerial photgraphs, although in view of the evidence for Roman activity in the vicinity (Chapter 12, below), a later date for these features cannot be excluded. The flaked stone recovered from Brinor, also to the north of the railway (Chapter 2, above), suggest extensive Neolithic–Bronze Age activity in the immediate area.

Although the site lies in an area named 'Castle Hill', the earliest reference to the name is in 1823 in the documents of the Kennaway family in the Devon Record Office (DRO 961/T8). Benjamin Donn's 1765 map of Devon called the area 'Tower Hill' (Weddell 1991, 23).

Topography, Geology, and Land-use

The site lay on a slight south-east facing slope between 68 and 72 m AOD and *c.* 450 m north-west of the River Otter near Fenny Bridges, centred on SY 1065 9850 (Figs 2 and 5). The angle of the slope steepened noticeably to the north of the eastern end of the site. The underlying geology is Upper Sandstone with Valley Gravels not far to the north-west (Geological Survey of

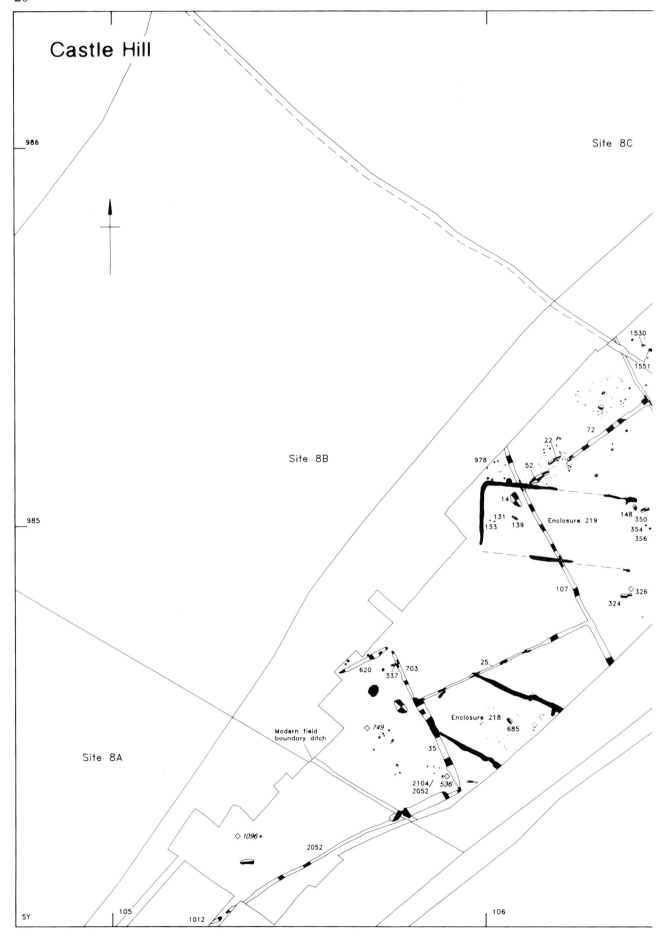

Figure 6   Castle Hill: plan of excavations

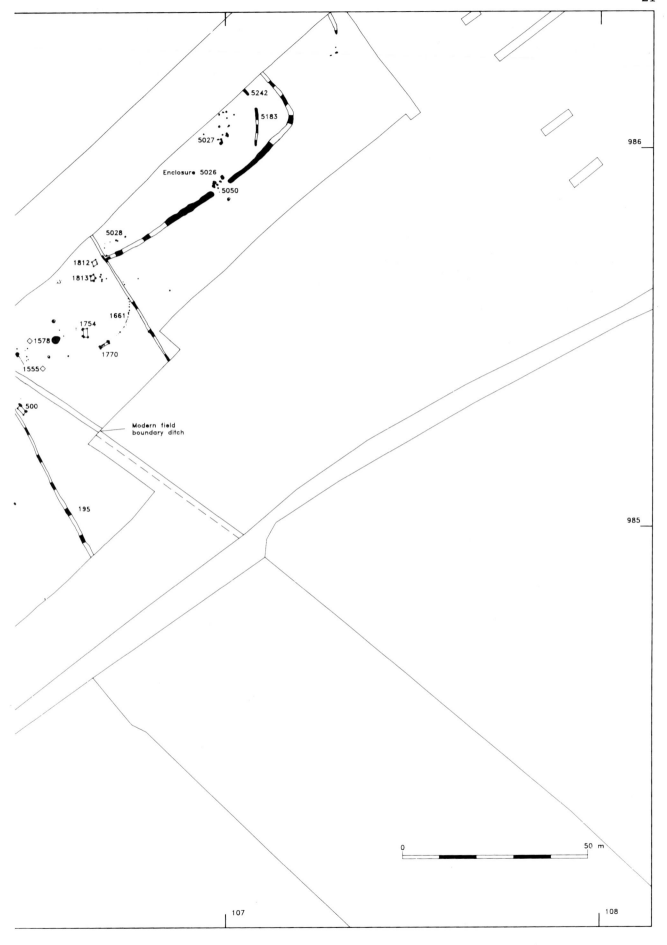

5242
5183
5027
Enclosure 5026
5050
5028
1812
1813
1661
1754
1578
1770
1555
500
Modern field
boundary ditch
195

986

985

107   108

0   50 m

Key

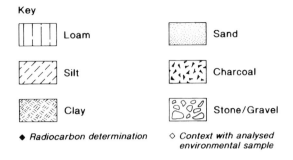

Loam

Silt

Clay

Sand

Charcoal

Stone/Gravel

◆ *Radiocarbon determination*   ◇ *Context with analysed environmental sample*

Figure 7   Drawing conventions for feature fills

Great Britain, Drift, Sheet 326 and 340, Sidmouth). The predominant natural soils encountered, however, were silty clays with intermittent spreads of gravel and occasional sandy patches, but there was much localised variation across all the trenched areas.

The site extended across three fields which were under grass at the time of the excavation but which had previously been in cultivation.

Excavation Areas

The site (W2414.8) was sub-divided into three areas, 8A, B and C (from south-west to north-east), of which 8B was the main excavation area (Fig. 5). Eleven Strip and Record trenches (1–9, 23, and trench 24 as a southward extension from trench 5) were opened in area 8A, with more extensive stripping in the eastern part of the area eventually leading to the amalgamation of trenches 7, 8, and 9 and the area surrounding them with the large trench in 8B. Of the 13 Strip and Record trenches (10–22) opened in area 8C, seven (trenches 10–13, 17–19) were absorbed into an extensive eastern enlargement of the main trench. The total area investigated was 14,443 m². The excavations were carried out between April and October 1997.

Methods

A number of features of natural origin and some isolated possible post-holes are not described here; details can be found in archive. Details of the many possible

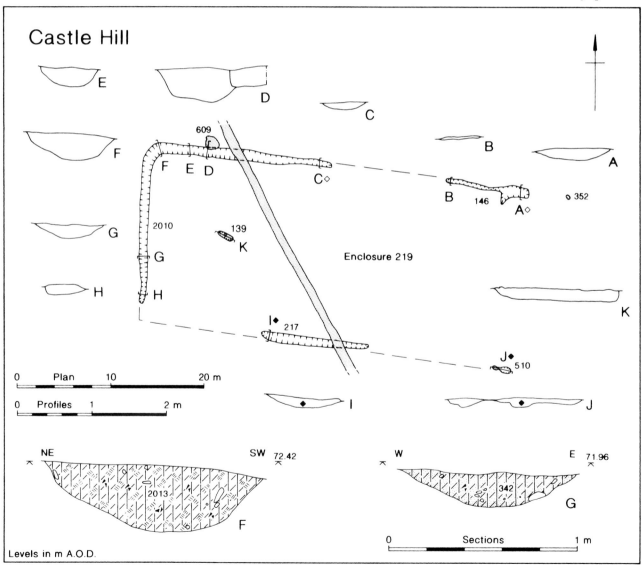

Figure 8   Castle Hill: plan and sections of Neolithic enclosure 219

stake-holes which were intermittently dispersed about the site are also in archive. The conventions used in the drawings are given in Figure 7.

Results

Neolithic

Enclosures 219 and 218

Stratigraphically, the earliest features at Castle Hill were two groups of discontinuous ditches in area 8B, which formed sub-rectangular enclosures 218 and 219 (Figs 6, 8, 9; Pl. 2). At their closest the enclosures were 33 m apart, with 219 to the north and slightly east of 218. They were similarly but not identically orientated; the long axis of 219 was aligned almost directly west–east, but 218 was angled more to the south-east. Both were fully excavated. Two radiocarbon dates were obtained from enclosure 219, 3610–3140 cal. BC (AA-30670; 4630±50 BP) and 2920–2600 cal. BC (Beta 78183; 4220±60 BP), placing both in the Neolithic. Peterborough Ware was recovered from 218.

Enclosure 219

Enclosure 219 (Fig. 8) was less well preserved than 218, but more of it, possibly the full surviving extent, was within the excavation area. It consisted of three definite stretches of ditch plus a short and rather doubtful possible fourth, giving a maximum overall length of c. 42 m and maximum width of c.19.5 m. The longest ditch, 2010, was 36.5 m long, forming almost the whole of the western side (c.17 m), the north-western corner and part of the northern side. After a break of 12 m the north side was completed by 146, c. 9 m long, and the south side by 217, c. 13 m from 2010 and c. 11.5 m long. A second short possible section of ditch, 510, 1.9 m long, further along the projected line of the south side does not increase the overall dimensions of the enclosure. A doubtful post-hole, 352, was on the same alignment as, and c. 3.9 m from, the eastern end of the northern ditch. The ditches appeared to peter out rather than end in terminals. There was no sign of a connecting eastern ditch within the excavation area.

The largest ditch section, 1.2 m wide and 0.34 m deep, was at the north-western corner; nowhere else was it more than 1 m wide, and it was usually less than 0.2 m deep. The ditches appeared to be fairly consistent in profile, being generally rounded, but this apparent similarity could have been an effect of the shallowness of many sections with any variation in the truncated upper profiles having been lost. No stake-holes were recorded in or near any part of the ditch. In the evaluation, which was undertaken in the winter, it had proved possible to distinguish a secondary fill but when the site was excavated in the dry summer months, despite the spraying of features with water, only a single fill was recorded in each section excavated. There was, however, much variation between sections, from light greyish–brown sandy loam through mid reddish–brown sandy clay loam or sandy silt loam, to yellowish–brown or dark brown silty clay loam. Charcoal was rare, but enough blackthorn charcoal was recovered from the southern segment of the western end of section 217 to

allow radiocarbon dating to be undertaken; yielding a date of 3610–3140 cal. BC (AA-30670; 4630±50 BP). As the ditch was so truncated at this point (Fig. 8, section I), it seems likely – but cannot be proved – that the surviving deposits are the primary fill. The possibility that this small quantity of charcoal is residual from the Early Neolithic activity evidenced by the flaked stone should also be acknowldeged.

The date from the secondary fill of segment 510 examined in the evaluation is 2920–2600 cal. BC (Beta 78183; 4220±60 BP). The charcoal for that assay was not identified to species or whether it represented heartwood or sapwood, however, both dates are consistent with an origin in the later part of the earlier Neolithic, with activity continuing into the middle Neolithic.

A few widely dispersed features, some of which were probably of natural origin, were recorded inside the enclosure (Figs 6 and 8). Amongst these were two possible post-holes, 131 and 133, and a pit, 139, near the western end of the enclosure. Over to the east were another two possible post-holes, 354 and 356, an irregularly shaped feature, 148, and another possible pit, 350. Details of these features are held in archive. A large pit, 14, was also within the enclosure but dates from a later period and is described below.

Enclosure 218

Enclosure 218 consisted of two almost parallel ditches, both running out of the excavation area to the south-east (Figs 6 and 9). The enclosure had a maximum known length of c. 25.9 m and the ditches were between 17.4 m and 19.4 m apart, the wider distance being at the south-east. The north-western ends of the enclosure ditches were cut by the ditches of the Middle Bronze Age field system (see below), although the northern one, 26, extended slightly beyond its interceptor. The enclosure may have been open at the western end. There was no ditch there, and two intercut possible gullies, 29 and 2088, in approximately the right location and orientation to have been part of the enclosure were more probably the result of root and/or animal disturbance, of which there was much in the area.

Each side of the enclosure was formed from two separate ditches, which were almost, but not quite continuous. These sectional ditches may have been of similar length: the two most complete, 26, at the north and the corresponding southern ditch, 36, measured 17.1 m and a little over 16 m respectively; the western end of 36 was, however, cut by field system ditch 35 (see below). The terminals of ditches 26 (west) and 532 (east) turned away from each other slightly, leaving 0.1 m of unexcavated ground between them. The equivalent area for the southern ditches, 36 (west) and 2074 (east), was obscured by root disturbance and intrusive Late Bronze Age pottery was found (Fig. 25, 45), but they appeared either to be misaligned or, perhaps, incomplete. Ditch 2074 narrowed abruptly from a width of c. 1.5 m near the trench edge to c .0.86 m at the probable terminal; it was also narrower than ditch 36. There may have been a gap of c. 0.2 m between the terminals. It is not possible to say whether this arrangement represents an extension to the west of the

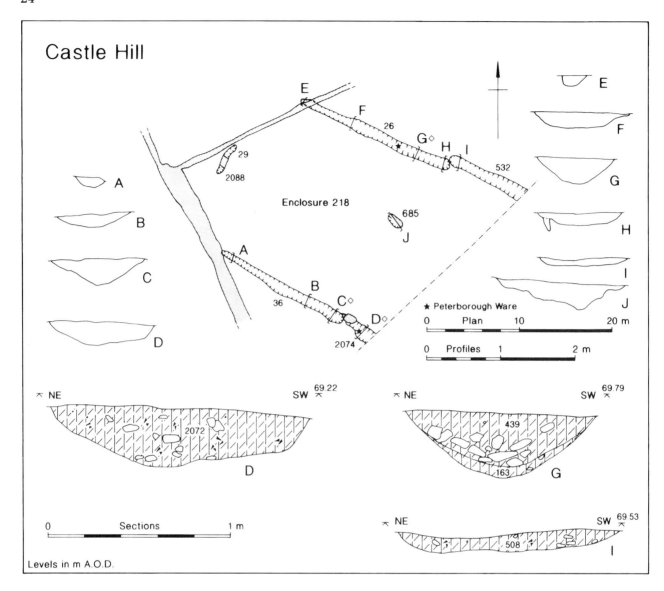

Figure 9   Castle Hill: plan and sections of Neolithic enclosure 218

enclosure, or whether it represents the digging of the ditches in segments.

The ditches of enclosure 218 varied considerably in size. The greatest width, 1.5 m, was recorded in 532; the maximum depth was 0.35 m in 36, but this ditch also had the smallest section with a width of 0.6 m and depth of 0.13 m. The ditches were irregular in profile, varying from gently sloping sides and rounded or almost flat base to V-shaped; the sides were more steeply angled in the smaller sections. Most of the ditches contained only one fill, and these were less variable than for enclosure 219, mostly yellowish, mid, or dark brown silty loam with occasional charcoal.

The Peterborough Ware was found in both sides of the enclosure, but the majority was found in one of the few segments in which a secondary fill was identifiable in north-eastern ditch 26. The secondary fill was identified in both the evaluation and the excavation. The remainder of the Peterborough Ware came from the southern half of the terminal of segment 2074 in which only a single fill (2072) was recognisable. Only one

concentration of flaked stone was noted, in segment 26, 2 m to the east of the Peterborough Ware bowl. The material from the north-eastern ditch included a number of refitting chert flakes and core.

A number of possible stake-holes were recorded in the sides and bases of the terminals of ditches 26 and 532: 10 in the north-western terminal, a further 22 in the south-eastern one, and another 16 in the surrounding area. Three were noted in the base of ditch 36 on the other side of the enclosure, but none was recorded in the terminals on that side. Up to 51 were recorded in the area between the ditches. Full details of these features are in archive; similar features noted in a root-disturbed area adjoining (and extending into) 532 were described by the excavator as being the result of root and/or animal disturbance and this was likely to have been the case elsewhere. Certainly, the lack of consistency or pattern in the location and arrangement of these features suggests that natural disturbance was a probable cause, although their presence and/or absence could also reflect difference of experience,

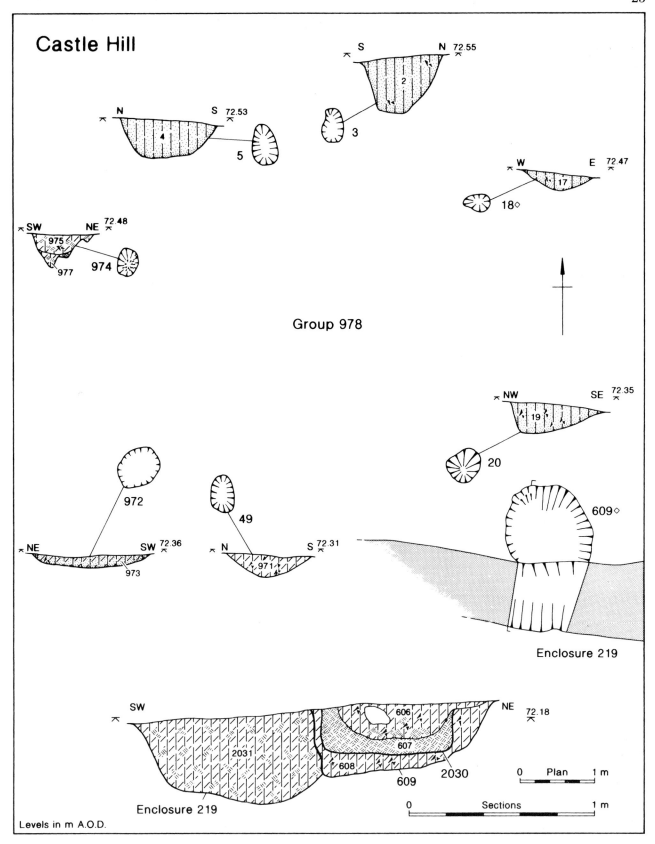

Figure 10   Castle Hill: plan and sections of Bronze Age post-hole group 978 and pit 609

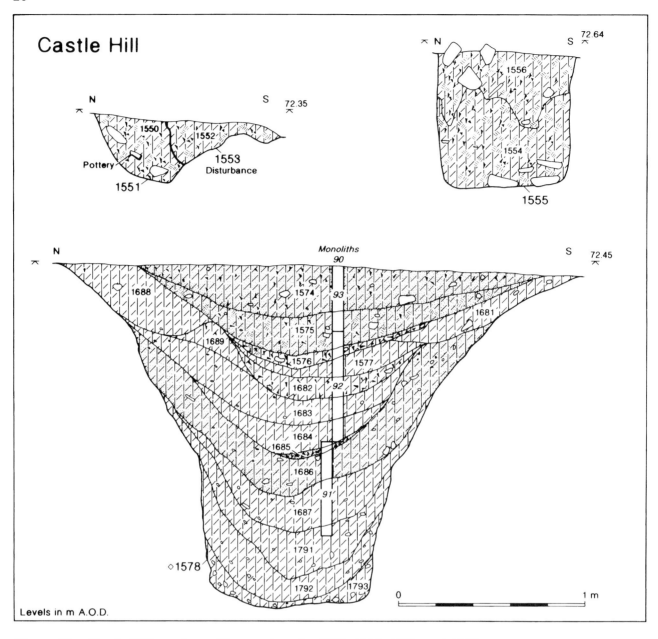

Figure 11   Castle Hill: sections of Bronze Age pits 1578, 1551, 1553, and 1555

observation and technique amongst the excavators. Only one other feature, 685, possibly also the result of root disturbance, was recorded in the interior of the enclosure. It was roughly oval in plan, 1.5 m long, 0.9 m wide, and 0.3 m deep, and was filled with charcoal-flecked, brown silty loam. Its location, midway in an open end of the monument, and perhaps at the very end of it in any first phase, might suggest that it once held a timber post. As it survived, the feature was very shallow, but this may be due the extensive truncation of the archaeological deposits.

Bronze Age

Early Bronze Age
Beaker pottery was recovered from five features: two small pits (or large post-holes) in the eastern part of the site, 1551 and 1555; pit 609, which cut the northern ditch

of enclosure 219; post-hole 7; and from a large tree-throw hole, 1602 (not on plan).

Pits 1555, 1551, and 1530
The eastern group consisted of one shallow and two deeper pits or large post-holes, 1555, 1551, and 1530 (Figs 6 and 11). Beaker pottery was recovered from the primary and secondary fills of 1555, from 1551 (which was disturbed by an animal burrow), and from a large tree-throw hole, 1602. Relatively large amounts of Middle Bronze Age pottery were also found in pits 1530 and 1555. Flaked stone cores and flakes, some refitting, scrapers, and a broken hammerstone were also found in pit 1555, and there were two scrapers in 1531.

Middle Bronze Age
The majority of the remaining features on the site, principally a field system and enclosure with associated post-hole groups, were of Middle Bronze Age date. A

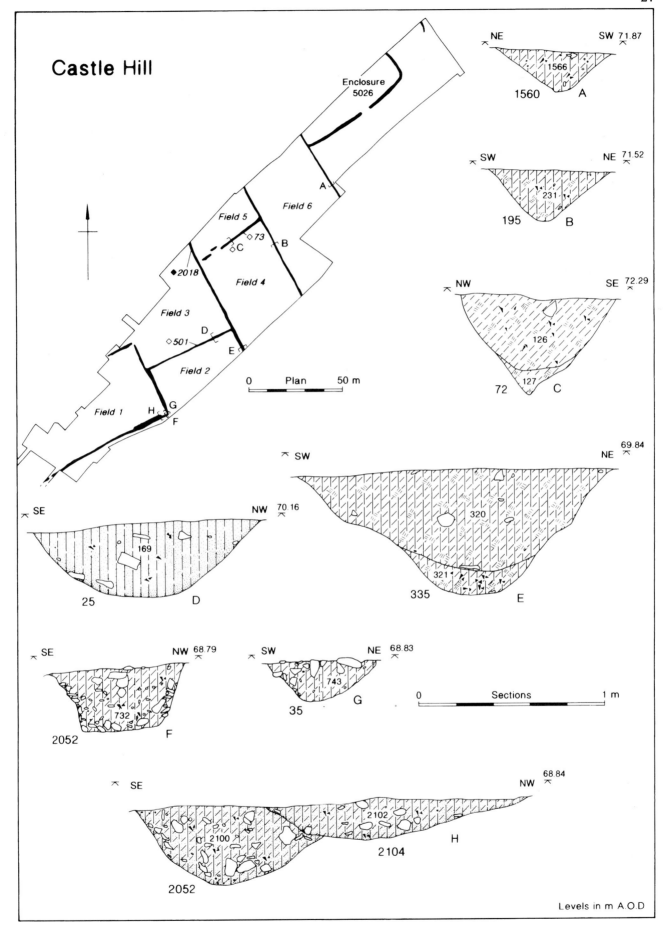

Figure 12   Castle Hill: plan and sections of Bronze Age field system

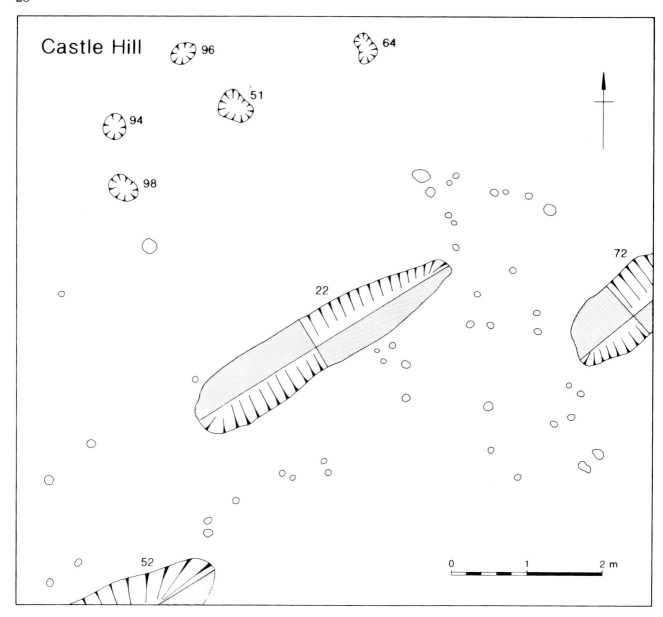

Figure 13   Castle Hill: plan of entrance between Bronze Age fields 4 and 5

radiocarbon date of 1440–1150 cal. BC (AA-30671; 3060±55 BP) was obtained for ditch 107.

Field system ditches
Superimposed across 218 and 219 were the ditches of a coaxial field system with, at its east, part of an associated enclosure (Figs 6 and 12). At least five fields could be identified but the extent of the field system is unknown. No ditches were seen in the Strip and Record trenches beyond the enclosure to north-east and only one crossed the additional trenches to the south-west of the main excavation area but, despite the evidence of aerial photography, its extent to the north and south is not known. A short shallow ditch near the northern tip of the extended excavation area in 8C was not directly linked with the field system. Six boundaries were within the main excavation trench, giving the fields widths of *c.* 40 m (four) and *c.* 50 m (two), but no complete measurements were recorded. The longest ditch extended for at

least 150 m. There were no paired parallel ditches that might have flanked tracks or droveways. The orientation of the field system was at variance with modern field boundaries but followed the natural (south-east facing) slope of the land.

Although part of a planned layout, differences of size and profile showed that the ditches were dug in sections. This was shown most clearly at the south-west corner of the main block of fields where a steep-sided flat-bottomed ditch, 2052, met a shallow, V-shaped ditch less than half its size, 35 (Fig. 12, F, G). Further to the north-west, ditch 35 cut ditch 25 (which divided fields 2 and 3) but was itself cut by 703, a much smaller ditch, which continued the boundary further to the north-west. Few recuts were recorded but at the south-west corner of the main group 2052 was cut by 2104, a broad, shallow ditch, which was, however, only *c.* 15 m long; ditch 2052 continued south-westwards (as 1012) and out of the excavation area. A second possible recut, of ditch 35, was recorded in one section only.

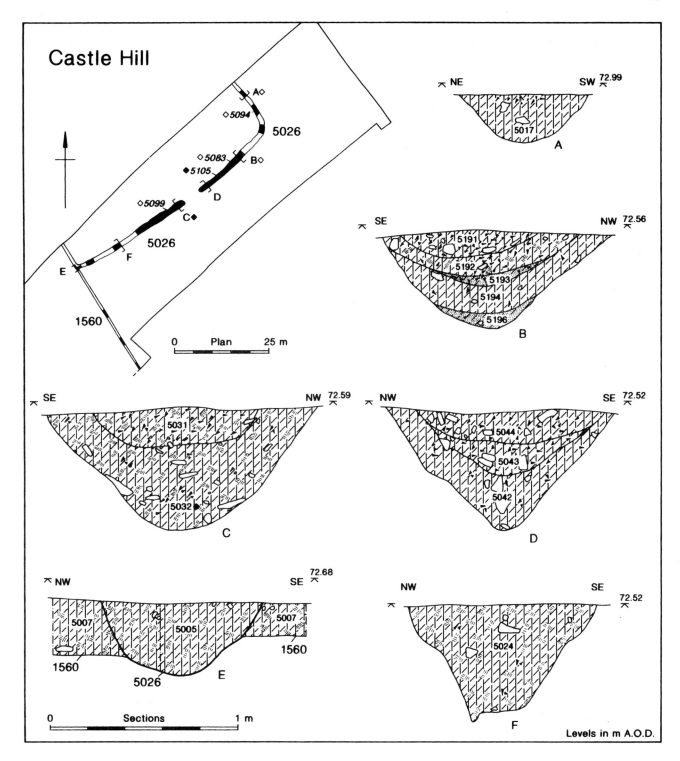

Figure 14   Castle Hill: plan and sections of Bronze Age enclosure 5026

The ditches ranged in width from 0.4 m to 2.4 m (but most were less than 1 m wide) and in depth from 0.13 m to 0.65 m. They were variable in profile; generally broad, shallow, and with flat bases to the south-west, they were narrower, rounded but sometimes V-shaped to the north-east. Few ditch sections contained more than one fill, but these were usually clay, silty clay, and/or silty loam, or, less frequently, sandy silt, and ranged in colour from dark brown through reddish- to yellowish- or light brown. Finds were scarce.

Four gaps were recorded, some but not all of which, were entrances. One certain entrance 1.6 m wide separated outlying ditches 2052 and 1012 on the south of field 1. There may have been an entrance at the north-eastern corner of the same field, between ditches 703 and 620, where there was a gap of 1.2 m. Although both ditches appeared to terminate short of the corner by design, 703 was very shallow and may have been truncated; it did not resume within the excavation area. A short trench, 337 (1.4 m long), may have been

Plate 3 Castle Hill: enclosure 5026 viewed from the east in the early stages of excavation, with the dark upper fills of the ditch clearly visible

Plate 4 Castle Hill: Bronze Age field system ditch 1560 viewed from the south

associated with this gap; it was parallel to 620 and joined 703 *c*. 3.4 m south of the 'terminal'. There may have been another entrance at the north-western corner of field 4 between ditch 107 and short ditch 52, where there was a gap of almost 1.8 m. (The ditch of Neolithic enclosure 219 would, coincidentally, have passed through this gap, but would, by this period, have been infilled.) A more complex entrance was located only 6 m along the same boundary between fields 4 and 5 (Fig. 13). It consisted of three elements: ditch 52; ditch 72, on the same alignment but *c*. 5.5 m from 52; short ditch, 22, on the same alignment as 52 and 72 but offset by *c*. 1 m to the north-west. Five post-holes, 51, 64, 94, 96, and 98, between 2.5 m and 2.8 m north of ditch 22, may have been associated features. They were between 0.38 m and 0.7 m wide and 0.05–0.28 m deep, and were, for the most part, filled with charcoal-flecked, greyish–brown silty clay or silty loam; 64 was filled with reddish–brown loamy sand. Clusters of possible stake-holes were noted in and around the entrance and in the east corner of the field (Fig. 13). Although the second group formed a roughly oval spread, no convincing structural patterns were discernible.

A number of post-holes were recorded in the east of field 1. It was not possible to convincingly ascribe them

to groups but is possible that they derive from post-built structures. The charred plant remains and charcoal from post-holes 536, 749, and 1096 (not on plan) do not suggest that any buildings were used for storing crops.

Post-hole group 978; pit 609
A group of eight possible post-holes, 978, was just to the north of enclosure 219 (and west of field system ditch 107) (Figs 6 and 10). The group may represent a post-built round-house, although the plan is almost certainly incomplete if this is so. Seven post-holes, 3, 5, 18, 20, 49, 972, 974, formed an irregular circle *c*. 4.8 m in diameter. Post-hole 2030, 0.7 m south-east of post-hole 20, could have formed part of a south-east-facing entrance but, if this was the case, there was no evidence. It appeared to be be cut more or less centrally through infilled pit 609. If this was the case, however, there was no evidence for a matching post to complete the entrance. The area within the post-holes showed much evidence of animal activity and a number of possible stake-holes recorded there and in or near some post-holes were most probably the result of such disturbance (details are held in the archive), as perhaps were some of the post-holes.

The post-holes were variable in size, from 0.34 m to 0.71 m wide and 0.07 m to 0.3 m deep, and in their fills. These ranged from loamy sand, through silty loam to

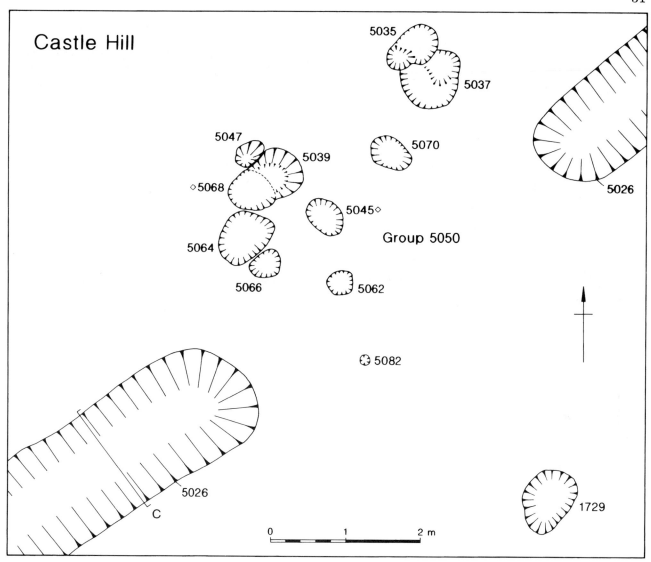

Castle Hill

5035

5037

5047

5039

5070

◇5068

5045◇

5064

Group 5050

5066

5062

⊙ 5082

5026

5026

C

1729

0   1   2 m

Figure 15   Castle Hill: plan of entrance to Bronze Age enclosure (group 5027)

silty clay loam, but were predominantly reddish–brown in colour. Most contained some charcoal, although usually in limited quantities. The base and sides of 2030 were filled (or lined) with clean dark pink clay. The upper fill was mid greyish–brown silty loam, with large pieces of chert and patches of clay. Flaked stone, including scrapers, a piercer, and knapping waste were found in and around 978 and pit 609.

Pit 609 cut the northern edge of infilled enclosure ditch 219, and appeared to be cut by post-hole 2030 which may, however, have been a distinctive fill of the original pit. The pit was *c.* 1.7 m long, 1.4 m wide and 0.36 m deep and the undisturbed part was filled with charcoal-flecked, light brown silty loam. Beaker sherds were found in 606, the upper fill of 2030, where they were associated with Trevisker Ware (Figs 23, 5–9; 24, 21). It is possible that the Beaker sherds are redeposited from enclosure ditch 219.

Pit 1578
This large pit lay within Field 6, and was *c.* 2.35 m in diameter at the surface, narrowing to *c.* 0.8 m at the

base, and was 1.8 m deep; the base was flat (Figs 6 and 11). The lower two-thirds of the pit were filled with a series of layers of dark yellowish–brown or dark brown predominantly silty loam, although a small central lens of sandy loam (1685) overlaid a layer of sandy silty loam (1686) almost half way up. Nearer the top, as the pit widened, dumps of 'dirty', charcoal-flecked or sometimes ashy material (e.g. 1576, 1574) filled the centre of the pit, with cleaner soil, probably the result of natural erosion and slumping, towards the edge. There were no finds and insufficient pollen was present to allow pollen counts to be made, although after extensive scanning a few grains of cereal type were noted. The poor survival of pollen may be due to extensive oxidation or ground water fluctuations.

The pit, which may have been a well, has been attributed to this phase on the basis of the charcoal in the upper fills which may derive from the occupation the nearby enclosure 5026. It is possible, however, that the pit is of earlier date; either Neolithic or Early Bronze Age. There is no evidence to suggest that it held a large timber post.

Plate 5   Castle Hill: enclosure 5026 with field ditch 1560 in the early stages of excavation, viewed from the west

Post-hole alignment 1661

A curving post- and stake-hole alignment, 1661 (Fig. 6) may have been cut by and thus pre-date Middle Bronze Age field system ditch 1560 but there is no certain evidence that this was the case. The alignment, or fence line, consisted of 15 post-holes and 13 possible stake-holes in a broad north to south-south-west arc with an overall length of *c*. 15.5 m. Two post-holes and one stake-hole were to the east of ditch 1560 with the remainder to its west. The post-holes were at intervals of 0.45–1.3 m, but became more widely spaced and interspersed with more possible stake-holes to the south-west. The post-holes ranged in width from 0.13 m to 0.4 m and in depth from 0.04 m to 0.28 m; 13 had depths of 0.15 m or less. Most were filled with dark yellowish- or reddish–brown silty loam, usually but not always charcoal-flecked. A group of five post-holes, 1770, at the south-western end of 1661 may have continued the alignment, perhaps forming an entrance and giving a possible overall length of 21.2 m. It is, however, considered more likely that group 1770 represents two or four-post structures. There was a notable concentration of flaked stone tools to the north of 1661 and it is possible that the fence defined an area where stone objects were made and used.

Enclosure 5026 and post-hole group 5050

Enclosure 5026 was at the north-eastern end of the field system, making use of a field boundary as its

south-western side (Figs 6, 14, 15). The enclosure ditch cut field boundary ditch 1560 (Pl. 5), suggesting that the enclosure was added to the field system or that its ditch was recut. It is possible that the enclosure was originally free-standing and that the field system was laid out around it, but any evidence that this might have been the case was destroyed by the recutting of the ditches and it cannot be demonstrated on the evidence available.

Since the radiocarbon date for the primary fill of the western terminal, 1400–1050 cal. BC (AA-30673; 2985±50 BP), is later than the date for the primary fill of the eastern ditch of 1510–1260 cal. BC (AA-30675; 3115±50 BP), it seems more probable that the western ditch was recut after the enclosure had become established. The full size of the enclosure is not known since it extended beyond the northern edge of the road landtake, but its width, the only complete dimension, was *c*. 64 m. An entrance 4.9 m wide entrance was sited near the middle of the south-eastern side.

The ditches either side of the entrance varied in width between 0.7 m and 1.6 m and in depth between 0.28 m and 0.72 m; the entrance terminals were slightly smaller than the larger of these dimensions. In profile the ditches were steep-sided, the bases usually round but flattened in small number of sections. The ditch fills were markedly more variable than those of the field system ditches, particularly to the north-east of the entrance (and nearer to the cluster of features inside the

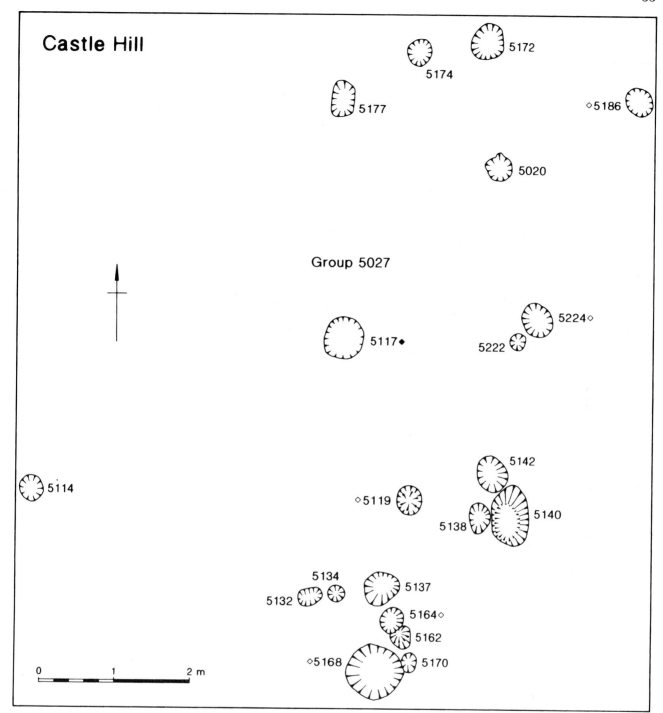

Figure 16   Castle Hill: plan of post-holes in eastern part of Bronze Age enclosure (group 5027)

enclosure; see below). Dark yellowish–brown to reddish brown sandy silt, sandy loam, and silty clay loam predominated and many of the upper fills in this part of the ditch were charcoal-rich. To the south-west of the entrance, fewer fills were recorded and primary fills were often much deeper (up to 0.5 m), consisting principally of dark greyish–brown to reddish–brown silty clay and silty clay loam. Charcoal from the primary and upper fills of one section from near the terminal of the eastern half of the ditch gave radiocarbon dates of 1400–1050 cal. BC (AA-30673; 2985±50 BP) and 1420–1130 cal. BC (AA-30674; 3035±50 BP) res-

pectively. It is not clear whether the enclosure was defined by an internal bank of any size rather than, for example, a hedgerow. There is little evidence for an internal bank having eroded into the enclosure ditch.

The posts of gates or some other form of barrier were represented by a group of 11 post-holes, 5050, at the entrance (Fig. 15). Two intercut pairs of post-holes, 5037 cut by 5035 at the east and 5039 cut by 5068 at the west, showed that the structure was replaced, at least in part. The earlier post-holes of each pair were 1.67 m apart and 1.19 m and c. 2.25 m respectively from the east and west terminals of the enclosure ditch. The later ones

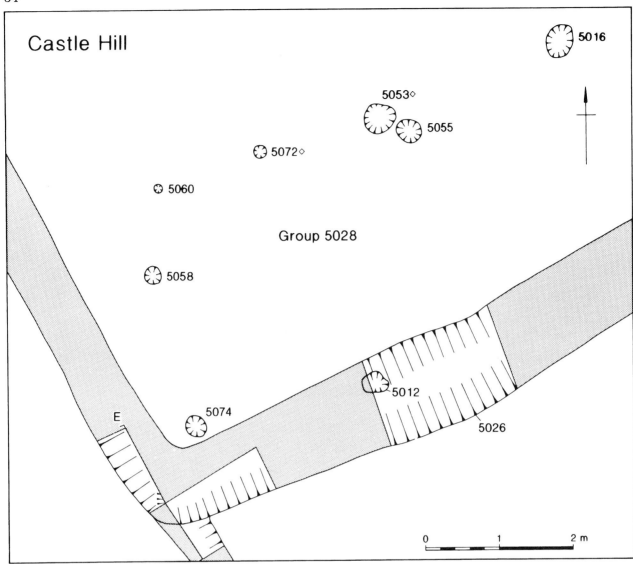

Figure 17   Castle Hill: plan of post-holes in south-western part of Bronze Age enclosure 5026

were *c.* 2.2 m apart and 1.7 m (east) and 2.04 m (west) from the ditch terminals. A small post-hole, 5047, was immediately north-west of 5039 (i.e. further inside the enclosure) and a much larger one, 5064, was south of 5068. Three post-holes, 5066, 5045, and 5070, were ranged in a line across the middle of the entrance. Post-hole 5045 contained a large quantity of oak sapwood and heartwood which may be from a post. An ill-defined possible post-hole, 5062, was situated between the ditch terminals (closer to the western one) and a small post-hole, 5082, was not far to the south-east. One other large post-hole, 1729, was almost 4 m outside the entrance.

Features within the enclosure; post-hole groups 5027–8 and ditches 5183 and 5242
Inside the enclosure but not necessarily contemporary with it were two short ditches and two groups of post-holes, one north of the entrance and the second, smaller, one in the southern corner (Figs 6, 16, 17).

Post-hole group 5027, consisting of 20 features to the north of the enclosure entrance and west of ditch 5183

(Fig. 16), showed no obvious or complete structures, but elements of structural groups are represented. An arc of four post-holes, 5177, 5174, 5172, and 5186, may be one such, but there are many other possible alignments. It is equally possible, that a number of two, or perhaps four-post structures are represented. None of the features was very deep, only two being more than 0.2 m, and some may have been the result of root and/or animal disturbance. However, post-hole 5168 contained thin slivers of oak, probably heartwood, which may be the charred base of a post. Two sherds of Middle Bronze Age pottery were recovered from post-hole 5140, which was the deepest feature at 0.28 m.

Seven post-holes in the southern corner of the enclosure, group 5028 (Fig. 17), may in fact post-date it if an eighth post-hole, 5012, forms part of the group, for it cut the infilled ditch. The group was approximately rectilinear in plan, two 'sides' running almost parallel with the south-eastern and south-western enclosure ditches. Post-hole 5012 could have been accommodated within such a structure as part of a third side. As with group 5027, some of the features may have been caused

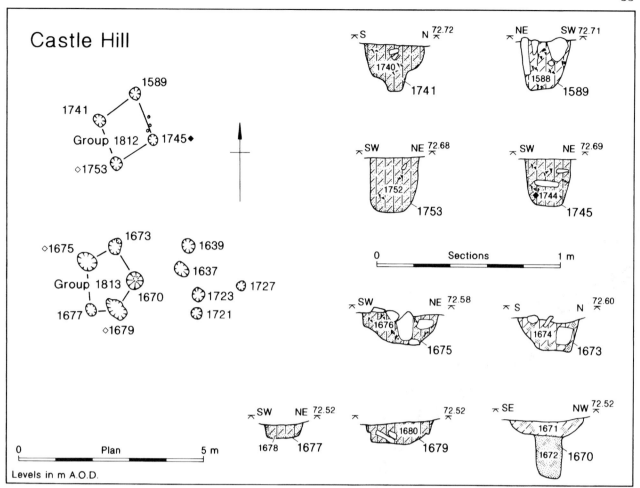

Figure 18   Castle Hill: plan and sections of Bronze Age four-/five-post structures 1812 and 1813

by root or animal activity and all were quite shallow, not more than 0.18 m deep (except for 5012, which was 0.33 m). No finds were recovered from any feature.

Ditch 5183, slightly curved in plan and *c.* 10 m long, lay towards the eastern corner of the enclosure but was nowhere very near to the enclosure ditch. The southern terminal of 5183 was *c.* 11 m from the eastern entrance terminal (and 1.8 m from the nearest part of the enclosure ditch); the northern terminal was 7 m from the north-eastern enclosure ditch. Separated from 5183 by a gap of *c.* 3.8 m, ditch 5242 headed out of the trench to the north-west. No finds were recovered from either ditch.

Post-built structures 1812 and 1813 and associated features

There were several post-built structures in the field immediately south-west of enclosure 5026 (Figs 6 and 18). Few of these features could be dated and while it might be assumed that most are contemporary with the enclosure, a radiocarbon determination from group 1812 suggest that it is, in fact, slightly later.

What appear to be two four-post structures, 1812 and 1813, within 1.76 m of each other, were a short distance south-west of the enclosure. The northern one, 1812, was *c.* 1.5 m square. The post-holes (1589, 1741, 1745, 1753) were between 0.26 m and 0.3 m in diameter

0.25 m and 0.28 m deep. Three were filled with greyish–brown sandy silty loam, the other with silty loam; two were heavily charcoal-flecked. Charcoal from 1745 gave a radiocarbon date of 1080–820 cal. BC (AA-30672; 2765±50 BP). Three possible stake-holes were recorded near post-hole 1745 at the eastern corner. Structure 1813 may have been of five rather than four-posts, since the south-east side appeared to have been augmented by a fifth post-hole, 1679, albeit slightly off-line. The structure was less regular than 1812, the shortest side measuring *c.* 1.3 m and the longest *c.* 1.73 m. The principal post-holes (1670, 1673, 1675, 1677) were between 0.21 m and 0.42 m in diameter and 0.08 m and 0.3 m deep. They were filled with reddish- or yellowish–brown sandy silty loam or silty clay loam; charcoal was present only in post-hole 1675 where the large fragments (up to 103 mm) of oak sapwood and heartwood may have been from a post. Post-hole 1679 had a diameter of 0.35 m and was 0.12 m deep; it too was filled with reddish–brown sandy silty loam.

Two possible two-post structures lay to the east of 1813 (Fig. 18): one pair, 1637 and 1639, was within 0.9 m of 1813, and the other, 1721 and 1723, was 1.4 m away. Post-holes 1637 and 1639 were 0.3 m apart. They were 0.3 m and 0.28 m in diameter and 0.06 m and 0.15 m deep respectively; both were filled with reddish–brown silty loam, lightly charcoal-flecked in the case of

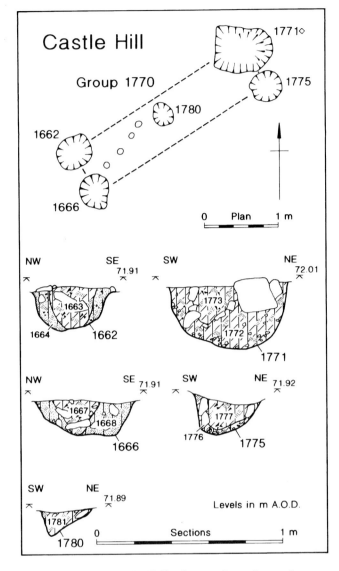

Figure 19   Castle Hill: plan and sections of five-post structure 1770

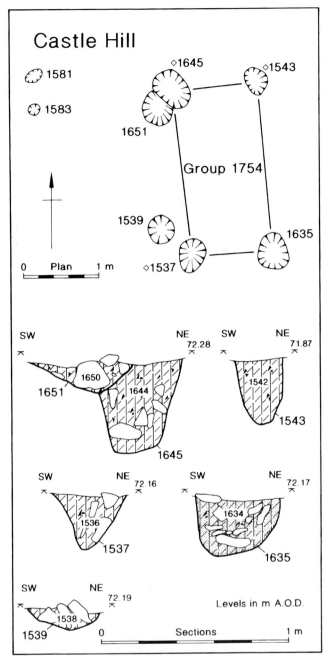

Figure 20   Castle Hill: plan and sections of six-post structure 1754

1637. Post-holes 1721 and 1723 were 0.4 m south-east of 1637 and were 0.14 m apart. They were 0.33 m and 0.31 m in diameter and were both 0.13 m deep. They were filled with charcoal-flecked reddish–brown silty clay loam. A fifth post-hole, 1727, was 0.87 m east of the second pair.

A cluster of 15 possible stake-holes within an area approximately 1.4 m square was recorded *c.* 5 m to the west of four-post structure 1813.

Five-post group 1770
Post-hole group 1770 was *c.* 3.7 m south-west of curvilinear alignment 1661 (Figs 6 and 19). It consisted of two pairs of post-holes, 1771, 1775, and 1662, 1666, *c.* 2.1 m apart, with post-hole 1780 midway between them. The paired post-holes were 0.4–0.7 m wide and between 0.16 m and 0.32 m deep; 1780 was 0.25 m in diameter and 0.1 m deep. Four possible stake-holes were recorded between 1780 and the western post-holes. Filled mainly with reddish- to greyish–brown silty clay loam, the outer post-holes also had pieces of chert as possible packing.

There were no finds. It is possible that this represents a very narrow four-post structure, but it is perhaps more likely to represent the remains of a rebuilt two-post structure.

Six-post group 1754
A group of six post-holes, 1754, lay *c.* 3.5 m north-west of 1770, of which four (1537, 1635, 1543, 1645) formed a structure with maximum dimensions of 2.3 m by 1.15 m (Figs 6 and 20). Post-holes 1651 and 1539 may have replaced or provided further support at the west; post-hole 1651 cut 1645 and 1539 was only 0.25 m north-west of 1537. If, however, post-holes 1651 and 1539 superseded the earlier ones this would suggest a two-post structure replacing a four-post one. The

post-holes ranged in width from 0.25 m to 0.5 m and in depth from 0.3 m to 0.5 m. Three were filled with greyish- or reddish–brown silty loam with the fourth containing very dark brown sandy silty loam.

Four-post structure 500

An isolated four-post structure was recorded less than 1 m from the junction of field system ditches 72 (Fig. 6) and 195 (Fig. 12). The north-western and south-western post-holes of the group, 198 and 403, were 1.96 m apart and *c.* 0.7 m from the other pair, 290 and 292. A fifth post-hole, 299, was immediately north-west of 290. Post-holes 290 and 292 and were 0.65 m and 0.62 m wide and 0.15 m and 0.18 m deep respectively, both showing possible stone packing around post-pipes.

The other pair of post-holes were smaller in diameter at 0.38 m and 0.35 m, but were similar in depth at 0.19 m and 0.13 m; 299 was 0.43 m in diameter and 0.12 m deep. Post-hole 403 was filled with reddish–brown silty clay, but the others contained yellowish–brown silty loam or silty clay loam; all fills were lightly charcoal-flecked.

Pit 14

A large, almost wedge-shaped pit, 14, lay with its long axis almost parallel to and 1.5–1.6 m west of field system ditch 107 (and *c.* 1.3 m from the northern ditch of enclosure 219) (Fig. 6). The pit was a little over 4 m long, 2 m wide, and up to 0.82 m deep. It was filled with generally 'clean', mainly silty, clay.

Features 324 and 326

Two tree-throw holes or pits, 324 and 326, from which Middle Bronze Age pottery was recovered were recorded to the south of enclosure 219 (Fig. 6). The features were only 0.13 m apart and both were sub-rectangular in plan with steep sides and undulating bases. The larger of the two, 324, was 2 m long, *c.* 1.1 m wide, and 0.32 m deep; 326 was 1 m long, 0.8 m wide, and 0.29 m deep. Both were filled with dark brown silty loam, quite heavily charcoal-flecked in the case of 324 but less so for 326. No other features were recorded in the vicinity.

Pits 1130, 1132, 1135, 1137

Four shallow pits, a group of three less than 1 m apart, 1132, 1135 and 1137, and one *c.* 9 m to the north-east, 1130, were recorded during the Watching Brief in June 1998 in the area to the north of Trench 14 (Fig. 5). All four features were roughly circular or ovoid in plan, ranging in size from a maximum of 1.4 m by 1 m (1335) to 0.7 m in diameter (1137), and all were truncated, with depths of 0.09 m (1132) to 0.16 m (1130).

The pits all contained charcoal, which in 1135 and 1137 completely blackened the silty fills; the fills were otherwise grey, brownish–grey or very dark brown silty clay and sandy silt. Burnt flint was present in large quantities in all except pit 1137, but no other finds were recovered. A radiocarbon date of 2470–2138 cal. BC (AA-32606; 3850±60 BP) was obtained for pit 1130.

Finds

Flaked Stone, by Peter S. Bellamy

The assemblage consists of a total of 799 pieces (20,317 g) of both worked flint and chert including 541 pieces (14,155 g) from stratified contexts (Table 3). It has been examined in terms of its condition, composition, technology, and distribution in order to characterise its functional and chronological affinities and investigate its depositional patterning. Further details are given in Appendix 2.

Raw material

The raw material utilised comprises 49.8% flint and 50.2% chert. The flint ranges from dark brown lustrous flint with slight mottling, through mottled grey and brown flint with cherty inclusions and mid grey and white mottled flint to a rather cherty opaque pale grey flint. It includes both chalk and gravel flint in approximately equal quantities. The proportion of gravel flint may be higher as it is clear from a small number of pieces that worn pebble surfaces and relatively fresh-looking cortex can occur together on the same piece of parent material. The gravel flint is likely to have been procured from the immediate vicinity, perhaps from the local valley gravels and similar partially eroded flint pebbles are found in the soil on site. Some of the chalk flint has rather eroded cortex and may have been derived from a secondary source, perhaps from the alluvium or from the clay-with-flints, both occurring in the immediate vicinity of the site. Several pieces have reddish–brown staining just below the cortex and may have derived from the clay-with-flints. The nearest known source of chalk flint is at Beer, about 15 km to the south-east on the Devon coast and flint similar to the chalk flint from Castle Hill can be found at Beer (Tingle 1998). There is also an outcrop of Upper Chalk at Wilmington, about 7 km to the west of the site, but no flint has been found in this outcrop to date (*ibid.*, 90).

The chert is primarily golden brown in colour with a smaller quantity of darker brown banded chert. It was probably derived from the Upper Greensand of the Blackdown facies which forms the Blackdown Hills to the north of Honiton and also forms the steep scarp of Honiton Hill, Gittisham Hill and Westgate Hill on the southern edge of the Otter valley about 2 km to the south of the site (Edmonds *et al.* 1975). Most of the chert on the site appears to have come from pebbles or cobbles. A single piece of Portland Chert was recovered.

Assemblage description

Flint

The assemblage contains elements of two separate industries: a long flake/blade industry and a broad flake industry. No evidence for core tool production was recognised. The two industries can be distinguished only on the basis of technology. Although there is a slight differentiation in the flint types used, this not enough to

Table 3: Castle Hill, flaked stone assemblages by type (no./wt(g))

	Cores	Broken cores	Flakes	Broken flakes	Burnt flakes	Blades	Broken blades	Burnt blades	Tools	Broken tools	Chips	Misc. debitage	Total	Tool type
Chert														
Neo enclosure 218	2/601	–	27/540	16/96	–	–	–	–	–	–	15/5	–	60/1242	
Neo enclosure 219	–	–	3/117	2/16	1/7	–	–	–	–	–	1/1	1/5	8/146	
Field boundary 1001	–	–	1/6	–	–	–	–	–	–	–	–	–	1/6	
Field boundary 2052	–	–	4/25	1/15	–	–	–	–	1/16	–	–	–	6/56	scraper
Field boundary 35	–	–	6/129	1/6	–	–	–	–	–	–	–	–	7/135	
Field boundary 703	–	–	4/107	5/29	–	–	–	–	–	–	–	–	9/136	
Field boundary 620	–	–	2/28	–	–	–	–	–	–	–	–	–	2/28	
Interior field 1	–	–	3/42	2/19	–	–	–	–	2/113	–	–	–	7/174	scraper, ret. flake
Field boundary 107	3/1387	–	17/256	7/43	–	–	–	–	1/36	–	–	1/15	29/1737	scraper
Field boundary 25	–	–	1/4	1/12	–	–	–	–	–	–	–	–	2/16	
Interior field 30	–	–	1/5	1/4	–	–	–	–	–	–	–	–	2/9	
Pit 609/203	2/264	–	3/49	2/9	–	–	–	–	–	–	–	–	7/322	
Structure 978	–	–	5/94	7/86	–	–	–	–	2/101	–	3/3	1/5	18/289	2 ret. flakes
Field boundary 72/22/52	2/1039	–	30/456	12/79	–	–	–	–	–	–	6/4	1/53	51/1631	
Field boundary 195	–	–	2/35	–	–	–	–	–	–	–	–	–	2/35	
Interior field 4 (S)	–	–	2/20	–	–	–	–	–	–	–	–	1/4	3/24	
Field boundary 1560	–	–	2/24	1/8	–	–	–	–	–	–	–	–	3/32	
Interior field 6	6/1981	–	22/1189	12/352	–	–	–	–	–	1/160	–	7/212	48/3894	broken hammerstone
Enclosure ditch 5026	6/961	–	18/491	6/67	–	–	–	–	–	–	–	1/38	31/1557	
Trench 15	–	–	1/6	–	–	–	–	–	–	–	–	–	1/6	
Trench 16	–	–	6/53	–	–	–	–	–	1/5	–	–	–	7/58	ret. flake/notch
Trench 2	–	–	–	1/3	–	–	–	–	–	–	–	–	1/3	
Trench 5	–	–	2/18	1/34	–	–	–	–	–	–	–	–	3/52	
Unstratified	6/1953	–	42/1195	25/217	–	3/114	1/1	–	5/263	–	3/4	8/540	93/4287	4 scrapers, ret. flake
Sub-total chert	27/8186	0	204/4889	103/1095	1/7	3/114	1/1	0	12/534	1/160	28/17	21/872	401/15,875	
Flint														
Neo enclosure 218	–	–	1/4	1/14	–	–	–	–	3/54	–	6/1	1/5	12/78	fabric., ut. blade, scraper
Interior 218	–	–	–	–	–	–	–	–	1/9	–	1/0	1/60	3/69	ut. flake
Neo enclosure 219	–	–	3/20	5/18	–	1/1	1/3	1/3	4/53	–	2/0	–	17/98	scraper, 3 ut. flakes
Field boundary 2052	–	–	1/1	–	–	–	1/1	–	–	–	1/0	–	3/2	
Field boundary 35	–	–	1/9	–	–	–	1/1	–	–	–	–	–	2/10	

Table 3: (continued)

	Cores	Broken cores	Flakes	Broken flakes	Burnt flakes	Blades	Broken blades	Burnt blades	Tools	Broken tools	Chips	Misc. debitage	Total	Tool type
Flint														
Field boundary 703	–	–	2/14	1/1	–	–	–	–	–	–	3/2	–	6/17	
Interior field 1	–	–	4/22	1/20	–	–	–	–	2/74	–	1/1	1/9	9/126	2 scrapers
Field boundary 107	1/69	–	5/53	4/9	–	–	–	–	4/54	–	3/3	–	17/188	2 scrapers, 2 ret. flakes
Field boundary 25	–	–	2/4	–	–	–	1/1	–	–	–	–	–	3/5	
Pit 609/2030	–	–	1/12	–	–	3/17	1/1	–	2/18	–	–	1/2	8/50	scraper, ret. flake
Structure 978	–	–	14/134	8/45	–	3/17	2/1	–	7/127	2/23	6/3	2/5	44/355	6 scrapers+2 broken, piercer
Interior field 3	–	–	–	1/2	–	–	–	–	–	–	–	–	1/2	
Field boundary 72/22/52	1/51	–	5/50	2/2	–	–	2/5	–	2/27	–	–	2/8	14/143	scraper
Field boundary 195	–	–	1/12	–	–	–	–	–	–	–	–	–	1/12	
Interior field 4 (S)	–	–	–	1/1	–	–	–	–	–	–	–	–	1/1	
Interior field 4 (N)	–	–	–	–	–	–	–	–	–	1/4	–	–	1/4	broken ut. flake
Field boundary 1560	–	–	–	1/1	–	–	–	–	1/8	–	–	–	1/1	scraper
Interior field 6	2/108	5/208	28/290	11/56	–	–	1/11	–	14/283	1/5	8/4	11/93	81/1058	10 scrapers+1 broken, 4 ret. flakes
Enclosure ditch 5026	1/245	–	4/58	2/14	–	1/9	1/1	–	4/91	1/3	–	–	14/421	3 scrapers, 1 ut. flake
Interior enclosure 5026	–	–	1/5	1/1	–	1/1	2/4	–	–	–	–	1/9	6/20	
Trench 1	–	–	–	–	–	–	–	–	–	–	2/1	–	2/1	
Trench 2	–	–	–	–	–	–	–	–	–	–	1/1	–	1/1	
Trench 3	–	–	–	2/9	–	–	–	–	–	–	–	–	2/9	
Trench 4	–	–	–	1/4	–	–	–	–	–	–	1/0	1/14	3/18	
Trench 5	–	–	4/73	1/1	–	–	–	–	–	–	1/0	–	6/74	
Trench 6	–	–	1/4	–	–	–	–	–	–	–	–	–	1/4	
Trench 15	–	–	1/6	1/5	–	–	–	–	–	–	–	–	2/11	
Trench 24	–	–	–	1/1	–	–	–	–	1/59	–	–	–	2/60	scraper
Unstratified	3/177	1/14	39/451	19/132	1/1	–	3/6	–	29/540	3/54	23/17	13/186	134/1578	leaf arrowhead, chisel arrowhead, 22 scrapers+1 broken, piercer, notch, 3 ret. flakes+2 broken
Sub-total flint	8/650	6/222	118/1222	64/354	1/1	9/45	16/35	1/3	74/1397	8/89	59/33	34/381	398/4442	
Total	35/8836	6/222	322/6111	167/1449	2/8	12/159	17/36	1/3	86/1931	9/249	87/50	55/1263	799/20,317	

reliably assign individual pieces to one or other industry. The flint from both was in a similar condition being predominantly in mint or sharp condition with a smaller proportion of slightly rolled pieces. None of the flint is patinated except for a single unstratified broken blade which has a bluish white patination. A small number of pieces have been burnt.

The first industry represents probably no more than 10–15% of the flaked stone assemblage. It consists mainly of small parallel-sided blades (c. 15–45 mm long) with narrow plain butts, 1–3 mm, thick together with a smaller number of larger trimming flakes. Platform abrasion is present on almost all the flakes and blades. There appears to be some preferential selection in favour of very dark grey flint, though a range of different flint types is present. Two small blade cores, both unstratified, may belong to this industry. One is a small opposed-platform blade on a mottled grey flint gravel nodule; the other is broken and burnt.

The tools related to this industry include three utilised flakes or blades with trimming and slight polishing along one edge (Fig. 21, 1); two scrapers with abrupt retouch forming a slightly irregular scraping edge (Fig. 21, 2), and one fabricator with traces of wear at the distal end (Fig. 21, 3). A single leaf arrowhead (Fig. 21, 4), found unstratified, may be related to this industry but could also be an accidental loss. Also of interest is a fragment of a probable polished perforated mace head of pale grey opaque flint which had been reused as a core with the removal of a couple of small flakes (Fig. 21, 5). A single microburin was also found. The character of this industry together with the occurrence of artefact types such as fabricators and maceheads would suggest an Early Neolithic date, though the presence of a microburin suggests that some of the material is Mesolithic, but this could still be very late in the period.

The second industry comprises material from all stages of the reduction process as well as a number of tools and utilised pieces (Table 3). The material is, in general, much larger. Many of the pieces are made from mid to dark grey mottled flint with a thin pale cortex. The cores are all multi-directional flake cores (Fig. 21, 8), one of which is on a thick flake. They were flaked from a number of different angles depending on the shape of the nodule or the presence of irregularities in the flint and the majority had been worked out or had been abandoned due to faults in the raw material. There is little sign of any platform preparation. The flake scars indicate that the flakes were removed primarily by a hard hammer and the majority of the final flakes removed terminated in a hinge fracture.

The flakes are generally broad in shape between 30–70 mm in length and 20–50 mm in width with either plain or thermal butts averaging about 10 mm wide. Where it can be determined with a degree of certainty, the flakes were removed with a hard hammer. The flakes included preparation flakes (c. 22.5%), core trimming flakes (c. 46%), and other 'waste' flakes. Two side-blow janus flakes were recovered suggesting that butt thinning was undertaken, though no flint flakes with thinned butts were found.

The tools and other pieces showing signs of utilisation (including the pieces mentioned above which may be related to the earlier industry) comprise about 20% of the assemblage (Table 3). Scrapers are the most numerous tool type and include a number of different forms but generally they have regular abrupt retouch forming a convex scraping edge, though occasionally they have an irregular scraping edge. A significant proportion of the scrapers have been made on broad flakes with retouch extending down both sides, a form common in Late Neolithic and Bronze Age assemblages (Fig. 21, 9 and 10). The majority of the rest of the pieces are retouched flakes or utilised flakes.

Chert

Two industries can also be recognised in the chert assemblage, similar to those described above for the flint, though the differences are less marked and it is difficult to provide reliable quantified data. A single core from the earlier industry has been found — a single platformed core with flake removals from one face of a Greensand pebble. A number of flakes refitted onto this core (Pl. 6). There was a general trend towards long thin flake removals, including core preparation flakes, from this core. One scraper on a long flake, found just outside Neolithic enclosure 219, may belong to this industry (Fig. 21, 6).

The material from the later industry is characterised by a greater tendency towards broader thicker flakes and less controlled use of cores with fewer ridged flakes and more evidence for the removal of flakes from a number of different directions. Almost all the cores from the later industry are multi-platformed, where the cores were rotated to use flake scars as subsequent platforms and there is no evidence of careful platform preparation (Fig. 21, 12). The differences between the two industries grade into one another and it is difficult to be certain about separating the bulk of the material into one or other industry. The differences are perhaps masked by the fact that the vast majority of the chert from the features containing Neolithic pottery are core preparation or core trimming flakes, which have a tendency towards being more irregular, and very few other flakes or blanks.

The flakes from the later industry are generally broad with thick plain or thermal butts (5–25 mm) and normally removed with a hard hammer. About 73% of the flakes are core preparation or core trimming flakes, generally as broad or broader than they are long, measuring up to 90 mm in length, 90 mm in width and 30 mm in thickness. There is a tendency for the other flakes to be smaller in size but similar in shape. Overall the chert flakes are larger in size than the flint flakes, probably a result of the different size of raw material.

Thirteen chert tools and utilised pieces have been recovered from the site, mainly unclassified retouched flakes (Table 3). The majority of these are probably part of the later industry but two scrapers – one on a long flake (Fig. 21, 6) and one small Portland chert scraper (Fig. 21, 7) – may belong to the earlier industry. The other scrapers had abrupt retouch on the distal end of thick flakes (Fig. 21, 13). The retouched flakes included

Plate 6   Castle Hill: refitting chert core from segment 26 in the northern side of enclosure 218

two that have had their bulbs removed or thinned down (Fig. 21, 14). One broken chert pebble hammerstone was also found (Fig. 21, 15).

Distribution

The flaked stone occurred as a general spread across the whole of the excavated area, with the greatest quantities in the areas with the greatest concentration of archaeological features. The earlier industry was concentrated around the two enclosures 218 and 219 with the majority of the material coming from the enclosure ditches. More flaked stone was recovered from enclosure 218 including a number of refitting chert flakes and core from the northeastern ditch. The chert from both enclosures comprised mainly knapping waste but the flint includes many more tools and utilised pieces and possible blanks. A microburin was found in the south-western ditch of enclosure 218.

The material from the later industry occurred mainly in the Middle Bronze Age field boundary ditches with most material coming from the ditches in the centre of the site. The largest concentration of flaked stone came from field 6 immediately to the west of enclosure 5026, or more particularly from post-hole 1555 and pit 1530 in the northwestern corner of this field. Post-hole 1555 contained a number of cores and broken cores (e.g. Fig. 21, 12) and many preparation and core trimming flakes (including several refits) of both flint and chert together with a broken hammerstone (Fig. 21, 15). In addition to this knapping waste a large number of scrapers (9) and retouched flakes (4) were found in this feature (Fig. 21, 9–10). Pit 1530 also contained two scrapers. This was the greatest concentration of tools on

the site and strongly suggests that both production and use of flaked stone artefacts took place in this area.

Another lesser concentration of flaked stone occurred around structure 978 and in pit 609 in the area immediately north of enclosure 219 (Table 3). This concentration contained a mixture of material from both the earlier and later industries and included both knapping waste and tools including eight scrapers and one piercer (Fig. 21, 11).

Discussion

The flaked stone assemblage from this site contains elements from a number of different periods from the Mesolithic through to the Middle Bronze Age, although only two different industries can be identified with any certainty and which undoubtedly reflects the two main periods of use of the site. Evidence for Mesolithic activity is confined to a single microburin, which could date to very late in the period, and the Late Neolithic is represented by only one chisel transverse arrowhead, both of which could of course be accidental losses.

The Early Neolithic material is concentrated around the two enclosures 218 and 219 and includes evidence for chert knapping in enclosure 218. The evidence for flint knapping on site is less strong. Much of the flint appears to be chalk flint and may have been brought to the site, perhaps from Beer. The Portland chert scraper points to contacts further afield. The tools point to a range of activities on site but given the small numbers present this is hard to categorise. The tool types present on this site find parallels at the nearby causewayed enclosure at Hembury (Liddell 1930; 1931; 1932; 1935).

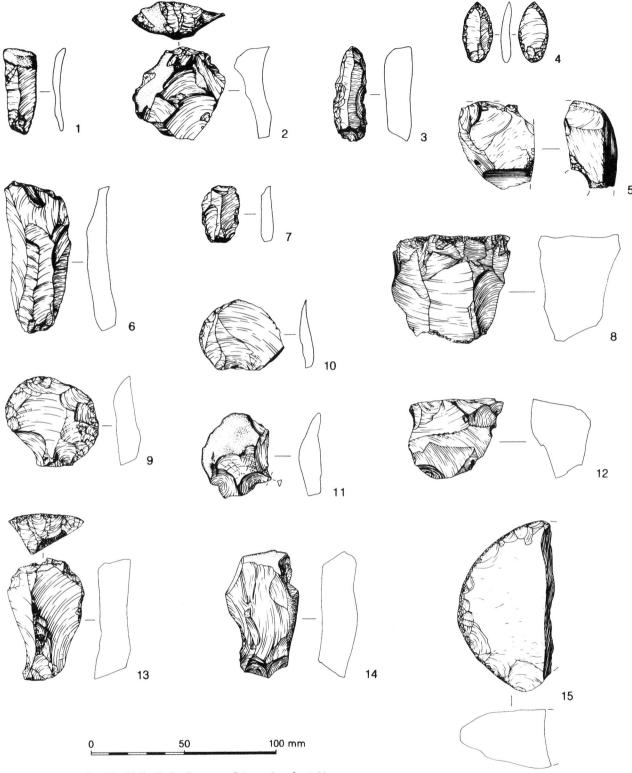

Figure 21   Castle Hill: flaked stone objects (scale 1:2)

It is interesting to note that the macehead fragment was made from the same distinctive flint as all of the flint axes at Hembury. There does appear to be a greater use of Greensand Chert at Castle Hill than at Hembury. At Hembury it formed only 6% of the assemblage, and much of that may be related to the Mesolithic activity at the site (Berridge 1986). The Castle Hill Early

Neolithic assemblage fits into a pattern of Early Neolithic lithic scatters (often mixed with Mesolithic material) in river valleys in this part of east Devon (Miles 1976). This is particularly evident in the lower Exe valley (Silvester *et al.* 1987) and the Yarty valley (Berridge 1985), although these apparent concentrations may be the result of the amount of fieldwork carried out in those areas. The recent work in the Otter valley (p. 17, Chapter 1) indicates that a similar pattern probably exists here too.

The Middle Bronze Age material is present as a background scatter across the field system, though the tailing off of the amount of material recovered away from the central excavated area of the site suggests that there was a concentration of activity in this middle part of the site, which appears to be greatest along the northern edge, particularly in field 6. In general, however, there are insufficient data to allow intra-site patterning to be explored in any detail. There is evidence for both stone tool production and use exploiting locally available raw material – both flint and Greensand chert occur in almost equal amounts, though there does seem to be a preference for flint for tool manufacture. The large number of scrapers present may only reflect their ubiquitous nature as tools, but it could point to some specialised activity.

Illustrated objects
(Fig. 21)
1. Utilised flint blade. Context 26, enclosure 218.
2. Flint scraper. Context 163, enclosure 218.
3. Flint fabricator. Context 2006, northern half of the terminal of segment 2074 in ditch 218.
4. Flint leaf arrowhead. Unstratified.
5. Flint macehead fragment, re-used as core. ON 5, context 2002, tree-throw 2003.
6. Chert scraper. Context 2019, ditch group 107.
7. Portland chert scraper. Context 1, topsoil.
8. Flint flake core. Context 1554, post-hole 1555.
9. Flint scraper. Context 1554, post-hole 1555.
10. Flint scraper. Context 1554, post-hole 1555.
11. Flint piercer. Context 6, pit 609.
12. Chert core. Context 1554, post-hole 1555.
13. Chert scraper. Context 670, post-hole 671.
14. Retouched chert flake. Context 6, pit 609.
15. Chert hammerstone. Context 1556, post-hole 1555.

Other Objects of Worked Stone, by M. Laidlaw, with stone identifications by D.F. Williams

A total of 18 pieces of stone was retained as worked or possibly utilised, including whetstones and quern fragments. With the exception of one whetstone, all of the stone types probably came from a fairly local source.

One small greenstone whetstone, recovered from enclosure ditch 5026 (section 5002), has a drilled perforation at one end and narrow sharpening grooves on both surfaces (Fig. 22, 2). A second possible whetstone, rectangular in section with two smooth worn surfaces and one concave surface, was recovered from an unstratified context (Fig. 22, 1). This is in a fine-textured sandstone, probably from the local Permian.

Ten small fragments of Permian lava, with a probable source in the Exeter area, probably derive from querns, although the form is uncertain. All came from Middle Bronze Age enclosure ditch 5026.

Five pieces of quartzite, again all from enclosure 5026, and including one large, rounded pebble, are apparently unworked, as is an irregularly shaped, worn

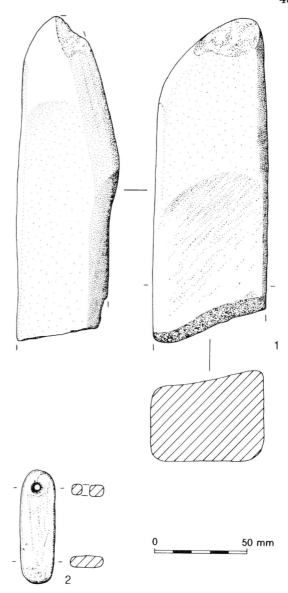

Figure 22   *Castle Hill: other objects of worked stone*

fragment of ?Permian sandstone with small natural perforations from ditches 955/957.

Illustrated objects
(Fig. 22)
1. Sandstone whetstone, broken. Unstratified
2. Small perforated greenstone whetstone. ON 53, context 5151, enclosure ditch 5026.

Pottery, by M. Laidlaw and Lorraine Mepham

Introduction
A total of 774 sherds (9701 g) was recovered and includes pottery ranging in date from the Middle Neolithic to Late Bronze Age; the small quantity of Romano-British, medieval, post-medieval, and unidentified sherds (18 sherds; 88 g) are not discussed further here. The bulk of the pottery is attributed to the Middle Bronze Age, with

Table 4: Castle Hill, pottery, fabric totals

Fabric	No.	Wt (g)	% of period by wt
Middle Neolithic			
R16	135	1252	91.9
R17	10	104	7.6
Q16	1	6	0.5
Total	146	1362	–
Bronze Age			
Grog-tempered fabrics			
G1	111	991	12.0
G2	8	58	0.7
G3	72	705	8.5
G4	146	2039	24.7
G5	22	276	3.3
G6	29	1143	13.9
Sandy fabrics			
Q2	3	19	0.2
Q6	8	48	0.6
Q7	1	17	0.2
Q8	1	9	0.1
Q9	4	74	0.9
Q12	1	40	0.5
Chert-tempered fabrics			
R1	29	110	1.3
R2	83	1154	14.0
R4	3	11	0.1
Volcanic fabrics			
R3	77	1417	17.2
R9	2	3	0.1
Fabric containing quartz/sandstone			
Q10	10	137	1.7
Sub-total	610	8251	–
Later pottery			
R-B	8	27	–
Medieval	2	5	–
Post-med	5	53	–
Unident.	3	3	–
Total	774	9701	

smaller quantities of Middle Neolithic, Early Bronze Age and possible Late Bronze Age material. The condition of the assemblage varies; sherds are in general relatively unabraded, although the extreme friability of many of the fabrics, particularly the Middle Neolithic fabrics and the Middle Bronze Age chert-tempered fabrics, has led to a high degree of fragmentation (mean sherd weight 12.7 g.). A significant number of diagnostic sherds (rims, decorated sherds, etc) are present. Full details of fabric types and vessel forms are given respectively in Appendix 3. Fabric totals are given in Table 4.

Middle Neolithic

Pottery dating to the Middle Neolithic period is represented by at least three Peterborough Ware vessels deriving from enclosure 218, one from the northern ditch (525), and two from the southern ditch (2073). In addition, a small number of decorated body sherds in similar fabrics were recovered as residual sherds from post-hole 743 (two sherds) and enclosure 5026 (six sherds).

Two of the vessels, one from the northern ditch and one from the southern ditch, survive as almost complete profiles. Both vessels occur in similar rock-tempered fabrics (R16 and R17), and both are of Mortlake style. The vessel from ditch 525 (fabric R16) is slightly more complete, although in a very poor, friable condition. The form is typical of the Peterborough Ware tradition, comprising a bowl with a concave neck and carinated shoulder; the rim is quite sharply everted, creating a marked 'overhang' over the neck (Fig. 23, 1). The decoration comprises all-over twisted cord 'maggots' in rows of alternating diagonals. A small number of sherds in the same fabric from ditch 525 are slightly thicker walled, have a different decorative pattern and may represent a second vessel (Fig. 23, 2).

The vessel from ditch 2073 (fabric R17) is in slightly better, less friable condition, although less survives. This bowl is of similar form to the example from ditch 525, although with a more upright rim and a less well defined concave neck (Fig. 23, 3). The decorative scheme is also very similar, although augmented by a narrow band of incised cross-hatching inside the rim.

One small rim sherd in a coarse chert-tempered fabric (Q16) was also recovered from ditch 2073, and derives from a further Peterborough Ware vessel, of Fengate style (Fig. 23, 4). Both fabric and decoration are quite distinct from the two Mortlake style vessels. The rim has impressed cord decoration externally, and ?fingernail impressions around the inside of the rim.

A sample sherd from the vessel from ditch 525 (fabric R16) was submitted for petrological analysis. The full petrological report appears here as Appendix 4.

David Williams writes:

> The sherd contains quartz, orthoclase and plagioclase felspar, biotite, tourmaline and some pieces of granite. The comparative coarseness of the fabric is reminiscent of South Devon Ware, for which a source south of Dartmoor has been postulated (Bidwell and Silvester 1988). Although this fabric is more commonly associated with Roman pottery, the writer has noted similar prehistoric fabrics in the region.

Fabric R17 is likely to have a similar source; it is distinguished here from R16 merely on the basis of the smaller size of the inclusions.

Peterborough Ware vessels, indeed all Middle/Late Neolithic ceramics, are rare occurrences in Devon. Three Peterborough Ware sherds are recorded from the Late Neolithic settlement at Topsham, all identified, with varying degrees of confidence, as Fengate style (Smith 1975). Two further sherds from Beer Head have been very tentatively identified as Peterborough Ware (Cleal

1998a, 28). Other comparable vessels are mainly recorded from sites further to the east, such as Windmill Hill and the Marlborough Downs in Wiltshire.

The dating of Peterborough Ware has not yet been satisfactorily resolved. It now appears that the traditional sequential division of Peterborough Ware styles from Ebbsfleet through Mortlake to Fengate may no longer be valid. A recent programme of radiocarbon dating from 15 sites in England and Wales has produced dates ranging from c. 3400–2500 cal. BC, and suggests that Peterborough Ware should be regarded 'as a developed (but not necessarily late/final) stage of the British Neolithic' (Gibson and Kinnes 1997, 67). Dates for the Mortlake style vessels, selected from ten sites, covered the whole of this range, and there is therefore no reason to suppose that the Mortlake style and possible Fengate style vessels from Castle Hill were not in use at the same time.

Early Bronze Age
The Early Bronze Age material includes a small quantity of Beaker pottery in the grog-tempered fabrics G1 and G2. These fabrics are very similar in nature and vary only slightly in the abundance and size of the quartz grains. These sherds have been identified on the basis of decoration and the thinness of the vessel walls in comparison to the remainder of the grog-tempered sherds from this site; the fabrics alone are indistinguishable, and are also found with diagnostic Middle Bronze Age traits.

The Beaker sherds are all decorated with square-toothed comb impressions (Fig. 23, 5–11); while this is also found in Trevisker-style assemblages and some of the Castle Hill pottery was found with Trevisker-related material, the motifs found here are more characteristic of the Beaker tradition. With the exception of three very small rims recovered from post-hole 7 and pit 609, the other Beaker sherds are body sherds.

Beaker vessels in similar grog-tempered fabrics with comb-impressed decoration are recorded elsewhere in the south-west from Honeyditches, Seaton (Silvester 1981), Kent's Cavern, Torquay (Silvester 1986), and Beer Head in Devon (Cleal 1998b), and from Ham Hill (Morris forthcoming) and Brean Down (Harrison 1990) in Somerset.

Middle Bronze Age

Fabrics
A total of 16 fabric types has been recorded and includes grog-tempered, rock-tempered and sandy fabrics, the most common fabric types being grog-tempered. This group of grog-tempered fabrics is visually quite homogeneous, and distinctions between fabrics are not always clear-cut; fabrics have been distinguished on the basis of the slight variations in the size and frequency of inclusions. Fabric totals are presented in Table 4.

Samples of five fabrics (R1, R2, R3, R4 and Q10) were submitted for petrological analysis. The full petrological report is included here as Appendix 4. The fabrics were found to fall into three broad fabric groups on the basis of the principal inclusions: chert (R1, R2, R4), quartz/sandstone (Q10) and volcanic (R3). All three groups are likely to be of relatively local origin. Fabric R3 contains fragments of volcanic rock for which an origin in the Permian rocks in the Exeter region is postulated. Similar inclusions were found in fabrics from the Iron Age assemblages from Blackhorse and Long Range (see below), but it is worth noting that the occurrence of volcanic fabrics in Middle Bronze Age assemblages in Devon is rare – Williams notes two other examples, from Heatree, Manaton, and Hayes Farm, Clyst Honiton (Williams 1991; Woodward and Williams 1989).

On the basis of macroscopic comparison with the thin-sectioned samples, one further fabric (R9) was assigned to the group containing volcanic fragments. The six grog-tempered fabrics (G1–G6) and four remaining sandy fabrics (Q7–Q9) contain no geologically distinctive inclusions, and are presumed to be of local origin.

Forms
Four vessel forms were defined. The occurrence of each vessel form by fabric type is listed in Table 5.

MBA1: Jars with inturned rounded rims, generally plain (Fig. 24, 12–16).

MBA2: Jars/bowls with expanded rims, generally decorated (Fig. 24, 17–25).

MBA3: Jars with slightly constricted neck, rounded and flattened rims, generally with applied cordons (Fig. 24, 26–30).

MBA4: Small bowl, open vessel, applied lugs (Fig. 24, 31).

At Castle Hill the most commonly occurring form is the straight-sided bucket-shaped or ovoid jar with an expanded rim (MBA2), which occur more commonly in grog-tempered fabrics, particularly fabric G4. Smaller numbers of jars with inturned rims (MBA1) and necked jars (MBA3) tend to be produced in the finer grog-tempered fabrics. Only one example of type MBA4 was recorded. None of the vessels have handles or perforated lugs, and the only possibly carrying mechanism observed is the large impressed 'dimple' above the cordon on a vessel of form MBA3 (Fig. 24, 29), which does not appear a particularly functional feature.

The four forms do appear to occur within distinct, although overlapping size ranges, although this is based

Table 5: Castle Hill, Middle Bronze Age pottery, vessel forms by fabric type (no. occurrences)

Form	Grog-tempered					Chert		
	G1	G4	G3	G5	G6	R2	R3	Total
MBA1	1	2	2	–	–	–	–	5
MBA2	–	7	–	–	2	3	5	17
MBA3	–	2	1	2	–	–	1	6
MBA4	–	1	–	–	–	–	–	1
Unid.	–	1	1	–	–	1	–	3
Total	1	13	4	2	2	4	6	32

purely on rim diameters since, in the absence of complete profiles, the rim diameter:height ratio is unknown. The largest vessels are those of form MBA2, rim diameters ranging from 120 mm to 340 mm, with seven of the 11 measurable examples falling between 180 and 240 mm. The jars of form MBA1 are smaller (diameters 120–160 mm; six measurable examples), and those of MBA3 ranging from small to medium (100–200 mm; four measurable examples). The single example of MBA4 falls at the smallest extreme (diameter 100 mm).

Form MBA2 can be correlated with style 3/4 in Parker Pearson's proposed revised classification for Trevisker wares, MBA3 with his style 5 and MBA4 with his style 6 (Parker Pearson 1990; slightly revised 1995). The plain form MBA1 is less easily attributable to ceramic tradition, but would not be out of place within a Deverel-Rimbury style assemblage; one vessel has finger-impressed decoration around the rim (Fig. 24, 16), a characteristic decorative trait of this ceramic tradition.

Decoration and surface treatments
A significant proportion of the Middle Bronze Age assemblage is decorated (84 sherds; 14% of the total assemblage by number), but the range of techniques and motifs is fairly restricted. Decorative motifs by fabric

type are presented in Table 6. The techniques used include incision, impression, stabbing, and the application of cordons and lugs; techniques can be combined on a single vessel. The most common decoration motif comprises deeply incised cross-hatching, generally occurring just below the rim (Fig. 24, 25). Variants of this include diagonal hatching on applied cordons (Fig. 24, 39) and shorter diagonal slashing (Fig. 24, 38). Simple stabbed or impressed decoration is found on rims (Fig. 24, 16, 22–4) and applied cordons (Fig. 24, 40–42). Plain applied cordons occur on form MBA3 vessels, just below the rim. One open vessel of form MBA2 has a series of applied bosses below the rim, and incised cross-hatching on top of the rim (Fig. 24, 21), and applied bosses also occur on the single example of form MBA4 (Fig. 24, 31).

Surface treatments are limited to smoothed surfaces, particularly on grog-tempered fabrics G3 and G4. The majority of sherds have smoothed external surfaces with smaller numbers smoothed internally including around the rim. Traces of wipe marks are visible on three sherds in G6 and R3.

Residues
Very small numbers of sherds have traces of sooting and are restricted to three fabrics (G1, G4, R3). Eight sherds are sooted internally and two have traces of soot on their

Table 6: Castle Hill, Middle Bronze Age pottery, decorative motifs by fabric type (no. sherds)

Motif	Grog-tempered					Chert	Vol.	Q/sand	
	G1	G2	G3	G4	G6	R2	R3	Q10	Total
Impressed									
Combed	37	2	–	–	–	–	–	–	39
Fingernail (body)	4	–	–	–	–	–	–	–	4
Fingertip (cordon)	–	–	–	–	3	–	–	–	3
Fingertip (rim)	–	–	–	1	1	1	–	–	3
Triangular impressions	3	–	–	–	–	–	–	–	3
Dots (body)	–	–	–	–	–	–	3	–	3
Dots (rim)	–	–	–	–	–	1	–	–	1
Dots (cordon)	–	–	–	–	–	1	–	–	1
Tooled lines	–	–	–	1	–	–	–	–	1
Incised									
Parallel lines	1	–	–	–	–	–	–	–	1
Diagonal hatching	1	–	–	–	1	3	1	4	10
Applied									
Bosses	–	–	–	1	–	–	–	–	1
Plain cordon	–	–	–	4	–	–	–	–	4
Combination									
Bosses+lattice	–	–	–	6	–	–	–	–	6
Cordon+dimple	–	–	1	–	–	–	–	–	1
Hatching+cordon	–	–	–	–	–	–	1	–	1
Diag. slash+cordon	–	–	–	2	–	–	–	–	2
Total	46	2	1	15	5	6	5	4	84

Table 7: Castle Hill, pottery by feature (no./wt (g))

	Neolithic	Grog	Sandy	Chert	Volcanic	Quartz/ sandstone	Later	Total
Neo enclosure 218	138/1336	2/5	4/33	1/2	–	–	–	145/1376
Neo enclosure 219	–	1/1	–	3/29	–	1/6	–	5/36
Post-hole 7	–	61/521	–	3/11	–	–	–	64/532
Pits 1530/1551/1555	–	112/987	–	–	–	–	–	112/987
Structure 978	–	18/83	–	–	2/32	–	–	20/115
Field boundary 72	–	4/23	–	–	2/3	–	–	6/26
Field boundary 107	–	6/26	3/19	–	1/2	–	7/26	17/73
Field boundary 335	–	1/1	–	–	–	–	–	1/1
Field boundary 1654	–	1/2	–	–	–	1/5	–	2/7
Enclosure 5026	6/18	133/2987	–	75/1105	38/942	5/51	–	251/5085
Post-hole group 5028	–	–	–	–	6/69	–	–	8/69
Post-hole group 5050	–	4/6	–	3/16	4/49	–	–	11/71
Structure 1813	–	–	–	16/52	–	–	–	16/52
Structure 1754	–	4/13	1/17	13/58	–	–	–	18/88
Other features	2/8	2/21	3/27	–	11/253	–	1/3	18/309
Total	146/1362	349/4676	11/96	114/1273	66/1350	7/62	8/29	701/8848

external surfaces. Two sherds in fabric G4 have slight traces of some form of residue surviving. None of these sherds can be related to a specific vessel form.

Distribution
Beaker pottery was recovered from six features: three small pits (or large post-holes) in the eastern part of the site, 1530, 1551 and 1555, from pit 609, from post-hole 7; and from a large tree-throw hole, 1602. The sherds from pit 609 (Fig. 23, 5–9) may be redeposited from the northern ditch of enclosure 219. They were associated with a bucket-shaped vessel of Trevisker style, with applied lugs (Fig. 24, 21). The sherds in 1555 may be residual but only Beaker pottery was found in the nearby pit 1551.

The largest group of Middle Bronze Age pottery came from ditch 5026 (276 sherds)(Table 7; Fig. 26). The volume of the excavated sections is comparable, so it is possible to be confident about the validity of the observed distribution, which shows that most came from the south-eastern section (198 sherds), with smaller quantities from the section excavated south-west from the western terminal (59 sherds). This group includes examples of vessel forms MBA1, MBA2, and MBA4, and a variety of decorated vessels, all in a range of grog-tempered and chert-tempered fabrics (Fig. 24, 12–16, 18–20, 22–5, 31, 35–37, 39–42). Radiocarbon dates of 2985±50 BP (AA–30673; 1400–1050 cal. BC) and 3115±50 BP (AA–30675; 1510–1260 cal. BC) were obtained from the primary fills of, respectively, the western terminal and the eastern ditch; the western ditch was probably recut.

Smaller groups came from pits 1530 (57 sherds) and 1555 (47 sherds) in field 6 which also contained relatively high quantities of flaked stone. Both groups consisted entirely of sherds in grog-tempered fabrics; pit 1530 contained no diagnostic material, while post-hole 1555 included three MBA3 vessel forms (Fig. 24, 26–8)

and two comb-decorated sherds (Fig. 24, 32–3). The remaining pottery was dispersed in small quantities in a number of features across the site and the totals are too small to allow for meaningful discussion of intra-site distributions.

Discussion
It is worth emphasising at the outset that this is the first assemblage of its kind from east Devon, and its importance lies not only in its addition to the distribution of Bronze Age ceramics in the county but in its occurrence in an area where two ceramic traditions merge. The Middle Bronze Age pottery from Castle Hill, although demonstrably mainly of local manufacture, clearly shows influences from the Deverel-Rimbury tradition of Wessex and the Trevisker style of south-west England. The plain, barrel-shaped vessels (MBA1), with occasional finger-impressed decoration on rims and applied cordons, find parallels in numerous Deverel-Rimbury assemblages in Dorset, such as Simons Ground (White 1982) and Eldon's Seat (Cunliffe and Phillipson 1969). Simple rims from biconical vessels are recorded from Norton Fitzwarren and Brean Down (unit 6) in Somerset and at Shaugh Moor in Devon (Woodward 1989, fig. 19, 23; Woodward 1990, fig. 88; Wainwright and Smith 1980).

A large proportion of the pottery, however, has closer affinities with the Trevisker wares of the south-west. The various Trevisker-related stylistic traits seen at Castle Hill include straight-sided vessels with expanded rims, plain and decorated cordons, applied bosses, and deeply incised decoration. Grog-tempered fabrics are characteristic of Trevisker assemblages from east Devon and Somerset, such as Brean Down and Norton Fitzwarren (Woodward 1990; Woodward 1989); there is no use of greenstone inclusions here, such as is found in assemblages from around Dartmoor in the west of the county.

Overall, in its mixture of cultural traits, this assemblage finds perhaps its closest parallel in an assemblage just across the Dorset Border at Chard Junction Quarry (Quinnell unpubl. a), which has produced a range of comparable vessel forms and decorative motifs in which traits from both Deverel-Rimbury and Trevisker traditions can be seen, sometimes on a single vessel.

This is, however, an assemblage of restricted range, in terms of both vessel forms and decorative styles, and it is interesting to observe what is absent as well as what is present. The Trevisker Style wares from Castle Hill all find parallels within other assemblages from the south-west, most notably from Brean Down (Woodward 1990) and Trethellan Farm, Cornwall (Woodward and Cane 1991), the two largest assemblages of Trevisker Style wares in the south-west. When compared with overall schemes of classification for the Trevisker Style, however, such as that of ApSimon (ApSimon and Greenfield 1972) or the revised scheme proposed by Parker Pearson (1990; 1995), it becomes apparent that certain classes of vessel which are well defined elsewhere are absent here, in particular, the large, handled vessels with cord-impressed decoration (ApSimon and Greenfield 1972, style 1; Parker Pearson 1990, style 1), and smaller vessels with similar decoration and with a range of handles, lugs and impressed 'dimples' (ApSimon and Greenfield 1972, styles 1/2; Parker Pearson 1990, styles 2 and 5).

ApSimon saw the various Trevisker styles as representing a chronological progression within the tradition, with larger, more elaborate, cord-impressed vessels (ApSimon and Greenfield 1972, style 1) superseded by smaller, simpler vessels with incised motifs (styles 3/4). Recent re-evaluation of the evidence, however, suggests that the various styles are more likely to represent functional differentiation within the Trevisker tradition (Parker Pearson 1990). In the latter scheme, which is largely size-dependent, the large, handled, cord-impressed vessels are seen as storage vessels, small vessels as eating and drinking wares (*ibid.*, styles 5 and 6), with medium-sized vessels (styles 2 and 3/4) having a range of functions relating to storage, cooking and eating/drinking. Nevertheless, Parker Pearson allows the possibility of chronological progression from cord-impressed to incised decoration, and that the large handled vessels of style 1 are replaced by smaller style 2 vessels with lugs (*ibid.*, 10).

Following this scheme, then, the Castle Hill assemblage can be seen as consisting of a restricted range of small to medium-sized vessels which could have fulfilled the range of functions relating to food storage, preparation and consumption. The assemblage is dominated by food preparation and cooking vessels of styles 3/4, which are the predominant forms on settlement sites in the south-west (Woodward and Cane 1991, fig. 53). The plain vessels with closer links to the Deverel-Rimbury tradition would also fit within this range. The dominance of incised motifs and the complete absence of cord-impressed decoration suggests a date range later in the Trevisker sequence. This is supported by the absence of large decorated storage vessels of Parker Pearson's style 1, although other factors may be at work here; style 1 vessels occur more often in funerary contexts than on settlement sites – the settlement site at Trethellan Farm is unusual here in its high proportion of style 1 vessels (*ibid.*).

In a wider regional context, the mixture of cultural affinities seen in the Castle Hill assemblage is not unexpected. As Parker Pearson notes, the boundary between the Trevisker styles of the south-west and the Wessex Biconical and Deverel-Rimbury styles centres on Dartmoor, with some degree of overlap between the two (1990, 22, fig. 12). Wessex styles rarely penetrate further west, which could be explained by a strongly maintained cultural identity and rejection of outside cultural influences in the south-west. To the east of the 'frontier zone' less conformity is apparent, and Trevisker styles have a wide distribution in Devon, Somerset and beyond, where they are frequently found in association with other ceramic styles such as Deverel-Rimbury. In the case of Castle Hill, fabric analysis has shown that this mixing of styles is resulting from influences on local potters rather than actual movement of vessels, and again this reflects the wider pattern in Devon, where the emphasis is on local production rather than the gabbroic industry of Cornwall (*ibid.*, 16–18).

Late Bronze Age

A small quantity of sherds in four sandy fabrics (Q6, Q7, Q8, Q9) have been tentatively attributed to the Late Bronze Age on the basis of both fabric type and associated vessel forms. Neither fabrics nor forms are particularly chronologically distinctive, but the sandy fabrics are not matched within the recognisable Trevisker/Deverel-Rimbury assemblage, and the vessel forms present represent smaller, thinner walled vessels. Two vessel forms were identified:

LBA1: Jars with inturned rounded rims (Fig. 25, 43–4).
LBA2: Jars with slight neck constrictions (Fig. 25, 45–6).

Two concentrations of very small sherds were recovered from stake-hole 77 and post-hole 79.

Similar simple inturned rims in sandy fabrics are recorded from Dainton, Devon (Silvester 1980), unit 4 at Brean Down (Woodward 1990, fig. 93–5), Norton Fitzwarren (Woodward 1989, fig. 19, 27–8), and Cadbury Castle phase 4 (Alcock 1980), all falling within Barrett's post Deverel-Rimbury plain ware tradition (Barrett 1980). Similar rim forms, although not in sandy fabrics, were found at Hayne Lane, which has radiocarbon dates ranging from mid 2nd to early 1st millennium cal. BC (see below, Chapter 5, pp. 111–12).

Illustrated vessels
(Figs 23–5)

Middle Neolithic
1 Peterborough decorated vessel, complex rim (form MNEO.1), fabric R16. Pottery Record Number, (hereafter PRN) 388, context 163, enclosure 218.
2. Peterborough Ware body sherd, possibly from same vessel as No. 1. Fabric R16. PRN 388, context 163, enclosure 218.

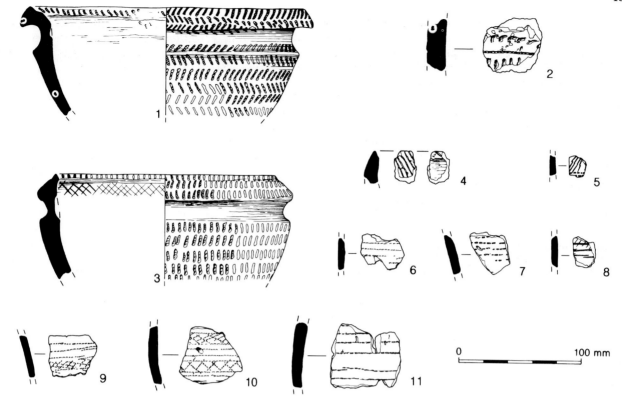

Figure 23   Castle Hill: Middle Neolithic (1–4) and Early Bronze Age (5–11) pottery. Scale 1:3

3. Peterborough decorated vessel and rim (form MNEO.1), fabric R17. PRN 476, context 2072, enclosure 218.
4. Small decorated rim, form possibly MNEO.1, fabric Q10. PRN 477, context 2072, enclosure 218.

Early Bronze Age
5–8. Four decorated Beaker sherds, fabric G1. PRN 363, context 606, pit 609.
9. Two conjoining decorated Beaker sherds, fabric G2. PRN 362, context 606, pit 609.
10–11. Two decorated Beaker sherds, fabric G1. PRN 578, ON 11, context 5154, unstratified.

Middle Bronze Age
12. Jar, plain inturned rim (form MBA1), fabric G4. PRN 487, context 5021, enclosure 5026.
13. Jar, plain inturned rim (form MBA1), fabric G4. PRN 488, context 5021, enclosure 5026.
14. Jar, slightly thickened, inturned rim (form MBA1), fabric R3. PRN 552, context 5150, enclosure 5026.
15. Jar, inturned, flattened rim (form MBA1), fabric G4. PRN 558, ON 40, context 5151, enclosure 5026.
16. Jar, inturned, flattened rim (form MBA1), fabric R2; finger-impressed decoration. PRN 551, context 5150, enclosure 5026.
17. Jar, expanded rim (form MBA2), fabric R3. PRN 417, context 1501, pit/post-hole 1502, feature group 1500.
18. Jar, expanded rim (form MBA2), fabric G4. PRN 563, ON 43, context 5151, enclosure 5026.
19. Biconical jar, expanded rim (form MBA2), fabric R3. PRN 568, ON 47, context 5151, enclosure 5026.
20. Jar, slightly expanded rim (form MBA2), fabric G6. PRN 539, ON 36, context 5150, enclosure 5026.

21. Bucket-shaped jar, expanded rim (form MBA2), fabric G4; incised decoration on top of rim, row of applied bosses below rim. PRN 373/398, context 606, pit 609.
22. Bucket-shaped jar, expanded flat topped rim (form MBA2), fabric R2; stabbed on rim. PRN 495, context 5032, enclosure 5026.
23. Biconical jar, expanded rim (form MBA2), fabric G4, incised around outside of rim. PRN 530, ON 29, context 5102, enclosure 5026.
24. Biconical jar, expanded rim (form MBA2), fabric G6, incised around outside of rim. PRN 564/570, ON 44/52, context 5151, enclosure 5026.
25. Bucket-shaped jar, expanded rim (form MBA2), fabric G6, incised cross-hatched decoration. PRN 543. ON 38, context 5150, enclosure 5026.
26. Small jar, slightly thickened rim (form MBA3), fabric G1. PRN 440, context 1554, post-hole 1555.
27. Jar, slightly thickened rim (form MBA3), fabric G4; plain neck cordon. PRN 442, ON 13, context 1556, post-hole 1555.
28. Jar, slightly thickened rim (form MBA3), fabric G4; plain neck cordon. PRN 435, context 1554, post-hole 1555.
29. Jar, plain rim (form MBA3), fabric G3; plain neck cordon with large impressed 'dimple'. PRN 479, ON 10, context 2105, unstratified.
30. Ovoid jar, thickened rim (form MBA3), fabric G1. PRN 577, ON 11, context 5154, unstratified.
31. Small open vessel, (form MBA4), fabric G4; applied bosses. PRN 486, context 5021, enclosure 5026.
32. Two conjoining decorated body sherds, fabric G1; comb-impressed decoration. PRN 439, context 1554, post-hole 1555.
33. Base, comb-impressed decoration, fabric G1. PRN431, ON 17, context 1550, post-hole 1551.

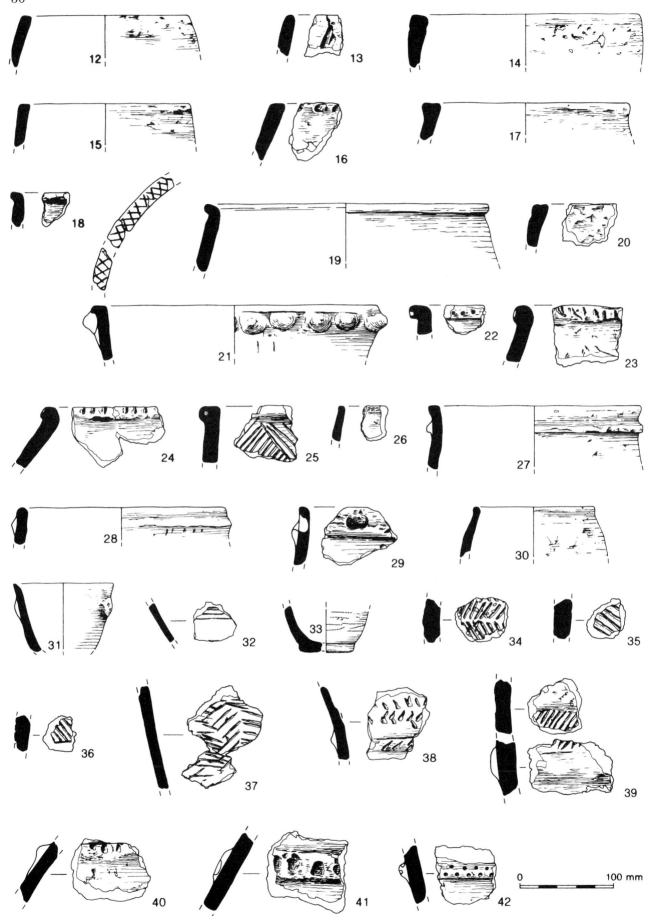

Figure 24   Castle Hill: Middle Bronze Age pottery (12–42). Scale 1:4

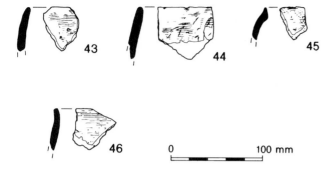

Figure 25   Castle Hill: Late Bronze Age pottery (43–6). Scale 1:4

34. Body sherd with deeply incised cross-hatching, fabric Q10. PRN 412, context 1005, tree-throw 1004.
35. Body sherd with deeply incised cross-hatching, fabric Q10. PRN524, ON 26, context 5102, enclosure 5026.
36. Body sherd with deeply incised cross-hatching, fabric R3. PRN 518, context 5101, enclosure 5026.
37. Body sherds with incised cross-hatching, fabric R2. PRN 493, ON 23, context 5022, enclosure 5026.
38. Body sherd with applied cordon and diagonal slashing, fabric G5. PRN 574, ON 11, context 5154, unstratified.
39. Body sherd with applied cordon and incised diagonal hatching above, fabric R3. PRN510, ON 25, context 5084, enclosure 5026.
40. Body sherd with applied, finger-impressed cordon, fabric G6. PRN 502, ON 51, context 5084, enclosure 5026.
41. Body sherd with applied, finger-impressed cordon, fabric G6. PRN 542, ON 35, context 5150, enclosure 5026.
42. Body sherd with applied, stabbed cordon, fabric R2. PRN 507, ON 24, context 5084, enclosure 5026.

Late Bronze Age
43. Jar, plain inturned rim (form LBA1), fabric Q7. PRN 459, context 1644, pit 1645, feature group 1754.
44. Jar, plain inturned rim (form LBA1), fabric R1. PRN 462, context 1680, post-hole 1679; four-post structure 1813.
45. Jar, internal rim bevel (form LBA2), fabric Q8. PRN 467, context 2006, southern half of the terminal of segment 2074 in enclosure 218.
46. Jar, slight neck constriction (form LBA2), fabric Q6. PRN 465, context 1790, post-hole 1585.

Environmental Analyses

Charred Plant Remains,
by Alan J. Clapham

Forty-two samples of charred plant material from a representative range of features were selected for analysis (see Appendix 7). Preservation of the material was generally good, permitting the identification of most of the remains. Seeds and fruits dominated the remains, although most samples also contained charred grass rootlets, and some samples had parenchyma tissue present.

Neolithic
Six samples from Neolithic contexts were analysed, three each from the ditches of enclosures 218 and 219 (Table 8). The preservation of the material was poorer than that from Bronze Age contexts. There were few cereals; a single emmer (*Triticum dicoccum*) spikelet fork found in enclosure 218. The most common remains were rootlets of onion couch grass (or false oat-grass), *Arrhenatherum elatius* and fragments of indeterminate cereal grains. The samples from enclosure 218 were the richest (Table 8) and the majority of the taxa are representative of arable, waste ground, and scrub/hedge habitats, such as *Persicaria maculosa* (redshank), *Chrysanthemum segetum* (corn marigold), *Galium aparine* (cleavers), and *Prunus spinosa* (sloe). Ditch segment 2074 contained leaf fragments of *Calluna vulgaris* (ling), suggesting the use of the moorland environment. The presence of grassland was indicated by the presence of pignut (*Conopodium majus*) tuber fragments. Damper woodland was indicated by the presence of *Ajuga reptans* (bugle) in enclosure ditch 219. Apart from the scarce finds of cereal crops within the samples, other food sources may be indicated by the presence of hazel (*Corylus avellana*) nutshell fragments, along with pignut, sloe, and bramble (*Rubus fruticosus*).

There is very little difference between enclosures 218 and 219, as both sets of samples contain taxa representative of similar habitats. The environment surrounding the enclosures was grassland, with possibly patches of scrub consisting of sloe, elder (*Sambucus nigra*), and hazel. It is difficult to ascertain the main cereals grown and whether or not they were processed locally due to the lack of cereal grains and chaff remains.

Early Bronze Age

Pit 1555
Two of the lower fills of pit 1555 contained a small quantity of charred plant remains (Table 9). Grains of bread and emmer wheat were recovered, as were spikelet forks and glume bases of emmer, and barley was also identified. Non-cultivated species present in the two samples were indicative of arable habitats, while the presence of hazel nutshell may represent a source of wild food.

Post-hole group 978; pit 609
The sample from post-hole 18 in possible round-house 978 contained very few plant remains (Table 9) as did the large pit 609 where the assemblage appears to represent a background flora as there is no evidence of material from crop processing or storage.

Middle Bronze Age

Field system ditches
Samples from ditch groups 2052, 25, and 72 contained very little in the way of plant remains, most of the material being indeterminate fragments of cereal grains (Table 10). An emmer grain and rachis fragment were recovered from ditch 2052 along with a single find of flax

52

Table 8: Castle Hill, charred plant remains from Neolithic enclosures 218 and 219

	Enclosure	218	218	218	219	219	219
	Feature type	Ditch	Ditch	Ditch	Ditch	Ditch	Ditch
	Feature / section	26/G	2074/D	36/C	146/A	2010/C	217/I
	Context	163	2072	2008	144	61	136
	Sample	21	29	30	40	32	31
	Flot size (ml)	20	25	10	42	5	30
Cereals							
Triticum dicoccum spikelet fork		–	1	–	–	–	–
Cerealia indet.		19f	9f	9f	–	5f	–
Weeds							
Corylus avellana nutshell		2f	–	–	4	3	–
Chenopodium sp.		–	–	1f	–	–	–
Persicaria maculosa		–	–	–	–	–	1
Rumex acetosella		–	–	–	1	–	–
Viola sp.		–	–	1	–	–	–
Calluna vulgaris leaf frags		–	3	–	–	–	–
Rubus fruticosus		–	–	–	1f	–	1
Prunus spinosa		–	–	–	–	–	2f
Rosaceae thorn		1	–	–	–	–	–
Vicia sp. cotyledons		2	–	–	–	–	–
Conopodium majus tuber		–	1	–	–	–	–
Ajuga reptans		–	–	–	–	–	3
Galium aparine		–	–	–	1f	–	3f
Sambucus nigra		–	–	–	1	–	1
Chrysanthemum segetum		–	2	–	–	–	–
Asteraceae cypsela		–	1f	–	–	–	–
Arrhenatherum elatius rootlets		2f	32f	9f	1	6f	–
Avena sp. awn fragments		1	–	–	–	–	–
Small Poaceae		–	1f	–	–	–	–
Cenococcum geophilum		–	–	–	2	–	–
Unident.		1f	–	–	–	–	–

f = fragment

(Linum usitatissimum). Ditch group 25 also contained few remains, no cereals were recovered but single finds of wild radish (Raphanus raphanistrum) and vetch (Vicia sp.) were, and these are cornfield weed species. Hazel nutshell fragments were also found, though only in small numbers.

The material from ditch 72 was similar and it can be said that the remains in all these samples represent the environments surrounding the ditches and may reflect a background flora, there is no evidence for the dumping of crop processing waste.

Pit 1578
Samples 195 and 196 from contexts 1574 and 1575 represent the two top fills of the pit respectively, while 1682 is a lower context. In general, the number of plant remains was low, with the richest sample was from the uppermost fill (1574; Table 10). Cereals were re-presented by emmer grain and chaff fragments and the weed seeds also indicate an arable environment. The samples from context 1682 did not contain cereals, though the non-cultivated species present are indicative of an arable environment.

Enclosure 5026
Five samples from the enclosure ditch were analysed, one sample from the south-western arm and four from the north-eastern arm (Table 11). Only two (from ditch sections 5094 and A) were rich in remains. Cereals were represented by grains of bread (Triticum aestivum), emmer wheat, and hulled barley (Hordeum vulgare). Chaff remains of emmer were represented by spikelet forks, glume bases, and rachis fragments, a single find of a spelt (Triticum spelta) glume base was also identified. Barley rachis fragments were also found in the two richest samples. Apart from cereal remains,

Table 9: Castle Hill, Early Bronze Age charred plant remains from features south-west of enclosure 5026

Feature group			988	
Feature type	Pit	Pit	PH	Pit
Feature no.	1555	1555	18	609
Context	1554	1554	17	608
Sample	51	52	16	14
Flot size (ml)	92	110	5	10
Cereals				
Triticum aestivum grain	–	1	–	–
T. dicoccum grain	–	4	–	–
tail grain	–	1	–	–
glume bases	1	1	–	–
rachis frags	–	1	–	–
Triticum sp. grain	2	1	–	–
Hordeum vulgare grain	–	1+1f	–	1
tail grain	–	1	–	–
Cerealia indet.	4f	56f	–	7f
Weeds				
Ranunculus ficaria tuber	–	2	–	–
Corylus avellana nutshell	1f	4f	1f	–
Chenopodium album	1	–	–	–
Persicaria lapathifolia	–	1	–	–
Rumex acetosella	–	1	–	–
Rumex sp.	1f	–	–	–
Vicia tetrasperma	–	1	–	–
Festuca sp. type	–	1+1f	–	–
Arrhenatherum elatius rootlets	–	5f	–	1
Avena ap.	–	–	–	1f
Poaceae culm bases	–	–	2	–
Leaf frags	–	1	–	–
Buds	–	1	–	–
Unident.	2	–	–	–

other cultivated crops were a single find of flax from ditch section 5094 and a fragment of a pea (*Pisum sativum*) in ditch section A.

The weed flora is indicative of arable land, with scrub habitats represented by finds of bramble and sloe. A grassland environment is represented by finds of pignut and false oat-grass, though the latter can also be a pernicious arable weed. A wetland/fen habitat was indicated by the presence of great fen sedge (*Cladium mariscus*).

The charred remains from ditch sections A and 5094 are most likely to be dumped material from domestic hearths, whereby the chaff and weed seeds from crop processing was used as a fuel. The presence of the weed species and other crop processing waste suggests that the crops were grown and processed locally.

Post-holes within enclosure 5026
Seven samples from post-holes within enclosure 5026 were analysed from groups 5028, 5027, and 5050 (Table 12). Identifiable cereal remains were rare but include finds of emmer spikelet forks, glume bases, and rachis fragments. The weed seeds are representative of an arable environment. A find of corn marigold identified from post-hole 5224 is indicative of a sandy soil and the presence of cross-leafed heath (*Erica tetralix*) leaf fragments in the same sample suggests the exploitation of a moorland habitat. One sample from a post-hole at the entrance of enclosure 5026 (post-hole 5068, group 5050) contained three rootlets of false oat-grass and two fragments of indeterminate cereal grains.

Post-holes south-west of enclosure 5026
Seven samples from this group of features were analysed and in general, they were the richest samples in terms of both number of remains and number of taxa (Table 13). The post-holes in group 1754 were the richest, being dominated by cereal remains. Post-hole 1537 contained emmer in the form of grains and chaff remains of spikelet forks, glume bases, and rachis fragments. In some cases the spikelets were so well preserved that the rachis was still attached to the glumes. Barley was also present. Post-hole 1537 contained the largest number of chaff fragments. Other cultivated plants identified from these samples include flax in post-holes 1537 and 1543.

The weed species associated with the cereals are typical arable species. A grassland habitat may also be represented by a fairy flax (*Linum catharticum*) capsule along with the greater numbers of Poaceae finds in post-hole 1537. Small fragments of pine (*Pinus*) charcoal were also identified in two post-holes (1537 and 1645), though this was not present in the charcoals analysed from these features.

These remains are most likely to represent the final sieving of crop-processing whereby the larger weed seeds and chaff fragments (such as culm nodes) have been removed previously. The charred remains suggest that structure 1754 may be a grain store.

Post-built structures 1812 and 1813
Four samples from this possibly Late Bronze Age group were examined (Table 13). Two samples from group 1812 contained emmer including chaff and grains, and barley but the commonest crop was flax. The weed species are indicative of an arable environment, though a hawthorn (*Crataegus* sp.) fruit fragment and a fragment of hazel nutshell represent a scrub element.

Within post-built structure 1813, post-hole 1675 contained emmer wheat grain, spikelet forks, glume bases and rachis fragments, and also barley. There were very few weed species in post-hole 1675, with only redshank present. The other non-cultivated species include fragments of pignut tubers and false oat-grass rootlets, both of which can be found in grassland habitats. Elder seeds were also present and may represent a scrubland habitat.

The samples from this group contained less material than that from group 1754 so it is more difficult to determine whether or not they indicate that the

Table 10: Castle Hill, Middle Bronze Age charred plant remains from the field system ditches and pit 1578

	2052	25	72			
Feature group	*2052*	*25*	*72*			
Feature type	*Ditch*	*Ditch*	*Ditch*	*Pit*	*Pit*	*Pit*
Feature / section no.	*F*	*501*	*73*	*1578*	*1578*	*1578*
Context	*734*	*502*	*190*	*1574*	*1574*	*1682*
Sample	*46*	*45*	*17*	*195*	*196*	*200*
Flot size (ml)	*5*	*10*	*18*	*24*	*20*	*5*
Cereals and other crops						
Triticum dicoccum grain	1	–	–	2	–	–
rachis frags	1	–	–	–	–	–
spikelet forks	–	–	–	1	–	–
glume bases	–	–	–	1	–	–
Cerealia indet.	19f	3f	3f	7f	9f	–
Linum usitatissimum	1	–	–	–	–	–
Weeds						
Ranunculus ficaria tuber	–	–	1	–	–	–
Corylus avellana nutshell	2f	1	3f	–	2f	1f
Chenopodium album	–	–	–	–	–	1
Atriplex sp.	–	–	–	2f	–	–
Persicaria maculosa	–	–	1f	–	–	–
Raphanus raphanistrum capsule frag.	–	1	–	–	–	–
Rumex acetosella	–	–	–	1	–	–
Rubus fruticosus	–	–	1	–	–	–
Crataegus sp. fruit frag.	–	–	1	1	–	–
Vicia sp.	–	1	1f	–	1	1
Lathyrus pratensis	–	–	–	–	–	1
Trifolium sp.	–	–	–	1	–	–
Anthemis cotula	–	–	–	–	1	–
Arrhenatherum elatius var. *bulbosum* tuber	–	–	2+1f	2f	–	–
A. elatius rootlets	5	6	6	15f	8	2
Avena sp.	1	–	–	–	–	–
Bromus / Avena sp.	–	1f	–	–	–	–
Small Poaceae	–	–	–	–	1	–
Poaceae culm nodes	–	1	–	–	–	–
Buds	–	1	–	–	–	–
Pinus charcoal	–	–	–	*	–	–
Parenchyma	–	–	–	–	–	1f
Cenococcum geophilum	1	–	–	–	2	1
Unident.	–	–	–	1	–	–

* = present

structure was used for storing crops. The presence of flax in post-built structure 1812 hints that it may have been used to store flax seeds.

Four-post structure 500
Post-hole 292 contained a single identifiable wheat grain though the weed species are indicative of an arable environment, while post-hole 299 contained indeterminate cereal grains and one hawthorn fruit (Table 14).

Post-holes in Field 1
Post-hole 749 contained fragments of hazel nutshell, as did post-hole 536. Otherwise these samples contained little in the way of plant remains, though those that were present were indicative of arable environments. Post-hole 1096 contained very few charred plant remains, though these included three wheat grains, one emmer glume base and eleven fragments of hazel nutshell.

Table 11: Castle Hill, Middle Bronze Age charred plant remains from the eastern arm of enclosure ditch 5026

	5099	5094	5083	B	A
Feature			*5026*		
Feature type			*Ditch*		
Feature / Section no.	*5099*	*5094*	*5083*	*B*	*A*
Context	*5097*	*5091*	*5084*	*5191*	*5018*
Sample	*100*	*92*	*95*	*104*	*99*
Flot size (ml)	*20*	*60*	*950*	*220*	*100*
Cereals and other crops					
Triticum aestivum grain	–	–	–	–	2
T. spelta glume bases	–	–	–	1	–
T. dicoccum grain	–	8	–	–	7
spikelet forks	–	2	–	–	2
glume bases	–	9	–	–	–
rachis frags	–	1	–	–	1
Triticum sp. grain	–	2	–	3	4
spikelet forks	–	4	–	–	–
glume bases	–	20	–	1	1
Hordeum vulgare grain	–	8	–	3	16
tail grain	–	1	–	–	2
Hordeum sp. rachis frags	–	2	–	–	1
Cerealia indet.	–	136f	32f	26f	123f
Linum usitatissimum	–	1	–	–	–
Pisum sativum cotyledons	–	–	–	–	1
Weeds					
Corylus avellana nutshell	–	1f	–	–	–
Chenopodium album	1	2	–	–	1
Persicaria maculosa	–	4+1f	–	–	1f
Polygonum aviculare	–	2f	–	–	–
Fallopia convolvulus	–	–	–	–	3+3f
Rumex acetosella	–	–	–	–	1
Rumex sp.	–	–	–	1	2
Rubus fruticosus	–	–	–	–	1
Prunus spinosa	–	–	–	–	1f
Rosaceae thorn	–	–	–	–	1
Medicago sp.	–	–	–	–	2
Vicia hirsuta	–	1	–	–	–
Vicia sp.	–	2	–	–	–
Conopodium majus tuber	–	10f	–	–	–
Plantago lanceolata	–	–	–	–	2
Sambucus nigra	–	2	–	–	–
Cladium mariscus	–	2	–	–	–
Arrhenatherum elatius var. *bulbosum* tuber	1	–	–	–	1f
A. elatius rootlets	–	28	8	–	23f
Poaeceae culm bases	4	–	–	–	–
culm nodes	4	–	–	–	–
stem	1	–	–	–	–
Unident.	–	6	–	–	1
Buds	–	1	–	–	–
Cenococcum geophilum	–	–	–	–	1

Table 12: Castle Hill, Middle Bronze Age charred plant remains from post-holes inside enclosure 5026 and post-hole 5068 at the entrance

	Feature group 5028	5028	5027	5027	5027	5027	5050
	Feature type			Post-holes			
	Feature no. 5053	5072	5119	5164	5186	5224	5068
	Context 5045	5073	5118	5163	5187	5223	3067
	Sample 145	134	142	130	116	141	81
	Flot size (ml) 3	5	20	30	5	30	90
Cereals							
Triticum dicoccum spikelet forks	–	–	–	1	–	–	–
glume bases	–	–	–	1	–	1	2f
rachis frags	–	–	–	1	–	1	–
Triticum sp. grain	–	–	1	–	–	1	–
Hordeum vulgare grain	–	2f	2	–	–	–	–
Cerealia indet.	2f	3f	31f	5f	2f	102f	–
Weeds							
Chenopodium album	–	–	–	3	–	2	–
Atriplex sp.	–	–	–	–	–	1	–
Stellaria media	–	–	–	–	–	3	–
Rumex acetosella	–	1	–	1	–	2	–
Rumex sp.	–	–	–	–	–	3	–
Polygonaceae indet.	–	–	1	1	–	–	–
Erica tetralix leaves	–	–	–	–	–	2	–
Chrysanthemum segatum	–	–	–	–	–	1	–
Tripleuropermum inodorum	–	–	–	–	–	1	–
Arrhenetherum elatius var. *bulbosum* tuber	–	–	1	–	–	–	–
A. elatius rootlets	–	4	15	5	1	13	3
Buds	1	–	–	–	–	1	–

Undated features

Four samples from features that are strictly undated were analysed. Of these pit 1578 has been attributed to the Middle Bronze Age (Table 10). The other sample is from a possible tree-throw 326 (Table 14) which contained very few charred plant remains; two fragments of hazel nutshell and three fragments of indeterminate cereal grains. There were also single finds of corn marigold and a grass culm node. These remains probably represent a background flora.

Discussion

Charcoal fragments, modern seeds and roots dominated all 42 samples from Castle Hill, although several samples were found to be very rich in charred plant remains. The presence of modern seeds and roots may introduce some level of mixing of plant remains through the profiles of the features, but this was not observed.

Samples were analysed from a variety of features and contexts, including ditches, post-holes, and pits (Tables 8–14). Six samples were analysed from the Neolithic enclosures 218 and 219. Thirty-two samples were analysed from the Middle Bronze Age and four from undated features and contexts. The richest samples were from features south-west of enclosure

5026 (Table 13) and those samples from the enclosure ditch itself (Table 11).

It is not possible to usefully discuss any changes in the crops cultivated due to the rarity of remains from the Neolithic. The majority of the plant remains from this period are representative of arable, scrub, and grassland environments, while the presence of ling leaf fragments suggests the utilisation of a moorland habitat.

In the Middle Bronze Age, the dominant cereal is emmer wheat, which is represented by grains and chaff fragments. Other cereals such as spelt and bread wheat were also recorded though not in such large quantities. Hulled barley grains and rachis fragments were also identified but again it appears to have been a minor crop as were flax and peas.

The majority of non-cultivated species represent an arable environment and is most likely to have been growing with the cultivated crops. The small size of the weed seeds suggests that they probably represent fine sieving residues (Hillman 1981) from crops that were grown locally and processed and stored on-site.

Unambiguous evidence for storage buildings such as granaries is sparse, though the plant remains suggests that post-hole group 1754 may be one. Here the

Table 13: Castle Hill, Middle–Late Bronze Age charred plant remains from post-holes south-west of enclosure 5026

	1754	1754	1754	1812	1812	1813	1813
Feature group							
Feature type				Post-hole			
Feature no.	1537	1543	1645	1753	1745	1679	1675
Context	1536	1542	1644	1752	1744	1680	1676
Sample	57	54	56	75	69	71	60
Flot size (ml)	32	28	20	30	30	20	60
Cereals and other crops							
Triticum spelta grain	2	1	–	–	–	–	–
glume bases	34	7	–	–	–	–	–
T. dicoccum grain	26	7	8	–	4+1f	–	8
tail grain	8+10f	–	3	–	–	–	–
spikelet forks	50	4	5	–	1	–	2
glume bases	284	23	28	1	–	–	9
rachis frags	111	3	–	–	–	–	1
Triticum sp. grain	31f	4f	2+3f	4f	1	–	2
spikelet forks	20	–	5	–	–	–	4
glume bases	311	45	22	–	–	–	20
Hordeum vulgare grain	5+8f	3	5	2	6+2f	–	8
tail grain	4+3f	1	–	–	–	–	1
6-row rachis frags	6	–	–	–	–	–	–
Hordeum sp. rachis frags	8	1	1	–	–	–	2
Cerealia indet.	466f	78f	68f	48f	50f	–	136f
Embryos	5	–	2	–	–	–	–
Sprouts	2	–	–	–	–	–	–
Linum usitatissimum	4f	2+2f	–	9+18f	19+25f	–	–
Weeds							
Ranunculus ficaria tuber	2	–	–	–	–	–	–
Ranunculus subgenus *ranunculus*	–	–	–	–	2	–	–
Corylus avellana nutshell	–	–	1f	1f	–	1f	1f
Chenopodium album	22+3f	4+9f	3	2f	3+3f	–	–
Atriplex sp.	2	–	–	–	–	–	–
Stellaria media	–	–	–	1	–	–	–
Persicaria maculosa	–	–	5+5f	–	–	–	4+1f
P. lapathifolia	14+3f	2+3f	–	–	–	–	–
Fallopia convolvulus	–	2f	–	–	–	–	–
Polygonum aviculare	–	–	–	–	1	–	–
Rumex acetosella	5	–	–	1	1+1f	–	–
Rumex sp.	2	3	–	8+1f	1	–	–
Polygonaceae indet.	3f	10f	–	–	1f	–	–
Anagallis arvensis	1	–	–	–	–	–	–
Crateagus sp. fruit frag.	–	–	–	1	–	–	–
Vicia cracca	–	–	1+2f	–	–	–	–
Vicia sp.	10	2	–	–	3+1f	–	–
Trifolium sp.	2	–	–	–	–	–	–
Linum catharticum capsule	1	–	–	–	–	–	–
Mentha sp.	1	–	–	–	–	–	–
Conopodium majus tuber	–	–	–	–	–	–	10f
Plantago lanceolata	1	1	–	–	2	–	–
Odonites vernus	–	1	–	–	–	–	–
Galium aparine	–	1f	–	–	–	–	–
Sambucus nigra	–	–	–	–	–	–	2

Table 13: (continued)

	1754	1754	1754	1812	1812	1813	1813
Feature group	1754	1754	1754	1812	1812	1813	1813
Feature type				Post-holes			
Feature no.	1537	1543	1645	1753	1745	1679	1675
Context	1536	1542	1644	1752	1744	1680	1676
Sample	57	54	56	75	69	71	60
Flot size (ml)	32	28	20	30	30	20	60
Tripleurospermum inodorum	4	–	–	–	–	–	–
Asteraceae cypsella	2	–	–	–	–	–	–
Arrhenatherum elatius var. *bulbosum* tuber	–	–	4f	–	3	–	–
Arrhenatherum elatius rootlets	15	7	14	7	–	1	28
Avena sp.	–	–	–	1	–	–	–
awn frags	14f	–	–	1	–	–	–
Bromus/Avena sp.	13f	–	–	–	4+1f	–	–
Small Poaceae	7+1f	1	–	1f	–	–	–
Poaceae culm nodes	3	–	–	–	–	–	–
Leaf frags	5	–	–	–	–	–	–
Pinus charcoal	2f	–	1f	–	–	–	–
Parenchyma	–	–	1	–	–	–	–
Unident.	2	–	4	–	3f	–	–
Cenococcum geophilum	–	3	–	–	–	–	–

Table 14: Castle Hill, Middle Bronze Age charred plant remains from other post-holes and undated tree-throw

	500	500		Field 1		1770	
Feature group	500	500		Field 1		1770	
Feature type			Post-holes				Tree-throw
Feature no.	292	299	749	536	1096	1771	326
Context	294	297	748	535	1095	1773	325
Sample	4	5	8	10	47	73	24
Flot size (ml)	10	2	10	20	40	20	5
Cereals							
Triticum dicoccum glume bases	–	–	–	–	1	–	–
Triticum sp. grain	1f	–	–	–	3	–	–
glume bases	–	–	–	1	–	–	–
Hordeum vulgare grain	–	–	–	–	–	–	–
Cerealia indet.	1f	8f	2f	11f	3f	2f	3f
Sprouts	–	–	–	–	1	–	–
Weeds							
Papaver rhoeas type	1	–	–	–	–	–	–
Corylus avellana nutshell	–	–	7f	3f	11f	–	2f
Chenopodium album	–	–	–	1	–	–	–
Rumex sp.	1	–	–	–	–	–	–
Viola sp.	1	–	–	–	–	–	–
Crataegus sp. fruit frag.	–	1	–	–	–	–	–
Trifolium sp.	1	–	–	–	1	–	–
Linum catharticum	–	–	–	–	–	1	–
Plantago lanceolata	–	–	–	1	–	–	–
Chrysanthemum segetum	–	–	–	–	–	–	1
Arrhenatherum elatius rootlets	4	–	1	1	–	2	–
Avena sp.	–	–	–	–	–	–	–
Poaceae culm bases	–	–	–	–	–	–	–
culm nodes	–	–	–	4	–	–	1

post-holes contained many charred plant remains, especially cereals. The association of weed species and cereals suggests that the crops were stored semi-cleaned and only fully processed when required.

Overall, the samples analysed show that crops of emmer, spelt and bread wheat along with barley and flax were grown and processed locally and possibly stored in a semi-cleaned state. Other possible uncultivated food sources were represented by finds of hazel, sloe, bramble, pignut and onion couch grass tubers, although it is possible that the latter species was more likely to be representative of arable habitats.

Charcoal, by Rowena Gale

Charcoal occurred widely and samples from a range of features were selected to provide data on possible structural elements, the use of local species for fuel, and environmental information. Twenty-nine samples were studied: three from ditches from the Neolithic enclosures, and 26 from Middle Bronze Age ditches, post-holes, and pits.

The charcoal was generally poorly preserved and friable, and a coating of sediments on the walls of the cells often obscured diagnostic details. Large samples were sub-sampled as follows: sample 96, 25%; sample 84, 50%. The results are summarised in Table 15. The anatomical structure of the charcoal was consistent with the taxa (or groups of taxa) given below. It is not usually possible to identify to species level. The anatomical similarity of some related species and/or genera makes it difficult to distinguish between them with any certainty, e.g. members of the Pomoideae, Leguminosae, and Salicaceae. Classification is according to *Flora Europaea* (Tutin *et al.* 1964–80).

Aquifoliaceae. *Ilex* sp., holly
Betulaceae. *Alnus* sp., alder; *Betula* sp., birch
Corylaceae. *Corylus* sp., hazel
Fagaceae. *Quercus* sp., oak
Leguminosae. *Ulex* sp., gorse and/or *Cytisus* sp., broom. These genera are anatomically similar.
Oleaceae. *Fraxinus* sp., ash
Rosaceae. Pomoideae: *Crataegus* sp., hawthorn; *Malus* sp., apple; *Pyrus* sp., pear; *Sorbus* spp., rowan, service tree and whitebeam. These generally are anatomically similar. Prunoideae: *Prunus* spp., which includes *P. avium*, wild cherry; *P.padus*, bird cherry; *P. spinosa*, blackthorn. Although it is sometimes difficult or impossible to differentiate between the species, the charcoal from Castle Hill was more characteristic of blackthorn.
Salicaceae. *Salix* sp., willow; *Populus* sp., poplar. These genera can not be distinguished using anatomical characters.

Neolithic

Enclosure 219
Charcoal from ditch 146, section A, consisted of a large quantity of hazel roundwood up to 25 mm in diameter. Although fragmented, at least 11 growth rings were seen on some pieces. Charcoal from ditch 217, section I included blackthorn, the hawthorn group and willow/poplar.

Enclosure 218
The sample from ditch 26, section G, included less charcoal than in the previous samples. Oak heartwood and blackthorn were identified.

Early Bronze Age

Pit 1555
Two samples (51 and 52) from the lower fill (1554) included oak sapwood and heartwood, alder, holly, and also in sample 51, blackthorn, and hawthorn type.

Middle Bronze Age

Field system ditches
Field system ditch 107, section 2018 was sited just north of the Neolithic enclosure 219. Charcoal from the ditch included oak roundwood, sapwood, and heartwood, hazel roundwood (some with wide growth rings), alder, blackthorn, hawthorn type, and willow/poplar.

Pit 1578
Dumps of charcoal occurred in the mid–upper levels of the pit. Although some pieces of material were up to 10 mm thick it was crumbly and difficult to examine. Samples from contexts 1682 and 1686 from the mid-levels consisted of oak, probably heartwood, but was too degraded to be certain; context 1574, from the upper level, included oak sapwood and heartwood, and also alder. The charcoal appeared to have accrued from the burning of poles/billets of wood wide enough to have developed heartwood and, in contrast to the charcoal residues from most other contexts at the site, the samples were predominantly oak. Only from the upper level (1574) was a small quantity of alder recorded. The purpose of the pit is, at present, enigmatic. Its large dimensions and the absence of general refuse, apart from charcoal and seeds, is puzzling and suggests a function dedicated to a specific activity.

Post-hole alignment 1661
The sample from a single post-hole from the southern end of the arc of stake- or post-holes, group 1770 (post-hole 1771; Table 15) consisted of oak heartwood, ash, alder, blackthorn, and probably hawthorn type.

Enclosure 5026
The sample from the southern terminal (ditch section C) of the entrance to the enclosure included fragments of alder, blackthorn, gorse/broom, and oak heartwood. Three samples from the northern ditch were examined. Samples from ditch sections 5094 and 5105 from near the ditch terminal at the entrance were poorly preserved.

The sample from the upper level of ditch section 5105, contained a considerable quantity of charcoal (from which a 25% sub-sample was examined) and identified as blackthorn, oak roundwood, sapwood and heartwood, ash, hawthorn type, and probably alder, or hazel. The sample from the base of ditch section 5105 was composed of small fragments which included alder, oak sapwood and heartwood, possibly ash, and a quantity which was either alder or hazel (but too degraded to verify). The sample from ditch section 5094 from the south-west to north-east aligned section of ditch included blackthorn and alder, and a few pieces of oak, fast-grown sapwood and heartwood.

Entrance group 5050

The sample from post-hole 5045 included a large quantity of charcoal. A 50% sub-sample was examined and identified as oak, sapwood and heartwood. Some sapwood fragments included growth rings as wide as 8 mm and although the material was too fragmented to assess likely diameters. It is probable that a fairly wide pole(s) is indicated.

Features inside enclosure 5026

It is uncertain whether the cluster of post-holes in the north-east corner was contemporary with the enclosure. Although preservation was poor, charcoal from three of the post-holes within group 5027 was examined.

That from post-hole 5117 consisted of hazel, blackthorn, gorse/broom, and hawthorn type. Further fragments were identified as hazel/alder. Post-hole 5168 contained thin slivers of oak, probably heartwood. By implication this could be interpreted as the remains of the post, perhaps burnt *in situ* or from the charred base of a post. The sample from post-hole 5224 included oak, alder and blackthorn.

Post-built structures 1812 and 1813

Two samples were analysed from four-post structure 1812, from post-holes 1745 and 1753. Both produced oak heartwood and hazel, and (?) alder, 1745 yielded a radio-carbon date in the Late Bronze Age.

The charcoal from post-hole 1675 in four-post structure 1813 included large fragments (up to 103 mm) of oak sapwood and heartwood and may be from a post. Post-hole 1679 included rather slow-grown oak sapwood and heartwood, and alder.

Six-post group 1754

The sample from post-hole 1537 mostly consisted of thin slivers of oak sapwood and heartwood but also alder, gorse/broom and hawthorn type. Post-hole 1645 contained very fragmented charcoal representing the same range of taxa, including some alder with a diameter of 5 mm and 3 growth rings. The material extracted for the analysis of the charred plant remains from post-holes 1537 and 1645 contained very small fragments of pine charcoal (Table 13) but this species was not present in the material extracted for the charcoal analyses. The sample from post-hole 1543 consisted of oak, narrow roundwood and heartwood, birch, hazel, blackthorn, hawthorn type, and gorse/broom. A small piece of coal was also recorded.

Post-holes in Field 1

Some post-holes at the southern end of the site were more randomly distributed, although it is possible that they derive from post-built structures of some sort. Between them they produced fragments of oak, hazel, gorse/broom, and probably blackthorn. Post-hole 1096, one of the southernmost features of the site, consisted of small fragments of oak heartwood, and hazel/alder.

Undated features

Several tree-throw holes were found on site, some of which contained small amounts of charcoal. The sample from tree-throw hole 326 included small fragments of hazel, alder, and hawthorn type.

Discussion

Charcoal occurred in numerous features but although deposits were frequently abundant, the preservation was often poor. In most contexts the charcoal consisted of a range of taxa and can, fairly confidently, be attributed to discarded hearth debris.

However, a quantity of hazel roundwood (ditch 146, section A) was identified from Neolithic enclosure 219. The roundwood consisted of stems measuring up to 25 mm in diameter (when charred) and, by implication, the charcoal could represent the burnt remains of structural components, e.g. wattle hurdles or narrow stakes.

Three samples from the Middle Bronze Age post-holes may represent the burnt remains of oak posts (post-hole 5168 from a group (5027) of post-holes inside the eastern enclosure; Group 5027; post-hole 5045 (group 5050) from the entrance to the enclosure; and post-hole 1675 from a group (1813) of post-holes south-west of the eastern enclosure.

The undated pit 1578 was notable for its large size. Charcoal deposits occurred in the middle and upper levels. Oak, probably heartwood, was identified from two mid-level samples, while the upper level comprised mainly of oak but also some alder. The charcoal appeared to have been dumped in the pit. The use of oak poles/ billets suggests that this material originated from a source other than a domestic hearth, in which a more likely use of fuel would have employed faggots composed of a mixture of species.

Assuming the charcoal from the remaining samples to represent spent fuel deposits it is clear that fuel was gathered from a wide range of species including alder, birch, hazel, ash, holly, blackthorn, oak, willow and/or poplar, gorse and/or broom), and member/s of the Pomoideae, e.g. hawthorn, apple, whitebeam, and wild service. Oak usually predominated and consisted of roundwood and wider billets or logs of wood, although occasionally oak was entirely absent, e.g. samples from inside the eastern enclosure, post-hole 5117, group 5027 and sample from the tree-throw hole 326. Alder, hazel, and blackthorn appear to have been used relatively frequently but other species probably more sporadically, e.g. holly, ash, and birch rarely occurred in the samples. Coal was sometimes used to supplement fuel – as testified by a small piece of coal in the sample from feature 1543, group 1754.

Environmental evidence

Neolithic features were confined to enclosure ditches and although only three charcoal samples were available from these for identification, the results indicate a landscape which included oak, hazel, black-thorn, willow/poplar, and member/s of the Pomoideae (hawthorn etc).

The much wider range of taxa identified from Bronze Age contexts undoubtedly reflects the larger number of samples examined and, in addition to those named

Table 15: Castle Hill, charcoal (no. fragments identified)

Feature	Context	Sample	Alnus	Betula	Cor	Frax	Ilex	Pom	Prunus	Quer	Sal	Ul/Cyt
Neolithic ditches												
26G	163	21	–	–	–	–	–	–	4	2h	–	–
146A	144	40	–	–	57r	–	–	–	–	–	–	–
217I	136	31	–	–	–	–	–	21	15	–	3	–
Early Bronze Age												
Pit 1555	1554	51	11	–	–	–	2	3	2	27s,h	–	–
	1554	52	1	–	–	–	3	–	–	18s,h	–	–
Group 1770												
Post-hole 1771	1773	73	3	–	–	1	–	(3)	2	19h	–	–
Middle Bronze Age												
Field system ditches 107												
2018	2019	26	10	–	16	–	–	1	6	15r,s,h	–	3
Pit 1578	1574	195	3	–	–	–	–	–	–	27,s,h	–	–
	1682	200	–	–	–	–	–	–	–	24	–	–
	1686	204	–	–	–	–	–	–	–	53	–	–
Enclosure, S ditch section 5026												
C	5032	78	8	–	–	–	–	–	10	2h	–	–
Enclosure, N ditch section 5026												
5094	5091	92	20	–	–	–	–	–	26	3s,h	–	–
5105	5101	96	17	–	(1)	3	–	3	6	9r,s,h	–	–
	5103	103	2(10)	–	(10)	(1)	–	–	–	7s,h	–	–
Features inside E enclosure 5026, group 5027												
5117	5115	131	(15)	–	1(15)	–	–	2	3	–	–	1
5168	5166	137	–	–	–	–	–	–	–	55h	–	–
5224	5223	141	5	–	–	–	–	–	1	5h	–	–
Entrance area group 5050												
5045	5040	84	–	–	–	–	–	–	–	69s,h	–	–
Features SW of enclosure 5026												
Group 1812												
1753	1752	75	2	–	12	–	–	–	–	9h	–	–
1745	1744	69	(2)	–	8(2)	–	–	–	–	15h	–	–
Group 1813												
1679	1680	71	3	–	–	–	–	–	–	35,s,h	–	–
1675	1676	60	–	–	–	–	–	–	–	49s,h	–	–
Group 1754												
1537	1536	57	12	–	–	–	–	1	–	24s,h	–	1
1543	1542	54	–	2	2	–	–	4	1	14r,h	–	1
1645	1644	56	4r	–	–	–	–	(1)	–	5s,h	–	1
Post-holes in field 1												
749	748	8	–	–	3	–	–	–	–	1h	–	–
536	535	10	–	–	4	–	–	–	6	2s,h	–	2
1096	1095	47	(1)		(1)	–	–	–	–	15h	–	–
Undated												
Tree-throw												
326	325	24	1	–	2	–	–	1	–	–	–	–

Key: Cor = *Corylus*; Frax = *Fraxinus*; Pom = *Pomoideae*; Quer = *Quercus*; Sal = Salicaceae; *Ul/Cyt* = *Ulex/Cytisus*
r = roundwood; s = sapwood; h = heartwood; ( ) = unverified identification.

above, added alder, birch, ash, holly, and gorse and/or broom.

The site lies on a south-east facing slope in a dry valley about 450 m north-west of the River Otter. The soils consist of silty clays interspersed with spreads of gravel and occasional sandy patches. The taxa identified are characteristic of acid soils and suggest that the dominant woodland was probably oak, perhaps mixed with hazel, or in more open woodland with birch and gorse. Ash, holly, and members of the Pomoideae such as hawthorn, wild service, and apple are woodland trees, although ash, holly, and hawthorn also grow in marginal woodland or open aspects, e.g. holly and hawthorn in scrub. Blackthorn is shrubby and quickly colonises cleared areas to form dense thickets. Alder, willow, and poplar grow in damp or seasonally wet soils. The banks or environs of the nearby River Otter probably provided a suitable habitat although more local damp patches/ponds may have existed closer to the site.

The evidence for coppicing was inconclusive. The charcoal was mostly too fragmented to assess the use of coppiced wood although fast-grown oak sapwood was noted in the sample from the southern ditch section 5094 of the eastern enclosure, and fast-grown hazel round-wood in the sample from the field system ditch 107.

Conclusion

Charcoal samples from the Neolithic and Bronze Age features identified the use of a wide range of taxa. Most of the charcoals almost certainly derived from fuel refuse but some material may have had structural origins, e.g. posts or components from hurdles.

The taxa identified included alder, birch, hazel, ash, holly, blackthorn, oak, willow and/or poplar, gorse and/or broom and member/s of the Pomoideae, e.g. hawthorn, apple, and wild service. These taxa suggest a wooded landscape characteristic of neutral to acid soils, probably with scrub or shrubby growth in open areas, and alder and willow in damper parts.

Land Snails, by Michael J. Allen

The identification of fresh- and brackish-water species in the assessment phase was of interest as there is no obvious habitat for the survival of these species today. Snails from 10 out of the 15 samples where snails were present were extracted for analysis (Table 16).

Most samples were 15 litres (Appendix 7) and all were processed by bulk flotation with the flot retained on a 0.5 mm mesh and the residues on a 1 mm mesh. The loss of shells in the residue in the 0.5–1 mm fraction will have occurred, but in view of the low numbers of shells and very general interpretation level undertaken this is not considered a difficulty. All shells were extracted under a x10–x30 stereo-binocular microscope by Sarah F. Wyles.

Shell numbers were very low in view of the large sample size, and in some samples most were obviously modern. Three samples contained obvious modern species and these specimens have not been included in the totals; all other specimens were worn and likely to be part of the palaeo-, rather than modern or sub-modern, fauna.

The assemblages

Shell numbers were very low throughout, (no more than three, excluding modern and burrowing specimens), so only some general comments can be made. Further, most of the samples in which shells were present were post-holes for which the taphonomy of how and when the shell was incorporated into the context is undetermined.

The terrestrial component is too small to say more than that of the shells that do survive, open country species seem to be most prevalent, as would be expected on an occupation site of the Middle Bronze Age. However, nearly 50% of the Middle Bronze Age features examined contained slum or fresh-/brackish-water species, and where they did occur they were the only non-recent species. They included *Anisus leucostoma* and *Valvata piscinalis*, which are common in bodies of water. *A. leucostoma* prefers soft water and is widely distributed and typically in ponds lakes, of slow flowing rivers and their adjacent marshes (Macan 1977), where as *V. piscinalis* is common in running water providing the current is not too fast. The slum species *Oxyloma pfeifferi* is restricted to wet land habitats such as water meadows, river banks, fens and sedge beds.

Of the terrestrial species no obligatory marsh species (e.g. Vertiginids), nor species common in wet grassland (such as *Vallonia pulchella*) were present, but *Arianta arbustorum* which is common in fairly damp situations including water meadows, marshes (Stratton 1954) and valley bottoms as well as drier habitats was present (Cameron and Palles-Clark 1971).

The preservation of the slum and fresh-/brackish-water species may be a combination of a different source or origin; i.e. from an area were shell formation was better, in combination with their being incorporated into archaeological deposits rather than being in an active soil where decay is more likely to occur. The presence of these species either indicates the nature of the local site environment, or perhaps more likely, that they have been transported to this site by animal or human activity. The site is above the floodplain of the River Otter which flows c. 0. 5 km to the east. For isolated single shells of fresh- or brackish water species, accidental transport to the site in mud on the feet of birds is often invoked (*cf.* Thomas 1977), but on this site the occurrence seems to be too common for this explanation. Instead it seem likely that the shells were incorporated with resources brought from the River Otter valley; all the shells could have been included within clay/mud or vegetation brought to site. This is likely to have included reeds and sedges for thatching, fodder, and bedding, or clays collected to be used in, for example, daub for walls, rather than in materials used for manuring fields (*cf.* Allen 1997, 175).

Although the assemblages are small, they indicate that a distinct wet (river side meadow land) element was exploited, probably for vegetation for thatching and bedding and animal fodder or clay for building. The remaining element in the assemblages was, in contrast, predominantly typical of open dry grassland.

Table 16: Castle Hill, land snails

	Date	Neo	Middle Bronze Age							
	Feature type	Ditch	Field ditch	Pit		Post-holes					
	Feature	146	735	1578	279	1555	1635	1679	1771	1753	5070
	Sample	40	46	204	5	52	55	71	73	75	85
	Context	144	734	1686	299	1554	1634	1680	1773	1752	5069
	Vol (litres)	15	15	15	3	15	15	15	15	10	15
MOLLUSCA											
Pomatias elegans (Müller)		–	–	+	–	–	–	–	–	–	–
Oxyloma pfeifferi (Rossmässler)		–	–	–	–	–	–	–	–	1	–
Pupilla muscorum (Linnaeus)		1	–	1	–	–	–	–	–	–	–
Vallonia costata (Müller)		–	–	1	–	–	–	[1]	–	–	–
Discus rotundatus (Müller)		–	–	+	–	–	–	–	–	–	–
Cecilioides acicula (Müller)		–	2	–	–	–	–	–	–	–	–
Clausilia bidentata (Ström)		–	–	–	–	1	–	–	–	–	–
Candidula intersecta (Poiret)		–	–	–	[1]	–	–	–	–	–	–
Helicella itala (Linnaeus)		–	–	1	–	–	–	–	–	–	–
Trichia hispida (Linnaeus)		–	[1]	–	–	1	–	–	–	–	–
Arianta arbustorum (Linnaeus)		–	–	–	–	+	–	–	–	–	–
Cepaea spp.		–	–	–	–	+	–	–	–	–	–
FRESH-/BRACKISH-WATER											
Valvata piscinalis (Müller)		–	–	–	–	–	–	–	–	–	1
Anisus leucostoma (Millet)		–	1	–	–	–	2	–	–	–	–
Taxa		1	1	3		2	1	1	–	1	1
Total		1	1	3	0	2	2	1	+	1	1

Totals exclude *Cecilioides acicula*. Modern specimens indicated by [ ]

Magnetic Susceptibility,
by Hayley F. Clark

A total of 120 magnetic susceptibility samples was taken and in general they produced low readings.

All the features of Neolithic date have low readings except 2073 (part of enclosure 218). This anomaly could possibly be due to root or animal disturbance rather than human activity, but Peterborough Ware was also found here. The readings were higher in the enclosure ditch (5026) of the Middle Bronze Age settlement and pits and post-holes 5186, 1530, 1551, and 1555, some of which are of Early Bronze Age date, also had higher readings than other post-holes on the site.

The higher readings in the enclosure ditch are most likely to reflect the disposal of refuse there. The low readings from the other Middle Bronze Age features, principally the field system, seem most likely to indicate less intensive use.

Radiocarbon Dates, by Michael J. Allen

Seven radiocarbon determinations were obtained on charcoal from contexts excavated during the evaluation and excavation phases (Table 17; Fig. 26).

Neolithic Enclosures 218 and 219

The two determinations from enclosure 219 (Table 17) clearly date different events. The determination from ditch segment 217 (AA-30670, 4630±50 BP) is from the small roundwood pieces of *Prunus* from mixed charcoal of blackthorn, hawthorn group, and willow/poplar. It is only *assumed*, therefore, that this determination provides a date for the digging of the ditch and its infilling and it is possible that the charcoal is redeposited from earlier activity. The charcoal (not identifed to species) from ditch 510 recovered during the evaluation (Beta 78183, 4220±60 BP) suffers from the same taphonomic ambiguities. Nevertheless, although the dates are separated by four centuries, both determinations fall within the range of dates recovered from other Neolithic monuments.

Middle Bronze Age Enclosure 5026 and Field System 107

Four determinations were made on charcoals from the ditches of enclosure 5026 and field system 107. We can model these four determinations as a phase indicating that the enclosure and field systems, or at least the dis-

Table 17: Castle Hill, radiocarbon dates

Context	Material	Lab. No.	Result (BP)	$\delta^{13}C\%_0$	Calibration BC (2σ)
4-post group 1812, single fill PH 1745	*Quercus* (heartwood) charcoal	AA-30672	2765±50	-25.9	1080–820
W terminal enclosure ditch 5026, primary fill	*Prunus* charcoal	AA-30673	2985±50	-26.6	1400–1050
Enclosure ditch 5026, top fill	*Prunus* charcoal	AA-30674	3035±50	-24.7	1420–1130
Field system ditch 107, single fill	Mixed charcoal*	AA-30671	3060±55	-24.6	1440–1150
Enclosure ditch 5026, primary fill	*Quercus* (sapwood) charcoal	AA-30675	3115±50	-23.7	1510–1260
Pit 1130	*Corylus* charcoal	AA-32605	3850±60	-23.7	2470–2130
Enclosure 219, terminal N side	?charcoal	Beta 78183	4220±60		2920–2600
Enclosure 219, terminal S, side, single fill	*Prunus* charcoal	AA-30670	4630±50	-25.0	3610–3140

* *Corylus*, Pomoideae, *Prunus*, *Quercus* (sapwood), Salicaceae, *Ulex / Cytisus*

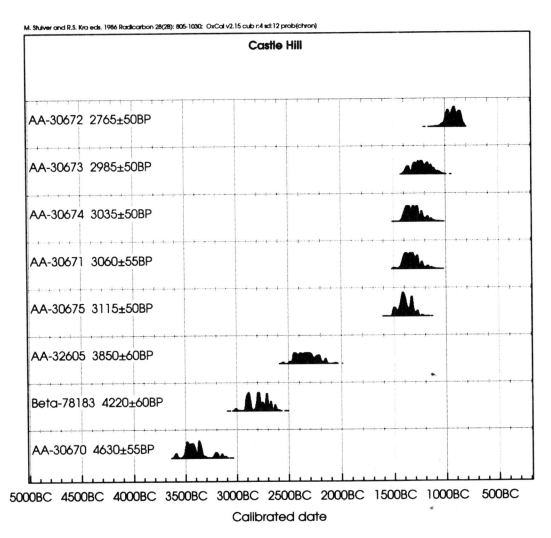

Figure 26   Castle Hill: probability distributions of radiocarbon dates

posal of charcoal in their ditches, is contemporaneous. These fall within a range of about 1500–1150 BC, i.e. firmly within the Middle Bronze Age.

Late Bronze Age Four-post Structure 1812

Charcoal from one of the post-holes (post-hole 1812) provided a date later than the phase of the enclosure and field systems. The charcoal from the samples was solely oak, and may represent the timber post. Only heartwood was present and this could provide an offset of up to about 100 years for a timber post 300 mm diameter, although realistically this is unlikely to be no more than 50 years (R. Gale pers. comm.). It is therefore possible to determine that this structure is later than the phase of activity represented by the enclosure and field systems, while the determination itself is also significantly different (Ward and Wilson 1978).

Discussion, by A.P. Fitzpatrick

The Neolithic Monuments

The apparently segmented and very uneven character of the ditches of enclosures 218 and 219 at Castle Hill is typical of Neolithic monuments, and a range of rectangular-shaped monuments of this date is known; cursuses, long barrows, free standing mortuary enclosures, and long mortuary enclosures. The wider context of the monuments is discussed in Chapter 9. What seems to be the full extent of enclosure 219 – some 42 m – is known though, in view of the extreme truncation of the eastern end of the enclosure, it is possible that it was originally somewhat longer but there is no evidence to suggest that it was enclosed at its eastern end. The surviving evidence is, however, compatible with the whole plan of the monument having been recovered. Enclosure 218, at which two phases of activity may be represented by a lengthening of the enclosure, appears to have been open at its western end.

Although the incompleteness of the enclosure ditches could be due to the severe plough damage, causeways are found in the ditches of Neolithic mortuary enclosures and long barrows, as well as other monuments. At Castle Hill there was little evidence from the fills of the ditches for an eroded mound nor are the ditches substantial enough to have been the quarries for a substantial mound; irrespective of whether the upcast was placed over a core of turves. The fact that a Middle Bronze Age field system overlies the monuments emphasises the slight nature of any earthworks.

The Castle Hill ditches were excavated in the hot summer months when only a single fill was certainly identifiable in every section. It can only be said that in some places there were clear indications of secondary and tertiary fills, for example enclosure 218, segment 26 (Fig. 9, G). By contrast segment 510 of enclosure 219 was examined in the evaluation during the winter and a slump line of material derived from an internal bank was identifiable. This deposit could not be re-identified

during the excavation due to the significant truncation the site had suffered during the intervening years. Accordingly it is likely that, by analogy with some other monuments of Neolithic date, only a small internal bank stood behind the ditches.

There is also inferential evidence for an internal bank in the form of the narrowing of ditch 107 of the field system just after it crosses the enclosure ditches. The banks, which were presumably still upstanding, meant that the base of the ditch would not have been dug to the same depth into the subsoil. There is no certain evidence for a timber palisade having stood within the ditch segments. However, a number of possible stake-holes were recorded in the sides and bases of the terminals of ditches in enclosure 218 and in the surrounding area. Although the lack of consistency or pattern in the location and arrangement of these features suggests that some of them are natural disturbances, some of the charcoal from hazel roundwood from the other enclosure 219 may derive from wattle hurdles or narrow stakes. It is possible therefore that there was some form of superstructure, either within the enclosures or outside them. None of the other of the small number of features within the enclosures can be shown to be contemporary with them rather than being associated with subsequent Bronze Age occupation, and the general paucity of finds of Neolithic date is consistent with this. However, pit 139 appears to be centrally located on the axis of enclosure 219 (Fig. 8) and it may be suspected that it is contemporary with it. A similar, but very shallow, pit is sited in an analogous position in enclosure 218. The limited evidence from the charred plant remains suggests that the monuments were sited in grassland, perhaps with patches of scrub of sloe, elder and hazel. Emmer was certainly being cultivated, but not in the immediate vicinity of the monuments.

Pottery was found in the northern and southern sides of enclosure 218, but most was in the secondary fill of segment 26 (Fig. 9), with the remainder coming from the southern half of the terminal of segment 2074 where only a single fill was recognisable. As a substantial part of the Peterborough Ware bowl from segment 26 is present it is probable that it was deliberately placed there and the same is likely to be true of the bowl from 2074, where a second vessel may also be represented. The Beaker pottery in pit 609, which cut enclosure 219, may derive from the secondary fills of the enclosure ditch. Only one concentration of flaked stone was noted, in segment 26, 2 m to the east of the Peterborough Ware bowl. The material from the north-eastern ditch included a number of refitting chert flakes and a core (Pl. 8). The chert from both enclosures comprises mainly knapping waste but the flint included many more tools and utilised pieces and possible blanks. All of this is consistent with what is known of the sequence of the deposition of objects in similar contexts (Thomas 1991, 70, 92, fig. 5.9), but also, albeit to a lesser extent, their location towards the ends of monuments (Thomas 1984, 167; Cleal 1991, 184–5). In contrast to the pottery, much of the flaked stone may be ascribed to the Early Neolithic, suggesting activity in the area, perhaps before the enclosures were built, and early in their use.

However, given the long time scale involved, there is nothing to indicate whether the monuments are contemporary or separated by several centuries. No materials suitable for radiocarbon dating were recovered from enclosure 218 but two samples were obtained from enclosure 219, one each from the southern and northern sides. The oak charcoal from the western terminal of the southern segment (217) yielded a determination of 4630±50 BP, which calibrates to 3610–3140 cal. BC. As the ditch is so truncated at this point (Fig. 6, section I), it seems likely – but cannot be proven – that the surviving deposits are the primary fill. The determination from the secondary fill examined in the evaluation is 2920–2600 cal. BC (Beta 78183; 4220±60 BP). That charcoal was not identified to species or whether it represented heartwood or sapwood, however, both dates are consistent with an origin in the later part of the earlier Neolithic, with activity continuing into the middle Neolithic.

The Bronze Age Farm and Field System

The main Bronze Age settlement at Castle Hill was preceded by modest amount of Early Bronze Age activity associated with Beaker pottery. This pottery was found in a small group of pits to the west of the Middle Bronze Age settlement (1530, 1551, and 1555), and in one post-hole of what may be small post-built round-house 978, lying to the north of Neolithic enclosure 219. Pit 609 was cut by, but may have been associated with 978. Significant quantities of flaked stone tools and waste were found in both areas, suggesting that they were both made and used nearby. It is possible, though, that the possible building 978 is Middle Bronze Age in date and represents a small building set within the fields. Charcoal from the field system immediately adjacent to the building and thought to represent the clearing out of a hearth yielded a radiocarbon date in the Middle Bronze Age. What may be a curving fence line (1661) appeared to be cut by the later field system, although it is possible that it represents a sub-division of the Middle Bronze Age field system.

Little more can be said of this fragmentary data other than it indicates activity in the vicinity, perhaps to the north, prior to the establishment of the field system. This is supported by the flaked stone recovered from Brinor, only 250 m to the north-east, amongst which were Neolithic and Early Bronze Age elements (Chapter 2 above) and flaked stone was also found to the west of the excavations during the Watching Brief.

The stratigraphic evidence suggests that the enclosure 5026 is later than the coaxial field system, but this may only indicate that the enclosure ditch was recut. The radiocarbon determinations from the field system and the enclosure form a coherent group. The determinations from the primary and tertiary fills of the western terminal of the enclosure ditch are also virtually indistinguishable.

Due to the extent of the trenching to both the east and west of the main excavation area it is possible to be confident that the limits of the field system were defined in those directions. How much further it extended to the north and south is unknown, but what may be elements

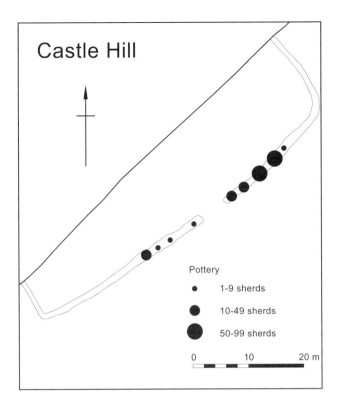

Figure 27 Castle Hill: distribution of pottery in Bronze Age enclosure 5026

of the same field system are visible on air photographs to the north (Griffith, Chapter 1), though there is also evidence for Roman activity in the same area (Chapter 12). The fields, which are mostly oriented south-east along the lie of the land, are not a consistent size, varying in width between 40–50 m. They appear to be rectangular rather than square.

Although they now appear as a coaxial system it is uncertain whether they were set out in one phase or cumulatively, for example the westernmost field (field 1) appears to be aligned at right angles to the remainder which could be read as suggesting that it is slightly later. However, the sequence of the cutting of the ditches between fields 1, 2, and 3 does show that the east–west ditch 25 was not a later addition or 'infilling' but was broadly contemporary and integral to the system as revealed by excavation. In places the ditches themselves appear to have been dug in short sections, which may suggest construction by gangs, but the stratigraphy within them generally appeared as a single homogenous fill. This homogeneity, perhaps due to recutting, may have destroyed any evidence for gang construction. The comparatively modest size of the field ditches would only have yielded a small bank sufficient to support a hedgerow. The wide range of species identified amongst the charcoal from the field ditches suggests that it is likely to derive from fires rather than hedge timmings or coppicing.

A large pit (1578) within field 6 remains undated. The small quantities of charcoal in the upper fills is, however, reminiscent of that occurring, albeit more intensely, in the fills of the nearby enclosure ditch and on this basis it is tentatively ascribed to the Middle

Plate 7   Castle Hill: view of the site from the north, from the old railway bridge, prior to excavation

Bronze Age. No pollen survived but the location of the feature, within a field, recalls the wells at sites such as Radley, Oxfordshire (Mudd 1995) and Reading Business Park, Berkshire (Moore and Jennings 1992) or the flax retting pits at the latter site. If it was a well, any evidence for wellhead structure or for fencing has been lost. Although the curving fence line 1661 appeared to be cut by the field system, it may represent a subdivision of the field nearest to the settlement which defined the range of two- and four-post structures immediately west of the settlement enclosure. Fence lines within Bronze Age ditched fields have been observed, for example at Shorncote in Gloucestershire (excavations by Wessex Archaeology), and again at Reading Business Park (Moore and Jennings 1992, 46).

There are several gaps in the field ditches at Castle Hill, such as that in the north-eastern corner of field 1 between ditches 620 and 703. Although most appear as simple causeways, the staggered entrance represented by ditches 22, 52 and 72 and the associated stake-holes in the north-west of field 4, recall in general terms, but not in their specifics, the arrangements at Fengate, Cambridgeshire, which Pryor has argued were for the handling and penning of sheep (Pryor 1996).

Only the southern part of enclosure 5026 was examined, showing it to have had an entrance structure of some sort that had been repaired and reworked on several occasions, and may be compared to the entrance of the Middle Bronze Age enclosure at Boscombe Down East, Wiltshire (Stone 1936, 470–2, pl. i–ii). One other large post (1729) stood 4 m outside the entrance and

presumably marked it in some way. Some of the postholes inside the enclosure immediately to the west of the entrance may have acted as a screen, guiding people to the eastern half of the enclosure where there is evidence for at least one building. The terminals of the ditch at this point were larger than most of the rest of the circuit, suggesting that the terminals had been recut at least once. Elsewhere the ditches were only slightly larger than those of the adjoining field system, which raises the possibility that the enclosure did not have an internal bank rather than a hedgerow. Certainly there is little evidence in the ditch fills for an internal bank, and there are large quantities of finds in the tertiary fills. The entrance to the enclosure is also not very deep, which might be thought to suggest that any internal bank was not a significant size. As it survives, the stratigraphic evidence suggests that the enclosure was added to the field system, as is known for other Middle Bronze Age sites such as South Lodge in Cranborne Chase, Dorset (Barrett *et al.* 1991, 182). The possibility that the enclosure was primary with the field system being laid out around it cannot be resolved on the evidence available.

One arc of four post-holes in the eastern half of the enclosure suggests that at least one of the buildings was circular, and so probably a round-house, but it has not proved possible to satisfactorily reconstruct this or any of the other buildings or structures represented by these remains. A number of two or four post structures may also be represented by the post holes – if they are contemporary with the enclosure. The small, interrupted, ditch 5183, which encompasses these post-holes, is reminiscent of the contemporary enclosure at Patteson's Cross. In view of the paucity of finds from this group of features, the possibility that it represents an earlier or later phase should be acknowledged. By the same token, there is no evidence to suggest that they are not contemporary with the larger enclosure and the quantity of finds from the enclosure ditch to the south strongly suggests that the post-holes and the buildings they formed part of are contemporary.

The only other features in the interior of enclosure 5026 is the group of post-holes 5028, but one of these appeared to cut the enclosure ditch, and there are also other hints that at least some of the other post-built structures in that area may be of a slightly later date. Immediately outside the enclosure are a number of post-built structures, including groups 1812 and 1813, which can be interpreted as four- or five-post structures which by analogy with later examples from elsewhere in Britain, can be interpreted as above ground granaries or stores. The charred plant remains from 1812 include a large number of flax seeds, suggesting that it may at one stage have been used as a store.

However, other interpretations are also possible, for example group 1754 could represent a four-post structure which was then replaced by a two-post one (Fig. 20), although here there is a high proportion of residues from the final sieving in crop processing amongst the charred plant remains. Two-post structures, which presumably had a different purpose, such as drying racks for hay, also appear to be present, for example in group 1770 (Fig.19). It is likely therefore that a range of structures with different purposes is present. Certainly, if all the structures at Castle Hill were four-post granaries they would represent an early group. There is also a notable concentration of flaked stone of Middle Bronze Age date in this field that strongly suggests that stone objects were made, and perhaps also used, in the vicinity.

The radiocarbon date of 1080–820 cal. BC (AA-30672; 2765±50 BP) from four-post structure 1812 is slightly later than those from the enclosure ditch (below) and the field system. However, the pottery from the site forms a coherent group of Trevisker related wares for food storage, preparation and consumption and there are only slight hints of later material. Even so, one of the small number of sherds tentatively attributed to the Late Bronze Age on the basis of their fabric comes from a post-hole in the adjacent four- of five-post structure 1813.

Whether any of this provides secure enough evidence on which to suggest a, separate, later phase of activity is questionable. It should be recognised though, that the evidence within the excavated area for structures in and adjacent to enclosure 5026 that can be shown to strictly contemporary with it is slight. This is not to doubt that the enclosure represents the boundary of a settlement.

The enclosure ditch contained significant quantities of pottery and other material, which are consistent with settlement material. The distribution of the pottery from these deposits has a pronounced emphasis in the eastern half of the enclosure ditch, with the number of sherds outnumbering those from the western half by a ratio of 3:1 (198: 59 sherds) (Fig. 27). Radiocarbon samples from the primary and tertiary fills of the same section (5105) of the eastern ditch (Fig.26) respectively yielded determinations of 1510–1260 cal. BC (AA-30675; 3115±50 BP) and 1420–1130 cal. BC (AA-30674; 3035±50 BP). The primary fill of the western terminal, which is thought to have been recut, yielded a date of 1400–1050 cal. BC (AA 30673; 2985±50 BP).

The charcoal rich pits to the east of the enclosure (Fig. 6) may have been dedicated to a particular industrial function but they do recall the pits found beneath stone cairns immediately to the east in the Otter valley near to Honiton (Pollard 1967b; 1971) and to the west on Dartmoor (Wainwright *et al.* 1979, 29–31). The radiocarbon date of 2470–2138 cal. BC (AA-32606; 3850±60 BP) from pit 1130 is within the range known from related monuments. Even when they are found with monuments associated with mortuary practices, these pits often do not contain any cremated human bone. If there was only a low turf mound it is possible that the pits are all that remain of such a monument (*cf.* Griffith 1994, 92). The ring ditches known from aerial photography, and presumed to be of Bronze Age date (Pl. 22), are only 200 m to the north-east.

The charred plant remains from the enclosure ditches also include processing waste such as chaff and weed seeds, which may have been reused as fuel for hearths. This evidence points to the processing of cereals and their storage in a semi-clean state on site. As we have seen the four-/five-post structures immediately to the south-west of the enclosure, although possibly slightly later in date, appear to have been granaries.

On basis of the evidence from the enclosure ditches, emmer wheat was the dominant crop, with bread wheat and barley also being cultivated. Spelt, flax, and peas also appear to have constituted minor crops. Not surprisingly, the samples from the field ditches contained only small quantities of charred plant remains. These remains mainly provide an indication of the background flora, but there are occasional finds such as the wild radish and vetch which are of cornfield weed species.

It seems plausible that at least some of these cereals were grown in the fields surrounding the enclosure. The fields could also have been used to manage stock and the arrangement of at least one of the gates to the fields is reminiscent of those suggested to be for managing sheep (Pryor 1996). If the large, undated, pit 1578 was a well, its siting within a field would be consistent with providing water for animals penned near to the settlement.

The surrounding countryside was a mixture of woodland, scrub, grassland and arable, Charcoal from alder charcoal indicates the exploitation of a riverside habitat, almost certainly the River Otter not far to the south, with sedge indicating the use of wetland resources, confirmed by the rare survival of snail shells from fresh-brackish water species.

4. Patteson's Cross

by C.A. Butterworth

Introduction

The Preliminary Assessment of the Published Route (Weddell 1991, 22) noted that the *c*. 150 pieces of flaked stone in the Carter Collection in the Royal Albert Memorial Museum, Exeter which had been found in a field to the west of Patteson's Cross probably derived from a prehistoric settlement. Owing to the condition of the fields at the time that the pre-project evaluation was undertaken it was not possible to undertake systematic fieldwalking of the area, but further finds of flaked stone were found, adding further evidence for the existence of a settlement.

The subsequent geophysical survey concluded that;

> Topsoil magnetic susceptibility mapping shows a strong magnetic focus within this field. Limited access ... precluded follow-up gradiometer survey, but taking into consideration fieldwalking evidence for concentrations of flint and chert artefacts ... this field must be highlighted as having some archaeological potential. Topsoil magnetic susceptibility patterns recede approaching Patteson's Cross. (Johnson 1995, 3.74–5)

On this basis the it was recommended that further magnetometer survey and also Strip and Record works should tke place at the site. It was not possible to undertake any further work until the December of 1996, when a gradiometer survey of the western part of the area was carried, providing the following additional information:

> ... no specific pattern of anomalies was detected which may be confidently attributed on morphological grounds to a recognisable archaeological settlement or ritual site which might be associated with the surface (pre-historic) flintwork scatter and enhanced top-soil magnetic susceptibility measurements.
>
> However, unenclosed archaeological sites which do not comprise a high proportion of 'cut' features may remain largely invisible to gradiometer (or resistivity) survey, and it is possible that the enhanced topsoil magnetic susceptibility identity and surface artefacts represent the only indications of a dispersed horizon, perhaps associated with a truncated archaeological site. Significant denudation by prolonged ploughing in this field is confirmed by the total reduction of what must have been substantial former [medieval or post-medieval] boundary banks. (Johnson 1996, 4.1–2).

Topography, Geology and Land-use

The site (W2414.12) takes its name from a memorial cross erected in the late 19th century to the memory of John Coleridge, the missionary Bishop of Melanesia, who was murdered – by the indigenous population – in 1871. The memorial, which is sited at the crossroads of the A30 and Gosford Lane (Figs 28 and 29), is a Grade II listed building.

The site lay to the west of Patteson's Cross and north of the existing A30, centred on SY 0946 9766 (Fig. 2). The eastern end of the site was in the dry valley followed by the road between Ottery St Mary and Feniton, and from *c*. 60 m AOD there, the ground rose sharply to *c*. 65 m AOD at the top of the slope immediately to the west. Thereafter the ground was relatively level, rising gradually to *c*. 69. 5 m AOD at the west, where there was a slight south-eastward slope.

The underlying geology is Valley Gravel over Upper Sandstone (Geological Survey of Great Britain, Drift Sheet 326 and 340, Sidmouth). The natural soils encountered were of sandy silt or clay loam with gravel. The area, which extended across two fields, was under grass at the time of the excavation but the western field had previously been in cultivation.

Excavation Areas

A series of trenches was laid out to intersect the anomalies identified by the geophysical survey and to cover a representative sample of the area as whole (Figs 28–30). Some of these trenches were enlarged as considered appropriate by monitoring meetings, resulting in the final array seen in Figure 28. Eleven trenches in the eastern part of the site were supplemented by the enlargement of one trench and the addition of another three trenches in that area (Fig. 29). Another 11 trenches were excavated in the western part of the site (Fig. 30), most focused on areas of archaeological potential suggested by the gradiometer survey. Two areas, centred on post-built round-houses, were subsequently expanded. The total area investigated was 5,457 m², the work being carried out in stages between February and May 1997.

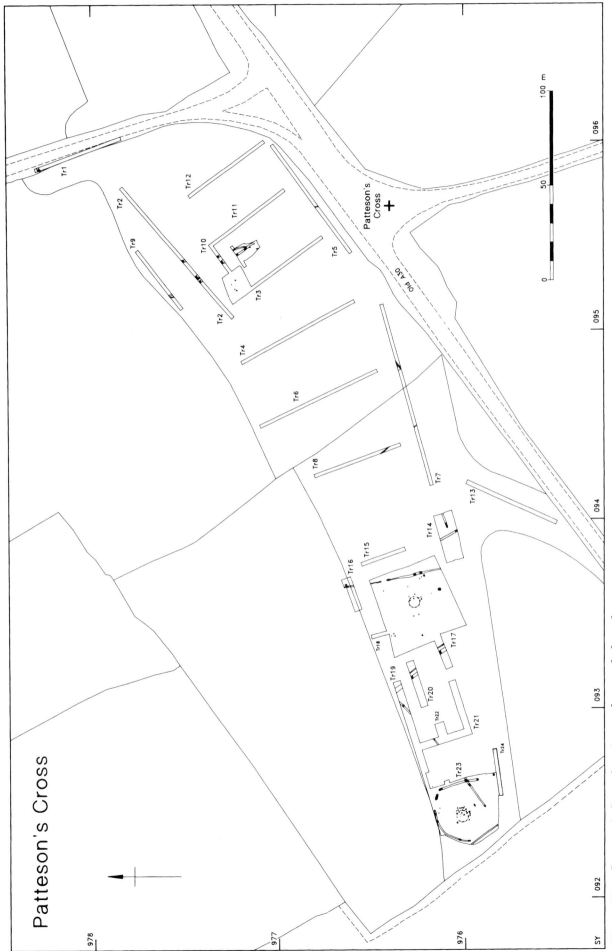

Figure 28   Patteson's Cross: location and general plan of excavaton

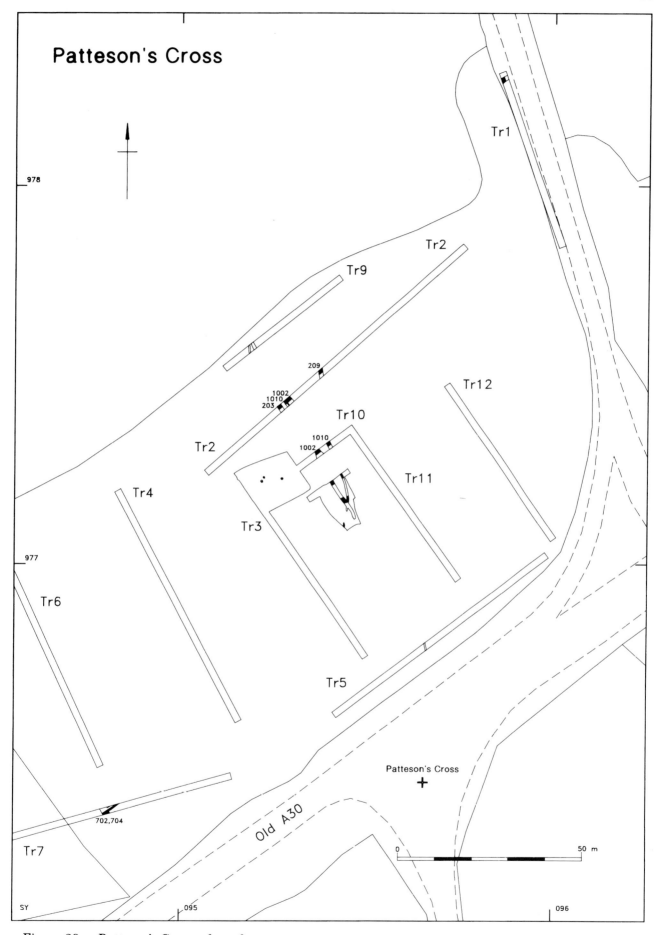

Figure 29   Patteson's Cross: plan of eastern area

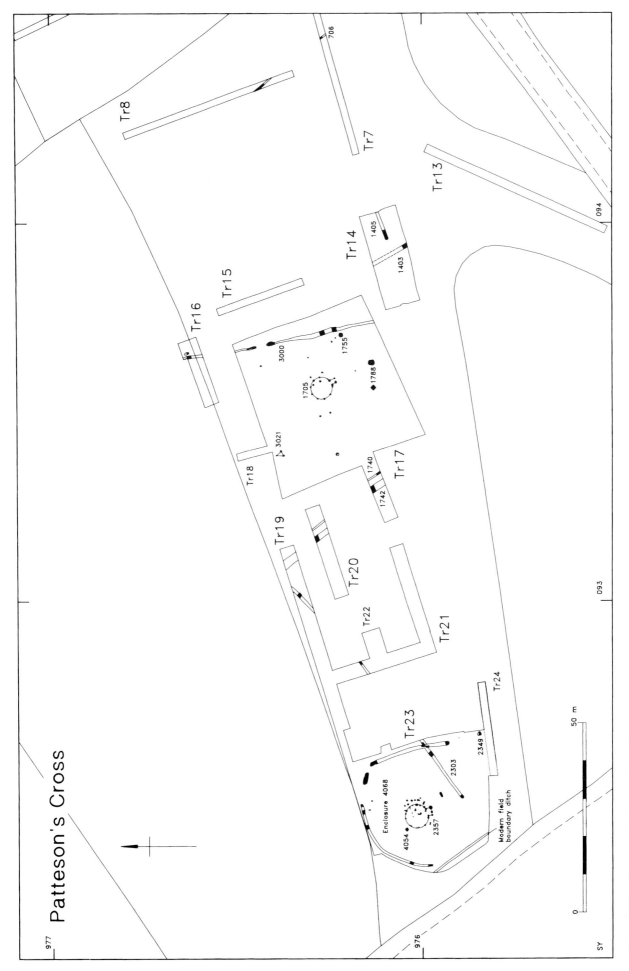

Patteson's Cross

Figure 30   Patteson's Cross: plan of western area

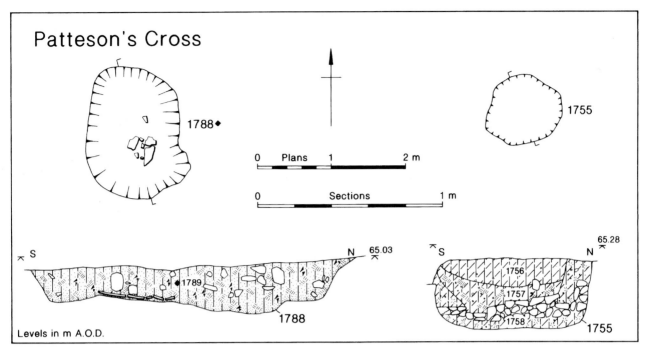

Figure 31   Patteson's Cross: plan and sections of pits 1788 and 1755

A number of features of natural origin and a few widely dispersed possible post-holes or pits were investigated but are not described in detail here; further information is available in the project archive.

Results

Pit 1788

A radiocarbon date of 2140–1880 BC (AA-30669; 3630±45 BP) was obtained from pit 1788, *c.* 11m south-east of round-house 1705 (Figs 30 and 31; Pl. 8). The pit was irregular in plan, measuring 1.75 m by 1.25 m, and was 0.25 m deep; the sides were irregular but generally steep, the base was uneven. Several large sherds of a bucket-shaped urn traditionally dated to the Middle Bronze Age rested on the base of the pit, below the single fill of charcoal-flecked, brown sandy clay loam.

Plate 8   Patteson's Cross: pit 1788 viewed from the east, with Bronze Age pottery in situ

Post-built Round-house 1705 and Associated Features

Round-house 1705 (Trench 17; Figs 30 and 32; Pls 9 and 10) was a simple, apparently unenclosed structure. The building was represented by 17 post-holes, 13 of which marked a circle *c.* 6 m in diameter with a south-south-east facing entrance; two of the remaining four post-holes were inside and two were outside the circle.

The post-holes of the main structure (1718, 1712, 1708, 1714, 1720, 1722, 1724, 1730, 1732, 1728, 1726) were at intervals of 1.45–1.9 m, except at the entrance where post-holes 1718 and 1726 were 0.23 m and 0.12 m respectively from 1712 and 1728. The outer post-holes of the entrance, 1734 and 1736, were 1.05 m and 0. 7 m from the inner ones and were 0.65 m apart. Both of the internal post-holes, 1706 and 1716, were in the eastern half of the structure, with the outer ones, 1710 and 1738, also to its east.

The post-holes were between 0. 2 m and 0.61 m in diameter and 0.02–0.23 m deep, with the inner post-holes of the entrance being among the largest. They were filled with a variety of soils, although each contained only one fill: dark reddish- or yellowish–brown silty loam predominated but sandy silt and sandy silty loam were also recorded. Charcoal was scarce, but that from post-hole 1734 gave a radiocarbon date of 1690–1440 cal. BC (AA-30666; 3280±45 BP).

A few post-holes were recorded further from the round-house, including a possible three-post structure 3021 *c.* 16. 5 m to the north-east (Fig. 33). The post-holes, which were spaced at intervals of 1.6 m, 1.4 m, and 0.98 m, were up to 0.44 m wide and between 0.22 m and 0.27 m deep. All three were filled with dark yellowish–brown silty loam, lightly charcoal-flecked in the case of 1774. Four metres to the west of the round-house was what appears to be a two post-structure; the posts were 2.4 m apart.

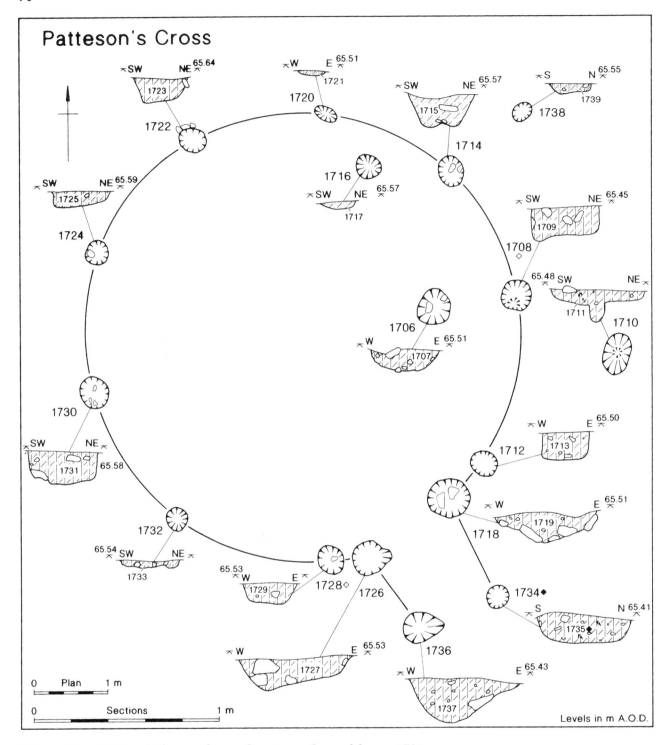

Figure 32   Patteson's Cross: plan and sections of round-house 1705

Pit 1755 was almost 10 m south-east of 1705 (Figs 30 and 31). It was roughly circular in plan with steep sides falling to a level base, and was *c.* 1.05 m in diameter and 0.37 m deep. A layer of dark reddish–brown silty loam with dark ash and gravel filled the base of the pit and was completely covered by chert cobbles as if to form a lining. More dark ashy material extended up the sides of the pit and was sealed by clean reddish brown silty loam.

Ditch 3000

Ditch 3000, which ran from north-north-west to south-south-east between 9 m and 10 m east of round-house 1705 (Fig. 30), may have been associated with it, but more probably as a field boundary than as part of an enclosure. There was a 2.8 m wide break in the ditch *c.* 14.5 m north-east of 1705, but thereafter it continued out of Trench 17, across and out of Trench 16.

Plate 9   Patteson's Cross: Round-house 1705, viewed from the north, during the course of excavation but before topsoil stripping was complete. Photograph: DAP/ABI 20 (1 May 1997), by Bill Horner, Devon County Council.

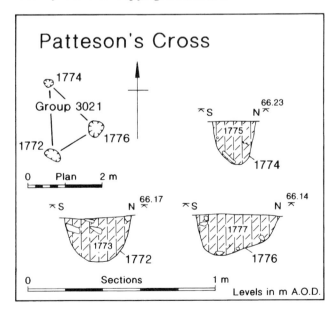

Figure 33   Patteson's Cross: plan and sections of three-post structure 3021

The ditch was up to 1.4 m wide and 0.45 m deep in section at the north side of the trench, where it also appeared to have been recut. Some sections showed the ditch to be asymmetrical, the west side being steeper

Plate 10   Patteson's Cross: round-house 1705 fully excavated, viewed from the east. The porch is to the left of the photograph

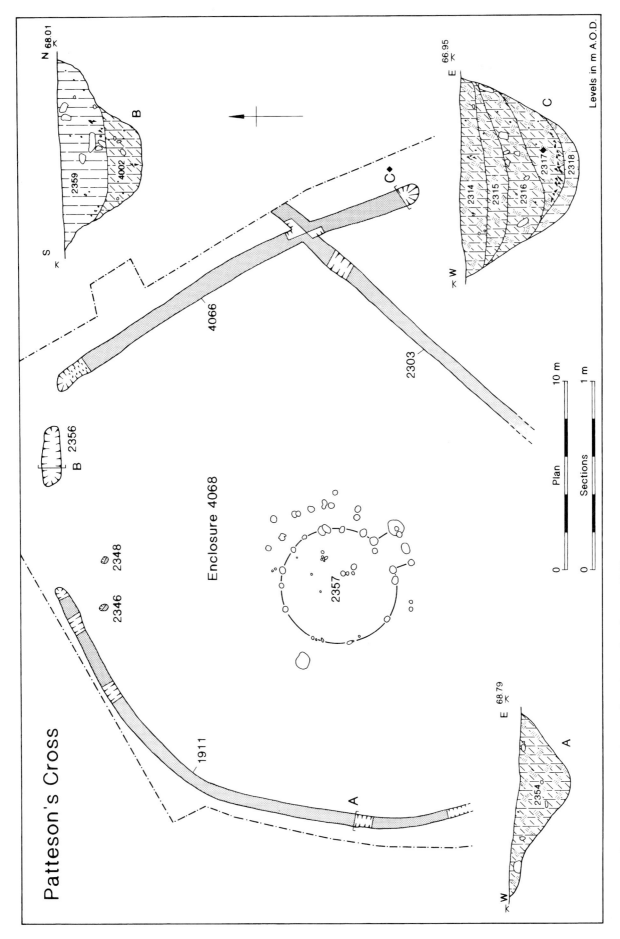

Figure 34   Patteson's Cross: plan and sections of enclosure 4068

than the east, but the base of the ditch was everywhere rounded. In the northern trench-edge section a thin primary fill of strong brown sandy silt was overlain by thicker dark yellowish–brown silty loam. Elsewhere only single fills were recorded in any one section but there was much variation between sections: dark yellowish–brown silty loam, dark greyish–brown silty clay loam, reddish–brown loam and yellowish–brown clayey silt were all encountered, with charcoal and gravel present in varying quantities. The recut ditch was 1.7 m wide and 0.4 m deep, cut slightly to the east of the earlier feature. It was filled with dark yellowish–brown silty loam. An intermediate soil layer lay between topsoil and natural to the east of the recut but was not present to the west of 3000, where the natural was higher.

Enclosure 4068

A probable enclosure, 4068, was marked by three ditches to the east, north and west of round-house 2357 (Fig. 34). The western ditch petered out near a modern field boundary and there were no features (in the trench) to the south of the round-house that might indicate whether the enclosure continued there. The enclosure was c. 95 m south-west of round-house 1705.

The eastern ditch, 4066, was 22.2 m long and ran from south-south-east to north-north-west with well-defined terminals at either end. The southern terminal was the deepest section of all three ditches, 1.1 m wide and 0.62 m deep, symmetrical in profile with a rounded base and steep sides. Five deposits filled the ditch, from the primary fill of reddish–brown clayey loam, through brown to dark brown silty clay loam with a patchy lens of charcoal, to gravelly, and then less stony dark yellowish–brown or brown silty clay loam in the upper part of the ditch. Charcoal from the secondary fill gave a radiocarbon date of 1430–1160 cal. BC (AA-30668; 3040±45 BP). The northern terminal was 1 m wide, 0.37 m deep and asymmetrical. Its two fills, both very lightly charcoal-flecked, dark yellowish–brown silty clay loam, were distinguishable only by the larger gravel in the upper fill. There were no finds. The ditch was probably cut by ditch 2303 and there was one pit, 2349, 1 m wide and 0.2 m deep, c. 7.7 m south-south-east of the southern end of 4066.

The short middle ditch, 2356, was at an angle to 4066 and was separated from it by a gap of almost 2 m. The ditch was really no more than a short trench, 3.38 m long, and with a maximum width of 1.16 m; it was 0.45 m deep. There were no finds in the primary fill which was a slightly gravelly, dark yellowish brown silty loam, but pottery, struck chert and flint were recovered from the overlying charcoal-flecked, stony, brown loam.

There was a gap of c. 5.27 m between the western end of 2356 and ditch, 1911, which curved from north-east round to the south. It was c. 28.3 m long but truncated, ending near a recently levelled hedgebank at the western edge of the site. The ditch had a maximum width of 1.0 m and maximum depth of 0.27 m. A single fill, usually charcoal-flecked yellowish- or dark yellowish–brown silty loam, was recorded in all except one section; there, reddish brown sandy clay loam was

overlain by a lighter coloured but otherwise identical soil.

Two post-holes, 2346 and 2348, may have been associated with ditch 1911. They were c. 1.1 m and 2.4 m south of the eastern terminal of the ditch and were 2.1 m apart. The post-holes were 0.75 m and 0.55 m wide and 0.26 m and 0.14 m deep respectively, and were filled with lightly charcoal-flecked dark yellowish–brown silty loam.

Post-built Round-house 2357

A second post-built round-house, 2357, was represented by a group of 54 post- and/or stake-holes (as elsewhere, features described as stake-holes may have been the result of natural disturbance) within enclosure 4068 (Figs 34 and 35). The building was incomplete and may have been of more than one phase. The group is most simply described as having two main components: a circle and a concentric outer arc at the east and south; the arc may represent the remnants of a double ring of posts. There were post-holes within the circle and outside the arc. The western post-holes were deep but were generally smaller in diameter than those at the east, and it is probable that shallow features would have been lost at that side. The building was slightly west of the centre of the enclosure and had a south-south-east facing entrance.

The diameter of the circle was a little over 6 m. It consisted of 13 post-holes (2335, 2333, 2361, 4060, 4058, 4012, 4008, 2379, 4039, 4037, 2327, 2339, 2337) and six possible stake-holes in two groups of three at the western side (2371, 2381, 2390, 2396, 2398, 4000). The post-holes of the eastern side were spaced at intervals of 0.46–0.98 m, the shortest distance, c. 0.8 m, being between 2327 and 4037 (which cut 4039). There were gaps of 1.3–1.9 m between the post-holes and stake-hole groups around the western half of the circle. The south-south-east facing entrance consisted of inner post-holes 2335 and 2337 with outer post-holes 2329 and 4004. Post-hole 4004 was cut by two smaller post-holes, 2325 and 2331, either or both of which may represent a rebuilt entrance with which post-holes 2363 and 2365 may also have been associated. A radiocarbon date of 1510–1260 cal. BC (AA-30667; 3120±50 BP) was obtained for charcoal from 4060.

The eastern post-hole arc was about 1 m outside the main circle and consisted of, from the south, 2394, 2341, 2373 cutting 2367, 2343, 2375 cutting 2377, 2384. At least another five post-holes and a small pit were ranged about the building. Some or all of these may have been part of an earlier structure or outer ring of post-holes; if the latter, the post-holes suggested above as outer posts of the entrance could have continued the second circle. They could, however, represent separate external structures.

Post- and possible stake-holes were found only in the eastern half of the interior, and were most common in the south-eastern quadrant, where they were in two clusters (4042, 4044, 4046, 4048; 4019, 4021, 4023, 4031, 4033). The three remaining features (4025, 4056, 4010) were ranged across the north-eastern quadrant.

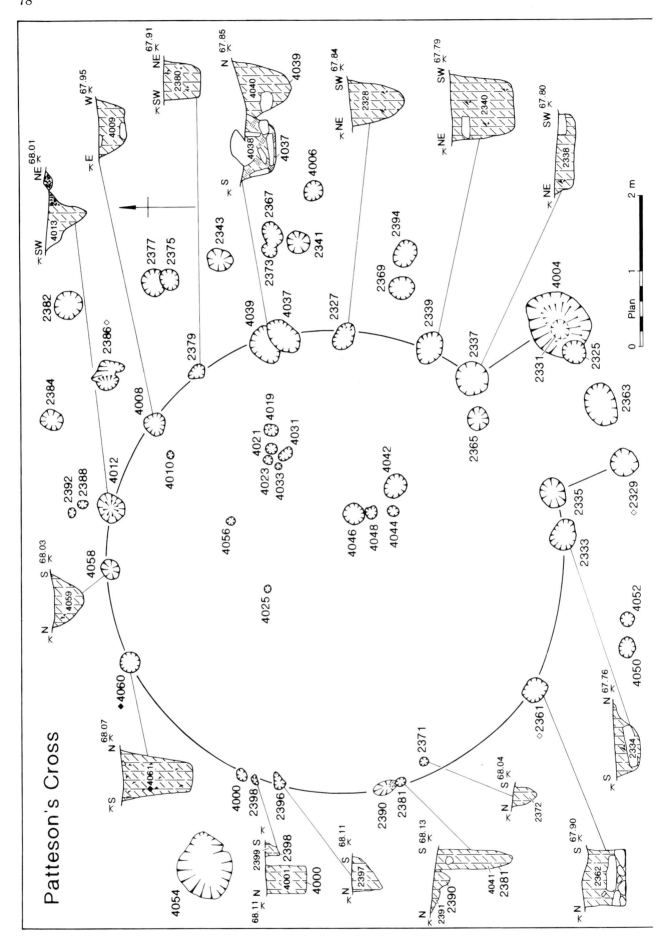

Patteson's Cross

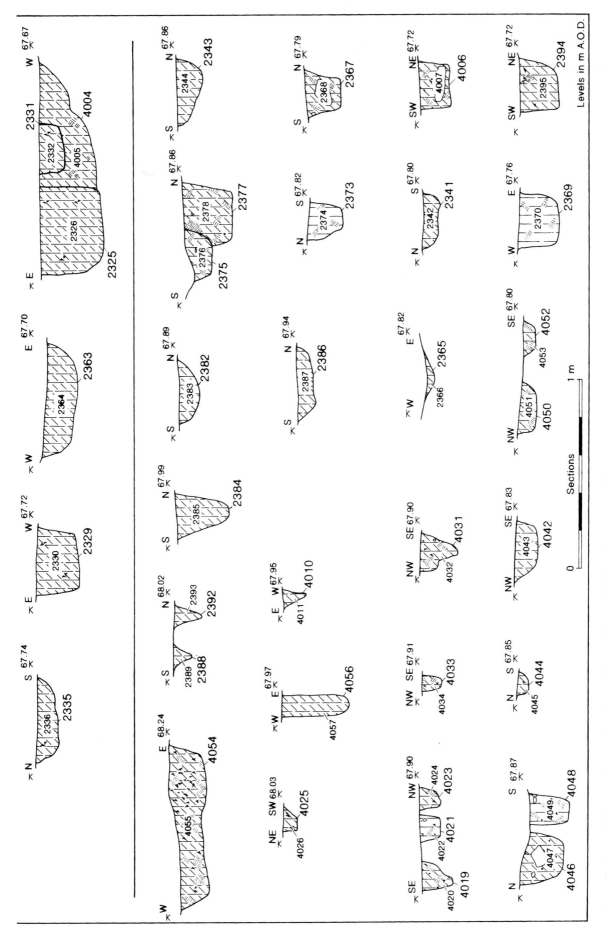

Figure 35   Patteson's Cross: plan and sections of round-house 2357 and associated features

With the exception of 4004, 2363 and 4054, the post-holes were between 0.16 m and 0.46 m wide and 0.09 and 0.38 m deep; 4004 was *c.* 1 m wide and 0.3 m deep, 2363 was 0.56 m wide and 0.42 m deep, and 4054 was 0.8 m wide and 0.2 m deep. Most were filled with dark yellowish–brown, dark brown or strong brown silty loam, although clay loam and silty clay were also recorded. There were few finds. Charcoal and possible packing stones were present in some but not all features; flat stones were noted at the bases of post-holes 2333 and 2361. The charcoal may be from the timbers of the building, and the fact that only oak sap- and heartwood was present in post-holes 2361 and 4060 is consistent with this. This might suggest that the round-house burnt down. If it did, it serves to emphasise the scarcity of finds.

Ditches 1405 and 1403

Trench 14 was intended to intersect two linear features suggested by geophysical survey but the two ditches found were differently orientated. Both were truncated and neither was seen elsewhere. Ditch 1405, which was more clearly defined, ran south-west from the eastern trench edge to terminate after *c.* 7.7 m (Fig. 30). The ditch, which was rounded with quite steeply sloping sides, was 0.6 m wide and 0.19 m deep. It was filled with flint and/or chert in lightly charcoal-flecked, reddish brown silt, although stone was absent from the upper 0.05 m of fill. Ditch 1403 ran south-east to north-west some 3.5 m west of 1405 and probably crossed the whole trench but could not be clearly traced in the northern half. It was wide but shallow, *c.* 1.3 m wide at the southern baulk but with a maximum depth of only 0.2 m, and was filled with lightly charcoal-flecked, strong brown sandy silt. There were no finds from either ditch but worked chert and flint were collected from topsoil and subsoil during machining. Although the alignment of 1403 was similar to that of post-medieval ditch 1742 (Trenches 17, 20, and 19), the ephemeral nature of both ditches suggests that they may have been of prehistoric date.

Post-medieval Field Boundaries

In the western part of Trench 17, post-medieval ditch 1742 was accompanied by a parallel gully, 1740, *c.* 1.5 m to its east (Fig. 30). Orientated from north-west to south-east, both features were also recorded in Trench 20 and the ditch in Trench 19.

Two ditches were recorded in Trench 7. The larger of these, 702, was on a similar north-west to south-east alignment to and not far from a recently removed fence (Figs 29 and 30). A smaller ditch, 704, joined 702 from the north-east. A similarly aligned shallow gully, 706, was recorded *c.* 30 m west of 702 and its continuation encountered in Trench 8.

Undated Features

A ditch crossed the northern end of Trench 1 from south-west to north-east. Ditch 1002 ran from north-west to south-east through Trenches 9, 2 and 10,

intersecting or intersected by an apparently meandering gully, 1010 (Fig. 29). Two other ditches, 203 and 209, were noted further to the west and east respectively in Trench 2. Ditch 209, on a north to south alignment, was not seen elsewhere. At the western end of Trench 10, four truncated post-holes or pit bases were recorded but no other features were seen in the vicinity.

Finds

Flaked Stone, by Peter S. Bellamy

The total flaked stone assemblage recovered comprises 153 pieces (3614 g) of flint and chert of which 89 pieces (2292 g) came from stratified contexts (Table 18). The small size of the assemblage and its dispersed distribution constrain the level of meaningful analysis possible on this material. The flint and chert was examined separately in order to assess any technological variations which may be due to the different raw material types but a rapid assessment indicated that, in general, the assemblage exhibited little technological or other variation. Further details are given in Appendix 2.

Raw material
The raw material utilised comprises 33% flint and 67% chert. The flint ranges from dark brown lustrous flint with no inclusions with a thin cream cortex to a pale grey and white mottled flint with cherty inclusions, though most is mottled grey with a thin pale brown cortex. It includes both chalk flint (22%) and gravel flint (33%). It is likely that the material came from the same range of sources as those of the Castle Hill assemblage (p. 37, Chapter 3, above). Two of the pieces from Patteson's Cross have reddish–brown staining just below the cortex and may have derived from clay-with-flints.

Assemblage description

Flint
The worked flint is in a sharp or slightly rolled condition and none of the pieces are patinated. The assemblage is dominated by flakes (Table 18). Some evidence for flint knapping on site is present in the form of two cores and a small quantity of core preparation and trimming flakes. The rest of the 'waste' consisted of small flakes and blades, generally less than 40 mm long. The trimming flakes were all removed with a hard hammer and the rest of the flakes and blades, where it can be determined, appear to have been removed with a soft hammer and a small number exhibit evidence of platform abrasion. The cores (one broken) are both multidirectional small flake cores on small rolled nodules – the complete core measures about 40 mm across. There is some evidence for platform preparation.

Four complete and four broken tools and utilised pieces were found, all unstratified. These comprise five scrapers (three broken), two broken flake knives, and a utilised flake. Two scrapers have regular semi-abrupt retouch round the distal end and partly down each side, the others are more irregular and one is made on a piece

Table 18: Patteson's Cross flaked stone assemblage by type (no./wt(g))

	Cores	Broken cores	Flakes	Broken flakes	Burnt flakes	Broken blades	Burnt blades	Tools	Broken tools	Chips	Misc. debitage	Total	Tool type
Chert													
Trench 2	–	–	2/26	–	–	–	–	–	1/50	–	–	3/76	piercer
Trench 6	–	–	–	1/9	–	–	–	–	–	–	–	1/9	
Ditch 104	–	–	2/54	–	–	–	–	–	–	–	–	2/54	
Ditch 203	–	–	1/6	–	–	–	–	–	–	–	–	1/6	
Ditch 209	1/190	–	–	–	–	–	–	–	–	–	–	1/190	
Ditch 1002	–	–	3/34	–	–	–	–	–	–	–	–	3/34	
Gully 1010	–	–	1/36	–	–	–	–	–	–	–	–	1/36	
Trench 10: other contexts	–	–	4/156	–	–	–	–	–	–	–	–	4/156	
Trench 14	–	–	6/109	2/26	–	–	–	1/122	–	–	–	9/257	ret. flake
Ditch 1911	–	–	–	3/38	–	–	–	1/16	–	1/1	–	5/55	ret/ flake
Ditch 3000	–	–	8/81	15/42	–	2/5	–	1/85	–	–	–	26/213	piercer
Trench 17: other contexts	–	–	6/137	3/25	–	–	–	–	–	–	–	9/162	
Trench 19: other contexts	–	–	3/43	–	–	–	–	–	–	–	–	3/43	
Trench 21	–	–	–	2/19	–	–	–	–	–	–	–	2/19	
Trench 22	–	–	1/22	–	–	–	–	–	–	–	–	1/22	
Round-house 2357	–	–	2/27	–	–	–	–	–	–	–	–	2/27	
Ditch 2356	2/1117	–	11/204	8/45	–	–	–	–	–	2/1	–	23/1367	
Ditch 2303	–	–	–	–	–	–	–	1/42	–	–	–	1/42	scraper
Ditch 4066	–	–	1/5	–	–	–	–	–	–	–	–	1/5	
Trench 23: other contexts	–	–	2/37	–	–	–	–	–	–	–	–	2/37	
Unstratified	–	–	1/29	1/2	–	–	–	–	–	–	–	2/31	
Sub-total chert	3/1307	0	54/1006	35/206	0	2/5	0	4/265	1/50	3/2	0	102/2841	
Flint													
Trench 6	–	–	–	–	–	–	–	–	1/20	–	–	1/20	flake knife
Ditch 1002	–	–	1/4	1/2	–	–	–	–	–	–	–	2/6	
Trench 10: other contexts	–	–	1/74	3/11	–	1/1	–	1/31	1/9	–	–	7/126	ut. flake, broken scraper
Trench 14	1/46	–	3/30	2/4	–	–	–	1/16	–	–	–	7/96	scraper
Round-house 1705	–	–	1/13	–	–	–	–	–	–	–	–	1/13	scraper

Table 18: (continued)

	Cores	Broken cores	Flakes	Broken flakes	Burnt flakes	Broken blades	Burnt blades	Tools	Broken tools	Chips	Misc. debitage	Total	Tool type
Flint													
Ditch 3000	–	–	–	1/9	1/6	–	–	–	–	–	–	2/15	
Trench 17: other contexts	1/97	–	2/88	2/8	–	–	–	–	–	1/0	–	6/183	
Ditch 1911	–	1/73	1/9	3/24	–	–	–	–	–	–	–	5/106	
Tench 19: other contexts	–	–	1/31	3/18	–	–	–	–	2/16	–	–	6/65	br. scraper, br. flake knife
Trench 21	–	–	–	–	–	–	–	–	–	–	1/4	1/4	
Round-house 2357	–	–	1/20	–	–	–	–	–	–	–	–	1/20	
Ditch 2356	–	–	2/45	–	–	–	1/1	–	–	–	–	3/46	
Trench 23: other contexts	–	–	1/9	–	–	–	–	1/17	–	–	1/4	3/30	scraper on core shatter
Unstratified	–	–	1/4	2/11	–	–	–	1/17	–	2/1	–	6/33	rough scraper
Sub-total flint	2/143	1/73	15/327	17/87	1/6	1/1		4/81	4/45	3/1	2/8	51/773	
Total	5/1450	1/73	69/1333	52/293	1/6	3/6	1/1	8/346	5/95	6/3	2/8	153/3614	

of core shatter. The flake knives both have fairly shallow invasive retouch, one along the right side and the other has inverse retouch on distal end of a short broad flake. The utilised flake is about 70 mm long with irregular microscars along the right edge. These implements are not very chronologically diagnostic but perhaps fit best into a Late Neolithic or Early Bronze Age context.

Chert
The chert is in a sharp or slightly rolled condition. The assemblage comprises elements from all stages of the reduction process: core preparation and trimming flakes, 'waste' flakes, flake tools and cores. About 31% of the flakes are core preparation/trimming flakes which are generally between 45–70 mm in length and 10–17 mm in thickness and usually have large thick striking platforms and prominent bulbs of percussion. The other flakes are generally smaller and thinner (30– 55 mm long and 3–7 mm thick). In general the 'waste' flakes are fairly irregular with cortex on one side or distal end, but a small number of flakes are 'blade-like' with roughly parallel sides. These flakes also have thinner platforms and slightly less prominent bulbs of percussion, though it is unclear whether they were re- moved with a hard or a soft hammer. The dorsal scars on all the flakes indicate that a single striking direction was used. Two of the three cores recovered are multi- directional – a single platform was in use at one time, when this platform was exhausted or abandoned due to flaws in the raw material, the core was rotated and another platform established utilising the previous flake beds. The third core is roughly discoidal with flake removals around the margins of a fairly flat nodule (Fig. 36, 4).

Three tools were recovered, all on larger or thicker blanks – a rudimentary scraper with minimal abrupt retouch on the distal end of a flake (Fig. 36, 2), a broken piercer with irregular bifacial retouch along the right side (Fig. 36, 1), and a flake knife with irregular semi-abrupt retouch on the distal end and along the right side of a squat hinge-fractured flake (Fig. 36, 3).

Distribution
The flaked stone has a wide distribution across the whole of the site with little evidence for any discrete concentrations. Many features did not produce any flaked stone at all and that found in the majority of the features could easily be the result of the accidental incorporation of residual material scattered across the site.The good condition of the pieces does suggest that the material has not been subject to much movement or wear before deposition. Only two features (ditches 2356 and 3000) contained more than the occasional piece of flint and chert (Table 18).

Ditch 3000 contained small quantities of flaked stone along the whole of its excavated length but in the southern terminal was a group of 22 small chert flakes and blades, two of which refitted and most of the others clearly came from the same core and probably represent debris from a single knapping episode. It had either been deliberately deposited in the feature or had come from immediately adjacent knapping activity. The small length of ditch 2356 contained 26 pieces of flint and chert including two cores (Table 18). The material from this ditch was more heterogeneous than the assemblage in

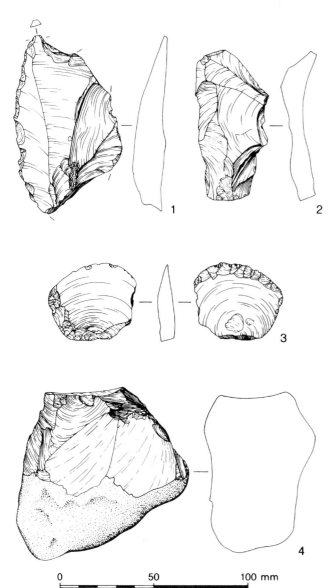

Figure 36   Patteson's Cross: objects of flaked stone. Scale 1:2

ditch 3000 and probably does not represent a single episode of activity but it is unclear whether this material was deliberately deposited in this feature or was the result of accidental incorporation from activity in the vicinity. Only a very small quantity of material was recovered from the immediate environs of the round-houses 1705 and 2357 which suggests that any activity involving the use of flint and chert was not focused on these structures.

Discussion

The analysis of the assemblage by material type has not shown any major significant differences in the technology used for the different raw material types and the whole assemblage appears to belong to a single industry producing flakes and using some measure of control in the flaking of the cores. The large proportion of chert in the assemblage is worthy of comment as it has previously been noted that in west Somerset and east Devon that there was a marked preference for Greensand chert during the Mesolithic, but in Neolithic

assemblages flint is the preferred raw material and tends to predominate (Norman 1975; Silvester *et al.* 1987). This is clearly not the case with the present assemblage and there are no demonstrably Mesolithic elements present to explain the high proportion of chert, so a different explanation must be sought.

Most of the Mesolithic sites in east Devon, survive as artefact scatters which also contain some Neolithic material (Berridge 1985; Silvester *et al.* 1987). Therefore, it is possible that Neolithic use of chert has been masked or underestimated by the presence of the Mesolithic material, but this does not significantly alter the general pattern which occurs on stratified Late Neolithic sites in Devon such as Topsham (Jarvis and Maxfield 1975) as well as on unstratified multiperiod sites like Churston (Parker Pearson 1981), and Dainton (Silvester 1980), where the raw material used was almost exclusively flint, mainly gravel or beach flint. It might be argued that the greater use of Greensand chert at Patteson's Cross was a result of its proximity to significant Upper Greensand deposits. However, at Hembury, only 5 km to the north, chert formed only 6% of the flaked stone assemblage (Tingle 1998, 94).

One possible explanation for this anomaly at Patteson's Cross may be that a significant proportion of the chert is a result of Bronze Age activity as is well-attested at nearby Castle Hill and Hayne Lane. The occurrence of refitting chert flakes from the terminal of ditch 3000 might be best interpreted as knapping activity contemporary with the ditch. The character of the stone-working with the accent on long narrow flakes is, however, more typical of an earlier Bronze Age industry. Other than this material the distribution of the finds bears little relation to the location of the principal archaeological features, and as a whole the assemblage fits comfortably into a Late Neolithic or Early Bronze Age context.

Illustrated objects
(Fig. 36)
1.   Chert piercer. Context 3016, ditch 3000.
2.   Chert scraper. Context 2304, ditch 2303.
3.   Chert flake knife. Trench 6, unstratified.
4.   Chert core. Context 2359, enclosure ditch 4068 (section 2356).

Pottery, by M. Laidlaw

The pottery comprises 244 sherds, weighing 3627 g. This includes six sherds of medieval and four of post-medieval date which are not discussed here. The prehistoric assemblage is dominated by sherds derived from two large, bucket-shaped urns of Middle Bronze Age type. The remaining sherds are small, plain and lack diagnostic features, such as decoration and identifiable vessel forms, but on the basis of fabric types these are also attributed to the Middle Bronze Age. Overall the mean sherd weight is 15 g.

Fabrics

Seven fabric types are present at Patteson's Cross. Six of the seven fabrics occur also in the Middle to Late

Table 19: Patteson's Cross, pottery fabric totals

Fabric	No. sherds	Weight (g)	% of period by wt
Grog-tempered			
G1	5	8	0.2
G4	14	28	0.8
G5	46	262	7.3
Sandy			
Q2	2	2	0.1
Q11	1	3	0.1
Chert-tempered			
R2	140	2947	82.2
R7	26	334	9.3
Sub-total	234	3584	
LATER POTTERY			
Medieval	6	16	
Post-med	4	27	
TOTAL	244	3627	

Table 20 Patteson's Cross, pottery by feature (no./wt (g))

Feature	Grog	Sandy	Chert	Total
Pit 1788	–	–	46/2542	46/2542
Round-house 2357	3/1	–	9/44	12/45
Ditch 3000	1/6	2/2	–	3/8
Enclosure 4068	59/284	106/689	–	165/973
Total	63/291	108/691	55/2586	226/3568

Bronze Age assemblages from Castle Hill and/or Hayne Lane (see Chapters 3 and 5, and Appendix 3). Fabric type Q11 (found only unstratified here) was identified also at Langland Lane. A detailed list of fabric descriptions is presented in Appendix 3 and pottery fabric totals are presented in Table 19.

Forms, decoration and surface treatments

Diagnostic sherds from five vessels were identified. Two came from pit 1788, comprising an expanded rim in fabric R7 (Fig. 37, 2) and an applied cordon in fabric R2 (Fig. 37, 3), both from large, bucket-shaped vessels. The cordon on the latter vessel appears not to have been continuous around the body. Other recognisable vessel forms comprise two jars with inturned rims (form MBA1) (Fig. 37, 1). Another small rim sherd, slightly externally expanded (MBA3) has a deep diagonal groove just below the rim (Fig. 37, 4), although it is uncertain whether this is decorative or purely fortuitous.

Surface treatments are also scarce and are restricted to one of the vessels from pit 1788 (fabric R7), which has smoothed surfaces. A small number of sherds in fabric R2 from ditch 4068 have traces of sooting.

Distribution

Three sherds were recovered from ditch 3000, two grog-tempered (G4) and one sandy (Q2); none are diagnostic (Table 20). The remaining 46 sherds from trench 17 derived from pit 1788, all chert-tempered, and including the two large bucket-shaped vessels (Fig. 37, 2, 3). A radiocarbon date of 2140–1880 (AA-30669; 3630±45 BP) was obtained from the pit.

Nearly three-quarters of the total assemblage came from fills of the enclosure ditch 4068, all from the short, discrete length of ditch (2356) in the north-east corner of trench 23. The secondary fill of an adjacent section of ditch (4066) yielded a radiocarbon date of 1430–1160 cal. BC (AA-30668; 3040±45 BP). Fabrics present include grog-tempered (G1, G4, G5) and chert-tempered fabrics (R2), and this group includes three of the five diagnostic forms from the site: ovoid jars with inturned or slightly everted rims (Fig. 37, 1, 4). Round-house 2357 produced only 12 sherds, grog-tempered (G4) and chert-tempered (R2), and included no diagnostic material.

Discussion

Pit 1788 represents the earliest well – dated activity on the site, and the radiocarbon date from this feature (2140–1880 cal. BC) places the bucket-shaped vessels from this feature in the Early Bronze Age. Bucket-shaped urns with cordons find numerous parallels amongst the later Deverel-Rimbury assemblages of Wessex; comparable assemblages from south Dorset, for example, include Simons Ground (White 1982) and Eldon's Seat (Cunliffe and Phillipson 1969). Fabrics vary regionally, from the grog-tempered fabrics of south Dorset to the flint-tempered fabrics of north Dorset and Wiltshire; grog-tempered fabrics have as yet rarely been identified in south-western Bronze Age assemblages, but are not unknown (Quinnell 1993, 92). Plain, flat-cordoned bucket urns are recorded from Burrowshot Cross, Axminster (*ibid.*, fig. 32); similar flat-cordoned vessels are present in Trevisker assemblages, such as from Trethellan, Newquay (Woodward and Cane 1991), but are invariably decorated, as are flat-rimmed, bucket-shaped Trevisker-related vessels from Brean Down (Woodward 1990, figs 89–90).

Material from other features on the site is less closely attributable on stylistic grounds. Similar fabrics and forms have been recorded within the assemblages from Castle Hill and Hayne Lane, for which radiocarbon dates cover a wide range in the Middle–Late Bronze Age; radiocarbon dates from Patteson's Cross would place the pottery from round-house 2357 and enclosure ditch 4068 (1510–1160 cal. BC) broadly contemporary with Castle Hill. The more highly decorated forms of the Trevisker sequence are absent in the Patteson's Cross assemblage though whether this is due to subtle chronological varaiation, the small size of the assemblage or the nature of the site is uncertain.

List of illustrated sherds
(Fig. 37)
1. Jar with inturned rim (form MBA1), fabric G5. PRN 786, context 4016, enclosure ditch 4068 (section 2356).

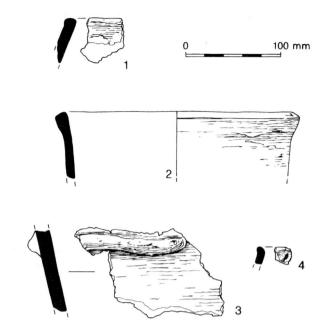

Figure 37   Patteson's Cross: Bronze Age pottery. Scale 1:4

2. Jar with expanded rim (form MBA2), fabric R7. PRN 783, context 1789, pit 1788.
3. Applied cordon from bucket-shaped vessel, fabric R2. PRN 781, context 1789, pit 1788.
4. Jar slight neck, rounded rim, decorated. Form MBA3, fabric R2. PRN 770. Context 2359, enclosure ditch 4068 (section 2356).

Environmental Analyses

Charred Plant Remains, by Alan J. Clapham

Two samples from the post-holes of round-house 1705, four from the post-holes of round-house 2357, and one from pit 1788 were analysed. In general, the plant remains were adequately preserved to allow full species identification where possible. Modern roots were found in most of the samples but very few intrusive modern seeds were identified from the samples suggesting that there has been very little contamination from either modern or ancient sources. The majority of the remains recovered were of weed species (Table 21).

Pit 1788

No cereal grains or chaff were found and the only remains of cultivated plants were indeterminate cereal grains. The other species are indicative of cultivated and other disturbed land and may have been growing in the vicinity of the pit. The presence of a leaf fragment of cross-leaved heath suggests that a heathland habitat was being exploited.

Round-house 1705

Cereals and other cultivated crops were rare, being represented by indeterminate cereal fragments and one basal rachis fragment in post-hole 1708 (Table 21). The

rest of the remains were representatives of cultivated or waste ground. Species identified included fat hen (*Chenopodium album*), black bindweed (*Fallopia convolvulus*), sheep's sorrel (*Rumex acetosella*), vetch/vetchling (*Vicia/Lathyrus* sp.), onion couch grass (*Arrhenatherum elatius* var. *bulbosum*) and brome/oats (*Bromus/Avena* sp.). Other species found within the sample were more representative of grassy (*Stellaria graminea* and *Prunella vulgaris*) and scrub (*Prunus spinosa*) habitats. A heathy/moor habitat may be represented by the find of a single leaf fragment of cross-leaved heath (*Erica tetralix*).

The lack of cereal chaff does not suggest the presence of crop processing products and while the small weed seeds may be representative of crop processing waste, if this was so, the remains of chaff would be expected to be present (Hillman 1981). Instead it is most likely that the charred plants remains represent the flora growing at, or near to, the base of the round-house.

Round-house 2357

In general, the remains of cereals and other crops were poorly represented. No identifiable cereal grains were recovered though two samples provided glume bases of spelt wheat (*Triticum spelta*) and another a glume base of emmer wheat (*T. dicoccum*) (Table 21). A single seed of flax (*Linum usitatissimum*) was also found. The other plant were mainly segetals and ruderals indicative of cultivated or other disturbed habitats. A high number of fat-hen seeds were found in post-hole 4060. The presence of henbane (*Hyoscyamus niger*) in one post-hole (2357) may suggest a habitat of high nitrogen content such as can be found on manure heaps. The find of stinking mayweed (*Anthemis cotula*) (2329) is usually indicative of heavy soils. A possible wild food source is indicated the hazel (*Corylus avellana*) nutshell fragments.

The general lack of cereals and chaff suggests that the charred plant remains again represent the flora growing around the base of the round-house, which may have been burnt down.

Discussion

The samples are notable for the lack of cereal remains in the form of grains or chaff. Remains of emmer and spelt wheat chaff were identified along with a seed of another crop, flax. Due to the paucity of crop remains it is difficult to establish if they were grown and processed locally, although it might be expected that this was the case. What may be wild sources of foods are indicated by the presence of sloe and hazel nuts. The ruderal and segetal species are interpreted as representative of the flora growing at the base of the round-houses. Other habitats that may have been exploited include heathland, as indicated by finds of cross-leaved heath leaf fragments. In general the environment surrounding the site can be interpreted as being open, with grassland, scrub and arable components.

Charcoal, by Rowena Gale

Charcoal was generally sparse and its preservation varied. It was necessary to subsample (50%) the large

Table 21: Patteson's Cross, charred plant remains

Feature group	Round-house 1705		Round-house 2357				
Feature type			Post-holes				Pit
Feature	1708	1728	2361	2329	4060	2386	1788
Context	1709	1729	2362	2330	4061	2387	1789
Sample	2	14	24	31	39	47	21
Flot size (ml)	4	5	74	20	50	2	30
Cereal remains and other crops							
Triticum spelta glume bases	–	–	–	3	6	–	–
T. dicoccum rachis frags	–	–	1	–	–	–	–
Triticum sp. glume bases	–	–	–	–	5	–	–
Cerealia basal rachis frags	1	–	–	–	–	–	–
Cerealia sprouts	–	–	–	1	–	–	–
Cerealia indet.	7f	3f	3f	14f	41f	3f	9f
Linum usitatissimum	–	–	–	–	–	1	–
Weeds							
Ranunculus subgen *Ranunculus*	–	–	–	–	2f	–	–
Ranunculus ficaria tuber	–	–	–	1	–	–	–
Corylus avellana nutshell	–	–	–	–	–	4f	–
Chenopodium album	–	1	4+15f	4+3f	135+65f	–	12+26f
Atriplex sp.	–	–	3	–	–	–	–
Stellaria media	–	–	–	–	3	–	–
Stellaria graminea	1	–	–	–	–	–	–
Spergula arvensis	–	–	1	–	1	–	6
Persicaria maculosa	–	–	2+1f	–	1	–	8+14f
Persicaria lapathifolia	–	–	–	–	–	–	2+4f
Fallopia convolvulus	1	–	2	–	7+11f	–	1+11f
Rumex acetosella	2	–	1	–	1	–	4
Rumex sp.	–	–	–	1	–	–	–
Polygonaceae indet.	–	–	–	1	4f	–	23f
Erica tetralix leaf frag.	–	1	–	–	–	–	1
Prunus spinosa	1f	–	–	–	–	–	–
Vicia hirsuta	–	–	–	–	–	–	–
Vicia tetrasperma hilum	–	–	–	–	–	–	1
Vicia/Lathyrus sp.	–	3c	–	1	1+8c	–	6c
Melilotus sp.	–	–	–	–	–	–	2
Trifolium sp.	–	–	–	5	4	–	–
Apiaceae indet.	–	1	–	–	–	–	–
Hyoscyamus niger	–	–	–	1	–	–	–
Solanum nigrum	–	–	–	–	–	–	1
Prunella vulgaris	–	1	–	–	–	–	–
Plantago lanceolata	–	–	–	1	–	–	–
Galium aparine	–	–	2	–	1	–	–
Anthemis cotula	–	–	–	1	–	–	–
Asteraceae indet.	–	–	–	–	1	–	1

Table 21: (continued)

Feature group	Round-house 1705		Round-house 2357				
Feature type			Post-holes				Pit
Feature	1708	1728	2361	2329	4060	2386	1788
Context	1709	1729	2362	2330	4061	2387	1789
Sample	2	14	24	31	39	47	21
Flot size (ml)	4	5	74	20	50	2	30
Arrhenatherum elatius var. *bulbosum* tuber	12f	8f	–	–	–	–	–
A. elatius rootlets & culm bases	27	14	–	5	–	3	30
Avena sp. awn frags	–	–	–	–	–	–	1
Bromus/Avena sp.	2f	–	–	–	–	–	1f
Small Poaceae	–	–	2	–	4	1	–
Poaceae culm bases	–	–	–	–	3	–	–
culm nodes	–	–	–	–	4	–	–
Unident.	1	1	–	–	1	–	–
Buds	–	–	1	–	–	–	1
Cenococcum geophilum	10	–	–	–	2	1	1

c = cotyledon; f = fragment

quantity of charcoal from post-hole 4060 in round-house 2357, but conversely the material from the associated enclosure ditch (4068) was particularly poor.

The results are tabulated in Table 22 and described below. The taxa identified include:

Aceraceae. *Acer* sp., maple
?Betulaceae. *Alnus* sp., alder
Corylaceae. *Corylus* sp., hazel
Fagaceae. *Quercus* sp., oak
Leguminosae. *Ulex* sp., gorse; *Cytisus* sp., broom. These genera can not be distinguished from their anatomy.
Oleaceae. *Fraxinus* sp., ash
Rosaceae. *Prunus* spp., which include *P. avium*, wild cherry, *P. padus*, bird cherry, and *P. spinosa*, blackthorn. It is often difficult to differentiate between the species but in this instance the structure was more characteristic of blackthorn.

Pit 1788
The charcoal-flecked loam fill of the pit included oak sap- and heartwood, ash, blackthorn, and gorse/broom.

Round-house 1705
Charcoal was sparse; post-hole 1708 included oak heartwood, hazel, probably narrow roundwood, and blackthorn roundwood, probably 20 mm in diameter with at least 14 growth rings. Post-hole 1728 contained oak roundwood and heartwood, and blackthorn, while 1734, part of the porch, included oak sapwood and heartwood, blackthorn and gorse/broom.

Enclosure 4068
The northern terminal of the eastern enclosure ditch included very poorly preserved charcoal. Some appeared only partially charred which could account for its degraded condition. The sample contained predominantly blackthorn roundwood (diameter 10 mm and wider), but also included oak sap- and heartwood, gorse/broom and hazel or alder.

Round-house 2357
The charcoal was better preserved and more abundant in the post-holes of this building. Post-hole 2361 consisted of a large quantity of slivers of fast-grown sap- and heartwood of oak. Post-hole 4060 included a large volume of charcoal, which was 50% sub-sampled, consisting of fairly wide slivers from oak sapwood and heartwood, while 2329 mostly consisted of oak sapwood and heartwood; maple was also recorded.

Discussion
Although the settlement was relatively small, consisting mainly of two round-houses and some enclosures, charcoal was still surprisingly sparse, especially in view of the large number of post-holes associated with the round-houses. The charcoal from the few productive post-holes at round-house 2357 was better preserved and more abundant than that from round-house 1705. Although the round-houses are of slightly different dates, the use of wood resources appears to have been consistent across the settlement.

With the exception of charcoal and charred cereal grains, no other artefactual remains were found. All samples examined from round-house 2357 consisted of large quantities of oak sapwood and heartwood. Post-hole 2329 also contained a small amount of maple. In all instances the oak derived from posts or poles wide enough to include heartwood. The absence of oak roundwood or residues from other taxa in samples from post-holes 2361 and 4060 strongly suggests an origin from the remains of oak posts used in the construction of the house. The similarity of the charcoal from post-hole 2329 to the previous samples suggests that all

Table 22: Patteson's Cross, charcoal (no. fragments identified)

Feature	Context	Sample	Acer	Alnus	Corylus	Fraxinus	Prunus	Quercus	Ulex/Cytisus
Round-house 1705 (post-holes)									
1708	1709	2	–	–	2r	–	2r	3h	–
1728	1729	14	–	–	–	–	1	4r,h	–
1734	1735	15	–	–	–	–	3	10s,h	2r
Round-house 2357 (post-holes)									
2361	2362	24	–	–	–	–	–	76s,h	–
2329	2330	31	2	–	–	–	–	35s,h	–
4060	4061	39	–	–	–	–	–	63s,h	–
Enclosure ditch 4068									
4066	2317	23	–	(1)	(1)	–	25r	2s,h	1
Pit 1788	1789	21	–	–	–	1	1	12s,h	–

Key: r = roundwood (diam. <20 mm); s = sapwood; h = heartwood ( ) = unverified identification

three had a common origin although, in this instance, the presence of maple tends to weaken the argument. The use of maple wood for domestic utensils has long traditions (Keller 1866; Morris 1984) and considering its association with the round-house, an artefactual origin for maple is feasible (particularly since maple was not identified from other likely fuel residues).

Three post-holes in round-house 1705 contained oak and blackthorn, with the addition of hazel in the former and gorse or broom in one post-hole. Despite the general absence of domestic refuse in these post-holes it is more likely that this charcoal represents fuel debris than structural components. Nonetheless, the species named have, traditionally, been used for construction, e.g. oak for posts, hazel and blackthorn for hurdles, and gorse for thatching (Lucas 1960), and similar uses/origins here can not be dismissed. Round-houses made from such flammable materials as wood and thatch must frequently have fallen victim to the flames from domestic hearths.

Charcoal deposits dispersed in enclosure ditch 4066 probably resulted from fuel debris. The apparent similarity of the taxa identified from the ditch (oak, blackthorn, gorse/broom and hazel/alder) and the deposits from the slightly earlier round-house 1705 to the east may suggest a more likely origin of the charcoal from the round-house as fuel. In common with most other charcoal from the site, oak predominated in pit 1788, although blackthorn and ash were also identified, and presumably represent fuel debris.

Fuel
Five of the eight samples (post-holes 1708, 1728 and 1734, ditch 4066, and pit 1788), can probably be interpreted as fuel debris. The evidence suggests that the preferred fuel consisted of oak, from poles/cord wood which included heartwood. This was combined with roundwood from oak, hazel, blackthorn, gorse/broom, and ash. These species provide energy efficient firewood and were probably gathered from the immediate vicinity of the settlement.

Environmental evidence
The settlement was situated on sloping land partly in a dry valley with underlying soils of sandy silt or clay loams with gravel. The charcoal examined probably originated from structural components and from firewood, and was undoubtedly selected for these functions. The relatively narrow range of taxa identified almost certainly reflects this choice and any interpretation of the landscape based solely on these results would be inaccurate. What can be stated with certainty is the existence of oak woodlands, possibly including ash, and maple, and more open areas supporting blackthorn, hazel, gorse and possibly broom. The character of the landscape (i.e. the modern topography and edaphic conditions) suggests a more diverse range of trees and shrubs for the Middle Bronze Age, but no such evidence was forthcoming from the charcoal.

Conclusion
Charcoal from the site provided evidence of fuel residues and possibly charred structural components. The latter consisted of possible remains of oak posts used in the construction of round-house 2357. Charcoal from the remaining contexts probably relates to fuel residues and identified the use of oak, blackthorn, hazel, gorse/broom, ash, and maple. The narrow range of taxa identified at Patteson's Cross when compared to, for example, Castle Hill (above), can probably be attributed to the paucity of suitable material from the site and anthropological selection of species for specific uses.

Radiocarbon Dates, by Michael J. Allen

Four determinations were obtained from charcoal from round-houses 1705 and 2357 and its associated enclosure ditch, and pit 1788 (Table 23; Fig. 38).

Pit 1788

This pit is nearly five centuries earlier than the round-houses and is part of an earlier, Early Bronze Age,

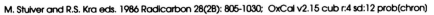

M. Stuiver and R.S. Kra eds. 1986 Radiocarbon 28(2B): 805-1030; OxCal v2.15 cub r:4 sd:12 prob(chron)

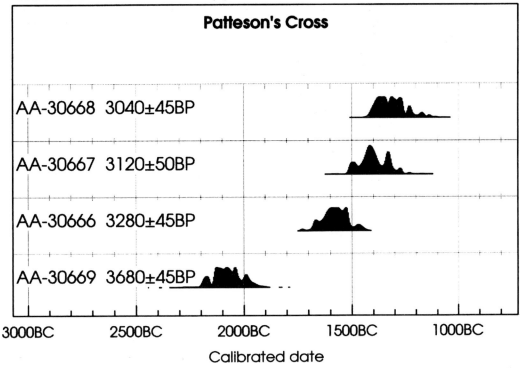

Figure 38   Patteson's Cross: probability distributions of radiocarbon dates

phase of activity, pre-dating the enclosure and round-houses.

Round-houses 1705 and 2357 and Enclosure 4068

Oak sapwood charcoal from the postholes may represent the timber posts of the buildings. The two determinations (AA-30666, 3280±45 BP and AA-30667, 3120±50) are not statistically indistinguishable at the 95% confidence level, and the probability distributions overlap (Fig. 38).

The results from the sample from enclosure 4068 and the round-house itself can be modelled as a phase. The probability distributions, although not statistically indistinguishable at the 95% level (Ward and Wilson

1987), do overlap indicating that they probably relate to the same phase of site activity.

Discussion, by A.P. Fitzpatrick

Patteson's Cross is the earliest of the Bronze Age sites examined in the project. Two round-houses, one of which lay within a small enclosure, were excavated and although the evidence is slight, it seems likely that the site was used over several centuries.

The earliest dated feature is pit 1788, which yielded a radiocarbon date of 2140–1880 cal. BC (AA-30669; 3630±45 BP). There is a possibility that the pit is a grave, with all traces of inhumed bone having been destroyed by the acidic soil conditions, although at this time a cremation burial is perhaps more likely. The

Table 23: Patteson's Cross, radiocarbon dates

Context	Material	Lab. No.	Result BP	$\delta^{13}C‰$	Calibration BC (2σ)
S terminal ditch 4066, enclosure 4068, secondary fill	Mixed charcoal*	AA-30668	3040±45	-25.5	1430–1160
Round-house 2357, post-hole 4060, single fill	*Quercus* sap/hearthwood charcoal	AA-30667	3120±50	-26.1	1510–1260
Round-house 1705, post-hole 1735, single fill	*Quercus* sapwood charcoal	AA-30666	3280±45	-25.1	1690–1440
Pit 1788, single fill	*Quercus* sapwood	AA-30669	3630±45	-27.7	2140–1880

* *Prunus, Quercus, Ulex/Cytisus* charcoal

radiocarbon date might be thought to be early for the parts of two bucket-shaped urns found in it, which find parallels with Middle Bronze Age assemblages further to the east. However, given the still limited knowledge of prehistoric pottery in east Devon this apparent discrepancy should not be over-emphasised. There is little evidence for cereals in the plant remains. The other species are indicative of cultivated and other disturbed land, while there is a hint of the exploitation of heathland, which may have grown on the sandy soils in the vicinity.

Ditch 3000 may be broadly contemporary with pit 1788 as the refitting chert flakes from one of the terminals have an emphasis on long narrow flakes, which is more characteristic of an earlier Bronze Age industry.

No pottery at all was found in nearby round-house 1705 but a radiocarbon date of 1690–1440 cal BC (AA-30666; 3280±45 BP) indicates that it is later than pit 1788 and perhaps ditch 3000. A scatter of two and three-post structures and other undated post-holes around the round-house may represent drying racks and the like – if they are contemporary with it. It may be that the field boundary 3000 and pit 1788 had long passed out of use when the round-house was built.

The paucity of finds from the round-house, which despite the additional post-holes in the eastern part of it, appears to be of a single phase, does not suggest that there was any significant domestic activity. The features that formed part of the round-house yielded little evidence of charred plant remains. Cereal remains are rare, and while the other charred plants suggest arable and waste land, grassland, or scrub, and possibly heath habitats are also indicated. Much of this could simply represent the plants growing around the house.

In conjunction with the paucity of material culture, the evidence for an open landscape, with grassland, scrub and arable components is consistent with the 'house' having stood at the margin of a perhaps disused field system or block of land in an area reserved for pasture. The Mid–Late Iron Age site at Langland Lane 250 m to the west was built within an earlier, but not otherwise dated field system, which could conceivably date to the earlier Bronze Age. This may hint at the foreshadowing of the division of land seen more clearly at Castle Hill in the Middle Bronze Age, but the evidence is to slight too provide more than a hint.

Round-house 2357 is slightly later in date and may either have been rebuilt, or have been more complicated in its architecture, having an outer or double ring of posts which has been severely truncated on the western side (Guilbert 1975, 215–17; 1981, 300). The house lay within a slight, and now heavily truncated enclosure. Charcoal from a post-hole from the round-house yielded a radiocarbon date of 1510–1260 cal. BC (AA-30667; 3120±50 BP) and charcoal from the secondary fill of the southern terminal of the eastern enclosure ditch gave a date of 1430–1160 cal. BC (AA-30668; 3040±45 BP). The quantity of pottery is small and though it is of Middle Bronze Age date, much of the lithic material could again be earlier. These dates indicate that round-houses 1705 and 2537 are not associated and do not form the pair of major house and ancillary building seen later at Hayne Lane (Chapter 5).

It is possible that the Patteson's Cross enclosure may originally have been circular, with the southern section being completed by either a hedge or fence, as is known at other contemporaneous settlements such as Down Farm in Cranborne Chase and Cock Hill in East Sussex (Barrett et al. 1991, 208, fig. 5.42). However, at those sites the enclosure ditches are more substantial than that at Patteson's Cross, and there is a wider range of ancillary buildings and structures, such as granaries, which may suggest that the occupation at Patteson's Cross was not intensive or long-lived. The only feature to yield relatively large quantities of flaked stone and pottery at Patteson's Cross was ditch segment 2356 and it is possible that this represents the deliberate deposition of material at an entrance. What may have been a wooden object is present amongst the charcoals.

The charred plant remains associated with round-house 2357 could once more represent the plants growing at the base of it. Some of the charcoal from the postholes is substantial enough to represent the timbers of the building, hinting that it may have been burnt down. There is, again, no evidence for crops having been processed on-site. The single find of flax may also represent a crop, as it is known to occur in Middle Bronze Age contexts elsewhere in southern England. These include the nearby sites at Castle Hill and Hayne Lane and a range of other sites, such as Bray (Barnes and Cleal 1995, 43, 51) and Reading Business Park (Moore and Jennings 1992, 41, 108) in Berkshire.

A few species hint at very specific habitats, for example the henbane found in a single posthole might have grown on or near manure heaps, but such hints are rare. Most of the other plants are indicative of cultivated or other disturbed habitats and this evidence is consistent throughout the activity at Patteson's Cross. Both round-houses lay near to cultivated land, perhaps at the edges of field systems, but crop processing did not take place at either of them. The disturbed habitat could conceivably include the thorny scrub that regenerates after free-ranging pastoralism or shifting agriculture and which has been noted at other Bronze Age sites (Jones 1978, 108). A range of habitats, including heathland as indicated by finds of cross-leaved heath leaf fragments, may also have been exploited. In view of the very small quantities of material culture, and the small range of associated structures, it is possible that these houses were only used seasonally.

5. Hayne Lane

by C.A. Butterworth

Introduction

This enclosed settlement was first identified as a cropmark by F.M. Griffith in 1984 (Pl.11; p.7, Chapter 1). The existing A30 and the laying of a pipeline in the roadside verge had already destroyed part of the northern arc of the enclosure. The geophysical (magnetometer) survey undertaken as part of the evaluation suggested that a possible entrance on the south-eastern side, but there was no clear pattern of internal features and only the enclosure ditch produced sharp magnetic anomalies. *Schedule 4 of the Construction and Handback Requirements, Part 1, Annex 4A, Appendix 1, section 2.4.1,* summarised the ensuing trial trenching thus:

> An evaluation trench was excavated [east–west] across the entire length of the enclosure by Exeter Museums Archaeological Field Unit. The excavation demonstrated that the site had been regularly ploughed to a depth of 0.25 m. The two enclosure ditches were located within the trench. At the western end only the butt end of the ditch was found, indicating a probable causeway at this point. The ditch on the eastern side was fully excavated where it was exposed within the trench. Within the interior, a shallow pit was recorded but no other features were identified. This may reflect the extremely dry conditions at the time which impeded soilmark identification. Further localised geophysical scanning within the trench produced no significant anomalies.

Finds recovered in the evaluation included later prehistoric pottery and part of a clay loomweight.

Topography, Geology, and Land-use

The site lay immediately south of the existing A30 centred on SY 1402 9965 *c.* 0.5 km west of Honiton (Figs 2, 39). It was on a slight north-west-facing slope, above the floodplain of the River Otter and the river itself, some 220–320 m away. From a maximum height of *c.* 80.5 m at the south, the ground fell to *c.* 79 m AOD at the north-west. There were streams to west and east of the site (although the eastern end of the trench was marked by a culvert).

The underlying geology is Valley Gravel, mainly chert, over Upper (Keuper) Marls. The western part of the main trench was on intermittently gravelly clay but the eastern part and the western extension trenches were more heavily gravelled, less clayey and rather better drained. The field was previously in cultivation.

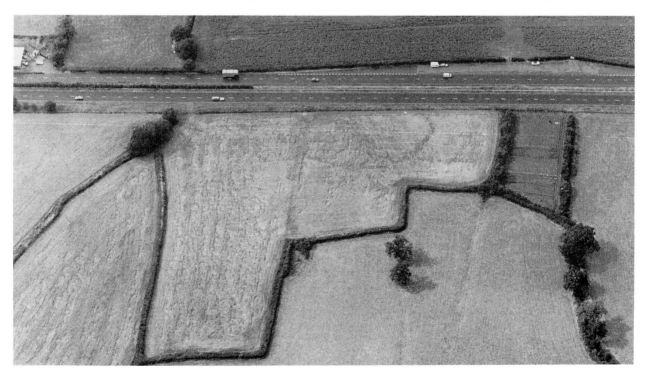

Plate 11   Hayne Lane: as discovered from the air on 12 July 1984, viewed from the south with the old route of the A30 immediately to the north. Photograph DAP/BX1, by Frances Griffith, Devon County Council. Copyright reserved

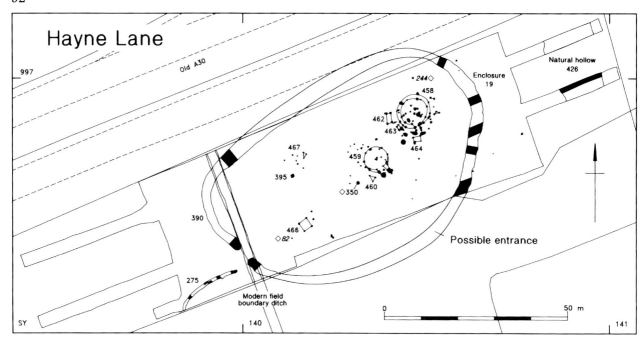

Figure 39   Hayne Lane: location and plan of excavation

Excavation Areas

The excavation trench (W2414.10) covered the full available extent of the enclosure, that is it excluded the ditch and parts of the interior outside the landtake to the south side, and a smaller area of interior and ditch to the north which were under the existing A30 westbound carriageway and verge (Fig. 39). Four extension trenches were opened from the main excavation area, two at the west and two at the east, together with an additional area at the south-western corner. The total excavation area was 4159 m². The excavations were carried out between May and August 1997. A number of features of natural origin were excavated but are not described here; details are in archive.

Results

All features, except gully 275, are inside enclosure 19; gully 275 is outside the entrance to the enclosure but is almost certainly associated with it. All features can be dated to the Middle/Late Bronze Age.

Enclosure Ditch 19

The long axis of the enclosure, which had an overall length of c. 81 m, was from south-west to north-east, and the maximum exposed width was c. 35 m (Figs 39 and 40). There was a single south-west facing entrance, marked by slightly inturned terminals, though the geophysical survey suggests that there may be a second entrance at the south-eastern side arc of the enclosure in the adjoining field.

Eight sections were excavated through the enclosure ditch: three 3 m long sections in the western arc, including both terminals (the northern one of which was located but not fully excavated during the evaluation) and four 2 m long sections (and one smaller one during the evaluation) in the eastern arc. The ditch lay beneath topsoil and subsoil with a combined depth of 0.5–0.55 m. A maximum depth of 2.3 m was recorded at the eastern side (Fig. 40, F). This was also the widest section but was oblique to the line of the ditch; the greatest true width was 3.42 m (Fig. 40, G). The northern terminal was 2.4 m wide and 1.38 m deep and the southern one only slightly larger at 2.63 m wide and 1.41 m deep (Fig. 40, B and C; Fig. 41, C). The smaller size of the terminals may have been the result of truncation by a pair of former field boundary ditches which crossed the southern terminal and clipped the northern one. The ditch was steep-sided and usually symmetrical but the base varied from broad and almost flat (Fig. 40, D, G) to narrow (Figs 40 and 41, H) or with a well-defined slot (Figs 40 and 41, A). A narrow step on the inner (western) side was recorded in one section (Fig. 40, G) and a second had a similar but broader step (Fig. 40, D), suggesting that the ditch may have been recut . The north-western section was relatively shallow but broad (1.29 m deep, 3.05 m wide), perhaps also indicative of a recut above an otherwise atypical shallow slot at the base (Figs 40 and 41, A).

The ditch was filled with brown to dark brown silty clay loam, silty loam, silty clay or clay, or combinations of a similar predominantly fine-grained nature, but occasionally with an admixture of sand. Stone was common in all sections, particularly at the east (naturally more gravelly), where some sections showed central 'columns' of larger stones (e.g. Fig. 41, H). These were probably an effect of the stability of the natural (demonstrated by the negligible erosion of excavated ditch sections and spoil heaps during prolonged heavy rain), the consequent slow infilling resulting in a gradual but steady accumulation of stones at the centre of the ditch as the soil within it slowly accumulated. No clear evidence of the redeposition of excavated material

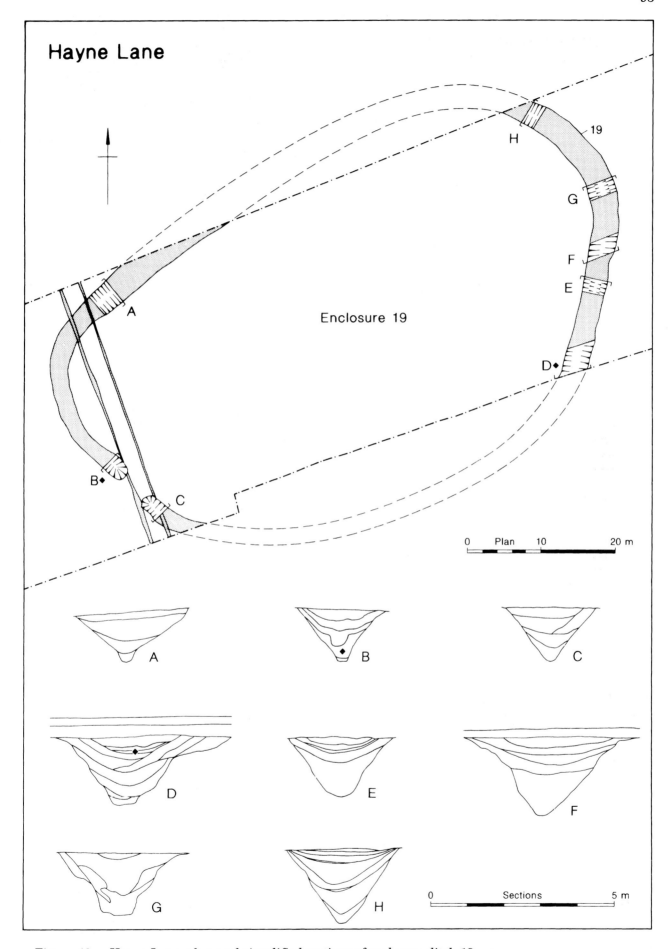

Figure 40   Hayne Lane: plan and simplified sections of enclosure ditch 19

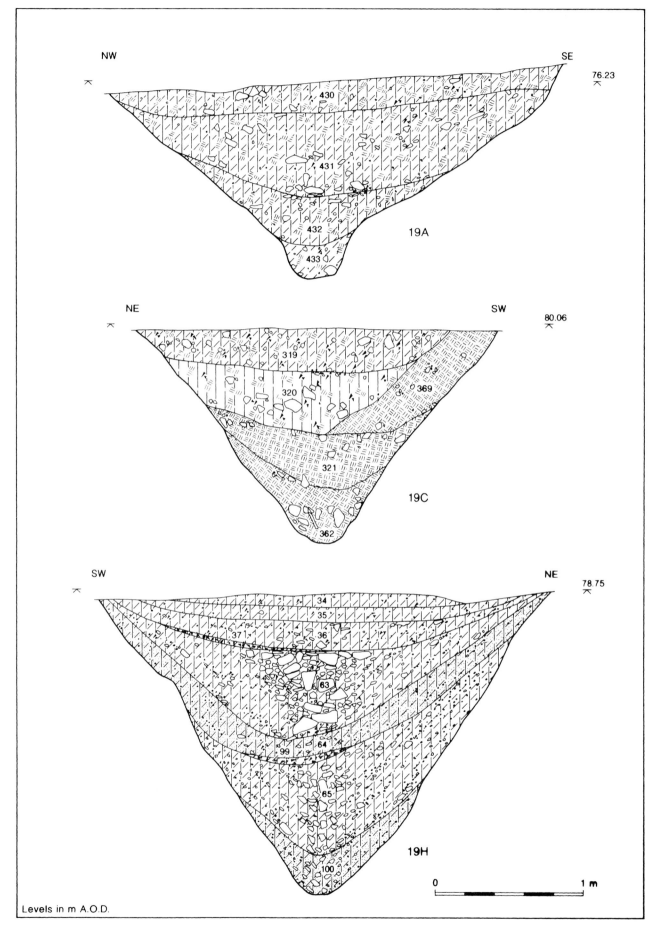

Figure 41   Hayne Lane: sections 19A, 19C, and 19H through enclosure ditch 19

from a bank was recognisable, although occasional higher densities of stone on the inner (western) side of some eastern sections may have been so derived.

The position of a bank may have been marked by an area largely clear of features between the eastern ditch and the main concentration of post-holes inside the enclosure.

Finds from the ditch were scarce but pottery and worked flint and/or chert were recovered from most sections in varying quantities. The largest collection of pottery, 212 sherds, was from the southern terminal; three groups of refitting pieces of chert (11 pieces in total) were found in the northern section, eastern side. The western sections were generally cleaner and contained less charcoal, but enough was recovered from near the middle of the partly infilled northern terminal to give a radiocarbon date of 1400–1040 cal. BC (AA-30677; 2980±50 BP). The charcoal was from a single species, blackthorn, and it is suggested that that it may have been the result of scrub clearance in the vicinity of the ditch. 'Dirty' material, charcoal and burnt flint, was more commonly found in the eastern ditch, nearer to the main density of internal features, with the amount dumped appearing to have increased during the lifetime of the enclosure. Charcoal from near the top of the infilled eastern ditch gave a radiocarbon date of 1000–810 cal. BC (AA-30676; 2725±50 BP).

Gully 275

A curvilinear gully, 275, approached the entrance to the enclosure from the south-west, stopping c. 3.2 m from the southern terminal (Fig. 39). Although it contained only undiagnostic pieces of worked flint and/or chert and was therefore not closely dated, its location suggests that it was an associated feature. It was up to 0.96 m wide and 0.41 m deep, quite steep-sided and with a flat base, and was filled with dark yellowish–brown silty clay, lightly charcoal-flecked. No other features (with the exception of modern land drains) were recorded outside the enclosure in this area.

Structures Inside the Enclosure

The density of post-holes in the eastern part of the enclosure was such that few patterns and/or structural groups were immediately obvious in the field. Little help was offered during the analysis stage by the inconsistencies of size, there were few stratigraphic relationships, and the nature of the finds offers few indications towards groups, structural or otherwise. Despite this, the western round-house, 459, was relatively clear.

Post-built round-house 459

Post-built round-house 459 was marked by a group of at least 29 post-holes slightly east of the centre of the enclosure (Figs 39, 42, 43). The structure was c. 6.8 m in diameter and had a south-south-east facing entrance which appeared, together with the adjoining part of the main structure, to have been completely rebuilt at least once, and there may be evidence for other repairs. The rebuilt structure was elliptical, maintaining the earlier width but measuring c. 5.8 m from the north-west to the south-east. A radiocarbon date of 1520–1260 cal. BC (AA-30678; 3125±50 BP), the earliest of the series for the site, was obtained from post-hole 287, part of the earlier entrance.

In its earlier form, the round-house was outlined by nine post-holes, 56, 54, 249, 283, 269, 255, 441, 263, and 60, with one possible stake-hole, 265, near 249. It was not possible, with one exception, to determine the relationships of the intercut pairs of post-holes at the entrance. Post-holes 447 and 287 seem likely to be a pair, as do 449 and 278. By analogy with, for example, the porches of the round-houses at Patteson's Cross (Figs 32 and 35), there is likely to have been only a single pair of posts at the front. It is not possible to say at Hayne Lane which pair of posts replaced which. The elongated and seemingly amorphous nature of most of the post-holes is likely to be due to the replacement of the posts of the porch. The only recognisable stratigraphic relationship was that post-hole 287 was cut by 285, which could represent the replacement of a post or a further rebuilding. It was from post-hole 287 that the radiocarbon date of 1520–1260 cal. BC (AA-30678; 3125±50 BP) was obtained.

The entrance in both phases was c. 2 m wide. The rebuilt structure comprised post-holes 299 and 307, 54 to 441 from the earlier house, 261 and 241, with 60, 453, and 447 (west) and 285 and 278 (east) at the entrance. (Despite looking like a double post-hole in plan, 278 was not recorded as such). Two post-holes within the entrance(s), 58 and 451, may have been associated with the later phase since 451 cut 449. There were six internal post-holes, including a central one, 301, which just clipped 443; a third post-hole, 289, was only 0.07 m north of 301. The other three were in the north-eastern part of the interior.

The post-holes of the main structure were at intervals of 0.83–2.55 m. The gap between 249 and 283 was relatively large and was not reduced significantly (to 2.2 m) by the presence of possible stake-hole 253 near post-hole 249. The entrance post-holes were closely spaced, the outer pairs being less than 0.1 m apart. The post-holes ranged from 0.3 m in diameter to 1.25 m long and 0.7 m wide and in depth from 0.12 m to 0.45 m. They were filled predominantly with dark yellowish–brown or dark brown silty loam. Central post-holes 301 and 289 were capped with reddish–brown clay and lumps of similar clay were noted in 443, perhaps representing the remains of a floor or indicative of deliberate infilling. Charcoal was present in almost all post-holes, but was common in 255 and 263. Burnt stone and occasional pieces of fired clay were found in some features, most commonly in entrance post-holes, 56, 326, and 447. Three cylindrical fired clay loomweights were recovered, two from post-hole 60 and one from 56; undiagnostic pottery was found in four post-holes of or near the entrance, 278, 285, 447, and 58, and in 263 and 283.

Three-post structure 460 and pit 350

A possible three-post structure, 460, consisting of post-holes 247, 328 and 344, lay c. 1.2 m west of the entrance to round-house 459 (Figs 39 and 44). Post-hole 247, at the narrowest apex, was 1.3 m from 328 and 1.54

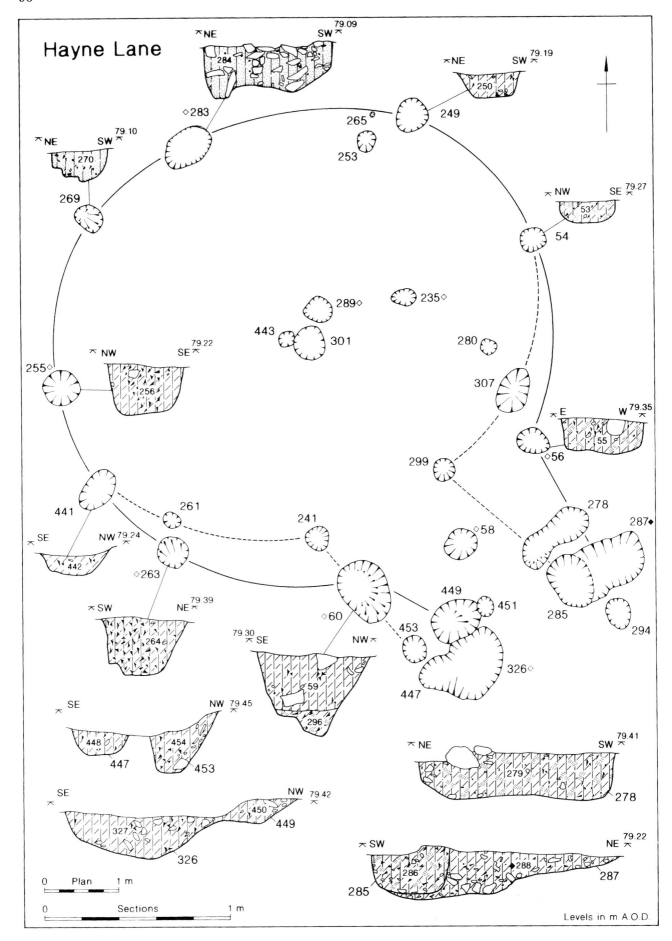

Figure 42   Hayne Lane: plan and sections of round-house 459

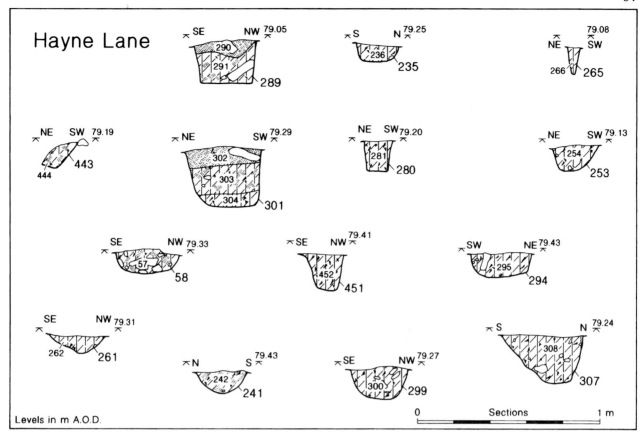

Figure 43   Hayne Lane: sections of features associated with round-house 459

m from 344; 328 and 344 were *c.* 0.95 m apart. The post-holes were between 0.23 m and 0.35 m wide; 247 and 344 were 0.07 and 0.08 m deep and 328 was deeper at 0.19 m. They were filled with lightly charcoal-flecked dark yellowish- or greyish–brown sandy silt loam or silty loam, but contained no finds.

Pit 350 was *c.* 3 m west of 460. The pit was 0.7 m in diameter and 0.21 m deep, and contained much charcoal, some pottery and 23 pieces of struck flint and chert (Figs 39 and 45).

Four-post structure 466 and other features

Two small clusters of features were recorded south-west and west of round-house 459 (Figs 39 and 46). The south-western group included a four-post structure and

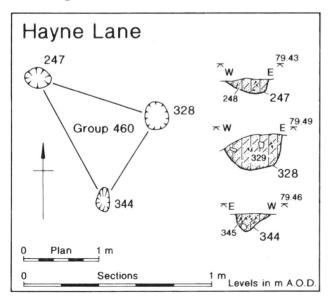

Figure 44   Hayne Lane: plan and sections of three-post structure 460

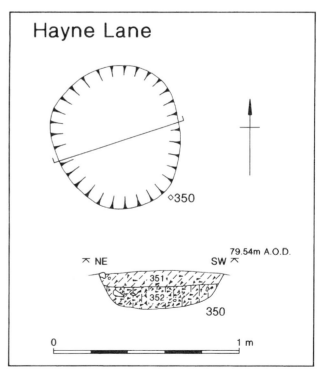

Figure 45   Hayne Lane: plan and section of pit 350

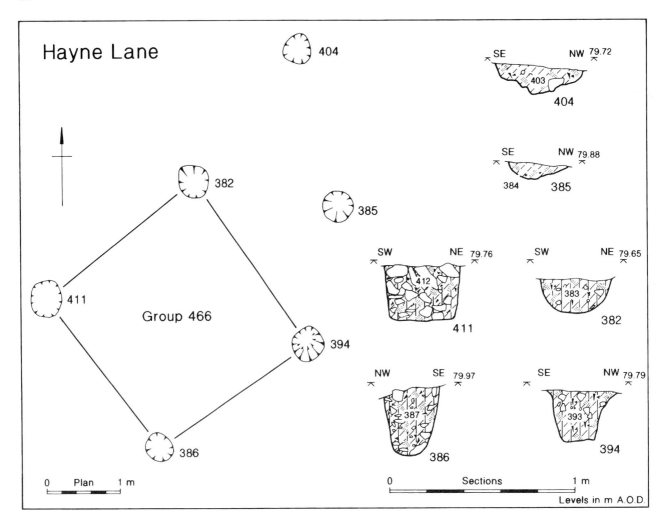

Figure 46   Hayne Lane: plan and sections of four-post structure 466

two post-holes to its north-east. The western group included one possible three-post structure, two paired post-holes and a much truncated pit.

Four-post-structure 466 was *c.* 22 m south-west of round-house 459. It was larger than the four-post structures near round-house 458, and was almost square with sides 2.4 m to 2.6 m long (Fig. 46). The post-holes, 382, 386, 394, and 411, were between 0.3 m and 0.43 m in diameter and 0.18 m and 0.34 m deep. They were filled with lightly charcoal-flecked dark yellowish–brown, brown or strong brown silty clay loam. Two post-holes, 385 and 404, 2.1 m apart, were *c.* 1 m north-east of 466 (Fig. 46). They were 0.37 m and 0.4 m in diameter and 0.08 m and 0.15 m deep respectively. Both were filled with lightly charcoal-flecked brown silty clay.

A possible three-post structure, 467, lay 16 m west of round-house 459 (Figs 39 and 47). The post-holes, 415, 419, and 427, were *c.* 0.9 m, 1.35 m, and 1.5 m apart. They were between 0.24 m and 0.32 m wide and 0.09 m to 0.19 m deep. Post-holes 415 and 419 may have been flanked by stake-holes but their irregular profiles were more probably the result of root or animal disturbance. The post-holes were filled with charcoal-flecked brown to dark brown silty loam.

Another five post-holes and one possible stake-hole were not far to the west of 467 and a pit lay to its south-west. The pit, 395, was sub-rectangular, 0.8 m by

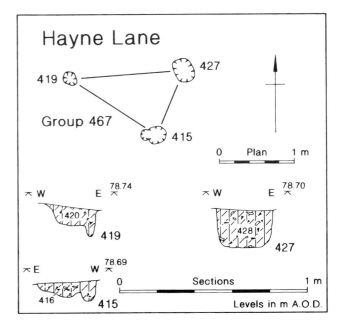

Figure 47   Hayne Lane: plan and sections of three-post structure 467

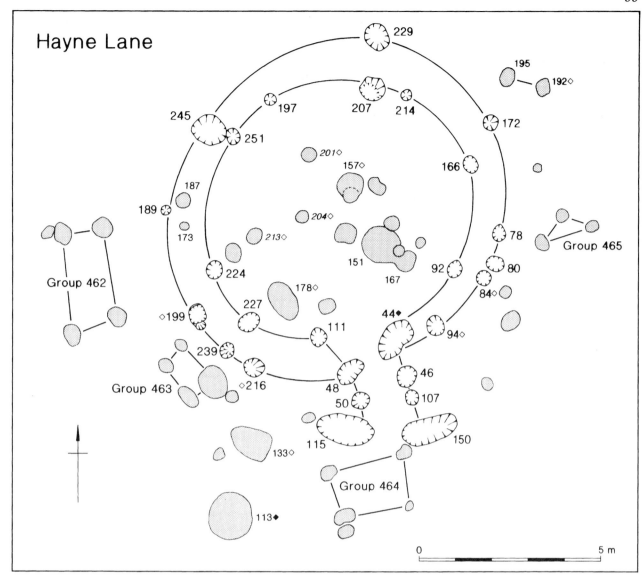

Figure 48   Hayne Lane: plan of round-house 458 and associated features

0.7 m, and was much truncated, with a surviving depth of only 0.06 m. It held one fill, fire-reddened, reddish–brown silty clay with a little charcoal and ash.

Post-built round-house 458

The second round-house, 458, has been extracted, after considerable deliberation, from the dense group of features at the eastern end of the enclosure (Figs 39, 48 and 49; Pl. 12). The interpretation offered is of a structure with a double ring of posts and a south-south-east facing entrance some 16 m north-east of round-house 459. This is, however, only one of several interpretations that could be put forward; some others are shown in Figure 61. There is a radiocarbon date of 900–800 cal. BC (AA-30679; 2715 ±50 BP) for one post-hole of the group.

The inner circuit consisted of ten post-holes, 111, 227, 224, 251, 197, 207, 214, 166, 92, 44, and had a diameter of *c.* 7.2 m. The last was shared with an outer circuit of 13 post-holes: 48, 216, 239, 199, 189, 245, 229, 172, 78, 80, 84, 94, and 44, with a diameter of *c.* 9.3 m. The

Plate 12   Hayne Lane: round-house 458 fully excavated, viewed from the east, with enclosure ditch 19 in the background

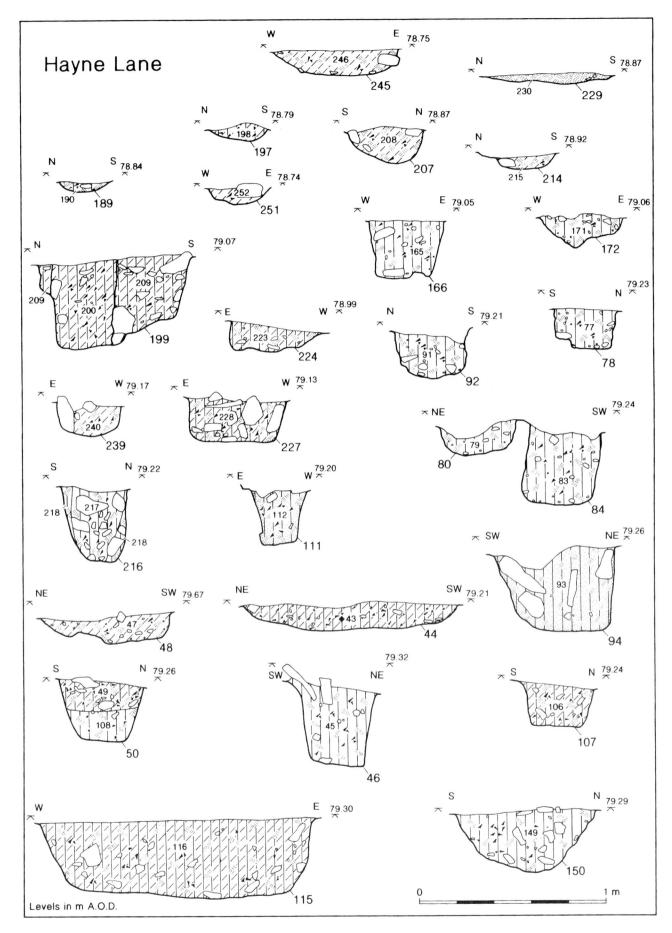

Figure 49   Hayne Lane: sections of post-holes of round-house 458

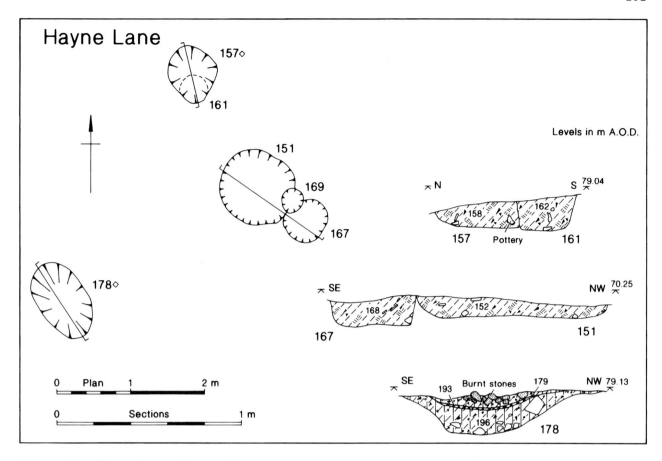

Figure 50   Hayne Lane: plans and sections of pits 178, 151/167, and 161/157

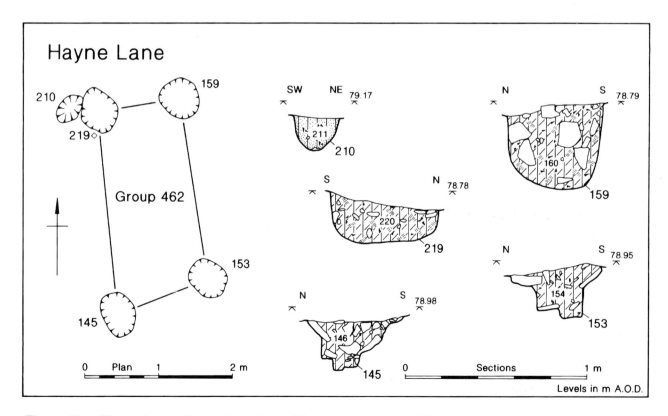

Figure 51   Hayne Lane: plan and sections of four-post structure 462

entrance consisted of post-holes 50 and 115 at the west and 46, 107, and 150 at the east. The post-holes of the inner ring were, for the most part, at intervals of 1.07–3.25 m, although there was only 0.44 m between 207 and 214. The outer post-holes were little as 0.1 m apart (84 and 80) and as much as 4.6 m (245 and 229). The outer circuit included two approximately symmetrical groups of three closely spaced post-holes to either side of the entrance: 84, 80, and 78 at the east and 216, 239, and 199 at the west. There were two post-holes, 173 and 187, 0.18 m apart, between inner and outer post settings.

The post-holes of the outer circuit ranged in width between 0.27 m and 0.8 m and were 0.08–0.47 m deep. Those of the inner one were generally smaller but showed less variation, ranging between 0.3 m and 0.55 m in width and 0.07 m and 0.35 m in depth. Post-hole 44, assigned to both inner and outer circuits, was 1.17 m long and 0.65 m wide but was only 0.15 m deep; it showed no recognisable sub-division into two or more features.

The outer post-holes of the entrance were large: 150 measured 1.55 m by 0.75 m and was deeper at the west, 0.34 m, than at the east, 0.24 m; 115 was only slightly smaller, 1.5 m long, 0.7 m wide and 0.45 m deep. The internal post-holes were similar in size range to those of the inner ring. Single fills, usually dark brown or dark yellowish–brown clay loam, silty loam, silty clay, and silty clay loam, were recorded in all except post-holes 50, 199, and 216; probable post-pipes were recorded in the last two. Small amounts of charcoal were present in almost all post-holes, but larger quantities were noted in 44 and 111 at the entrance, in 199, and in internal post-hole 201, a slight feature. Charcoal from 44 had a radiocarbon date of 900–800 cal. BC (AA-30679; 2715±50 BP) and, although 90 sherds of Middle Bronze Age pottery were found in the feature it also held two sherds of possible Early Bronze Age pottery. Large chert pebbles, probably packing, were recorded in 94, 80, 239, and 216 (outer ring), 227 and 111 (inner ring), and 46 (entrance), and in five internal post-holes. Many large pieces of chert were noted throughout the fills of 115 and 150. Pottery was recovered from six entrance post-holes, four of the inner circuit, one of the outer circuit, and six internal ones.

Within the round-house were 11 post-holes and four small pits or hearths. An irregular line of five, possibly six, post-holes (one may be a double post-hole) crossed the interior from south-west to north-east. There were five post-holes around the entrance and one to its north-west. The pits or hearths were also in the south-eastern half of the building, one west of the entrance, two to the north-east and the fourth slightly north-east of centre. The largest feature, 178 (Fig. 50), 1.1 m long, 1 m wide, and 0.22 m deep, contained much charcoal, burnt chert and quartzite pebbles and a fragment of fired clay in its upper fill. There was no evidence of burning on the sides of the pit, and no other finds were recovered. Pit 157 (Fig. 50) was smaller, 0.7 m by 0.5 m and 0.15 m deep, and was cut by post-hole 161, but it contained charcoal, a little (4 g) burnt animal bone and pottery, and fragments of fired clay. The other two pits 151 and 167 were 0.9 m and 0.55 m in diameter and 0.09 m and 0.1 m deep respectively. There was much

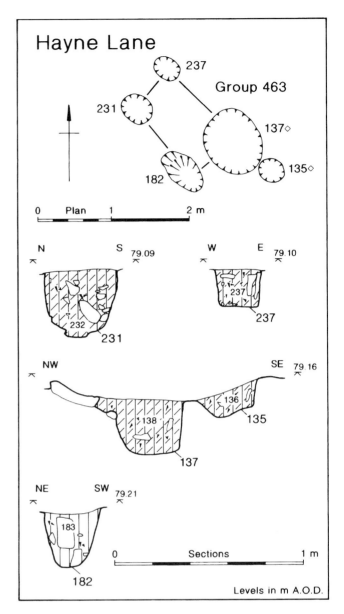

Figure 52   Hayne Lane: plan and sections of four-post structure 463

charcoal in 151, less in 167. Pits 178 and 157, and perhaps 151 are likely to have been hearths.

Four-post structures 462, 463 and 464 and other structural groups

Three four-post structures were recorded near round-house 458, two to its west and one immediately south-west of the entrance (Figs 48, 51–3). A fifth post-hole was contiguous with one post-hole of each structure (Fig. 48).

Structure 462 was less than 2 m west of the round-house and measured *c.* 2.7 m by *c.* 1.4 m, the long axis approximately north to south (Fig. 51). The post-holes (145, 153, 159, 219) were between 0.55 m and 0.6 m wide and 0.22 m and 0.6 m deep; the fifth post-hole (210) was 0.29 m in diameter and 0.16 m deep. All were filled with dark brown or very dark brown silty loam and silty clay loam. Charcoal was present in all five

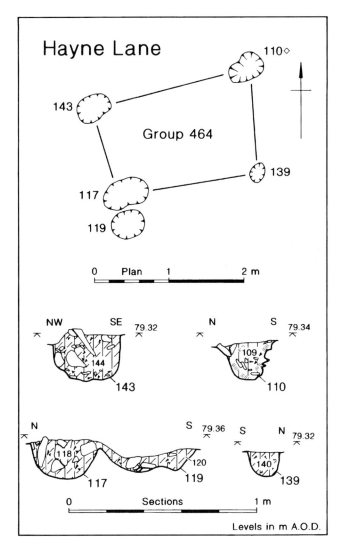

Figure 53   Hayne Lane: plan and sections of four-post structure 464

to north-west (Fig. 52). The largest post-hole of the group, 0.86 m wide and 0.35 m deep, was at the south-east corner where it was flanked by fifth post-hole 135, 0.25 m in diameter and 0.2 m deep. The south-western post-hole was 0.6 m wide and 0.3 m deep, but the other three were between 0.34 m and 0.44 m wide and 0.19 m and 0.34 m deep. Fills were mainly dark yellowish–brown silty loam, though sandy clay loam was noted in places beneath stone packing in 182 (although it did not occur in the drawn section). Packing was noted in all except post-hole 231; burnt chert was found in 135 and 137.

The third four-post structure, 464 (post-holes 110, 117, 139, 143), was almost certainly not contemporary with the round-house, since it would have obstructed the entrance; the north-eastern post-hole was only 0.06 m from the western end of entrance post-hole 150. The structure was up to 2.1 m long, and 1.4 m wide, the long axis from south-west to north-east (Fig. 53). The post-holes, with ancillary 119, were all between 0.55 m and 0.16 m in diameter and 0.13 m and 0.35 m deep. The fills were mainly dark yellowish–brown silty or clay loam, charcoal-flecked and with stone packing in 117 and 143 (burnt flint was also present in some quantity in 143).

A possible three-post structure, 465, lay 0.8 m east of round-house 458 (Figs 48 and 54). It was small, post-hole 72, at the northern apex, being 0.52 m from 70 and 74, which were in turn only 1.1 m apart. Post-holes 70 and 72 were 0.31 m and 0.35 m in diameter and 0.14 m and 0.19 m deep; 74 may have been larger, 0.53 m in diameter and 0.13 m deep, but was poorly defined. All were filled with lightly charcoal-flecked strong brown or brown gravelly clay loam.

Post-holes 195 and 192, c. 3 m north of 465, may have been associated. They were 0.43 m and 0.5 m in diameter and 0.16 m and 0.13 m deep, and were filled with brown clay loam. Although the fill of 192 was only lightly charcoal-flecked a concentration of charcoal was noted at the centre of 195.

Two pits, 133 and 113, were not far to the south-west of round-house 458 (Figs 48 and 55). Pit 133, 1.23 m west of entrance post-hole 115, was roughly boat-shaped in plan, 1.08 m long, up to 0.8 m wide and 0.4 m deep. It contained a single fill, heavily charcoal-flecked, dark yellowish–brown silty clay loam in which small chert pebbles were common. Charcoal from the pit gave a

post-holes and was common in 159. Stone packing was noted in 145, 153, and 159. Single sherds of pottery were found in 145, 159, and 219.

Structure 463 (post-holes 137, 182, 231, 237) was c. 1.35 m south-east of 462 and c. 0.5 m from the round-house. It was smaller than 462 with maximum dimensions of 1.3 m by 0.8 m, the long axis south-east

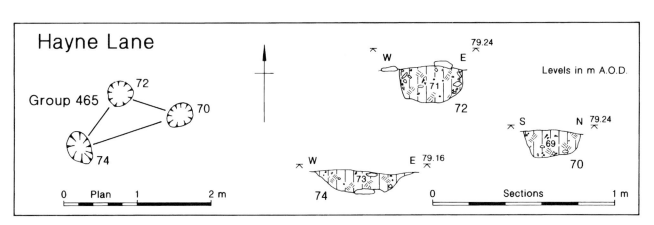

Figure 54   Hayne Lane: plan and sections of three-post structure 465

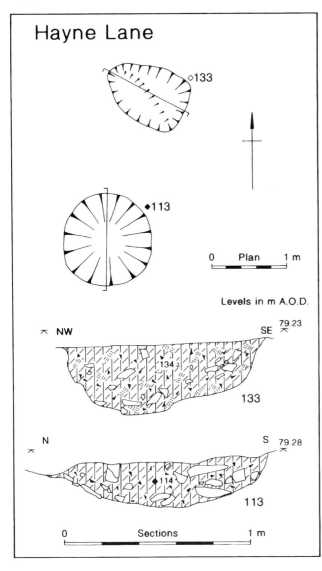

Figure 55   Hayne Lane: plans and sections of pits 113 and 133

radiocarbon date of 1000–800 cal. BC (AA-30680; 2730±55 BP).

Pit 113 was 1 m south west of 133. It was circular, 1.15 m in diameter and 0.27 m deep, and was filled with heavily charcoal-flecked very dark brown silty loam and chert pebbles, some of them burnt. There was no reddening of soil around the pit to show that burning *in situ* had taken place.

Finds

Flaked Stone, by Peter S. Bellamy

The assemblage consists of a total of 367 pieces (7946 g) of both worked flint and chert, of which 257 pieces (5493 g) were from stratified contexts (Table 24). Methods of analysis follow those outlined in Appendix 2.

Raw material
The raw material utilised comprises 53.7% flint and 46.3% chert and is likely to derive from the same sources

as were used for the Castle Hill assemblage (p. 37). The flint includes both chalk flint (12%) and gravel flint (30%). A single piece which is possibly of Portland Chert was recovered but as the piece has been burnt the identification is not certain.

Assemblage description

Flint
The worked flint is in a sharp or slightly rolled, unpatinated condition. A very small proportion has been burnt. The assemblage represents debitage from a flake industry with some material from all stages of the reduction process present as well as a number of tools and utilised pieces (Table 24). There are a small number of blades and blade fragments present also. No evidence for core tool production was recognised.

The cores are flake cores, with one unstratified small blade core with opposed platforms. This blade core, unlike any of the other pieces in the assemblage, is lightly patinated. The flake cores include three on rolled nodules originally measuring about 70 mm across, another on a small nodule of chalk flint, and two on flint gravel. One core has too little remaining cortex to allow the nodule to be characterised. Five of the cores are multi-directional with two being fairly systematically flaked, with one platform worked out then the core rotated and further flakes removed using an earlier flake scar as a platform, and three were rather less systematic with a number of flakes removed from many different directions. Three of these cores were abandoned because of thermal faults in the flint and two were worked out. Another core had a small number of flakes removed from one side using an unaltered thermal surface as a platform. The small core on chalk flint was different in character to the other cores. It was noticeably smaller (max. dimension 40 mm; 29 g) and showed signs of more controlled flaking with a greater tendency towards small parallel-sided flakes.

The flakes are generally broad in shape between 25 mm and 80 mm in length and 20–65 mm in width with either plain or thermal butts averaging *c*. 7 mm wide – and appear to have been largely removed with a hard hammer. The flakes include preparation flakes (*c*. 25%), core trimming flakes (*c*. 30%), and other 'waste' flakes. The small blades and 'blade-like flakes' present exhibit some technological differences to the rest of the assemblage – they are generally smaller than the other flakes with narrow butts some with evidence for platform abrasion and some were removed with a soft hammer. These pieces form about 8% of the total assemblage.

The tools and other pieces showing signs of utilisation comprise about 7.6% of the assemblage. Ten scrapers (three broken), one scraper/piercer, three broken piercers and two retouched flakes were identified (Fig. 56, 1). The majority of the scrapers are on heavy broad squat flakes with retouch round the distal end and down both sides, a type typically found in Late Neolithic/Early Bronze Age contexts. The piercers have minimal retouch to form a tip but in every example this had broken off. The scraper/piercer is illustrated as Figure 56, 2. The retouched flakes both have irregular retouch along one edge.

Table 24: Hayne Lane, flaked stone assemblage by type (no./wt(g))

	Cores	Broken cores	Flakes	Broken flakes	Burnt flakes	Blades	Broken blades	Tools	Broken tools	Chips	Burnt chips	Misc. debitage	Total	Tool type
Chert														
Natural hollow 426	–	–	2/16	–	–	–	–	–	–	–	–	–	2/16	
Ditch 19														
Section D	–	–	1/11	1/10	–	–	–	–	–	–	–	–	2/21	
Section E	–	–	8/326	1/20	1/23	–	–	–	–	–	–	–	10/369	
Section G	–	–	6/78	3/12	–	–	–	1/39	–	–	–	–	10/129	rough scraper
Section H	2/619	–	13/1033	8/133	–	–	–	–	–	–	–	–	23/1785	
Ditch 275	–	–	1/26	–	–	–	–	–	–	–	–	–	1/26	
Ditch 390, S terminal	–	–	9/76	1/4	–	–	–	1/46	–	–	–	–	11/126	ut flake
N terminal	–	–	1/20	2/15	–	–	–	–	–	1/0	–	–	4/35	
Section A	–	1/71	8/119	4/112	–	–	–	–	–	1/1	–	1/99	15/402	
Pits associated with round-houses 458 and 459														
113	–	–	7/308	2/26	–	–	–	–	–	–	–	–	9/334	
151	–	–	–	–	–	–	–	–	–	1/0	–	–	1/0	
167	–	–	–	1/1	–	–	–	–	–	1/0	–	–	2/1	
178	–	–	–	1/3	–	–	–	–	–	1/1	–	–	2/4	
134	–	–	2/47	1/9	–	–	–	–	–	–	–	–	3/56	
287	–	–	1/9	–	–	–	–	–	–	–	–	–	1/9	
350	–	–	3/80	1/4	–	–	–	–	–	–	–	1/11	5/95	
Pit 395	–	–	1/57	–	–	–	–	–	–	–	–	–	1/57	
Post-holes (NW enc.)	–	–	–	–	–	–	–	–	–	1/0	–	–	1/0	
Round-house 458	–	1/121	14/154	3/22	–	–	–	–	–	3/0	–	–	21/297	
Round-house 459	–	–	2/16	–	–	–	–	–	–	2/2	–	1/10	5/28	
Other features	–	–	3/76	2/30	1/11	1/1	–	–	–	–	–	–	7/118	
Unstratified	–	–	21/671	8/81	–	–	–	1/342	–	–	1/0	1/41	32/1135	ret flake
Sub-total chert	2/619	2/292	105/3131	39/482	2/34	1/1	0	3/427	0	11/4	1/0	4/165	170/5051	

Table 24: (continued)

	Cores	Broken cores	Flakes	Broken flakes	Burnt flakes	Blades	Broken blades	Tools	Broken tools	Chips	Burnt chips	Misc. debitage	Total	Tool type
Flint														
Natural hollow 426	1/174	–	5/30	2/29	–	–	–	–	–	–	–	–	8/233	
Ditch 19														
Section D	–	–	–	–	–	–	1	–	–	4/6	–	–	4/6	
Section E	–	–	5/36	2/17	–	–	1/3	1/26	–	2/1	–	–	11/83	scraper
Section F	–	–	1/22	–	–	–	–	1/10	–	–	1/0	1/18	4/50	scraper
Section G	–	–	5/36	–	–	1/1	1/2	–	–	1/0	–	–	9/40	
Section H	–	–	2/9	–	–	–	–	–	–	1/1	–	–	3/10	
Ditch 275	–	–	–	3/6	–	–	–	1/4	–	1/1	–	–	5/11	scraper/piercer
Ditch 390, N terminal	–	–	3/32	2/27	–	–	–	–	–	–	–	1/3	6/62	
S terminal	–	–	4/56	1/8	–	–	–	–	1/3	–	–	1/12	7/79	ret. flake
Section A	1/132	–	3/69	–	–	–	–	1/7	–	1/1	–	–	6/209	rough scraper
Pits associated with round-houses 458 and 459														
113	–	–	–	–	–	–	–	1/28	–	–	–	–	1/28	
115	–	–	–	2/3	1/13	–	1/1	–	–	1/0	1/0	–	6/17	
350	1/177	–	13/356	2/21	–	–	1/1	–	–	1/0	–	–	18/555	
447	–	–	1/5	–	–	–	–	–	–	–	–	–	1/5	
Post-hole 336	–	–	–	1/1	–	–	–	–	–	–	–	–	1/1	
Post-holes (SW enc.)	–	–	–	1/1	–	–	–	–	–	–	–	–	1/1	
Post-holes NW enc.)	1/53	–	–	–	–	–	–	–	–	1/0	–	–	2/53	
Round-house 458	–	–	8/77	4/24	1/14	–	–	–	–	6/3	–	1/7	20/125	
Round-house 459	–	–	1/2	–	–	–	–	–	–	2/0	–	1/1	4/3	
Other features	–	–	–	1/4	–	–	–	–	–	–	–	1/2	2/6	
Unstratified	6/309	–	22/339	19/73	2/4	3/35	4/6	4/126	5/41	4/5	4/3	5/377	78/1318	4 scrapers+3 broken, 2 broken piercers
Sub-total flint	10/845	0	73/1069	40/214	4/31	4/36	9/14	9/201	6/44	25/18	6/3	11/420	197/2895	
Total	12/1464	2/192	178/4200	79/696	6/65	5/37	9/14	12/628	6/44	36/22	7/3	15/581	367/7946	

Chert

The chert is in a sharp or slightly rolled condition. The assemblage comprises elements from all stages of the reduction process from core preparation and trimming flakes, 'waste' flakes, flake tools and cores. A number of conjoining flakes was found but none could be refitted back to a core. All the refitting flakes are core preparation flakes.

The two complete cores present are both single platform flake cores, one using a natural thermal fracture and the other had a platform prepared by the removal of a single flake. Neither core had been completely worked out, though one may have been abandoned due to faults in the raw material.

The flakes are generally rather squat with thick plain or thermal butts (5–25 mm) and generally removed with a hard hammer. The dorsal flake scars show that the majority of the flakes were removed from the same direction but a small number indicate at least one earlier flaking direction. About 60% of the flakes are core preparation or core trimming flakes, generally as broad or broader than they are long, measuring up to 80 mm in length, 130 mm in width, and 30 mm in thickness. There is a tendency for the other flakes to be smaller in size but similar in shape. Overall the chert flakes are larger in size than the flint flakes, probably a result of the different size of raw material – the refitting chert flakes indicate a nodule size greater than 200 mm across while the flint nodules appear to be no greater than about 80 mm across.

Three chert tools were recognised – a scraper with irregular abrupt to semi-abrupt retouch round the proximal end (Fig. 56, 3), a very large flake with abrupt retouch on the left distal edge and a flake with natural, cortical, backing along the right side, and traces of wear in the form of microscars along the left side (Fig. 56, 4). In addition there are a number of other naturally backed flakes which may have been utilised but no definite traces of wear could be seen.

Distribution

The flaked stone was found in features both inside and outside the enclosure (both to the east and west), however, the majority was found in the enclosure ditch (Table 24). No significant pattern could be seen in the quantity of material distributed round the enclosure ditch. There was no difference in the quantity or type of flaked stone deposited in the ditch terminals at the entrance to the enclosure. The most notable deposit was in the northern excavated segment (33, section H) of enclosure ditch 19, where eleven conjoining chert flakes were found (one group of 2 refits, one of 4 refits, and one of 5 refits) probably from two different nodules. No other refitting flakes were found on the site.

Flaked stone was found across the whole of the interior of the enclosure with a greater density in the north-eastern part and with a marked tailing off towards the entrance. This matches the distribution of cut features inside the enclosure, suggesting that this is the most significant factor, rather than a significant patterning of the flaked stone itself (Fig. 63). The majority of features inside the enclosure contained only one or two small pieces of flaked stone, strongly suggesting that it was accidentally incorporated into these features. Only two pits (113 and 350) contained more than the occasional piece (Table 24). Pit 350, on the south-western edge of post-hole concentration 459, produced 23 pieces (mainly of flint) including a flint core and a number of core preparation flakes. The flakes came from several different nodules and none obviously from the core. This material looks like a selection of pieces from knapping activity on the site, not necessarily from the immediate vicinity of the pit. It is not possible to tell whether this material was deliberately deposited or represents accidental incorporation. Pit 113, on the south-western edge of post-hole concentration 458, contained ten pieces (mainly of chert). The flakes are generally quite large and one has some fairly rudimentary retouch but otherwise this group is not noteworthy.

No significant pattern could be recognised in the distribution of cores – they were scattered across the whole of the site, both inside and outside the enclosure. Similarly the tools have a scattered distribution.

Discussion

It is clear that there is probably more than one period represented in the flaked stone assemblage. There is a small quantity of well-made blades and possibly one small core which are Early Neolithic in character. These pieces are all made from flint and appear to conform to the pattern of preferential selection of flint over chert during the Early Neolithic in this area (Silvester *et al.* 1987). This material represents only a very small proportion of the whole assemblage and primarily comprises small broken pieces which have a wide distribution across the site. This material represents a background scatter of Early Neolithic material attesting to an earlier period of activity on the site.

The bulk of the flaked stone assemblage from this site belongs to a flake industry producing broad flakes produced with little core preparation and control using raw materials available in the vicinity of the site. There is no apparent preferential selection of any particular raw material type, unlike in earlier periods (Berridge 1985; Silvester *et al.* 1987). This industry would fit best into the pattern of Bronze Age stoneworking technology. There are no chronologically specific type fossils present to enable a closer date range within the Bronze Age to be determined. A number of scrapers are of a type that is common on Late Neolithic and Early Bronze Age sites but not exclusively so. The majority of the features on the site are of Middle–Late Bronze Age date and it would seem reasonable to assume that the flint and stone working belonged to this period. The refitting flakes found in the northeastern part of the enclosure ditch would suggest that there was some knapping being carried out contemporaneously to the use of the enclosure. The nature of the flaked stone assemblage does not indicate any specialised activities and there is no evidence to associate the stoneworking with any particular feature or area on the site. It seems to represent a general spread of material across the whole area.

Illustrated objects
(Fig. 56)
1. Flint scraper. Context 28, enclosure ditch 19.

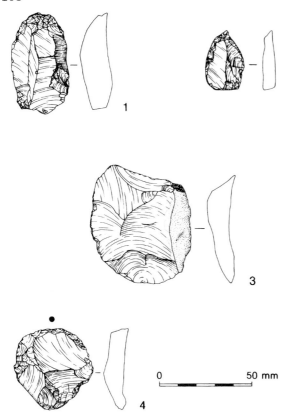

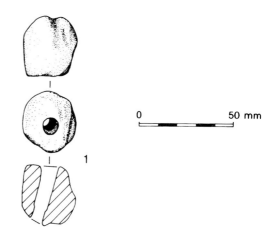

Figure 57   *Hayne Lane: stone spindle whorl.*
Scale 1:2

Figure 56   Hayne Lane: objects of flaked stone.
Scale 1:4

2.   Flint scraper/piercer. Context 277, gully 275 (east terminal).
3.   Chert scraper. Unstratified.
4.   Utilised chert flake. Context 319, enclosure ditch 390 (south terminal).

Other Objects of Worked Stone, by M. Laidlaw, with stone identifications by D.F. Williams

A very small quantity of worked stone was recovered, consisting of one possible spindle whorl and six small quern fragments; all from round-house 459. The spindle whorl, in a fine-textured ?Permian sandstone, is rather irregularly shaped, roughly cylindrical with worn surfaces and a central perforation (Fig. 57, 1). The quern fragments, all in Permian lava, are too fragmentary to attribute to type. Five fragments were recovered from post-hole 58 and one larger fragment from post-hole 241.

Illustrated object
(Fig. 57)
1.   Possible spindle whorl, worn on one side. ON 3, context 59, post-hole 58, round-house 459.

Pottery, by M. Laidlaw

The pottery assemblage consists of 937 sherds weighing 5058 g. The majority of sherds are small, plain body sherds, many of which are abraded due to the soft nature of the grog-tempered fabrics within this Middle/Late Bronze Age assemblage. Mean sherd weight is 5 g.

Fabrics
A total of 15 different fabric types was recorded, although the distinction between some of them is somewhat arbitrary as each fabric type covers a relatively broad range of inclusion size and frequency. Grog-tempered, sandy, and rock-tempered fabrics are present. Eleven of the fabric types identified occur also at Castle Hill (see Chapter 3 and Appendix 3). Fabric totals are given in Table 25.

Samples of five fabrics, one grog-tempered (G4) and four with rock inclusions (R5, R6, R7, R8), were submitted for petrological analysis. The full petrological report is presented here as Appendix 4. The five fabrics sampled were found to fall into four broad groups based on dominant inclusion type: grog/mudstone (G4), chert (R7), sanidine (R8), and granitic (R5, R6). The sample of G4 also contained sandstone. Inclusions in the sample of fabric R8 match those identified in an Iron Age fabric from Blackhorse (Chapter 8, fabric R13), which has been compared with Peacock's group 5 Glastonbury Ware, a source for which is postulated in the Permian rocks in the Exeter area (Peacock 1969). Chert as found in fabric R7 would have been easily available locally.

David Williams writes:

> Fabric R5 contains frequent grains of orthoclase and plagioclase felspar, large fragments of a tourmaline-granite, biotite and muscovite mica and quartz. The size and comparative freshness of the felspars and the granite suggests that these inclusions may not have travelled very far from the original granite outcrop. Although fabric R6 appears to lack fragments of granite, it does contain frequent discrete grains of orthoclase and plagioclase felspar, which may originally have derived from a granitic source. In all likelihood the two granitic fabrics each come from different sources, although perhaps both originate from the south-west of Exeter, either directly or indirectly tied to the large granite formations in that region.

Table 25: Hayne Lane, pottery, fabric totals

Fabric	No.	Weight (g)	% (wt)
Grog-tempered fabrics			
G1	4	9	0.2
G3	2	74	1.5
G4	614	2947	58.9
G5	2	10	0.2
G6	2	176	3.5
Sandy fabrics			
Q2	6	27	0.5
Q6	1	6	0.1
Chert-tempered fabrics			
R1	26	182	3.6
R2	46	344	6.9
R4	5	11	0.2
R7	183	859	17.1
Volcanic fabrics			
R3	11	32	0.6
Granitic fabrics			
R5	22	189	3.8
R6	2	6	0.1
Fabrics containing sanidine			
R8	3	139	2.8
Sub-total	929	5011	
Later pottery			
Post-med.	5	46	
Unident.	3	1	
Total	937	5058	

Macroscopic comparison with these petrological samples and with samples from other A30 sites reveals that there are three other chert-tempered fabrics (R1, R2, R4), and one fabric with volcanic inclusions (R3), the latter with a probable source again in the Permian rocks of the Exeter area. The chert-tempered, volcanic and sanidine fabrics are all likely to have an origin within the Exeter area, local (or at least fairly local) to the site. Four other grog-tempered fabrics and two sandy fabrics do not contain geologically distinctive inclusions, but are also likely to be of local origin. The granitic fabrics are the only demonstrably non-local wares.

Proportions of the various fabric groups are comparable with those from Castle Hill (Chapter 3), both dominated by grog-tempered fabrics with a lower proportion of chert-tempered fabrics, although at Hayne Lane the proportions of the two groups are closer in size (percentages calculated by weight). In both cases other fabric groups constitute less than 10% of the total assemblage. A similar range of fabrics is present at both sites, although the granitic and sanidine fabrics from Hayne Lane are not matched at the Middle Bronze Age settlement of Castle Hill, *c.* 3.5 km to the west.

Forms

Diagnostic rim forms are scarce from Hayne Lane and may be attributed to five Middle/Late Bronze Age vessel

Table 26: Hayne Lane, pottery, vessel forms by fabric (no. of occurrences)

Form	Grog G4	G5	Chert R1	R2	Vol. R3	Gran. R5	San. R8	Total
MBA2	2	1	–	–	–	1	1	5
LBA1	9	–	3	1	1	2	–	16
LBA2	1	–	–	–	–	–	–	1
LBA3	1	–	–	–	–	–	–	1
LBA4	1	–	–	–	–	–	–	1
Unid.	5	–	1	1	–	–	–	7
Total	19	1	4	2	1	3	1	31

forms, three of which also occur at Castle Hill (MBA2, LBA1, LBA3). Table 26 lists the occurrence of vessel forms by fabric. Full description of vessel forms can be found in Appendix 3.

MBA2: Jars with expanded rims. (Fig. 58, 2).
LBA1: Jars with inturned rounded rims. (Fig. 58, 1).
LBA2: Jars with slight neck constrictions. (Fig. 58, 3).
LBA3: Carinated vessel. (Fig. 58, 4).
LBA4: Lids (Fig. 58, 5).

The most common vessel forms are the ovoid jars with inturned rims (LBA1), which occur most frequently in grog-tempered fabrics, although there are examples in rock-tempered fabrics of three petrological groups (chert, volcanic, and granitic). The MBA2 jars are of more varied form than those from Castle Hill, and include two examples with internally bevelled rims (e.g. Fig. 58, 2). Jars of MBA2 form occur in small quantities in both the grog-tempered and rock-tempered fabrics, as do the two necked jars of form LBA2. Forms identified only at Hayne Lane consist of two small carinated vessels (LBA3) and a lid (LBA4). Seven rim sherds, mostly grog-tempered, are too small to attribute to specific vessel forms.

Decoration and surface treatments

Decoration on the pottery from Hayne Lane is very rare and includes two sherds with lightly scored lines in the fine grog-tempered fabric G1, possibly derived from a Beaker vessel. One lid fragment has finger impressions surviving around the rim, which may be due to manufacturing technique rather than deliberate decoration, and one sherd has seed-like impression on its external surface, again probably fortuitous rather than decorative. One grog-tempered sherd has a faint incised line, and another (very abraded) grog-tempered sherd has a possible applied boss.

A small number of sherds in fabrics G4 and R2 have smoothed internal surfaces while two sherds in fabric R1 have smoothed external surfaces. Wipe marks are visible on the external surface of one grog-tempered and one rock tempered sherd.

Residues

A moderate number of grog-tempered sherds have traces of sooting and possible food related residues surviving, mostly on internal surfaces. A substantial

Table 27: Hayne Lane, pottery by feature (no./wt (g))

	Grog	Sandy	Chert	Volcanic	Granitic	Sanidine	Total
Enclosure ditch 19							
Section A	17/39	–	14/122	–	–	2/132	33/293
Section C	21/131	–	180/830	1/8	4/43	–	206/1012
Section D	4/50	3/1	1/3	–	–	–	8/54
Section E	32/107	–	–	–	–	–	52/107
Section G	3/14	–	–	–	–	–	3/14
Section H	–	3/12	–	–	–	–	3/12
Round-house 458	285/1653	2/7	25/178	7/6	16/132	–	335/1976
Round-house 459	25/834	–	31/215	–	1/8	–	57/1057
Pit 350	26/125	–	–	–	1/4	–	27/129
Structure 462	3/35	–	–	–	–	–	3/35
Structure 463	73/181	1/8	3/40	–	1/4	–	78/233
Structure 464	6/18	–	1/1	–	–	–	7/19
Structure 466	1/2	–	1/2	–	–	–	2/4
Structure 467	1/2	–	1/1	–	–	–	2/3
Other features	5/17	–	3/4	–	–	1/7	9/28
Total	522/3208	9/28	260/1396	8/14	23/191	3/139	825/4976

Table 28: Hayne Lane, pottery, comparison of enclosure ditch 19 with round-houses 458 and 459

	Enclosure ditch 19		Round-house 458		Round-house 459	
Fabric	No./wt (g)	Diagnostic	No./wt (g)	Diagnostic	No./wt (g)	Diagnostic
Grog-tempered						
G1	1/1		3/8	scored decor.	–	
G3	–		2/74		–	
G4	96/340	LBA1	278/1356	MBA2; LBA1(x5); LBA3; LBA4	124/826	MBA2; LBA1; LBA2; ?boss
G5	–		–		1/8	MBA2
G6	–		2/176		–	
Q2	3/12		2/7		–	
Chert-tempered						
R1	–		19/148		3/21	LBA1
R2	12/100		4/18		28/194	LBA1
R4	1/3		1/4		–	
R7	182/852		1/2		–	
Volcanic						
R3	1/8		7/6		–	
Granitic						
R5	4/43	MBA2	15/130		1/8	LBA1
R6	–		1/2		–	
Sanidine						
R8	2/132	MBA2	–		–	
Total	302/1491		335/1931		157/1057	

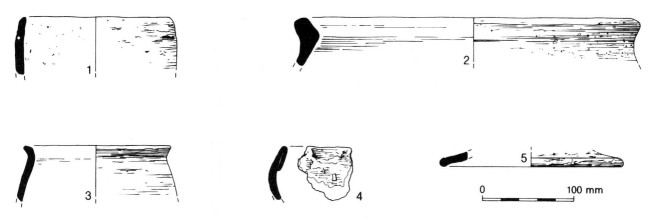

Figure 58   Hayne Lane: Bronze Age pottery. Scale 1/2

number of sherds in fabric G4 are sooted internally, although most of these sherds may be derived from the same vessel.

Distribution

Of the 926 sherds from stratified contexts, 306 sherds (33% of the total by number) came from the enclosure ditch 19/390, which includes a group of 206 sherds from the southern terminal, consisting largely of sherds probably from a single vessel (MBA2) in chert-tempered fabric R7 (from secondary fill 321). Accordingly, there are insufficient data to meaningfully assess either vertical or horizontal distributions within the enclosure ditch (Table 27).

Fabrics from the enclosure ditch comprise almost exclusively grog-tempered (G1, G4) and chert-tempered fabrics (R2, R4, R7), all of which are likely to be of local manufacture. Only three examples of regionally-produced fabrics (although still relatively local to the site) came from the ditch, all from secondary fills. These were one sherd in volcanic fabric R3, two joining sherds from the rim of a large MBA2 jar in sanidine fabric R8 (Fig. 58, 2), and an internally bevelled rim (MBA2 variant) in a very coarse version of granitic fabric R5.

A radiocarbon date of 1400–1040 cal, BC (AA-30677; 2980±50 BP) was obtained from near the middle of the partly infilled northern terminal, and another of 1000–810 cal. BC (AA-30676; 2725±50 BP) from near the top of the eastern ditch (19).

The remainder of the pottery derived mainly from two structures within the enclosure: round-houses 458 (335 sherds) and 459 (156 sherds). Within 458, the largest concentrations of pottery came from entrance post-holes 44 (92 sherds) and 50 (80 sherds), with a further 28 sherds from post-hole 199 on the western side of the outer circuit. There is a radiocarbon date of 900–800 (AA-30679; 2715±50 BP) for post-hole 44. The group from round-house 458 includes ten diagnostic forms: seven LBA1, one MBA2, one LBA3 (Fig. 58, 4) and one LBA4 (Fig. 58, 5). A further 78 sherds derived from four-post structure 463 to the south-east of round-house 458.

Within round-house 459, concentrations occurred in entrance post-hole 60 (39 sherds), and in post-holes 54 (51 sherds) and 56 (44 sherds) on the eastern side, all three post-holes belonging to the earlier form of the structure. The seven diagnostic forms from this structure comprised four LBA1, two MBA2, and one LBA2 vessel (Fig. 58, 3). A radiocarbon date of 1520–1260 cal. BC (AA-30678; 3125±50 BP) was obtained from a post-hole of the earlier phase, but the associated pottery is undiagnostic. The significance of the spatial distribution of the pottery (and other artefacts) within the two round-houses is explored further below (Fig. 62).

The round-house structures and the enclosure ditch produced comparable assemblages in terms of fabrics (Table 28). All three groups are dominated by grog-tempered fabric G4, and all three contained examples of chert-tempered and granitic fabrics; sanidine fabric R8 occurred only in the enclosure ditch, and volcanic fabric R3 only in the ditch and in structure 458. In terms of forms, there are some contrasts; the internally bevelled variants of MBA2 vessels occurred only in the enclosure ditch, and the only other diagnostic form was a single example of an LBA1 form, while the round-houses together produced examples of all five forms represented on the site.

Discussion

In terms of cultural affinities, the assemblage from Hayne Lane can be compared with that from Castle Hill; a range of similar fabric types (grog-tempered and rock-tempered) is represented, and some of the same vessel forms (MBA2, LBA1, LBA2). At Hayne Lane, however, the emphasis is on the later forms, and this is consistent with the radiocarbon dates from the two sites. While grog-tempered fabrics dominate both assemblages, and both also contain locally-produced chert-tempered fabrics, the fabric series from Hayne Lane also includes examples of regionally-produced fabrics in petrological groups not represented at Castle Hill (sanidine and granitic). Decoration and vessel forms typical of Trevisker styles, which are relatively common at Castle Hill, are scarce at Hayne Lane. The most common vessel form recorded is the smaller, plain jar with inturned rounded rim (LBA1) as opposed to the more decorative bucket shaped jars with flattened expanded rims (MBA2) recorded at Castle Hill. MBA2 forms do occur at Hayne Lane, including some in grog-tempered fabrics similar to the Castle Hill examples, but also present are two examples with internally bevelled rims, both in regionally-produced fabrics (granitic and sanidine respectively), which are not paralleled at Castle Hill. In terms of the range of vessel forms, the assemblage from Hayne Lane is broadly comparable with that from Dainton, which has been tentatively dated to the 10th century BC on the grounds of metalworking evidence (Silvester 1980, fig. 9; although note that a recent review (Needham *et al.* 1997) of radiocarbon dates for Wilburton metalwork potentially pushes the dating for this site back to the 12th century BC), and provides further evidence for a general pattern in the south-west of the replacement of Trevisker-style wares by plainer wares at this period (*ibid.*, 29). Other comparisons further afield can be sought with the Late Bronze Age 'post-Trevisker' (Quinnell 1994b, 77) components of assemblages from Norton Fitzwarren and Brean Down (Woodward 1989, fig. 19, nos 27–8; Woodward 1990, figs 93–5).

The apparent longevity of the site suggested by the radiocarbon dates (spanning 1520–800 cal. BC) is not reflected in the fairly homogeneous pottery assemblage. The occurrence of different fabric types in the same feature does not appear to be chronologically significant; rock-tempered fabrics are often associated with grog-tempered fabrics and there is no reason to suppose that they are not contemporaneous. The small number of sherds in the sandy fabrics also occur in a small number of features mixed with both grog-tempered and rock-tempered fabrics.

List of illustrated sherds
(Fig. 58)

1. Jar with inturned rounded rim (form LBA1), fabric G4. PRN 731, context 352, pit 350.
2. Jar with expanded and internally bevelled rim (form MBA2), fabric R8. PRN 745, context 432, enclosure ditch (west) 390.
3. Jar with neck constriction and everted rim (form LBA2), fabric G4. PRN 625, context 55, post-hole 56 in round-house 459 (first phase).
4. Shouldered jar with inturned rim, folded over (form LBA3), fabric G4. PRN 621, context 49, post-hole 50 in round-house 458.
5. Lid (form LBA4), fabric G4. PRN 619, context 49, post-hole 50 in round-house 458.

Other Objects of Fired Clay,
by M. Laidlaw

A total of 133 fragments of fired clay was recovered including three complete loomweights and two loomweight fragments. All five loomweights are cylindrical with impressed decoration and are in a range of sizes (Fig. 59, 1–4). The fabrics are similar, moderately soft and sandy with rare large stone inclusions. The three complete weights came from round-house 459 (post-holes 56 and 60), one weight fragment from pit 115 within round-house 458, and the second fragment from evaluation pit 554 (Fig. 63). All five weights are of a well-known type characteristic of the Bronze Age in southern England. The remaining fired clay fragments are small, abraded, featureless fragments found dispersed in small quantities across the site.

Illustrated objects
(Fig. 59)
1. Small cylindrical loomweight, impressed decoration at either end. ON 4, context 55, post-hole 56, round-house 459.
2. Medium cylindrical loomweight, impressed decoration at either end. ON 2, context 55, post-hole 56, round-house 459.
3. Large cylindrical loomweight, impressed decoration at either end. ON 1, context 59, post-hole 60, round-house 459.
4. Fragment of cylindrical loomweight, horizontal band of impressed decoration. Context 116, pit 115, round-house 458

Environmental Analyses

Charred Plant Remains, by A.J. Clapham

The charred plant macrofossil assemblages from Hayne Lane are the richest of all those from sites of prehistoric date analysed by the project in terms of number of taxa identified and the number of plant remains recovered. The majority of the macrofossils were well preserved allowing a high level of identification. In some cases the samples were sub-sampled and the size of the sample analysed is indicated in parentheses next to the volume of the sample in Tables 29–31.

Enclosure ditch 19 (section D, context 68)
The plant macrofossils from the best-preserved ditch sample still proved to be poorly preserved (Table 29). Hulled barley (*Hordeum vulgare*) was identified but it was not possible to determine whether this was six- or two-row because of the lack of barley rachis fragments. No other cereal remains were recovered, but weed species identified include *Chenopodium album* (fat-hen), blinks (*Montia fontana* ssp. *chondrosperma*), and a speedwell (*Veronica* sp.). Both fat-hen and the speedwell are indicative of disturbed habitats, while blinks indicates damp habitats which may reflect the location of the site above the floodplain of the River Otter.

Round-house 459
Eight samples samples from post-holes forming part of the round-house or lying within it were analysed. The preservation was good enough to allow identification of most of the remains (Table 29).

The only remains of crops were five fragments of indeterminate cereal grains but seeds of fat-hen, pale persicaria (*Persicaria lapathifolia*), vetch, and cleavers (*Galium aparine*) were found in small numbers. All these species are associated with arable and disturbed habitats, which are most likely to be found in the local area.

A large number of cultivated plant taxa was only found in post-hole 56, which formed part of a porch. A large quantity of hulled barley grains (107) and two grains of naked barley were recovered, as was spelt (*T. spelta*) chaff in the form of glume bases. Emmer wheat (*Triticum dicoccum*) chaff, also in the form of glume bases, and spelt wheat grain were also found, but the most common cereal taxon was that of indeterminate

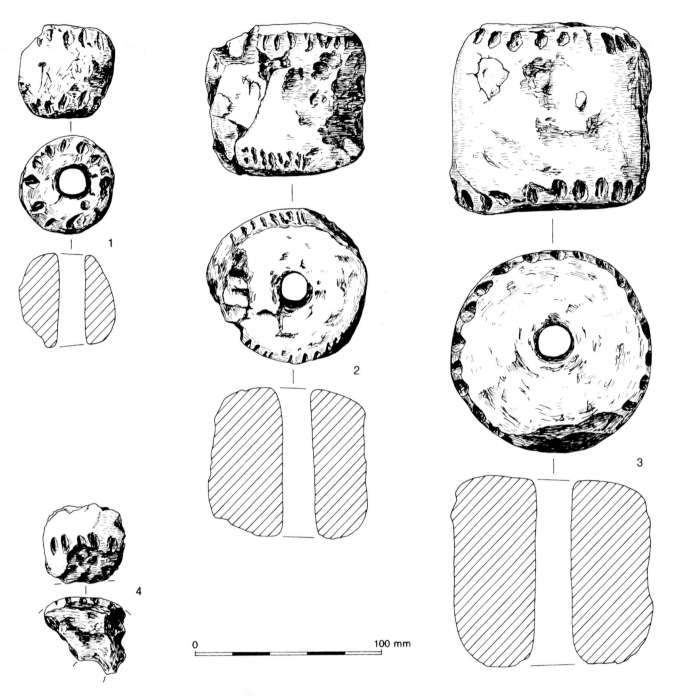

Figure 59   Hayne Lane: clay loomweights. Scale 1:2

cereal grain fragments. Other cultivated plants identified include a single fragment of flax (*Linum usitatissimum*) and finds of celtic bean (*Vicia faba*). Possible wild food resources are indicated by the finds of hazel (*Corylus avellana*) nutshell fragments.

The weed seeds found in small numbers in most samples are indicative of open and disturbed habitats such as agricultural fields. The species include fat-hen, chickweed (*Stellaria media*), redshank (*Persicaria maculosa*), pale persicaria (*Persicaria lapathifolia*), knotweed (*Polygonum aviculare*), black bindweed (*Fallopia convolvulus*), sheep's sorrel (*Rumex acetosella*), dock (*Rumex* sp.), vetches and vetchlings (*Vicia/Lathyrus* sp.), clover (*Trifolium* sp.), ribwort

plantain (*Plantago lanceolata*), cleavers (*Galium aparine*), stinking mayweed (*Anthemis cotula*), and corn marigold (*Chrysanthemum segetum*). Other possible cornfield weeds include, meadow grass (*Poa* type) and false oat-grass (*Arrhenatherum elatius*), including a tuber of onion couch grass (*A. elatius* var *bulbosum*). A single grass culm node was also recovered.

Round-house 458

Thirteen samples were analysed from features associated with this house. Three samples were from pits, eight were from post-holes of the round-house, and two were from post-holes from four-post structures outside the house (Tables 30–1).

Table 29: Hayne Lane, charred plant remains from enclosure ditch 19 and round-house 459

Feature group	Enc. ditch 19	Round-house 459						
Feature type	ditch	Post-holes						
Feature	19D	283	287	56	58	235	255	263
Context	68	284	288	55	57	236	256	264
Sample	3	91	93	73	79	70	82	83
Flot size (ml)	810(50)	50	60	110	40	90	60	150(20)
Cereal remains and other crops								
Triticum spelta grain	–	–	–	–	1	–	–	–
glume bases	–	–	–	5	–	–	–	–
T. dicoccum glume bases	–	–	–	1	2	–	–	–
Triticum sp. grain	–	–	–	2	–	3+3f	–	–
spkelet forks	–	–	–	–	1	–	–	–
glume bases	–	–	–	2	–	1	–	–
Hordeum vulgare hulled grain	16	–	–	107+35f	–	–	2	–
hulled tail grain	–	–	–	–	–	1	–	–
naked grain	–	–	–	2	–	–	–	–
Cerealia indet.	–	8f	5f	161f	4f	–	2f	83f
Vicia faba	–	–	–	–	–	–	1	30f
Linum usitatissimum	–	–	–	1f	–	–	–	–
Weeds								
Ranunculus ficaria tuber	–	–	–	–	–	–	1	–
Corylus avellana nutshell	–	–	–	–	–	–	1f	23f
Chenopodium album	16	–	–	–	1f	1	–	–
Chenopodium sp.	–	–	2+1f	4+3f	–	–	9	–
Montia fontana	16	–	–	–	–	–	–	–
Stellaria media	–	–	–	–	–	–	–	8
Persicaria maculosa	–	–	–	–	2	–	–	8
P. lapathifolia	–	–	1+1f	1	1	1	–	–
Polygonum aviculare	–	–	–	–	–	–	1	–
Fallopia convolvulus	–	–	–	1	–	–	–	–
Rumex acetosella	–	–	–	–	–	–	1	–
Rumex sp.	–	–	–	–	–	–	7+1f	–
Polygonaceae	–	–	–	–	1	–	–	–
Sinapsis sp. type	–	–	–	1	–	–	–	–
Vicia / Lathyrus sp.	–	1	1	8	–	–	1+2f	8+23c
Trifolium sp.	–	–	–	–	–	–	–	15
Plantago lanceolata	–	–	–	–	–	–	3	–
Veronica sp.	16	–	–	–	–	–	–	–
Galium aparine	–	–	2	2f	1f	–	3+3f	–
Anthemis cotula	–	–	–	–	–	–	1	–
Luzula campestris	–	–	–	–	–	–	1	–
Poa type	–	–	–	–	–	–	1	–
Arrhenatherum elatius rootlets/internodes	–	–	1	–	–	2	4	–
A. elatius var. bulbosum tubers	–	–	–	–	–	1	–	–
Bromus/Avena sp.	–	–	–	–	2f	–	–	–
Poaceae stems	–	–	–	1	–	–	–	–
Culm node	–	–	1	–	–	–	–	–
Small Poaceae	–	–	–	–	1	–	–	–

c = cotyledon; f = fragment

Table 30: Hayne Lane, charred cereal and other crop remains from features associated with round-house 458 and other features

Feature group	Round-house 458											4-post structure 646		Post-holes	
Feature type	Pits			Post-holes								Post-holes		Post-holes	
Feature	133	178	157	44	216	84	94	192	204	199	213	219	110	82	244
Context	134	179	158	43	217	83	93	191	203	200	212	220	109	81	243
Sample	27	45	41	2	61	8	10	48	55	56	59	65	17	133	75
Flot size (ml)	100(25)	400(50)	150(20)	220(54)	150(40)	200(40)	160	30	100	170	20	60	60	160(30)	150(18)
Triticum aestivum grain	–	–	–	–	–	–	–	–	–	–	–	–	–	–	–
T. spelta grain	–	–	–	–	–	–	–	3	–	–	–	–	–	–	–
tail grain	–	15	–	–	–	–	–	35	–	–	–	–	–	–	–
glume bases	12	–	–	–	8	–	–	2	–	–	–	–	–	–	8
spikelet forks	–	–	–	–	–	–	1	6	–	–	–	1	–	–	–
T. dicoccum grain	98+44f	8	8	144+112f	–	–	–	1	–	–	–	–	16+8f	–	16
tail grain	8	–	–	–	–	–	–	–	–	–	–	–	–	–	–
spikelet forks	–	16	–	–	–	–	–	4	1	–	–	–	–	–	–
glume bases	24	8	–	16	4	–	2	–	11	5	–	3	8	–	8
rachis fragments	–	8	–	–	–	–	1	–	1	1	–	1	–	–	–
Triticum sp. grain	–	–	23f	–	–	–	3+4f	12+18f	2	3	–	3	3	–	–
spikelet forks	4	8	–	–	–	–	–	2	–	–	–	1	–	–	8
glume bases	12	8	–	4	–	–	1	8	18	3	–	4	30	–	–
embryo	8	–	–	–	–	–	–	–	–	–	–	–	–	–	–
Hordeum vulgare hulled grain	100+28f	–	45+45f	196+24f	–	–	1	–	–	3+1f	–	1	–	–	–
Hordeum sp. rachis fragment	–	–	–	–	–	5	–	–	–	–	–	–	–	–	–
Avena sp. awns	–	–	–	–	–	–	–	–	–	–	–	1	–	–	–
Cerealia indet.	528f	8f	150f	–	4f	125f	39f	127f	105f	17f	–	9f	191f	110f	304f
Cerealia embryo	–	–	–	–	–	10	–	–	–	–	–	–	–	–	–
Vicia faba	4+4f	–	–	4+4f	–	5+5f	–	–	–	–	–	–	–	–	–
Pisum sativum	–	–	–	–	–	–	–	1	3small	–	1c(small)	–	–	–	–

f = fragment; c = cotyledon

Table 31: Hayne Lane, charred weed species from features associated with round-house 458 and other features

Feature group	Pits			Round-house 458								4-post structure 462					Pit
Feature type	Pits			Pits		Post-holes						Post-holes			Post-holes		
Feature	133	178	157	44	216	84	94	192	204	199	213	219	220	110	82	244	350
Context	134	179	158	43	217	83	93	191	203	200	212	220	220	109	81	243	352
Sample	27	45	41	2	61	8	10	48	55	56	59	65	65	17	133	75	112
Flot size (ml)	100(25)	400(50)	150(20)	220(54)	150(40)	200(40)	160	30	100	170	20	60	60	60	160(30)	150(18)	620(34)
Ranunculus ficaria tuber	–	–	–	–	8f	–	–	–	–	–	–	–	–	–	–	–	–
R. subgenus Ranunculus	4	–	–	20	–	5	3+2f	–	–	–	–	–	–	–	–	–	–
Papaver sp.	–	–	–	4	–	–	–	–	–	–	–	–	–	–	–	–	–
Corylus avellana nutshell	–	8	8	32f	–	–	–	–	10f	–	–	1f	–	–	5f	8f	612
Chenopodium polyspermum	–	–	–	–	–	–	–	–	–	1	–	–	2	–	–	–	–
C. album	–	16+8f	–	–	–	–	2+1f	–	2+2f	–	–	10+5f	–	–	–	–	–
Chenopodium sp.	8	–	8	8	4f	10	–	–	–	–	3	–	–	–	–	–	–
Atriplex sp.	–	–	–	–	–	–	2+1f	–	–	1f	–	–	–	–	–	–	–
Stellaria media	4	–	–	40	–	–	2	–	–	–	–	–	3	–	–	–	–
S. holostea	–	–	–	–	–	–	–	–	1	–	–	–	–	–	–	–	–
S. graminea	–	–	–	–	–	5	–	–	–	–	–	–	–	–	–	–	–
Spergula arvensis	–	–	–	–	–	–	–	1	–	–	1	–	–	–	–	–	–
Persicaria maculosa	–	–	8	–	–	5f	2	–	–	1	3+2f	1	–	–	–	–	–
P. lapathifolia	–	–	–	–	–	–	–	1	–	–	–	1	–	–	10f	–	–
Fallopia convolvulus	–	–	–	–	–	5f	–	–	–	–	–	1	–	–	–	–	–
Rumex acetosella	56	–	–	80	4	–	19	1	–	–	–	–	1	–	–	–	–
Rumex sp.	108	–	38	372	–	85	39+1f	–	2	–	1	1	–	–	–	–	–
Polygonaceae	–	–	8	12	–	5	–	–	1f	–	–	–	–	1	–	–	–
Malva sylvestris	–	–	–	–	–	–	–	–	1	–	–	–	–	–	–	–	–
Lepidium sativum	–	–	–	–	–	–	–	–	–	1	–	–	–	–	–	–	–
Erica tetralix leaf frags	–	–	–	–	–	–	1	–	–	–	–	–	–	–	–	–	–
Rubus fruticosus	–	–	–	–	–	5f	–	–	–	–	–	–	–	–	–	–	–
Prunus spinosa	–	–	23f	–	–	–	–	4f	–	–	–	–	–	–	5+10f	–	–
Vicia cracca	–	–	–	–	–	–	–	–	–	–	1	–	–	–	–	–	–
V. hirsuta	–	–	–	4	–	–	–	–	–	–	–	–	2	–	–	–	–
V. tetrasperma	–	–	8	–	–	–	–	–	–	–	–	–	–	–	–	–	–

	Round-house 458											4-post structure 462				Pit
Feature type	*Pits*					*Post-holes*						*Post-holes*				
Feature	133	178	157	44	216	84	94	192	204	199	213	219	110	82	244	350
Context	134	179	158	43	217	83	93	191	203	200	212	220	109	81	243	352
Sample	27	45	41	2	61	8	10	48	55	56	59	65	17	133	75	112
Flot size (ml)	100(25)	400(50)	150(20)	220(54)	150(40)	200(40)	160	30	100	170	20	60	60	160(30)	150(18)	620(34)
Vicia / Lathyrus sp.	28+20c	–	8+15c	64+20c	–	–	6+17c	–	2+3c+1f	1+4c	–	3+7c	2c	15c	8c	–
Melilotus sp.	4	–	–	20	–	–	–	–	1	–	–	–	–	–	–	–
Trifolium sp.	20	–	–	44	–	35	21+2f	–	–	–	1	–	–	–	–	–
Linum catharticum	–	–	–	4	–	5	–	–	–	–	–	–	–	–	–	–
Solanum nigrum	4	–	–	–	–	–	–	–	–	–	–	2	–	–	–	–
Prunella vulgaris	24+4f	–	8	64+4f	–	5	13	–	–	–	–	–	–	–	–	–
Plantago lanceolata	40	–	–	64	–	30	7+1f	–	1	1	1	–	1	–	–	–
Veronica arvensis	–	–	–	–	–	–	1	–	–	–	–	–	–	–	–	–
V. agrestris	–	–	–	8	–	–	–	–	–	–	–	–	–	–	–	–
Galium aparine	12+4f	–	–	44+4f	–	20+15f	17+17f	–	2+1f	–	2+1f	–	–	–	–	–
Lapsana communis	–	–	–	12+8f	–	–	3+6f	–	–	–	–	–	–	–	–	–
Chrysanthemum segetum	–	–	–	–	4	–	–	–	–	–	–	–	–	–	–	–
Leucanthemum vulgare	–	–	–	4	–	–	–	–	–	–	–	–	–	–	–	–
Tripleurospermum inodorum	–	–	–	–	–	–	1	–	–	–	–	–	–	–	–	–
Carex sp. (biconvex)	–	–	–	–	–	–	1	–	–	–	–	–	–	–	–	–
Carex sp. (trigonous)	–	–	–	–	–	–	–	–	–	–	–	–	–	5	–	–
Chrysanthemum segetum	–	–	–	4	–	–	–	–	–	–	–	–	–	–	–	–
Lolium type	64+28f	–	8	148+88f	–	100+35f	28+20f	–	–	–	–	–	–	–	–	–
Poa type	36	–	–	248	–	38	–	–	–	–	–	–	–	–	–	–
Arrhenatherum elatius culm bases	1	–	–	–	4	–	–	–	–	–	–	–	2	–	–	–
rootlets/internodes	4	–	–	128	–	135f	23	3	–	4	3	–	–	–	–	–
A. elatius var. *bulbosum* tubers	20+4f	8	–	16	–	–	–	–	–	–	–	–	–	–	–	–
Avena sp.	–	–	–	20	–	5	–	–	–	–	–	–	–	–	–	–
Phleum type	20	–	–	32	–	60	–	–	–	–	–	–	–	–	–	–
Bromus hordeaceus ssp. *hordeaceus*	8+12f	–	–	32+36f	–	–	7+31f	–	–	–	–	–	–	–	–	–
Bromus sp.	4	–	–	60f	–	–	–	–	–	–	–	–	–	–	–	–
Bromus / Avena sp.	–	–	–	–	4f	5+75f	–	–	–	–	–	1	2	–	2	–
cf *Elytrigia repens*	–	–	–	4	–	–	–	–	–	–	–	–	–	–	–	–

Table 31: (continued)

Feature group	Pits			Round-house 458								4-post structure 462		Post-holes		Pit
Feature type	Pits			Post-holes								Post-holes		Post-holes		Pit
Feature	133	178	157	44	216	84	94	192	204	199	213	219	110	82	244	350
Context	134	179	158	43	217	83	93	191	203	200	212	220	109	81	243	352
Sample	27	45	41	2	61	8	10	48	55	56	59	65	17	133	75	112
Flot size (ml)	100(25)	400(50)	150(20)	220(54)	150(40)	200(40)	160	30	100	170	20	60	60	160(30)	150(18)	620(34)
Poaceae stems	–	–	–	–	–	–	–	–	2f	–	–	–	–	–	–	–
Culm nodes	–	–	–	–	–	15	1	1	–	–	–	–	–	–	–	–
Small Poaceae	–	–	–	–	–	–	1	–	3	–	–	–	3	–	–	–
Leaf frags	–	–	–	–	4	–	–	–	1	–	–	–	–	–	–	–
Parenchyma indet	–	–	–	–	–	–	1f	–	–	–	–	–	–	–	–	–
Unident.	–	–	–	28	–	–	20	–	7	–	–	–	–	–	–	–
Cenococcum geophilum	–	–	–	–	–	–	–	–	–	–	–	–	1	–	–	–

c = cotyledon

Pits / hearths 133, 157, and 178

All three samples from these pits or hearths contained remains of cultivated plants. Pit 178, which is thought to be a hearth, contained the smallest number of cereals, while pit 133 was the richest, containing a large number of emmer wheat grains and hulled barley grains (Table 30). Smaller quantities of emmer (including tail grains) and barley were recovered from the other pits. In comparison with the grain remains, the amount of cereal chaff preserved within these features is negligible. Emmer glume bases were found in samples from pits 133 and 178. Emmer spikelet forks were identified from pit 178, whilst glume bases of spelt wheat were only recovered from pit 133 (Table 30). Indeterminate wheat chaff in the form of spikelet forks and glume bases were identified from pits 133 and 178. No chaff remains in any form were identified from pit 157.

Other cultivated crops identified from the pit samples included the remains of celtic bean from pit 133. The hazel nutshell fragments recovered from pits 157 and 178 may represent a source of wild food.

A large number of weed seed taxa was recovered from the pits (Table 31), the majority of which are indicators of open and disturbed environments, such as those associated with agriculture or pasture. Species included chickweed, sheep's sorrel, dock, vetch, and cleavers. Grass species were also common in these samples but especially in pit 133. These were represented by *Lolium*, *Poa*, and *Phleum* types and, linked with species such as *Bromus hordeaceus* ssp. *hordeaceus*, *Prunella vulgaris* (self-heal), ribwort plantain, and *Leucanthemum vulgare* (ox-eye daisy), indicate the presence of rough grassland in the vicinity, which may well be present at the edge of a cultivated field. The presence of tuber and culm nodes of false oat-grass also indicates the presence of cultivated land. Although in some cases, the presence of this species may indicate the recultivation of previously abandoned land.

Post-holes

The ten samples from round-house 458 and four-post structures 462 and 464 were not a rich as the samples from the pits or hearths, with the exception of post-hole 44 which contained a large number of emmer wheat grains and hulled barley grains. Emmer glume bases and indeterminate wheat chaff were also recovered (Tables 30–1). Cereal remains were rarer in the other post-holes but the most common wheat find was of spelt grains. Emmer glume bases were also found.

Other cultivated species include celtic bean and pea (*Pisum sativum*). The size of these pea remains were small but they are too large to be considered as vetches and therefore probably represent immature peas. The presence of hazel nutshell fragments (although in small numbers) along with *Prunus spinosa* (sloe) may again represent the remains of wild food resources.

The weed species associated with the cereal remains are in general representative of cultivated and therefore disturbed habitats. Although indicators of grassland such as self-heal, ribwort plantain and the grasses, *Bromus hordeaceus* ssp. *hordeaceus*, *Lolium* type, *Poa* type, and *Phleum* type are also present.

Other features: pit 350 and post-holes 82 and 244

The sample from the shallow pit 350 was dominated by charcoal and the only plant remains were fragments of hazel nutshell (Table 31), the large number of which suggests that they may have been a wild food resource. Post-holes 82 and 244 both contained cereal remains, hazel nutshell fragments and sloe.

Discussion

Comparison between those features associated with round-houses 458 and 459

In terms of the number of taxa identified and the number of remains recovered the features associated with round-house 458 were by far the richest (Tables 29–31). The remains from pit 133 and possible hearths 157 and 178 may have been charred by the fires in or near to those features. The seeds of the weed species associated with cereal remains have at least one dimension of a similar diameter to those of the cereals, and the seeds would therefore be present amongst the cereals until the final hand-sorting before being cooked (Hillman 1984).

The charred plant remains from the post-holes of both round-houses are similar, but naturally they occur in smaller numbers than those found in the large post-holes or pits. The low numbers of cereals present may indicate that the weed seeds may simply represent the vegetation that grew at the bases of the round-houses.

The crops

The cereals recovered from this site included, bread, spelt, and emmer wheat, although the bread and spelt wheat were not present in such a large quantity as the emmer. The most common cereal identified from this site was hulled barley. The lack of chaff remains has made it difficult to identify the variety of barley but the presence of a number of twisted grains suggests that it was of the six-row variety. It is most likely that the wheat and barley were grown in the vicinity of the settlement, but the lack of cereal chaff suggests that the processing of the crops may have taken place elsewhere.

Other crops grown in the vicinity include, celtic bean, peas, and flax. The evidence for this latter crop is scant as only a few remains were identified. Wild food resources such as hazel nuts and sloes were probably exploited to supplement the diet of the inhabitants. These wild foods would have been widely available in the scrubby habitats that were likely to be present in the vicinity of the site.

The weed species

The majority of the weed species (Tables 29; 31) represent open and disturbed habitats, and are usually associated with cereal crops. It is interesting to note that many of the species identified have a climbing or scrambling habit, such as the *Vicia* species, *Galium aparine*, and *Fallopia convolvulus*, whilst others can grow tall, suggesting that the crops may have been harvested by uprooting, (Hillman 1984). Other species present within the samples, such as the grass types, (*Lolium*, *Poa*, and *Phleum*), *Bromus hordeaceus* ssp.

hordeaceus, *Prunella vulgaris*, *Plantago lanceolata*, and *Leucanthemum vulgare* suggest that an element of grassland was also present in the area, possibly at the edge of the cultivated fields. Other habitats represented include scrub, as represented by the finds *Corylus avellana* and *Prunus spinosa*, and wetland as identified by the presence of *Montia fontana* and the sedge (*Carex* sp.) nutlets.

The identification of *Anthemis cotula* and *Chrysanthemum segetum* from the samples suggests that two soil types were exploited. *Anthemis cotula* is often used to indicate heavy soils which do not drain freely and it is a very early record of the species (V. Straker pers. comm.). *Chrysanthemum segetum* is often found on sandy (or free draining) acid soils. These two soil types are reflected in the underlying geology of the site, which consists of Valley Gravel over Upper (Keuper) Marls (see above). The western part of the settlement lay on clay, which is usually poorly drained (therefore preferred by *Anthemis cotula*), whilst the eastern part was heavily gravelled, less clayey and better drained (suitable for *Chrysanthemum segetum*). However, due to the small number of finds of each species, this interpretation must be viewed cautiously.

Conclusions

The crops inlcuded wheat (bread, spelt, and emmer), six-row barley, celtic bean, peas, and flax, which may have been supplemented by the wild foods of hazelnuts and sloes. The crops were grown on both heavy poorly-drained and light, better drained soils as reflected by the underlying geology of the site. The weed seeds show that the majority of the species were associated with the cultivation of the crops with grassland also being present, perhaps at the edges of the cultivated fields. The presence of remains of false oat-grass may suggest that some of the land has been brought back into cultivation after being abandoned, though after how long is unknown. Other habitats exploited included scrub and wetland.

Charcoal, by Rowena Gale

Charcoal deposits were present, often abundantly, in many of the samples from the enclosure ditch, the large post-holes/pits and post-holes of round-houses 458 and 459, and pit 350.

Most of the samples examined were relatively large with many pieces of charcoal measuring more than 5 mm in radial cross-section. The samples from the following features sub-sampled: pit 113, 50%; enclosure ditch 19 section B, 50%; enclosure ditch 19 section D, 10%; post-hole 201, 50%. With the exception of the sample from enclosure ditch 19 section B (context 333) preservation was generally good. A summary of the results is given in Table 32.

Aquifoliaceae. Ilex sp., holly
Betulaceae. *Alnus* sp., alder; *Betula* sp., birch
Corylaceae. *Corylus* sp., hazel
Fagaceae. *Quercus* sp., oak
Leguminosae. *Ulex* sp., gorse and/or *Cytisus* sp., broom. These genera are anatomically similar.
Oleaceae. *Fraxinus* sp., ash

Rosaceae. Pomoideae: *Crataegus* sp., hawthorn; *Malus* sp., apple; *Pyrus* sp., pear; *Sorbus* spp., rowan, service tree and whitebeam. These genera are also anatomically similar. Prunoideae: *P. spinosa*, blackthorn.

Salicaceae. *Salix* sp., willow; *Populus* sp., poplar. These genera are anatomically similar.

Enclosure ditch 19

Sample 3 from section D was from a burnt layer towards the top of the ditch, perhaps dumped material, which consisted of burnt soil, stones, and charcoal. Charcoal was very abundant; a 10% sub-sample was examined and identified as oak roundwood, sapwood, and heartwood, blackthorn, willow/poplar and member/s of the hawthorn group. A sample (138) from the northern terminal of the ditch (section B), included rather poorly preserved and fragmented material. A 50% sub-sample was examined and identified as blackthorn. It was not possible to assess the maturity or the dimensions of the wood before it was burnt but an origin other than fuel may be relevant in this instance (see below).

Round-house 459

The charcoal from post-holes 287 and 326 was relatively abundant, consisting mainly of oak (roundwood, sapwood, and heartwood), although in post-hole 287 alder was almost as frequent. Both post-holes also included blackthorn, and hazel and willow/poplar in 287.

The samples from post-holes 60 and 263 included mainly oak sapwood and heartwood, with smaller quantities of alder, hazel, and ash; and, in addition, in post-hole 263, blackthorn and a member of the hawthorn group. Fast-grown oak and hazel occurred in both pits; the latter as roundwood (charred diameter 10 mm).

Round-house 458, and four-post structures 462–4

The charcoal from two pits (113 and 157) was selected for analysis. The material did not appear to have been burnt *in situ*. The charcoal from both pits contained a fairly wide range of taxa. Oak sapwood and heartwood, hazel, and blackthorn were common to the other large post-holes or pits, but willow/poplar, alder, birch, ash, member/s of the hawthorn group (Pomoideae), and gorse/ broom occurred more sporadically (Table 32).

The samples from the post-holes included a more or less similar range of taxa to that identified from the pits, and although many of the post-holes contained packing stones, it is unlikely that any of the charcoal derived from the original posts. Oak occurred in all contexts and alder, birch, hazel, blackthorn, gorse/broom, and member/s of the hawthorn group were also common, but ash, holly, and willow/poplar were less frequent (Table 32). Fragments of roundwood from fast-grown hazel with charred diameters of up to 20 mm and four growth rings, and blackthorn (charred diameter 6 mm) occurred in post-hole 44. The oak generally consisted of sapwood and heartwood although narrow roundwood/ twiggy material (charred diameter 4 mm) occurred in pit 135/137; member/s of the hawthorn group also consisted of roundwood (charred diameter 4 mm). A small piece of what appears to be coal was also present in post-hole 199.

Post-hole 201 had been truncated, making interpretation difficult. It contained a large quantity of charred oak sapwood and heartwood, and the absence of other taxa may be significant, especially when compared with charcoal identified from pits nearby. It is possible that the post-hole was either dedicated to a specific function which involved the use of oak fuel (perhaps somewhere close-by) or that deposits in the post-hole accrued only from an activity for which oak fuel was preferred.

Pit 350

Charcoal was abundant in the base of this pit and consisted of many large pieces up to 30 mm in length. The charcoal was predominantly oak, mainly heartwood with minimal sapwood, with a small quantity of hazel roundwood (charred diameter up to 7 mm), and member/s of the hawthorn group.

Discussion

As with the charred cereal grains and seeds, charcoal was particularly well represented at this site. In addition to its general abundance, a high proportion of the charcoal consisted of large fragments exceeding 5 mm square in cross-section. Oak occurred in all the samples except that from enclosure ditch 19, section B, and was usually the dominant taxon. In addition, most samples included material from a wide range of trees and shrubs including alder, birch, hazel, ash, holly, hawthorn and/or other members of the Pomoideae, blackthorn, willow/poplar, and gorse/broom (Table 32).

Few contexts showed evidence of burning *in situ* and in many instances the charcoal was accompanied by other types of burnt material, e.g., flints, pot sherds, and organic material. It is probable that in most contexts the charcoal had accumulated from dumped fuel debris; there was no evidence to suggest origins from structural components.

Samples from the northern terminal of the enclosure ditch (section B) and post-hole 201 (in round-house 458) differed from the others in that they each contained only a single taxon. The sample from the enclosure ditch, consisted of a large quantity of blackthorn. It would have been unusual for domestic fuel to consist only of blackthorn, particularly when fuel residues from elsewhere indicate the widespread use of multiple species. Alternative origins could include a burnt object or the clearance of blackthorn scrub (or possibly hedge) growing close to the ditch by burning. The sample from post-hole 201 included a large volume of oak sap- and heartwood, indicating the use of fairly mature timber or billets. The truncation of feature hampers its interpretation, but the large deposit of oak may have some associated significance (see above).

The round-houses appeared to have been reconstructed at least once, and as repairs must also be considered likely, it is possible that the charcoal relates to different phases of the buildings. In general, however, the taxa identified from the fuel residues associated with the two houses were more or less similar. The absence of birch, gorse/ broom and holly from round-house 459 may only reflect the absence of hearths within it.

Table 32: Hayne Lane, charcoal from Middle–Late Bronze Age features (no. fragments identified)

Feature	Context	Sample	Alnus	Betula	Corylus	Frax	Ilex	Pom	Prunus	Quer	Salic	Ul/Cyt
Enclosure ditch 19												
D	68	3	6	–	–	–	–	16	20	11r,s,h	–	–
B	333	138	–	–	–	–	–	–	51	–	–	–
Round-house 459 post-holes												
287	288	93	–	–	4	–	–	–	1	36r,h	1	–
326	327	105	25	–	–	–	–	–	1	29s,h	–	–
60	59	89	6	–	1	1	–	–	–	35s,h	–	–
263	264	83	20	–	2r	1	–	1	2	91s,h	–	–
Round-house 458 and four-post structures												
Pits												
113	114	19	–	–	20	4r	–	6	2	23r,h	8	–
157	158	41	–	–	6	–	–	–	1	7s,h	–	–
Post-holes												
84	83	8	–	–	5	1	1	1	–	144s,h	–	1
201	202	54	–	–	–	–	–	–	–	71s,h	–	–
44	43	2	3	–	25r	1	–	6	10r	10s,h	12	2
219	220	65	1	2	1	–	–	2	1	14s,h	1	–
110	109	17	4	–	–	–	–	5	–	6s,h	–	–
135/137	136/138	24	4	5	34	–	—	26r	7	43r,s	–	3
204	203	55	7	1	3	–	–	–	1	45s,h	–	–
199	200	56	1	6	21	4	1	13	12	15r,s,h	2	1
Pit												
350	352	112	–	–	10	–	–	10	–	96s,h	–	–

Key: *Frax = Fraxinus*; Pom = Pomoideae; *Quer = Quercus*; Salic = Salicaceae; *Ul/Cyt = Ulex/Cytisus*
r = roundwood (diam. <20 mm); s = sapwood; h = heartwood

Fuel and wood resources
Assuming that the bulk of the charcoal derived from domestic fuel residues, and there was no evidence to indicate the use of industrial fuel, it is clear that fuel was gathered from many sources. The small deposits of charred cereal grains and weed seeds probably entered the fuel residues through food preparation, but the general absence of chaff suggests that cereal processing waste was not used as fuel or tinder. The greater part of the fuel derived from local wood resources. Oak evidently provided the major portion, and it was apparent that billets or timber mature enough to have developed heartwood was preferred. Although some narrow roundwood and twiggy material was identified this was comparatively infrequent.

Alder, hazel, blackthorn, and hawthorn or other members of the Pomoideae also frequently contributed to the log-pile, whereas birch, ash, holly, willow/poplar, and gorse/broom were used more sporadically. Apart from willow and poplar, the other members of the last group provide excellent firewood, and their general paucity/absence in the fuel deposits, particularly those associated with round-house 459, may be attributable either to ecological changes that occurred during the occupation of the settlement or to differential species distribution at, or near to, the site.

Although some fragments from oak and hazel included wide growth rings indicative of fast-growth there was no conclusive evidence for coppicing. Open woodland or stands of trees growing in favourable conditions with plentiful ground water could show similar growth patterns.

Environmental evidence
The proximity of the site to the floodplain of the River Otter and other local streams may suggest that pastoral farming may have been more appropriate in this area than arable farming. Local woodlands may, therefore, have been quite extensive in this period, with minimal land clearance for arable or other crops.

The charcoal analysis identified a wide range of trees and shrubs, but predominantly oak. Although this bias undoubtedly reflects the excellent qualities of oak as a fuel, it none the less demonstrates that oak was common in the environs and probably formed the dominant woodland component. In addition, the high ratio of oak heartwood to sapwood suggests that local woodlands were populated either with mature oak trees or possibly oak coppice on long-rotation, although evidence for the latter was slight. Oak woodlands tend to establish on damp soils, often on heavy clay, but not in waterlogged conditions. Associated woodland trees at Hayne Lane probably included hazel, ash, and holly. Such woodlands would have been more likely on soils away from the floodplain. Birch and gorse/broom are indicative of acidic or impoverished soils; these may have grown in open or marginal woodland, glades or scrub, or possibly have formed closed communities with other shrubby species such as hazel, hawthorn, and blackthorn. The floodplain and local streams would have provided the ideal habitat for wetland species including alder, willow, and possibly poplar.

Conclusion

Large quantities of well preserved material were recovered, most of which is attributable to the disposal of fuel residues, probably from domestic fires. Firewood appears to have consisted mainly of oak logs including heartwood, although wood from a range of other species was also used including alder, birch, hazel, ash, holly, hawthorn and/or other members of the Pomoideae, blackthorn, willow/poplar and gorse/broom. Slight differences between the two round-houses were apparent in the selection of species for fuel, which may relate to the different functions of the buildings.

The species in the charcoals from the main enclosure ditch 19 (section D) were similar to those from the pits and post-holes associated with the round-houses, and probably also derived from fuel debris. The origins of the charcoal from the northern terminal, section B of enclosure ditch 19, from which a large volume of blackthorn was identified were more obscure.

Environmental evidence testified to the existence of a varied tree/ shrub flora in which oak probably formed the dominant woodland element. Although oak and hazel both demonstrated rapid growth patterns there was insufficient evidence to implicate coppicing or woodland management.

Magnetic Susceptibility,
by Hayley F. Clark

One hundred and thirty-nine magnetic susceptibility samples were taken from this site. The results were very varied, showing a wide range of levels of activity across the site (Fig. 64, below). The readings from the terminals of the enclosure ditch 19 were low. The readings from a cluster of post-holes situated south west of round-house 459 which included a four-post structure, and those from a cluster of post-holes to the west of round-house 459 including a three-post structure and two paired post-holes were also low.

Round-house 459 itself showed readings, which ranged right across the scale but were higher to the south and west and this may suggest different activity areas within the building. The highest reading came from post-hole 255, which was probably a structural element of the round-house.

The readings from round-house 458 varied but overall, they were higher than those from round-house 459. The highest readings came from post-holes 201 and pit 157 inside the round-house and post-holes 44 and 150 from the entrance. The readings again indicate greater activity in the south-west, probably indicating different functional areas.

The three four-post structures to the west and south-west of 458 each had one post that yielded a higher reading than the other three. This may be related to the entrance into the structure that the posts supported. However, the three- and five-post structures at the western end of the enclosure all gave low readings

Radiocarbon Dates, by Michael J. Allen

Five radiocarbon determinations were obtained (Table 33; Fig. 60).

Round-house 459 and Associated Features

Charcoal from the porch of round-house 459 (post-hole 287) and from the secondary fills in the western terminal of the enclosure ditch 19 both produced results earlier than those discussed below. The probability histograms show very little overlap with these later dates, there being at least 100–400 years difference (Fig. 60).

Table 33: Hayne Lane, radiocarbon dates

Context	Material	Lab. No.	Result BP	$\delta^{13}C‰$	Calibration BC (2σ)
Round-house 458, post-hole 44, single fill	Mixed charcoal*	AA-30679	2715±50	-26.7	900–800
Pit 113, SW of round-house 458, single fill	Mixed charcoal**	AA-30680	2730±55	-25.0	1000–800
Enclosure ditch 19, E side, dumped burnt material	Mixed charcoal***	AA-30676	2725±50	-25.6	1000–810
N terminal, enclosure ditch 19, secondary fill	*Prunus* charcoal	AA-30677	2980±50	-28.9	1400–1040
Round-house 459, post-hole 287, single fill	*Corylus* charcoal	AA-30678	3125±50	-28.2	1520–1260

* = *Alnus*, *Corylus* (roundwood), Pomoideae, *Prunus*, *Quercus* (sapwood), Salicaceae, *Ulex/Cytisis*
** = *Corylus*, *Fraxinus*, Pomoideae, *Prunus*, *Quercus* (roundwood), Salicaceae
*** = *Alnus*, Pomoideae, *Prunus*, *Quercus* (sapwood), Salicaceae

M. Stuiver and R.S. Kra eds. 1986 Radicarbon 28(2B): 805-1030; OxCal v2.15 cub r:4 sd:12 prob(chron)

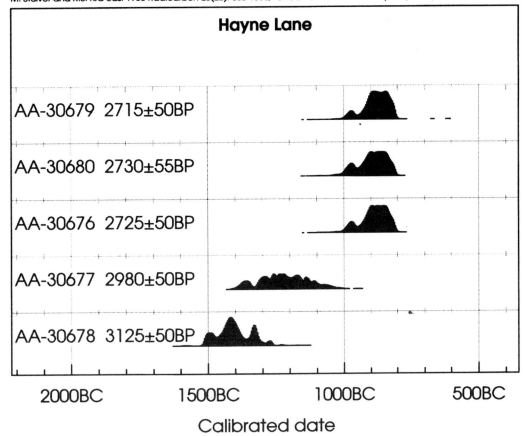

Figure 60   Hayne Lane: probability distributions of radiocarbon dates

The charcoal from the post-hole included hazel (dated), but also three other species (Table 33), and so does not represent the timber of the structure. The charcoal in the secondary fills of the ditch was dumped there.

Round-house 458 and Associated Features

Determinations from round-house 458, from pit 113 only 5 m south-east of the building, and from a deposit in the top of the adjacent enclosure ditch are statistically indistinguishable at the 95% confidence level, despite probably relating to different activities in the Bronze Age. As at least eight different wood species were identified, the charcoal in post-hole 44 is not from the timber post of the round-house (Gale above; Table 33). It may therefore be *assumed* that this charcoal represents activity associated with the structure (i.e. sweepings from hearths) that had found its way into the posthole during the life of the house, or after the post had been removed. The charcoal in the enclosure ditch was from a dump of material made late in its use.

Discussion

Despite the taphonomic ambiguities of some of the materials dated here, the results provide clear evidence for activity in the Middle Bronze Age at about 1500–1000 cal. BC and activity in the Late Bronze Age (1000–800 cal. BC). The Middle Bronze Age activity is broadly contemporary with that at Castle Hill and Patteson's Cross, but the Late Bronze Activity is later than most of the dated events on those sites.

Discussion, by A.P. Fitzpatrick

The majority of the oval enclosure was excavated revealing two or three round-houses set towards the rear of the compound with what appear to be four-post granaries standing front of them. In part the distribution of the buildings reflects the underlying geology, which is a heavy clay in the western part of the site, and a more free draining gravel in the eastern part. This variation in geology is also reflected in the carbonised plants brought in from the surrounding countryside to the settlement.

Two phases of occupation appear to be represented. The earlier is Middle Bronze Age, the later and apparently more significant, is Late Bronze Age. It is helpful to start with the dating evidence, which is modest and in places seemingly contradictory.

Dating and Sequence

The only recognisable *and dated* stratigraphic relationship was in round-house 459 where post-hole 287 was cut by the post-hole 285. Post-hole 287 yielded a date of 1520–1260 cal. BC (AA-30678; 3125±50 BP). It is not clear whether on its own, this replacement of 287

124

by 285 represents a repair, or a new building phase. The apparent pairing of post-holes 447 and 287 and post-holes 449 and 278 does suggest, however, that the porch was rebuilt at least once and it appears that the front of the building was also remodelled. Elsewhere it is equally difficult to distinguish between separate phases of building and repairs to an existing structure. This applies to both round-houses (e.g. post-hole 283 in building 459 and post-hole 199 in building 458). No other stratigraphic evidence for two phases was discernable but there is inferential evidence in that four-post structure 464 would seem to have stood right in front of the entrance to round-house 459 if they were contemporary.

One porch to round-house 458 is defined relatively clearly by post-holes 115 and 150 which have the characteristic oval shape created by the replacement of substantial timbers. A second porch is harder to define. Pit 133 appears to be the feature most likely to have supported the porch, with post-hole 115 being reused. This would echo the slight rotation to the west of round-house 459 in its second phase. The other Middle Bronze Age radiocarbon of date 1400–1040 cal. BC (AA-30677; 2980±50 BP) comes from the secondary fill of the north terminal of the enclosure ditch.

The Late Bronze Age radiocarbon date of 1000–810 cal. BC (AA-30676; 2725±50 BP) from the enclosure ditch on its eastern side is from near the top, in the tertiary fills. The stratigraphic position of the sample from which the date was obtained is consistent with a Middle Bronze Age enclosure continuing into the Late Bronze Age. The other Late Bronze Age dates are from round-house 458 (900–800 cal. BC; AA-30679; 2715±50 BP) and from pit 113 south west of round-house 458 (1000–800 cal. BC; AA-30680; 2730±55 BP). The longevity of the site attested by the radiocarbon dates is difficult to reconcile with the pottery assemblage or with the commonly accepted upper estimates for the life of timber round-houses (Harding *et al*. 1993, 103).

As a whole the pottery from the site is a homogeneous assemblage, largely of Late Bronze Age type, but there are small quantities of forms which originate in the Middle Bronze Age, but which do continue into the later Bronze Age (*cf*. Quinnell 1994b, 76). The examples at Hayne Lane could be typologically later than the Middle Bronze Age elements of the Castle Hill assemblage. One of these forms (MBA2) was found in the secondary fill of the southern terminal, which is consistent with the evidence of the radiocarbon dating.

There is insufficient diagnostic material from the primary fills for the enclosure ditch to confirm or refute that it was first dug in the Middle Bronze Age. In a few sections, though, what may be a recut is evident. The narrow step seen on the inner (western) side in two sections (Fig. 40, D and G) and the relatively shallow but broad ditch above the shallow slot in the base in section A, and perhaps in section B also (Figs 40, A–B; 41, A) may be all that remains of a first ditch which had been recut along part of its circuit.

One approach to the chronology of the site would be to be group only the dated features. For example, it could be argued that initially the enclosure contained only a few isolated features, such as post-hole 287, and that it was only later that the round-houses were built. But this

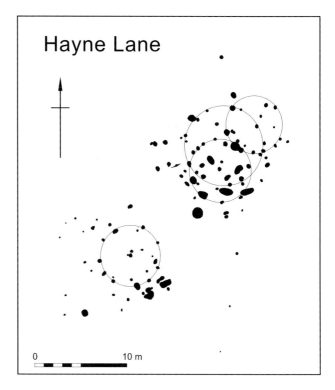

Figure 61   Hayne Lane: alternative reconstructions of buildings from the post-holes forming round-houses 458 and 459

would be to place an undue emphasis on those features with material suitable for radiocarbon dating, and it would require special pleading to separate the enclosure and the houses solely on chronological grounds.

It should, however, be clearly recognised that many of the perceived chronological difficulties arise from the presumptions of a continuous sequence of occupation, which may not have been the case and that the form of the settlement was essentially similar over time. The settlement could have been deliberately rebuilt, perhaps centuries later, on the site of an earlier, ancestral, one. It may also be that the post-holes interpreted here as the remains of sequential pairs of round-houses formed a rather different layout in an earlier phase which it has not been possible to determine. To disregard the seemingly inconvenient radiocarbon dates as being in some way 'rogue' dates has little to commend it.

The approach preferred here is to propose, with due caution, that the enclosure and houses are contemporary and to acknowledge the difficulties posed by the radiocarbon dates and the small and generally undiagnostic pottery assemblage.

Spatial Organisation

The precise details of the history of the settlement are difficult to disentangle from the plethora of post-holes, a familiar problem on sites of this type (Guilbert 1981, 308). Accepted at face value, and assuming that the features are all broadly contemporary, the organisation of the settlement recalls the well-known settlement module defined by Ellison at a number of Middle Bronze

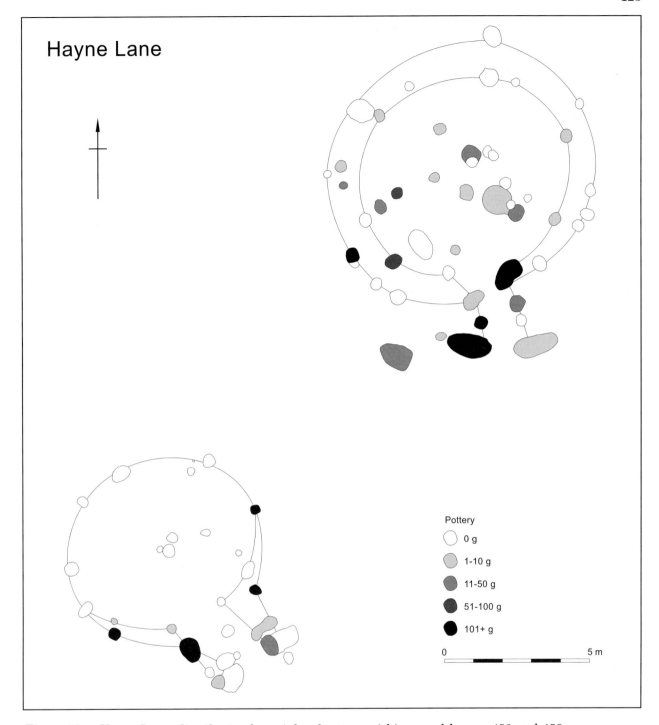

Figure 62   Hayne Lane: distribution by weight of pottery within round-houses 458 and 459

Age sites in southern England (1981; 1987; Russell 1996), including Shearplace Hill in southern Dorset (Rahtz and Apsimon 1962). The module consistes of a major residential house, an ancillary hut, storage facilities and areas for open air activities. Those interpretations have been developed using data from sites that have suffered relatively little disturbance from modern agriculture and where artefactual evidence is more abundant and animal bone is well preserved. Although some of those sites display evidence for rebuilding, it is not common and where it occurs it is usually immediately adjacent to the first phase, only rarely directly upon it. As a result it is difficult at Hayne

Lane to ascertain, for example, whether the double ring round-house 458 displays the axial symmetry seen so often in these buildings (Guilbert 1982).

Accordingly, the evidence from Hayne Lane is problematic and it is only possible, guided by those interpretations of settlement modules, to offer what is thought likely to be present amongst the mass of ill-focused data. The dating evidence from Hayne Lane would suggest that the settlement was laid out in this fashion in the Middle Bronze Age with occupation continuing into the Late Bronze Age.

Round-house 458 is interpreted here as a double ring round-house, perhaps the major residential house,

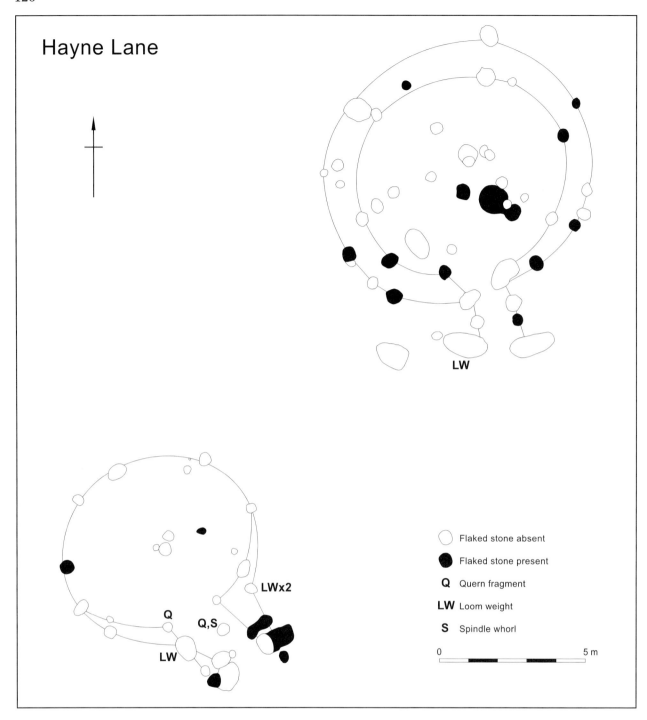

Figure 63   Hayne Lane: distribution by weight of flaked stone, and the presence of querns, loomweights, and spindle whorls within round-houses 458 and 459

while round-house 459 is the ancillary 'hut.' There is some evidence for the uses of these buildings, and this is clearest in round-house 459.

Three complete cylindrical fired clay loomweights were recovered from the inner post-holes of the phase 1 entrance of round-house 459, two from post-hole 60 and one from 56. A stone spindle whorl was also found in post-hole 58 also at the entrance to the building, but perhaps belonging to the phase 2 structure (Fig. 63). The fact that the loomweights are complete suggests that they are foundation deposits, with their placing perhaps

having been deliberately reversed when the second building was erected.

The loom weights signify that one of the uses of this building, perhaps the principal one, was the working of textiles. The postholes within the building could conceivably represent the settings for an upright loom as has been suggested at the contemporary site of Trevisker, which itself has a pair of houses, one of double ring construction, perhaps set within an enclosure (Apsimon and Greenfield 1972, 353).

All the fragments of quernstone from the site also come from 459, with fragments from postholes 58 and 241, both parts of, or within, the porch (Fig. 63). Most of these fragments are very small as the lava stone is very friable, and it is likely that they all come from one piece of a single quern stone. There is comparatively little pottery from round-house 459 (Fig. 62), but most of it is from what was the front of the house in both phases. The charred plant remains from the site are modest in number and the only feature to yield a large number of cultivated plant taxa was posthole 56, one of the inner supports of the porch of the Phase 1 building on the eastern side.

Apart from being a double ring round-house, building 458 is distinguished by a number of other features (Fig. 48). These include what are probably hearths, or where there are large quantities of pebbles or burnt stone, cooking troughs. The largest pit, 178 lies inside just to the west of the porch and contained much charcoal, burnt chert and quartzite pebbles and a fragment of fired clay, but no other finds. Pit 157 sited in the centre of the building was rather smaller and contained charcoal, pottery, fragments of fired clay and, notably, a little (4 g) burnt animal bone. Pit 151 also contained a significant quantity of charcoal, although there was less in 167.

One feature within the round-house which has been classified as post-hole, 201, contained a significant quantity of oak which may derive from billets, so it may be the truncated remains of a hearth. Other earth fast posts within the house(s) may represent internal partitions. Other methods of heating and cooking may be represented. Pits 133 and 113 lay immediately south-west of the round-house. Pit 133 contained a single fill, a heavily charcoal-flecked clay loam with many chert pebbles It is possible that this feature held a post for the porch of the second phase house. However, pit 113 was also filled with heavily charcoal-flecked silty loam and chert pebbles, some of which were burnt. There was no reddening of soil around the pit to show that the stone had been burnt *in situ*, but this would be consistent with the stones having been heated before being added to water in a cooking trough.

Round-house 458 also has a much greater quantity of pottery than round-house 459 (Fig. 62). The distribution of this material is blurred by the probability that there are two phases of the building, each on slightly different orientations. None the less, it is evident that the pottery is largely found in the front and centre of the house(s) and on the western side. There is very little pottery from the eastern side of the round-house(s). Most of the larger pieces of pottery come from the front of the house(s) and the porch(es), suggesting that it was used most intensively in that area.

Elsewhere within the building, the size and weight of the sherds are much smaller. Essentially the same range of pottery is found in round-houses 458 and 459, although the rare and potentially late forms are only found in round-house 458. This could reflect the use of a wider range of pottery, some of which had special uses. Likely as this may seem, in view of the difference in the size of the two populations little weight should be placed on this data. A single fragment of a loomweight was recovered from a post-hole 115 one of the outer post-holes at the porch to round-house 459. It is noticeable that it is fragmentary, in contrast to the complete examples from round-house 459.

The charred plant remains are also much more abundant than in round-house 459 and are represent the final stages of food preparation. Chaff is rare and there are few wheat glume bases and spikelet forks, particularly in the larger features such as the certain and possible porch foundations 44, 133, and hearth 157, which are most likely to have entrapped such evidence. The relatively high proportion of weed seeds in the assemblage from all of round-house 458 is likely to derive from the final hand sorting of cereals prior to cooking.

This evidence may be interpreted as indicating that the preparation, cooking, and probably consumption of food took place in the front and western parts of the house, while the occupants may have slept in the eastern parts. This pattern of use has been identified in Early Iron Age houses in Wessex (Fitzpatrick *et al.* 1995, 86–7, fig. 40). The more intensive use of the house is also borne out by the much higher magnetic susceptibility readings in round-house 458 compared to those in 459 (Fig. 64) Round-house 459 appears to have been used much less intensively. Spinning and weaving are suggested, and perhaps the storage of commodities in pots. The fragments of querns are very small but would suggest that some aspects of food preparation were undertaken in the round-house. Evidence of this sort has been interpreted as indicating a division of labour by sex, with some activities undertaken by females taking place in the ancillary hut, and perhaps of residence too (Drewett 1982, 342).

A number of two-, three-, and four-post structures, some of which may have been used to store unthreshed grain, stood around both round-houses. Midway between the round-houses and the entrance to the compound stood two separate groups of four-post or related structures (Fig. 39). If these groupings are contemporary, and not of successive phases, it is possible that they stood either side of a path to the houses. The western side of the enclosure could have contained middens as well areas of open space.

As the enclosure was not excavated completely (Figs 39 and 40) it is possible that there other structures within it. However, drains and ducts running along the verge of the old A30 road had destroyed any evidence within the unexcavated northern part of the enclosure. Only a small area at the south of the enclosure remains unexcavated, where it is possible that there was another entrance (above). However, as the internal bank, which may have been surmounted by a hedge or a fence would have covered much of these areas, it seems likely that most of the plan of the settlement has been recorded. On the evidence presently available it would appear that the houses were placed at the back of the settlement with – like many Middle Bronze Age houses – their entrances pointing to the south and south-south-east. This prescribed use of space and movement within the settlement may have been emphasised by the small enclosure 275, which would have guided access to the north of the entrance.

128

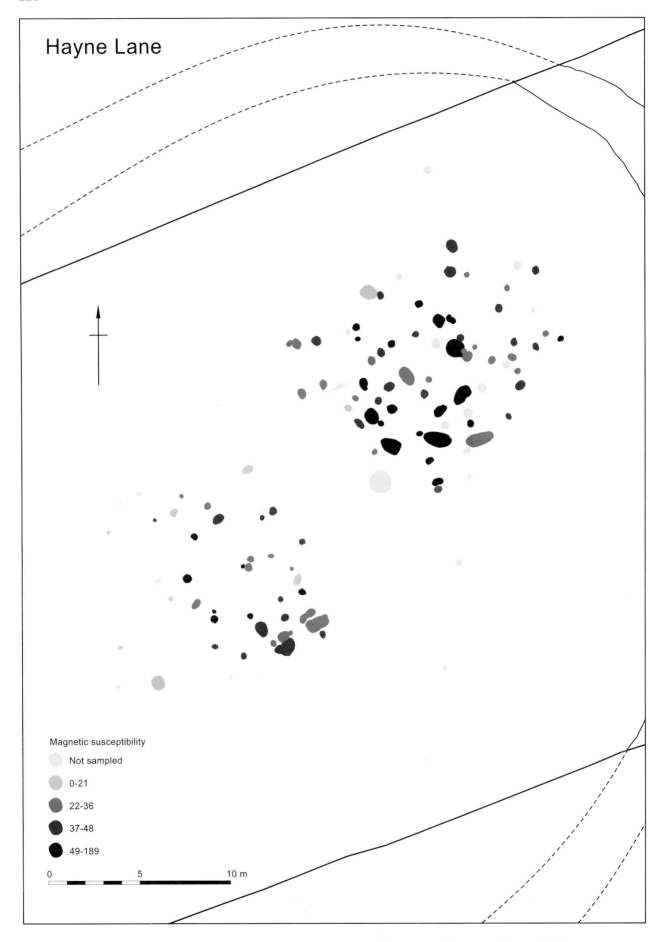

Figure 64   Hayne Lane: magnetic susceptibility readings within round-houses 458 and 459

Around them the people who lived in the settlement would have seen an open and cultivated landscape, with grassland also present. Areas of scrub and wetland as well as tracts of woodland were used. The charcoals from the site indicate that oak woodland predominated but holly, ash, and hazel were also present as well as trees such as willow/poplar which presumably grew close to the nearby River Otter. Despite the cultivation of a range of crops:- bread, spelt and emmer wheats, six-row barley, beans, peas, and flax; the landscape does not appear to have been intensively cultivated. The presence of false oat-grass at this site as well as the other sites of Bronze Age date, hints that some of the land was brought back into cultivation after a period of abandonment, a pattern which has been seen in Devon in recent times (Griffith 1994, 85–6).

6. Langland Lane

by C.A. Butterworth

Introduction

The site (W2414.15) was found *c.* 250 m west of the Middle Bronze Age site at Patteson's Cross during the watching brief over topsoil stripping (Pl. 13). The field in which it lay was one of five, which had been fieldwalked early on during the archaeological evaluation, but no finds were recovered.

Topography, Geology and Land-use

The site lay *c.* 250 m east of the River Tale, *c.* 300 m north-east of Fairmile, and a little over 100 m north of the existing A30 (Figs 65 and 66). The site was centred on SY 0910 9755. The ground sloped slightly from *c.* 71.5 m AOD at the north-west to *c.* 70 m AOD at the south-east. The underlying geology is Valley Gravel over Upper Sandstone and Lower Marls (Geological Survey of Great Britain, Drift, Sheet 326 and 340, Sidmouth). The main natural soil encountered was silty clay with gravel with occasional sandy patches.

The area had previously been under cultivation, but it was also the site of a Protestors' Camp immediately prior to the road building starting. As the site was first recognised as topsoil was being stripped by box scrapers, significant truncation of the archaeological features is likely to have occurred.

The Excavation

Once the site was identified, it was cleaned using mechanical excavators under constant archaeological

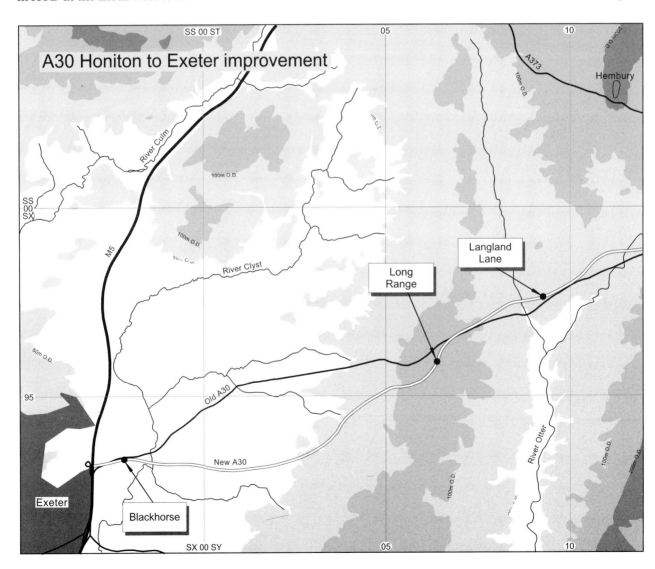

Figure 65   Location of the Iron Age settlements at Langland Lane, Long Range, and Blackhorse in relation to settlements known previously

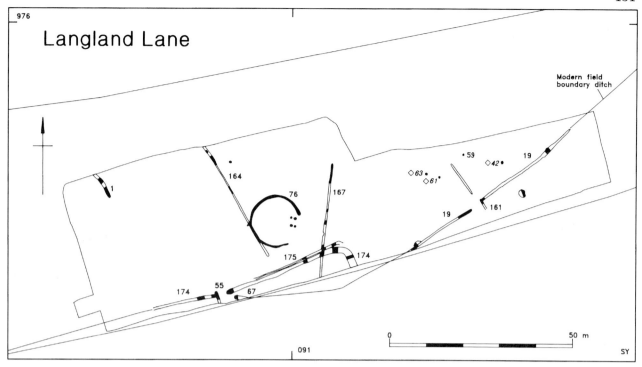

Figure 66   Langland Lane: plan of excavation

Plate 13   Langland Lane: the excavation, viewed from the east, surviving as an 'island' amongst the earth-moving. The River Tale, church of St Philip & St James's and woods of Fairmile are in the distance. Photograph (29 October 1997) by Bill Horner, Devon County Council. Copyright reserved

supervision. The total area investigated in October and November 1997 was 4623 m². A number of features of natural origin and a few widely dispersed post-holes (e.g. 61, 63; Fig. 66) were investigated but are not described here; further details are held in the project archive.

Results

The principal feature at Langland Lane, penannular gully 76, is dated to the Middle Iron Age by a single radiocarbon determination of 410–240 cal. BC (AA-30665; 2295±BP). Stratigraphic evidence suggests that some (ditches 164, and possibly 1 and 167) or all of the prehistoric linear features in the vicinity of the gully may be earlier in date. Post-medieval field boundaries were also recorded running across the southern part of the excavation area.

Ditch 167
This straight ditch crossed the site from north-east to south-west (Fig. 66). It terminated *c.* 10 m from the north-east corner of the northern edge of the excavation area but continued out of the trench to the south, and, in so doing, it was most probably cut by post-medieval ditch 174 and gully 175, although the stratigraphic relationship was not securely determined. The profile of ditch 167 varied from a wide, shallow V-shape (0.7 m wide, 0.19 m deep) to a vertical or steep-sided U (0.35 m wide, 0.27 m deep). It was filled with dark greyish–brown silty clay, from three pieces of chert were recovered.

Ditch 164
Ditch 164 ran from north-west to the south-east, and part of it was later recut and incorporated into

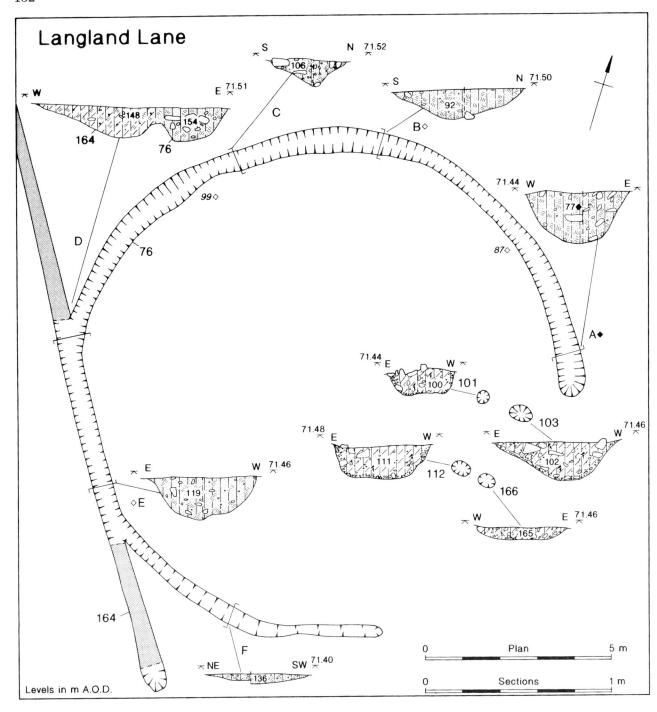

Figure 67   Langland Lane: plan and sections of penannular gully 76

penannular gully 76 (Fig. 66). The ditch was up to 0.68 m wide, had a maximum depth of 0.24 m, was rounded in profile and was filled with greyish–brown sandy or silty clay loam. A few flakes and chips of flaked stone were the only finds.

Ditch 1

Ditch 1, near the north-western corner of the excavation area, ran south from northern trench edge for a distance of almost 7.5 m before terminating (Fig. 66). It was up to 0.9 m wide and 0.35 m deep, sloping to a slightly rounded base *c.* 0.3 m wide. No finds were recovered from the single fill of dark reddish–brown silty clay.

Penannular gully 76

Penannular gully 76 had an overall diameter of almost 14 m and internal diameter of *c.* 12.5 m; the entrance faced south-east (Figs 66 and 67; Pl. 14). The gully was heavily truncated which may explain its irregularity in plan and the western side incorporated earlier ditch 164. The terminals were *c.* 8 m apart but the southern terminal and length of gully had been severely truncated by either topsoil stripping and/or cultivation. The size of the original gap in the gully can, however, be estimated from the positions of the better preserved northern terminal and of the four post-holes of the porch of the round-house. Assuming that the post-holes were

Plate 14   Langland Lane: penannular gully 76 fully excavated, viewed from the south-east

placed symmetrically relative to both terminals, the original gap would have been *c.* 4 m wide.

The gully had a maximum width of 0.74 m and maximum surviving depth of 0.27 m at the northern terminal but was elsewhere it was less than 0.6 m wide and no deeper than 0.14 m. Part of the western length of the gully incorporated the earlier ditch 164, which was recut here. In the better preserved lengths of the gully its sides sloped steeply to a rounded base, but elsewhere it was shallow, its base broad and flat, while only the base survived in much of the southern part. A single fill of a dark greyish–brown sandy clay loam, occasionally flecked with charcoal, was recorded throughout the whole length of the gully and all the pottery came from the northern terminal.

The porch measured *c.* 2 m by 1 m. Three of the post-holes, 101, 103, and 112, although truncated, were 0.63–0.33 m in width or diameter and ranged between 0.15 m and 0.21 m in depth. Both 101 and 112 were steep-sided with flat bases; 103 sloped more gently to a rounded base. The fourth post-hole, 166, was not well defined and, as originally excavated, was *c.* 0.5 m in diameter and only 0.07 m deep, with an apparently flat base. Further investigation to see if it was as large as the other three post-holes resulted in a deeper (0.23 m), but more angular and less convincing profile. All four post-holes were filled with mid greyish–brown silty loam. No other features survived within the gully.

Ditch 174 and gully 175
Ditch 174 and gully 175 crossed the southern side of the site from south-west to north-east (Fig. 66). Both features were thought to cut ditch 167. Ditch 174 had an overall length of *c.* 54 m but a gap 3.2 m wide separated it into two parts; the eastern part turned through 90° and continued out of the trench to the south; the western one petered out after *c.* 17 m. The ditch was at its broadest, 2.4 m, where it turned southwards, but was shallow with a maximum depth of 0.46 m; elsewhere it was between 0.57 m and 1.4 m wide and 0.11 m and 0.4 m deep. It varied in profile but most commonly had steep sides and a broad, flat, or almost flat, base. It was filled with brown to greyish–brown sandy silty loam. Fragments of clay pipe were recovered

from its western length, as were two pieces of flaked stone of prehistoric date.

Gully 175 was parallel with and *c.* 0.35 m north of 174 but was more truncated and could be traced for *c.* 25 m only. It also started to turn to the south at its eastern end but did not reach the edge of the excavation area. The gully was rounded in profile with a maximum width of 0.64 m and maximum depth of 0.29 m. Although no more than a single fill was recorded in any one section these ranged from dark brown sandy silty loam through dark reddish–brown to greyish–brown silty loam. Two pieces of flint were found in it.

Ditches 55 and 67
Two ditches, 55 and 67, approached the gap in ditch 174 (Fig. 66). Ditch 55 entered the trench from the south, passing *c.* 0.7 m east of the western terminal of ditch 174 and terminating slightly to its north. Rounded in profile and with steep sides, ditch 55 was 0.89 m wide and 0.38 m deep, and was filled with brown sandy silty loam. Ditch 67 ran towards the eastern terminal of 174 from the south-east but stopped *c.* 1.1 m short. It was slightly larger than ditch 55, 1.08 m wide and 0.41 m deep, but was of similar profile. The ditch contained a primary fill of reddish–brown sandy silty loam overlain by a similar but darker coloured secondary fill. There were no finds.

Ditches 19 and 161
Ditch 19 crossed the eastern part of the site from south-west to north-east on a similar but not identical alignment to and offset to the south-east of ditch 174 and gully 175 (Fig. 66). Ditch 19 was in two sections separated by a gap or entrance of *c.* 3.3 m, was again much truncated, having a maximum width of 1.1 m but a depth no greater than 0.15 m. It was filled with dark reddish brown to greyish brown silty loam. A second ditch, 161, ran towards and joined the eastern part of 19 from the south-east. It was of similar size and was filled with yellowish–brown silty clay loam. Another length of ditch ran north-westward after a gap of *c.* 2 m. Neither ditch contained any finds.

Finds

Flaked Stone, by Peter S. Bellamy

Twelve pieces of flaked stone, weighing a total of 168 g, were recovered (Table 34). The raw material used included both flint and Greensand chert, which was all, as far as it can be determined, derived from rolled nodules or gravel available in the immediate vicinity of the site. The vast majority of the pieces recovered were in a rolled condition. Only one piece, a broken bladelet of possible Mesolithic or early Neolithic date is worthy of note. Indeed, many of the other pieces may be accidental removals. The sparse scatter of flaked stone is likely to have been accidentally incorporated into the excavated features and represents no more than a background scatter of flaked stone debitage.

Table 34: Langland Lane, flaked stone by type

Context	Flakes	Broken flakes	Broken blades	Chips	Misc. deb.	Total
Chert						
Penannular gully 76	–	2/39	–	–	–	2/39
Gully 164	–	–	–	1/0	–	1/0
Gully 167	1/12	2/69	–	–	–	3/81
Gully 174	1/29	–	–	–	–	1/29
Sub-total	2/41	4/108	0	1/0	0	7/149
Flint						
Penannular gully 76	–	–	–	–	1/5	1/5
Gully 164	–	1/2	–	–	–	1/2
Gully 174	–	1/1	–	–	–	1/1
Gully 175	1/10	–	1/1	–	–	2/11
Sub-total	1/10	2/3	1/1	0	1/5	5/19
Total	3/51	6/111	1/1	1/0	1/5	12/168

Other Objects of Worked Stone, by Lorraine Mepham

Three joining fragments from a quernstone in Permian lava were recovered from ditch 167. One polished surface survives, but the form of the quern is uncertain.

Pottery, by M. Laidlaw

The small pottery assemblage from Langland Lane amounts to 53 sherds (61 g), all of which are small and abraded, and no diagnostic material is present. All the sherds came from two contexts in the northern terminal of gully 76, from which a radiocarbon date of 410–240 cal. BC (AA-30665; 2295±BP) was obtained.

The sherds are mostly in a moderately coarse, sandy fabric type (Q12), which has not been identified from any of the other sites examined during the current project. Three other fabrics are also represented, one grog-tempered (G4) and two sandy (Q2, Q11). Fabric Q2 appears to be a long-lived type; it occurs at the Iron Age sites of Blackhorse and Long Range, but also at the Bronze Age sites of Castle Hill, Hayne Lane, and Patteson's Cross. Fabrics G4 and Q12 also occur at these Bronze Age sites, so the sherd in fabric G4 may be residual here along with some of the flaked stone. Conversely, the only sherd in fabric Q11 from nearby Patteson's Cross was unstratified and could derive from the Iron Age activity at Langland Lane.

While this small and undiagnostic assemblage is not easily datable, a date within the Middle Iron Age, as suggested by the radiocarbon determination, would not be out of place.

Environmental Analyses

Charred Plant Remains, by Alan J. Clapham

Six samples from features certainly or probably of Iron Age date were analysed. Three samples were from penannular gully (ditch sections 87, B, and 99), one was from ditch 164 (ditch section E) and two from the undated post-holes 61 and 63 to the east of penannular gully 76 (Fig. 66). The preservation of the plant remains was poor and in general, the samples contained very few charred plant remains (Table 35).

Pennanular gully 76

The samples contained few charred plant remains and cultivated species were rare, with only one grain of emmer (*Triticum dicoccum*) wheat, two grains of indeterminate wheat grains (*Triticum* sp.) and three wheat glume bases from section B. No wheat remains were found in section 99, although one hulled barley grain was identified from this sample. The most common cultivated taxon was that of fragments of indeterminate cereal grains. The other charred plant remains found within the samples were indicative of arable or wasteland habitats with finds of fat-hen (*Chenopodium album*), sheep's sorrel (*Rumex acetosella*), smooth tare (*Vicia tetrasperma*), and cleavers (*Galium aparine*). Other arable indicators include tubers of onion couch grass (*Arrhenatherum elatius* var. *bulbosum*) in section 99 and rootlets of the same species in sections B and 99.

A hawthorn fruit fragment (*Crataegus* sp.) found in section 87 and a fragment of hazel nut (*Corylus avellana*) in section 99 may represent a scrub environment. These remains may represent wild food sources. The commonest taxon present in all of the samples was that of sclerotia of the soil fungus *Cenococcum geophilum*.

Ditch 164

The only remains of cultivated species identified from section E were of two indeterminate wheat glume bases and 11 fragments of indeterminate cereal grains. The other taxa found within the sample are indicative of arable/waste ground, with the dominant taxon within the sample being the sclerotia of the soil fungus *Cenococcum geophilum*. The rootlets of onion couch grass were also common.

Post-holes 61 and 63

The only cultivated plant remain from these post-holes was that of a single fragment of a cereal grain. The remainder of the remains are indicative of an arable habitat, with dock (*Rumex* sp.), oats (*Avena* sp.; represented by a single awn fragment), and onion couch grass rootlets present. However, the dominant remains

Table 35: Langland Lane, charred plant remains

Feature group		76		164		
Feature type		Penannular gully		Gully	Post-holes	
Feature / section	87	B	99	E	61	63
Context	86	92	98	119	62	64
Sample	1006	1008	1009	1013	1003	1004
Flot size (ml)	20	20	30	15	20	30
Cereal remains						
Triticum dicoccum grain	1	–	–	–	–	–
Triticum sp. grain	–	2	–	–	–	–
glume bases	–	3	–	2	–	–
Hordeum vulgare grain	–	–	1	–	–	–
Cerealia indet.	7f	24f	6f	11f	–	1f
Weeds						
Corylus avellana nutshell	–	–	1f	–	–	–
Chenopodium album	–	1	–	–	–	–
Silene sp. type	–	–	1f	–	–	–
Persicaria maculosa	–	–	–	1	–	–
Rumex acetosella	–	1	–	–	–	–
Rumex sp.	–	–	–	–	1	–
Crataegus sp. fruit frag.	1f	–	–	–	–	–
Vicia tetrasperma	–	2+1f	–	–	–	–
Vicia / Lathyrus sp.	–	–	–	3f	–	–
Trifolium sp.	–	–	–	1	–	–
Galium aparine	1f	–	–	–	–	–
Festuca sp. type	1	–	–	–	–	–
Arrhenatherum elatius var. *bulbosum* tuber	–	–	1+2f	–	–	–
A. elatius rootlets	–	15	48	51	7	10
Avena ap. awn frags	–	–	–	–	1	–
Small Poaceae indet.	–	–	1	–	–	–
Unident.	1	1	–	–	–	1
Sprout	–	–	–	–	1	–
Buds	–	–	–	–	–	2
Cenococcum geophilum	5	66	12	133	85	45

f = fragment

were again the sclerotia of the soil fungus *Cenococcum geophilum*.

Discussion
There is little evidence for the cultivation of crops at Langland Lane. A single grain of emmer, two indeterminate wheat grains, three glume bases, and a single barley grain were the only identifiable crops present. Other taxa present were indicative of an arable or waste ground habitat. The fragments of hazel nutshell and a fragment of a hawthorn haw indicate possible wild food sources. The most common remain was that of the sclerotia of the soil fungus, *Cenococcum geophilum* but because of its occurrence in a variety of habitats it is difficult to use this taxon as an indicator of cultivated fields (Jensen 1974). The small quantity and poor preservation of the remains makes it difficult to determine whether crops were cultivated or processed on the site. The other taxa present within the samples are indicative of arable or waste/open ground.

Charcoal, by Rowena Gale

Eight samples were examined and charcoal was extremely sparse. Although the deposits are too small to allow comparative analysis between features, they do provide information about the environment and local sources of fuel during the Iron Age. One sample (1001), from a burnt area on the eastern side of the site provided evidence for local fires and may well be of recent origin.

The charcoal samples were small, fragmented and poorly preserved. The results are given in Table 36 and described below. The taxa identified include:

Table 36: Langland Lane, charcoal (no. fragments identified)

Feature	Context	Sample	Alnus	Betula	Corylus	Prunus	Quercus	Salic	Ul/Cyt
Penannular gully 76									
A	77	1005	–	–	–	2	6r,h	–	9
87	86	1006	(1)	1	–	–	4h	–	10
B	92	1008	–	–	–	–	11s,h	(1)	–
99	98	1009	(1)	–	(1)	1	7s,h	–	1
Gully 164									
E	119	1013	–	–	–	(1)	1	–	1
Post-holes									
61	62	1003	–	–	–	3	3h	–	–
63	64	1004	–	–	–	1	1	–	–
Burnt patch									
42	41	1001	–	–	6	–	26s,h	–	1

Key: Salic = Salicaceae; Ul/Cyt = *Ulex / Cytisus*; r = roundwood; s = sapwood; h = heartwood; ( ) = unverified identification

Betulaceae. ?*Alnus* sp., alder; *Betula* sp., birch
?Corylaceae. *Corylus* sp., hazel
Fagaceae. *Quercus* sp., oak
Leguminosae. *Ulex* sp., gorse; *Cytisus* sp., broom. These genera can not be distinguished from their anatomy
Rosaceae. *Prunus* spp., which include *P. avium*, wild cherry, *P. padus*, bird cherry, and *P. spinosa*, blackthorn. It is often difficult to differentiate between the species but in this instance the structure was more characteristic of blackthorn
?Salicaceae. *Salix* sp, willow; *Populus* sp., poplar. These genera can not be distinguished using anatomical features.

Penannular gully 76

Charcoal occurred throughout this gully. Oak, roundwood, sapwood, and heartwood, was present in every sample. Other taxa identified included gorse/broom, blackthorn, birch, possibly alder or hazel, and willow/poplar.

Ditch 164 and post-holes 61 and 63

Charcoal from the point where ditch 164 was recut by the eastern arc of gully 76 was extremely sparse but included oak, gorse/broom, and possibly blackthorn. The two post-holes produced small quantities of oak and blackthorn.

Discussion

The charcoal from Langland Lane is likely to derive from fuel residues. A relatively narrow range of taxa was identified. Oak was present in every sample whereas birch, hazel, blackthorn, gorse/broom, and possibly alder and willow/poplar occurred more sporadically. Round-house 76 is nearby to the Middle Bronze Age round-houses at Patteson's Cross. Although neither of these sites produced much charcoal, a comparison of the fuels used at Langland Lane and Patteson's Cross suggests that they were gathered from a similar, or probably the same, environment.

Magnetic Susceptibility,
by Hayley F. Clark

Twenty-two magnetic susceptibility samples were taken from this site and their readings were consistently high across the site. It should be noted that a Protestors' Camp had occupied part of the site the previous year. The northern most post-hole (101) of the four-post entrance porch gave the highest reading. The readings from the two easternmost post-holes, 42 and 59, were lower than the two more westerly post-holes 61 and 63. The northern terminal of penannular gully 76 produced the highest magnetic susceptibility reading on the site.

The readings from this site may have been high as a result of modern contamination. Many of the samples for palaeo-environmental remains were rooty and contained uncharred weed seeds. However, the higher reading from the terminal of the eaves drip gully is coincident with the largest amount of pottery and this may indicate the disposal of refuse.

Discussion, by A.P. Fitzpatrick

Only the post-holes of the porch to round-house 76 and the gully had survived truncation. The radiocarbon date for charcoal from the north terminal of penannular gully 76, of 410–240 cal. BC (AA-30665; 2295±BP; Fig. 68) dates the round-house to the Middle/Late Iron Age. The dating of the pottery, if less precise, is at least not inconsistent with this. There were few other finds, a few pieces of flaked stone were also found in the penannular gully and in some other features, and three joining fragments of quern were found in ditch 167. Environmental evidence was similarly limited but some cereals were recovered, with seeds indicative of arable or waste ground. Charcoal, mainly oak, from the penannular gully derived from fuel rather than structural remains.

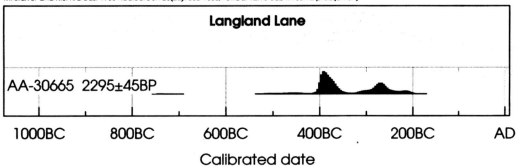

M. Stuiver and R.S. Kra eds. 1986 Radiocarbon 28(2B): 805-1030; OxCal v2.15 cub r:4 sd:12 prob(chron)

Figure 68   Langland Lane: probability distribution of radiocarbon date

Ditch 167, which is likely to have been cut by ditches 174 and 175, contained a few pieces of flaked stone and fragments of a quern. The apparent, but possibly fortuitous, reuse of an earlier boundary, 164, within penannular gully 76 is not seen at any of the other sites examined in the current project, although something similar may be seen at Long Range (Chapter 7) in the way that gully 69 approaches penannular gully 237.

The shared alignment of ditches 1, 161, and 164 at Langland Lane may suggest that they are of the same date and hint at the organisation of the landscape on a wider scale. As ditches 19 and the western arm of 174, which contained clay pipe, are shown on the 1891 Ordnance Survey map, this could be taken to suggest that the post-medieval field system echoes the layout of a prehistoric one. However, the slight dating evidence enjoins caution, and the possibility is beyond resolution on the evidence presently available.

7. Long Range

by C.A. Butterworth

Introduction

This site was identified by the geophysical survey during the pre-project evaluation as:

> a spread of relatively high magnetically susceptible topsoils some 80 x 30 m in extent, situated close to the B3180, [which] was investigated by gradiometer survey ... The resultant plot shows possible, though rather tenuous, curvilinear features. Soils in the vicinity contained several substantial pieces of burnt flint. (Johnson 1995, 3.64)

A trench 10 x 10 m was subsequently excavated by the Exeter Museums Archaeological Field Unit over this anomaly, revealing two small oval pits. A small quantity of undiagnistic prehistoric pottery was recovered from cleaning layers. It was concluded that there may have been a prehistoric settlement on the site and it was recommended for Strip and Record works.

Topography, Geology, and Land-use

The areas excavated (W2414.6) lay either side of the minor road B3180 on a ridge, West Hill, to the west of the River Otter (Figs 65 and 69). The excavation, centred on SY 0636 9592, which was on the crest of the ridge, was at a height of 160–163 m AOD.

The underlying geology consists of Budleigh Salterton Pebble Beds over Aylesbeare Mudstone. The bedrock exposed in the excavation trenches consisted principally of clay with intermittent patches of pebbles, but there was localised variation, with some areas of a more sandy, friable nature. Despite being on high ground, the soil drained very poorly in wet weather. The land to the east of the road was under grass at the time of the excavation but had previously been cultivated. Rhododendrons and some large trees had been felled and cleared from the area west of the road.

Excavation Areas

In the first instance two wide trenches (linked by a narrow trench at their northern ends) were excavated to the east of the B3180 within the 120 m long corridor initially recommended for Strip and Record works which included the area in which the geophysical survey and evaluation trenching had suggested prehistoric activity. This investigation did indeed reveal a number of features, and led to a second stage of clearance in the area between and around the original trenches. Further phases of trenching and stripping were subsequently carried out in the field to the north, the area of former woodland west of the B3180, and around and between the eastern trenches. The full investigation running between December 1996 and August 1997. The total area investigated was 7998 m^2 and was retrospectively reclassified as an excavation rather than a Strip and Record area (Fig. 69). A number of features of natural origin and a few widely dispersed possible post-holes were investigated but are not described here; details can be found in the project archive.

Results

Neolithic

Pit 241

Amongst the few features to the west of the B3180 road, a single pit, 241, contained sherds of Early Neolithic pottery and three pieces of flaked stone (Fig. 69). The pit was 0.41 m in diameter and had a maximum depth of 0.08 m. It was filled with light yellowish–brown sandy loam in which charred tubers of lesser celandine and a little oak charcoal were also present. In the area to the east of the road, a flint ovate of Neolithic date, broken and patinated in antiquity, was found in Iron Age pit 26.

Iron Age

The majority of features, including two complete penannular gullies and fragments of others, several post-built structures, a number of which may be three-post structures, and a number of post-holes and small pits, date to the Middle–Late Iron Age date. Radiocarbon dates from the two complete penannular gullies indicate that 269 was the earlier, with a date of 400–100 cal. BC (GU-7845; 2220±70 BP); a date of 350 cal. BC–cal. AD 10 (AA-30663; 2090±45 BP) was obtained for gully 4. It is assumed that the gullies surrounded buildings but few features were located within them and no traces of walls remained.

Penannular gully 269

Penannular gully 269 had an overall diameter of c. 15 m, an internal diameter of c. 13 m and an entrance 5.4 m wide which faced slightly south of east (Figs 69 and 70). The northern terminal, at c. 1.45 m wide and 0.64 m deep, provided the largest, but also one of the most poorly-defined, sections; elsewhere the gully was between 0.85 m and 1.22 m wide and 0.31–0.58 m deep. In profile it was generally symmetrical, V-shaped with steep sides. With the exception of the terminals and one section at the north-west side, each cutting contained one homogeneous fill, although this varied from reddish–brown sandy clay through yellowish–brown sandy clay, light greyish–brown clay loam to light brown sandy loam. A primary fill of silty loam sealed by a

Figure 69   Long Range: location and plan of excavation

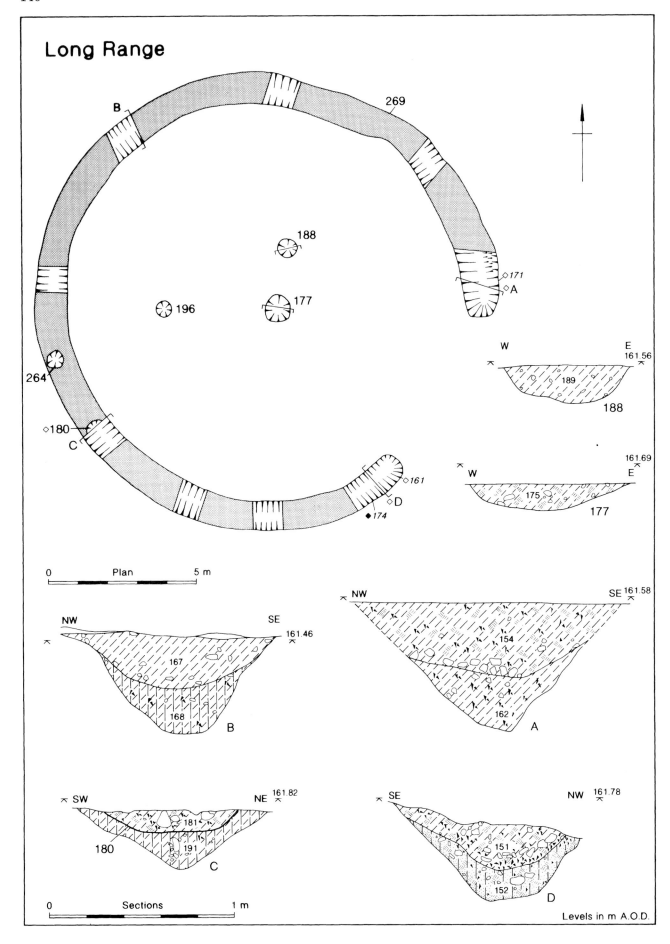

Figure 70   Long Range: plan and sections of penannular gully 269

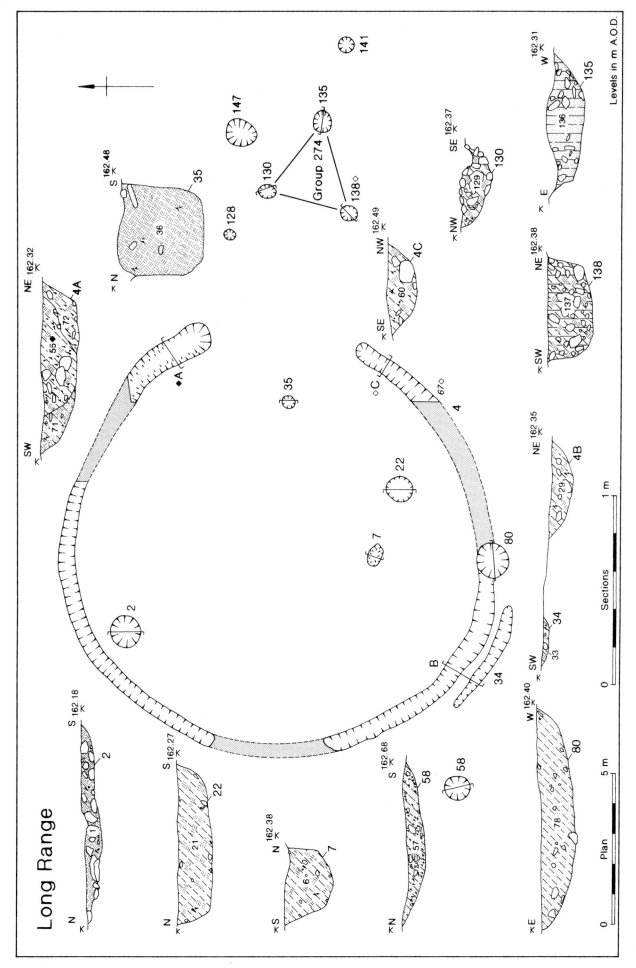

Figure 71   Long Range: plan and sections of penannular gully 4 and three- / four-post structure 274

Plate 15   Long Range: penannular gully 4 partially excavated, viewed from the east, with the terminal of the gully in the foreground. The apparent discontinuity in the gully is due to over-machining in the initial trenching

secondary deposit of silt was recorded in the north-western section. Charcoal was intermittently present throughout. Primary and secondary fills were also recorded in both terminals, where they were noticeably darker; the secondary fills in particular containing much charcoal. A variety of charcoal from the southern terminal gave a radiocarbon date of 400–100 cal. BC (GU-7845; 2220±70 BP). Two small pits or post-holes, 180 and 264, 2.08 m apart, cut the south-western arc of the infilled gully. There was some evidence of burning or scorching of the soil in 180, suggesting that either hot ash had been deposited or that the feature was used as a fire pit.

Two small pits or post-holes, 177 near the centre, 188, and a possible third, 196, were recorded within the gully. Features 177 and 188 were 0.68 m and 0.66 m in diameter and 0.08 m and 0.2 m deep respectively. Feature 196 had a diameter of 0.5 m but was much truncated and only 0.03 m deep (not illustrated). It was, however, mainly filled with charcoal, which was not present in the other two features and so may have been a hearth. There were no external features nearby.

Penannular gully 4 and associated features

The second penannular gully, 4, was c. 14 m south-east of 269 (Figs 69 and 71; Pl. 15). The gully had an overall diameter of almost 15 m and an internal diameter of c. 13.5 m. The entrance, which was 4.75 m wide, faced east.

The gully was not immediately recognised during the mechanical removal of overburden and parts of the arc were overcut. These are shown in tone on Figure 71.

Gully 4 varied in width between 0.35 m and 0.8 m, being at its widest at the northern terminal where it was also, at 0.2 m, deeper (but may have cut an earlier feature); elsewhere the maximum depth was 0.13 m. Generally rounded in profile, the base was slightly flattened at the northern terminal. The main body of the gully was filled with reddish–brown silty clay. Both terminals also contained dumps of darker, almost 'dirty' soil with much charcoal from a variety of woods, many pebbles and, particularly in the northern terminal, much pottery. Although only a single deposit, brown silty clay, filled the southern terminal, the northern terminal was more varied. There, reddish–brown silty clay and charcoal overlay deposits of dark brown sandy silty clay and silty clay at the sides of the gully. It is these deposits that may represent an earlier feature. Charcoal from the north terminal gave a radiocarbon date of 350 cal. BC–cal. AD 10 (AA-30663; 2090±45 BP).

The southern arc of the gully was thought to cut a pit, 80, although the relationship between the features was not securely determined. The pit had a diameter of 1.15 m, was 0.25 m deep and was filled with brown sandy silt.

A very slight gully, 34, was recorded on the same alignment but c. 0.4–0.24 m outside the south-western arc of 4. It was approximately 3.8 m long, 0.45 m wide, and 0.03 m deep. It was filled with reddish–brown silty clay. The gully may be part of another phase, or a fragment of an eavesdrip gully.

Four irregularly spaced post-holes and/or pits were recorded within the penannular gully. Two, 7 and 22, were not far from the southern arc, 2 was near the northern arc and 35 was more or less central to the entrance. Three ranged in diameter from 0.45 m to 1.0 m and in depth from 0.09 m to 0.45 m; 7 was 0.7 m long, 0.45 m wide, and 0.25 m deep. With the exception of 35, all were filled with dark yellowish–brown silty clay; 35 was filled with very lightly charcoal-flecked but otherwise clean dark red clay, with a possible stone lining or packing around its edge.

A pit or possible hearth, 58, lying c. 2.5 m to the south-west of the gully, may have been associated with it (Fig. 71). The feature, which was 0.85 m in diameter and 0.13 m deep, showed signs of burning at its base. It was filled with brown sandy silt, contained many charcoal fragments and flecks, together with a considerable number of burned and heat-fractured pebbles.

Other features in the vicinity of the gully include a cluster of five post-holes and one pit c. 4 m east of the entrance (Fig. 71). Although the group of post-holes could belong to a four- or five-post structure, post-holes 130, 135, and 138 were thought by the excavator to form a three-post structure (274) lying immediately east of the entrance to round-house 4. The post-holes were 2.36 m, 2.5 m, and 2.25 m apart, and were 0.57 m, 0.75 m, and 0.75 m wide respectively; they were 0.17–0.22 m deep. The remaining post-holes, 128 and 141, were 0.28 m and 0.46 m in diameter and 0.05 m and 0.2 m in depth. Pit 147 had a diameter of 1.06 m and was 0.36 m deep. As structure 274 is so close to the entrance of the round-house, it is possible that they may not be contemporary.

Penannular gully 237/63

This gully lay in two separate fields and as a result it was excavated in two stages (Figs 69 and 72). The area within the gully had been much disturbed by the field boundary and services.

Gully 63 was only 1.16 m long and was not traced beyond the northern edge of the original excavation trench, the foot of the hedge bank. It appeared to end with a clearly defined terminal at the south. The gully was almost U-shaped in profile, widening slightly with height and was 0.45 m wide and 0.3 m deep. It contained a single fill, gravelly, lightly charcoal-flecked, strong brown sandy clay in which six sherds of pottery were found. Gully 237 appeared as an interrupted curvilinear gully to the north of the former field boundary. It was in three parts with an overall length of 10.22 m, running in a rather flattened arc from west to north and east. The feature was badly truncated but its profile was probably U-shaped, with a maximum width of 0.54 m and maximum depth of 0.13 m. It was filled with stony, charcoal-flecked, reddish–brown clayey silt from which pottery was again recovered. The eastern end of the gully could not be traced south of a water-pipe trench cut along the north side of the former hedge bank.

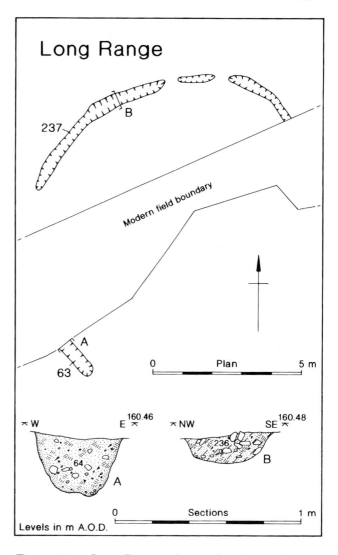

Figure 72   Long Range: plan and sections of penannular gully 237/63

Gully 245

A single length of curving gully 245 was recorded in the northernmost trench, 10 (Fig. 69). It was 4 m long, 1 m wide, and 0.6 m deep and filled with a silty clay. No finds were recovered. The monitoring meeting did not consider this feature to be a part of a gully associated with a round-house.

Three-/four-post structure 275

A small, diffuse cluster of post-holes was recorded near the north-west corner of the main excavation area (Figs 69 and 73). Amongst these was another possible three-post structure, 275, consisting of post-holes 118, 108, and 111, 2.5 m, 1.3 m, and 1.98 m apart. A fourth post-hole, 120, was only 0.44 m north-west of the triangle, and aligned, through 118, with 108 at the south. Charcoal from post-hole 118 gave a radiocarbon date of 410–200 cal. BC (AA-30664; 2275±45 BP) suggesting that the group may be associated with the nearer penannular gully, 269. All four post-holes were between 0.6 m and 0.7 m in diameter, but they varied in depth from 0.23 m (111) to 0.1 m (120). A smaller fifth post-hole, 123, lay 0.84 m east of 118; it was 0.28 m in diameter and 0.11 m deep. All were filled with pebbly,

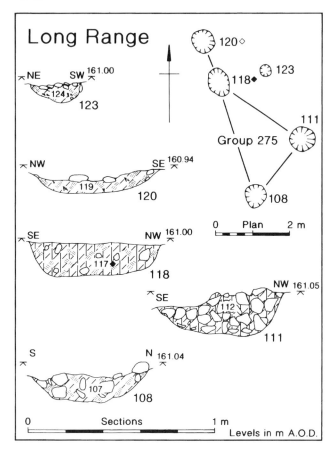

Figure 73   Long Range: plan and sections of three-/four-post structure 275

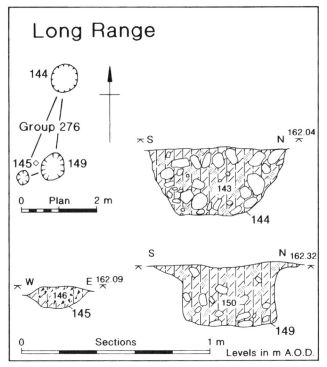

Figure 74   Long Range: plan and sections of three-post structure 276

reddish- or yellowish–brown silty clay and silty clay loam, 118, 120, and 123 with a little charcoal in addition.

A quern fragment was found in an isolated pit or post-hole, 41, in the north-western part of the site.

Three-post structure 276

A three-post structure, 276, was recorded *c.* 11 m north-east of penannular gully 4 and *c.* 11.5 m east of four-post structure 23 (Figs 69 and 74). It comprised two large post-holes, 144 and 149, 1.6 m apart, and a small post-hole, 145, 0.34 m west of 149. Post-holes 144 and 149 were 0.72 m and 0.7 m in diameter and 0.36 m and 0.33 m deep; they were filled with pebbly yellowish–brown and brown silty clay loam. Post-hole 145 was 0.3 m wide and 0.11 m deep, and contained almost stone-free but heavily charcoal-flecked, dark grey silty loam.

Four-/five-post structure 23

A four- or five-post structure, 23, lay c. 7 m north of penannular gully 4 and a slightly greater distance south-east of penannular gully 269 (Figs 69 and 75). It consisted of two pairs of post-holes c. 2.6 m apart, each pair consisting of one large and one smaller post-hole, 13 and 9, 15, and 11 respectively. The fifth post-hole, 25, was c. 1.75 m north-west of the southern pair and offset slightly to the north of a line projected from that pair. All five features were severely truncated, the deepest, 15, being only 0.16 m deep but having a diameter of 0.70 m, as did 13, which was 0.15 m deep. The smaller post-holes were 0.38 m and 0.33 m in diameter and 0.1

m and 0.16 m deep, and they were filled with pebbly, lightly charcoal-flecked brown sandy silt. Post-hole 25 was 0.45 m in wide and 0.09 m deep; it was filled with pebbly, brown silty sand.

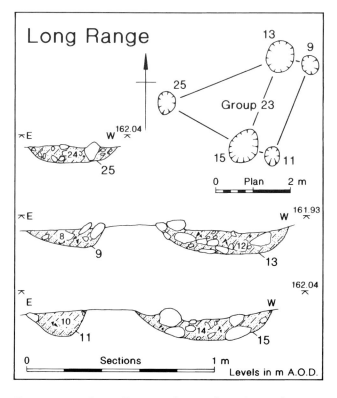

Figure 75   Long Range: plan and sections of four-/five-post structure 23

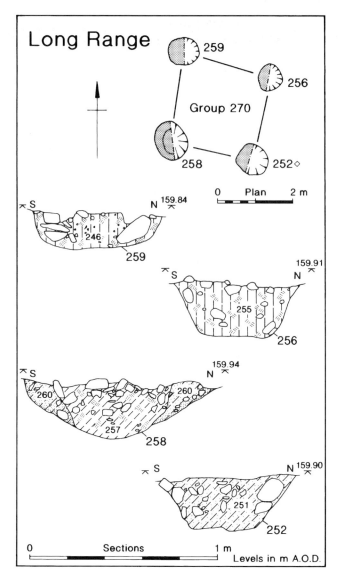

Figure 76   Long Range: plan and sections of four-post structure 270

Four-post structure 270

An apparently isolated, and undated, four-post structure, 270, *c*. 2.3 m square, was recorded near the northern end of the site in Trench 15 (and *c*. 23.5 m north of gully 237) (Figs 69 and 76). The post-holes (252, 256, 258, 259) were between 1.0 m and 0.62 m wide and from 0.18 m to 0.32 m deep. The fills varied from orange–brown slightly sandy silt through yellowish- or greyish–brown clay loam to brown silty clay, but all were quite stony. There were no finds.

Post-hole/pit group 273

A cluster of 12 post-holes and two pits, group 273, was *c*. 15.5 m north-east of pennanular gully 269 (Figs 69 and 77). The features occupied an area *c*. 11 m square. Although the group may represent a post-built round-house, the plan is clearly incomplete if this is so, and it would also be the only round-house on the site not marked by a gully. It seems more likely instead that the group represents the rebuilding of a number of three- or four-post structures.

Although no coherent structure was discernible there were two pairs of closely-spaced post-holes, 97 and 99, 104 and 113, each pair only 0.14 m and 0.19 m apart. The first pair were 0.62 m and 0.72 m in diameter and 0.16 m and 0.09 m deep; the second pair, although smaller in diameter at 0.47 m and 0.53 m, were slightly deeper at 0.17 m and 0.35 m. All four were filled with lightly charcoal-flecked reddish–brown silty clay. The other post-holes (88, 90, 91, 95, 106, 110, 116, 122) were between 0.25 m and 0.6 m in diameter, and all except two were no deeper than 0.14 m; 90 and 110 were 0.27 m and 0.28 m deep.

Pit 93, which cut post-hole 95, was 1.28 m long, 0.8 m wide, and 0.17 m deep. An irregular scoop, 102, to the south-east of the group was 1.4 m long, 0.7 m wide, and 0.07 m deep. Almost all features were filled with reddish–brown silty clay or silty clay loam, although 88 and 91 held brown silty sand; some, but not all fills contained charcoal.

Pit or post-hole 26 was *c*. 5.75 m south-east of group 273 (Fig. 69). It was 0.73 m in diameter and 0.09 m deep. The primary fill of dark yellowish–brown silty clay, in which the Neolithic ovate was found, was overlain by a thin layer of charcoal, possibly the remains of a post: it was this charcoal from which the radiocarbon date, 360–0 cal. BC (GU-7847; 2100±50 BP) was obtained. The natural soil into which the pit was cut had been burnt. There were no other finds.

Gully 69 and ?associated features

A straight gully, 69, crossed the north-eastern corner of the main excavation trench from north to south but did not extend beyond the field boundary which originally formed the northern limit of excavation (Fig. 69). The gully was up to 1.1 m wide and had a maximum depth of 0.38 m in a trench-edge section. In profile it was V-shaped with quite steeply sloping sides. Two fills were recorded in the trench-edge section, dark yellowish–brown silty clay primary fill beneath dark brown silty clay, both layers lightly charcoal-flecked; only one fill was recorded in each of the other four excavated sections.

Four post-holes were recorded near 69; three to its east and one to its west. Although not necessarily associated, the post-holes together formed an approximate right-angle. The eastern post-holes were 1.84 m and 2.14 m apart.

Pit 206, *c*. 10 m west of gully 69, 0.82 m in diameter and 0.25 m deep, was filled with heavily charcoal-flecked brown silty loam from which 38 sherds of pottery were recovered.

Hearth/pit 52

An isolated and much truncated feature towards the southern end of the site, 52 was 1.3 m long, 0.9 m wide, and 0.08 m deep (Fig. 69). It was filled with heavily charcoal-flecked dark brown clayey silt from which a single sherd of Iron Age pottery was recovered. The natural at the base of the feature appeared to have been burnt.

Hearth 1182

Another hearth was identified on the eastern edge of the excavated area during the Watching Brief as the batter

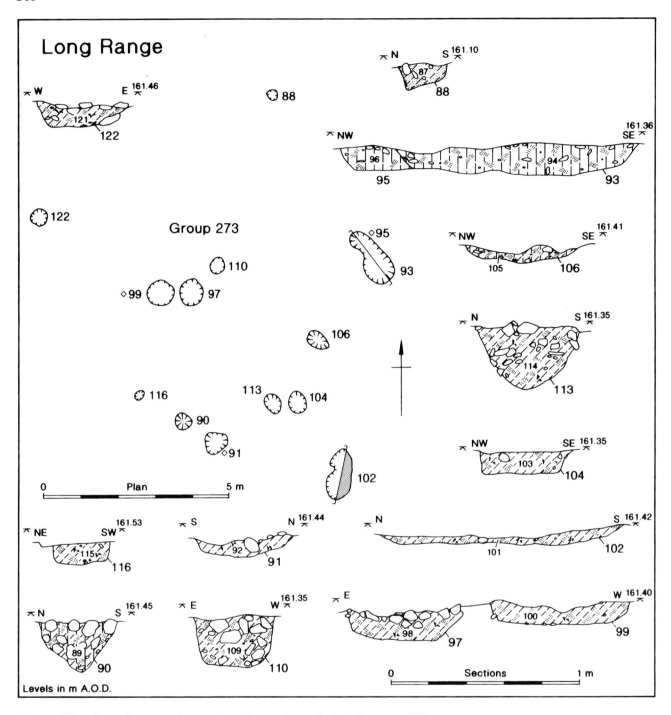

Figure 77   Long Range: plan and sections of post-hole/pit group 273

of the cutting was modified. The hearth was sub-circular feature with evidence of burning *in situ*. A thick layer of charcoal lay on the base of the hearth was similar to that from pit/hearth 52.

Finds

Flaked Stone, by Peter S. Bellamy

A total of 12 pieces (127 g) of flaked stone was recovered from stratified contexts (Table 37). A further 13 pieces

(190 g) were unstratified. The raw material used is predominantly flint and includes chalk flint, flint with a very eroded cortex which may have been derived from clay-with-flints, and gravel flint. It ranges from good quality very dark brown translucent chalk flint through a range of mottled greys and browns to coarse opaque light brown flint. Two flakes of Greensand chert were also recovered. Further details of the methods employed may be found in Appendix 2.

The assemblage mainly comprises small flakes and blades, the majority of which have narrow plain butts with some platform abrasion and are all of indeterminate hammer mode. A single two-platformed core

Table 37: Long Range, flaked stone assemblage by type (no./wt (g))

Context	Cores	Flakes	Broken flakes	Blades	Broken blades	Tools	Broken tools	Chips	Total	Tool types
Chert										
Pit 2	–	1/12	–	–	–	–	–	–	1/12	
Unstrat.	–	–	1/3	–	–	–	–	–	1/3	
Sub-total	0	1/12	1/3	0	0	0	0	0	2/15	
Flint										
Pit 26	–	–	–	–	–	–	1/53	–	1/53	ovate
Tree-throw 32	–	–	–	–	–	1/20	–	–	1/20	micro-dentic.
Penannular ditch 4	–	1/20	–	–	–	–	–	–	1/20	
N post-hole cluster	—	–	–	–	1/4	–	–	–	1/4	
Post-hole 125	–	1/4	–	–	–	–	–	–	1/4	
Penannular ditch 269	–	–	1/1	–	1/1	–	–	1/1	3/3	
Pit 241	–	1/8	–	–	2/3	–	–	–	3/11	
Unstrat.	1/85	4/16	3/9	1/2	–	2/74	–	1/1	12/187	piercer, ret. flake
Sub-total	1/85	7/48	4/10	1/2	4/7	3/94	1/53	2/2	23/302	
Total	1/85	8/60	5/13	1/2	4/7	3/94	1/53	2/2	25/317	

with evidence of small blade and flake removals was found unstratified. Three tools were also recovered. A large blade with micro-denticulations and gloss along the left side and semi-abrupt retouch along the other edge (Fig. 78, 1) came from context 31. This blade was much larger and thicker than the other blades from the site. A piercer on the distal end of a thick flake with large shallow inverse retouch along the right side was found unstratified. The other piece was a broken ovate (Fig. 78, 2) from pit 26. This artefact has an overall heavy creamy–green patina on all surfaces, including the broken edge, indicating that this was an ancient break.

Given the extremely small size of the assemblage, it is difficult to be certain of the chronology of this material but the presence of small blades with abraded platforms and a core from the same industry suggests that there is an earlier Neolithic component to this assemblage (Harding 1991; Brown 1991), confirmed by the occurrence of Early Neolithic pottery in the same context as some of this material (pit 241). The microdenticulate and the ovate would fit comfortably within a Neolithic assemblage but the piercer is more likely to be a Bronze Age type. Micro-denticulates have rarely been found on sites in Devon but where they have occurred, the assemblages have had both Mesolithic and early Neolithic components (Berridge and Simpson 1992; Sylvester *et al.* 1987). Several ovates have been found at Beer where it was remarked that they are the only tools that may have required specialised production (Tingle 1998, 62). They have also been claimed from several other sites in south-east Devon (Pollard 1966; Pollard and Luxton 1978) but these latter are all rather small and crudely made and very unlike the Beer and Long Range examples. It is interesting to note that like the one from this site, almost all of the ovates at Beer were broken or were unfinished – a pattern which Tingle

(1998) notes can be seen on other Neolithic sites such as Hurst Fen, Cambridgeshire (Clark 1960) and Orsett, Essex (Bonsall 1978).

The material is widely distributed across the site with no particular concentration apparent. The bulk of the material was either fresh or slightly rolled indicating that the material has not moved very far. However, it is likely that most of the assemblage was residual, except for pit 241, where the flint was found in association with Early Neolithic pottery. The most intriguing piece is the ovate from pit 26 which is very heavily patinated unlike the rest of the flints from the site, suggesting it may have been curated in a different way. It must have been buried, after breakage, for a sufficient length of time in an environment that produces a heavy patination (i.e. a calcium carbonate-rich environment). In other words, it must have been buried under different soil conditions than are available in the immediate vicinity. How this artefact arrived on the site and at what period is open to question. Is this an example of a discarded artefact of an earlier period being invested with new meanings and deliberately buried in an Iron Age pit?

Illustrated objects
(Fig. 78)
1. Utilised flint blade. Context 31, tree-throw 32.
2. Flint ovate. Context 28, pit 26.

Other Objects of Worked Stone,
by M. Laidlaw

The worked stone from Long Range (identified by D.F. Williams) comprises four quern fragments, all in Permian lavas with a probable source in the Exeter area. One saddle quern fragment was recovered from pit 41.

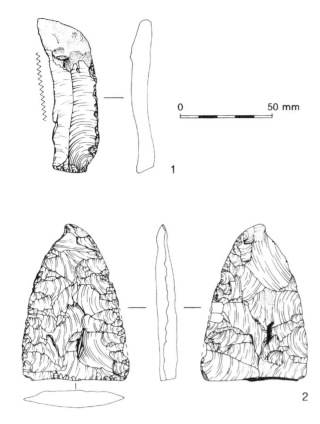

Figure 78   Long Range: objects of flaked stone.
Scale 1:2

This fragment is oval with an upper, very worn surface and part of one curved outer edge, which is also very worn.

Two smaller quern fragments, of uncertain form, were recovered respectively from three-post structure 276 (post-hole 144) and the southern terminal of penannular gully 269. A further very small fragment from gully 269 is probably from the same quern.

Pottery, by M. Laidlaw

The pottery assemblage (415 sherds; 3461 g) is predominantly of Iron Age date, with a small group of Early Neolithic vessels. One Romano-British and two post-medieval sherds were also found unstratified and are not discussed further here. The assemblage is in fair to good condition, with relatively unabraded edges and surfaces (mean weight 8.3 g). There are a number of diagnostic forms present, with large percentages of rim diameters surviving.

Early Neolithic

The Early Neolithic sherds are derived from at least three vessels all recovered on the western side of the site from pit 240. The sherds are in a good condition (i.e. relatively unabraded) although relatively small in size (mean sherd weight 6 g). The sherds are all attributed to sandy fabrics (Q13–Q15), although it should be noted that fabrics Q13 and Q14 also contain rare to sparse chert. All three fabrics show signs of some labour investment in the finishing of vessels; surfaces have been carefully smoothed and burnished.

The most complete vessel, in fabric Q13 (Fig. 79, 1), is a bowl which can be defined, using Cleal's classification, as a composite open form, carinated with a flared neck and slightly rolled rim (Cleal 1992); a slight, pinched-up cordon emphasises the carination. The bowl is burnished both externally and internally. Rim forms from two other vessels, in fabric types Q14 and Q15 respectively, consist of one simple closed form, and a second open form, possibly similar to No. 1. The first, possibly a cup, has an inturned neck and rolled rim (Fig. 79, 3), and the second a slightly rolled rim with traces of burnish on the exterior (Fig. 79, 2).

These vessel forms fall within the range of Early Neolithic forms recorded at sites in the south-west, such as Carn Brea, Cornwall and Hambledon Hill, Dorset (Smith 1983; Smith forthcoming), and characteristic of the Hembury or south-western regional style (Whittle 1977, 77–82); parallels for the two more complete vessels can be found at Hembury itself (Liddell 1932, pl.xviii, P232, P254). The inclusions within the three fabrics identified at Long Range were not geologically distinctive. The gabbroic wares identified in other Neolithic assemblages in the south-west, including Hembury, are apparently absent here, and there is nothing to suggest a non-local origin for any of the three fabrics. Local production on site or nearby is suggested at Hembury (Liddell 1931, 92). Fabrics Q13 and Q14 can be compared with a flint- or chert-tempered Early Neolithic fabric identified at Honeyditches, Seaton, and presumed to be of local manufacture (Smith 1981); a chert-tempered fabric was also identified at Hembury (Liddell 1931, 92).

Iron Age

Analysis of this part of the assemblage was carried out in tandem with the larger Iron Age assemblage from the excavations at Blackhorse. Discussion has focused on the latter as it is the larger assemblage of the two and it forms the main point of reference for this report (see Chapter 8).

Fabrics

A total of 12 fabrics was identified, comprising four sandy, seven containing rock inclusions and one with organic inclusions (see Table 38). Of these 12 fabrics, nine also occurred at Blackhorse (see Chapter 8 and Appendix 2).

A sample of one fabric (R11) was submitted for petrological analysis; the full report is presented in Appendix 3. The inclusions present within the clay matrix place this fabric within the group containing volcanic rock fragments, which are discussed within the Blackhorse report (Chapter 8). An origin in the Permian rocks of the Exeter region is suggested for this group (pp. 178–9), which matches that of Peacock's group 6 Glastonbury Wares (1969).

Correlation with other fabrics identified at Blackhorse, including those thin-sectioned, indicates that three of the same broad fabric groups are present at Long Range: volcanic, sanidine (Peacock's group 5) and quartz sand, but the gabbroic fabric of Cornish origin (R12) found at Blackhorse is not present at Long Range. One sherd of Durotrigian ware from Dorset was identified (Q17); a small quantity was also found at

Table 38: Long Range, pottery, fabric totals

Fabric	No. sherds	Weight (g)	% of period by wt
Early Neolithic			
Q13	34	209	73.8
Q14	11	65	23
Q15	2	9	3.2
Sub-total	47	283	
Iron Age			
Sandy fabrics			
Q2	102	797	25.3
Q3	13	45	1.4
Q17	1	2	0.1
Organic fabric			
V1	31	257	8.1
Volcanic fabrics			
Q1	3	38	1.2
R9	89	643	20.4
R10	45	314	9.9
R11	67	949	30.1
R14	7	71	2.3
R15	1	7	0.2
Fabrics containing sanidine			
R8	5	28	0.9
R13	1	4	0.1
Sub-total	365	3155	
Later pottery			
R-B	1	11	
Post-med	2	12	
Total	415	3461	

Blackhorse. Fabrics that have been identified at Long Range but which are not found at Blackhorse comprise the organic-tempered fabric V1, and fabric R11, which on macroscopic comparison with thin-sectioned samples has been placed in the volcanic group. There is a similar range here of fabrics with geologically non-distinctive inclusions (Q2, Q3, Q4, V1), but these form a lower proportion of the Iron Age assemblage than at Blackhorse – 35% (by weight) compared with 52% at Blackhorse. With the exception of the Durotrigian ware, all fabrics are likely to have been made within the local area, although several different sources are represented.

Forms
The range of vessel forms is limited to three types, all of which are also recorded from Blackhorse; the plain, rounded jars recorded at Blackhorse (form IA1) are absent here. The correlation between vessel forms and fabric types is listed in Table 39. A relatively large number of rims could not be attributed to specific rim forms due to the lack of a surviving profile – only 16 of the 26 rims recovered could be assigned to form with any degree of confidence. Full form descriptions are given in Appendix 3.

IA2: Round bodied jars/bowls with short necks, rounded or bead rims (Fig. 79, 4–6).
IA3: Jars/bowls with longer necks, upright or curved with plain or rounded rims (Fig. 79, 7–8).
IA4: Jars with slight neck constriction, upright plain rims (Fig. 79, 9–10).

The most common vessel form (ten examples) is the necked jar/bowl (IA3), which here occurs only in the volcanic fabrics R9 and R11. The proportion of beaded rim vessels (IA1) is much lower here than at Blackhorse. Rim diameters are within the ranges seen at Blackhorse: 100 mm for IA2 vessels (only 1 measurable example), 80–160 mm for IA3 (x8) and 100–160 mm for IA4 (x2).

Decoration and surface treatments
A high proportion of sherds are decorated (70 sherds; 19% of the total assemblage by number), but the range of motifs is restricted to shallow-tooled chevron bands (Fig. 79, 4, 7), cross-hatching (Fig. 79, 8) and rouletting (Fig. 79, 7); only one example has a more complex design, which merely combines chevrons and cross-hatching (Fig. 79, 8). A breakdown of decorative motifs by fabric is given in Table 40. Only four fabrics included decorated sherds; the largest number are recorded in fabrics R9 and R11 with smaller quantities in fabrics Q2 and R14. Decoration occurs only on IA2 and IA3 vessels.

Residues
A number of body sherds have surviving residues, mainly on internal surfaces, around the upper part of the body below the rim but also externally over the rim and neck area. As at Blackhorse, these residues are likely to be domestic in origin. The residues are common in fabrics Q2 and R11, with a slight emphasis on IA3

Table 39: Long Range, Iron Age pottery, vessel forms by fabric (no. of occurrences)

Vessel form	Sandy Q2	Organic V1	Q1	R9	Volcanic R10	R11	R14	Sanidine R13	Total
IA2	–	–	–	1	1	–	1	–	3
IA3	1	–	–	4	–	5	–	–	10
IA4	–	1	1	1	–	–	–	–	3
Unid.	4	–	–	1	3	1	–	1	10
Total	5	1	1	7	4	6	1	1	26

Table 40: Long Range, Iron Age pottery, decorative motifs by fabric type (no. sherds)

| | Sandy | | Volcanic | | |
	Q2	R9	R11	R14	Total
Chevrons	12	10	20	–	42
Cross-hatching	–	1	–	–	1
Chevrons+cross-hatching	–	11	–	–	11
Misc. rouletting	5	–	–	–	5
Misc. lines	5	1	4	1	11
Total	22	23	24	1	70

jars (including decorated examples), although small traces are also recorded on IA4 jars.

Distribution

All but 20 of the 365 Iron Age sherds recovered came from stratified contexts, and of the stratified material, the majority came from penannular gullies 4 and 269 (146 and 81 sherds respectively) (Table 41). A radiocarbon date of 400–100 cal. BC (GU-7845; 2220±70 BP) was obtained from the southern terminal of gully 269, and a date of 350 cal. BC–cal. AD 10 (AA-30663; 2090±45 BP) from the northern terminal of gully 4.

In both the complete penannular gullies, there was an obvious concentration of pottery in the terminals. From gully 4, all but nine of the 146 sherds (and all but two of the decorated sherds) came from the terminals (mostly the northern terminal), and from gully 269 all but 10 of the 81 sherds (and all but four of the decorated sherds) came from terminals (most from the southern terminal). Although the quantities of pottery involved do not permit detailed statistical analysis, some broad contrasts between the assemblages from the two gullies can be noted (Table 41). Gully 269 produced a higher proportion of decorated wares (35%, compared with 28% from gully 4), and included a much lower proportion of local (i.e. geologically non-distinctive) fabrics (6%, compared with 54% from gully 4). Decorative motifs from gully 269 consisted almost entirely of tooled or incised chevron designs, with one example of chevrons

and cross-hatching combined (Fig. 79, 8). The range from gully 4, despite the lower proportion of decorated wares, is greater, with the addition of more elaborate rouletted chevron motifs (e.g. Fig. 79, 7) to the techniques seen in gully 269. The single sherd of Durotrigian ware (Q17) came from gully 4, from an upper fill.

The remaining stratified pottery was recovered in much smaller quantities from several features and groups of features across the site: 28 sherds from gully 63/237, 38 sherds from pit 206, 37 sherds from post-hole/pit group 273, one sherd from three-post structure 274, and 12 sherds from pit 133. There is little amongst these sherds which is diagnostic, with the exception of one IA2 vessel from pit 133, and a sharply shouldered IA4 jar in organic-tempered fabric V1 from gully 63 (Fig. 79, 10).

Discussion

The assemblage from Long Range is closely comparable to the assemblage from Blackhorse; both sites have a range of similar fabrics and vessel forms. The presence of the organic-tempered fabric V1 at Long Range, however, is interesting. Similar fabrics have been recorded earlier in the Iron Age at Ham Hill, Somerset (Ellison and Pearson 1977; Morris forthcoming). Combined with the relatively crude appearance of the IA4 jar this might suggest a slightly earlier date for the small group from gully 63, the southernmost element of gully 63/237. However, the larger group from gully 237 is typical of the rest of the site assemblage and organic-tempered fabrics have also been identified at Meare Village East, Somerset, where they occur with decorated wares (Rouillard 1987).

The occurrence of coarse IA4 jars in association with finer decorated vessels in the Blackhorse assemblage (Chapter 8) is discussed below, and further illustrates the possibility of the continued use of plain wares alongside the decorated wares in the 3rd century BC. On stylistic grounds a similar date range to Blackhorse may be postulated for the assemblage at Long Range. However, the absence of bead rims and the more restricted range of decorative motifs and the lower proportion of geologically non-distinctive fabrics compared with the assemblage from Blackhorse suggest that the bulk of the Long Range assemblage is rather

Table 41: Long Range, pottery by feature (no./wt (g))

Feature	Sandy	Organic	Volcanic	Sanidine	Total
Penannular gully 4	80/666	–	63/692	3/23	146/1381
Gully 63	–	6/135	–	–	6/135
Pit 133	–	–	–	12/76	12/76
Pit 206	–	25/122	12/77	1/4	38/203
Penannular gully 237	–	–	22/115	–	22/115
Penannular gully 269	5/20	–	63/593	–	68/613
Post-hole/pit group 273	16/93	–	16/132	2/5	34/230
Three-post structure 274	1/5	–	–	–	1/5
Three-/four-post structure 275	–	–	2/3	–	2/3
Total	102/784	31/257	178/1612	18/108	329/2761

Table 42: Long Range, pottery – comparison of gullies 4 and 269 with Blackhorse

Fabric	Gully 4 No. sherds (no. decor.)	% of total	Gully 269 No. sherds (no. decor.)	% of total	Blackhorse No. sherds (no. decor.)	% of total
'Local' fabrics						
G7	–	–	–	–	2	1
I1	–	–	–	–	3	1
Q2	78(12)	53	5	6	135(40)	36
Q4	–	–	–	–	4(3)	1
Q5	–	–	–	–	30(5)	8
Q17	1	1	–	–	6	2
Volcanic fabrics						
Q1	–	–	1	1	4(3)	1
R9	14(7)	10	26(16)	32	26(14)	7
R10	27	19	–	–	34(8)	9
R11	16(20)	11	48(12)	59	–	–
R14	5(1)	4	1	1	18(3)	5
R15	–	–	–	–	1	–
Sanidine						
R8	3	3	–	–	61(16)	16
R13	–	–	–	–	44(8)	12
Gabbroic						
R12	–	–	–	–	3(2)	1
Total	144(40)	28	81(28)	35	371(102)	28

earlier in the date range. The radiocarbon dates from Long Range also suggest a slightly earlier start date and a longer time span for the settlement, with gully 269 at the earlier end of the range and gully 4 slightly later. This would place gully 4 more or less contemporary with the enclosure at Blackhorse, and it is interesting to note the comparisons between the pottery from Blackhorse and that from gully 4 (Table 42): both contained a similar proportion of decorated wares (28% from Blackhorse; 28% from gully 4) and 'local' fabrics (48% from Blackhorse; 54% from gully 4). The evidence is beginning to show a sequence within the South-Western style, in this area at least, of regionally-produced decorated wares being augmented and gradually superseded by locally produced copies with a lower incidence of decoration. The presence of Durotrigian ware in the upper fill of gully 4 can be compared with the sporadic occurrence of this ware at Blackhorse, where it appears to relate to the end of the sequence of activity.

List of illustrated vessels
(Fig. 79)

Early Neolithic
1. Carinated bowl with flaring neck and rolled rim (ENEO 1), fabric Q13. PRN 311, context 240, pit 241.
2. Simple closed form, inturned rim (ENEO 2), fabric Q15. PRN 316, context 240, pit 241.

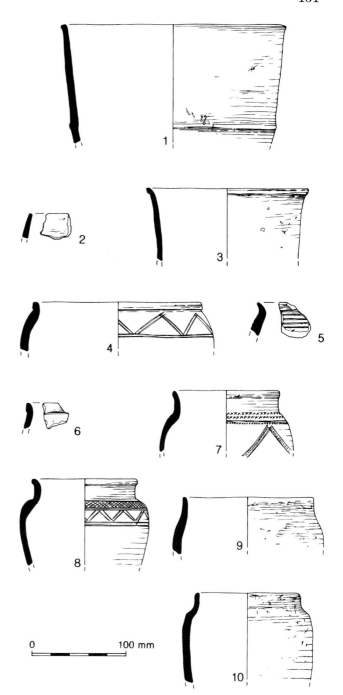

Figure 79   Long Range: Early Neolithic (1–3) and Middle–Late Iron Age (4–10) pottery. Scale 1:4)

3. Closed form, rolled rim (ENEO 3), fabric Q14. PRN 315, context 240, pit 241.

Middle–Late Iron Age
4. Rounded jar with beaded rim (form IA2), fabric R9. PRN 224–5, context 55, penannular gully 4 (N. terminal).
5. Rounded jar with short everted, pointed rim (form IA2), fabric R14; horizontal tooling on shoulder. PRN 228, context 55, penannular gully 4 (N. terminal).
6. Ovoid jar with beaded rim (form IA2), fabric R9. PRN 230, context 55, penannular gully 4 (N. terminal).

7. Rounded, necked jar (form IA3), fabric R11; band of horizontal rouletting around shoulder; chevrons around girth. PRN 223, context 55, penannular gully 4 (N. terminal).
8. Rounded, necked jar (form IA3), fabric R9; cross-hatched and chevron bands around shoulder. PRN 305, context 183, penannular gully 269 (S. terminal).
9. Plain, shouldered jar and upright rim (form IA4), fabric Q1. PRN 222, context 51, hearth/pit 52.
10. Plain, shouldered jar and upright rim (form IA4), fabric V1. PRN 249, context 64, gully 63.

Environmental Analyses

Charred Plant Remains,
by Alan J. Clapham

A total of 14 samples were analysed, one of Neolithic date, the remainder of Mid–Late Iron Age date. Overall, the samples contained fewer charred plant taxa than most other prehistoric sites examined in the project, but the preservation of the material generally permitted identifications to species (Tables 43–5).

Neolithic
The sample from pit 241 mainly consisted of modern root fragments but the charred remains were dominated by a large number of tubers of the lesser celandine, *Ranunculus ficaria* (Table 43). Other tuber remains recovered from the sample included a fragment of a pignut (*Conopodium majus*). The only cereal find within the sample was that of a fragment of a grain of barley (*Hordeum* sp.). A nutshell fragment of hazel (*Corylus avellana*) was also identified.

The find of barley suggests that agriculture may have taken place within the area although the possibility of later intrusion cannot be ruled out. There is no known nutritional value for the abundant lesser celandine tubers, although the plant has been used for medicinal purposes in the past. The most likely interpretation for the presence of these tubers is that they

Table 43: Long Range, charred plant remains from Neolithic pit 241

	Feature	Pit 241
	Context	240
	Sample	69
	Flot size (ml)	80
Cereal remains		
Hordeum vulgare hulled grain		1f
Weeds		
Ranunculus ficaria tuber		259
Corylus avellana nutshell		1f
Conopodium majus		1

f = fragment

represent an aspect of the local environment. The lesser celandine prefers damp, open grassland although it can also thrive in shady conditions; as the site drains very poorly in wet weather, suitable conditions for lesser celandine are present. The presence of a hazel nutshell fragment may represent the gathering of a wild food source.

Middle–Late Iron Age

Penannular gully 269
Two samples from each of the terminals of this gully were analysed. Samples from sections D and 174 were from the secondary fills, and samples from sections A and 171 were from the primary fills. In general, the samples were poor in the number of plant remains recovered. The upper fills mostly contained charcoal fragments and were sub-divided using a riffle box. The figures in Table 44 represent the multiplied number of remains, showing that there were few identifiable remains in the samples and that there appears to be little difference between the primary and secondary fills of the gully.

Cereal remains were found in all samples, including grains of emmer wheat and associated chaff remains such as spikelet forks, glume bases, and rachis fragments. The remains of spelt wheat were identified by the presence of glume bases in samples from gully sections D and A. A possible pea (*Pisum sativum*) was identified from section 171. Non-cereal remains were less evident but all the weed taxa are representative of an arable or disturbed habitat. It can be suggested that the samples represent the remains of crop processing waste, suggesting that the cereals were grown in the locality.

A post-hole or pit (180) in the gully mainly contained charcoal any may have been used as a fire pit. Apart from single finds of an emmer glume base and a fragment of indeterminate cereal grain, there were few cereals. Other taxa included single finds of redshank and pale persicaria (*Persicaria maculosa* and *P. lapathifolia*), two seeds of bramble (*Rubus fruticosus*), and sloe stones (*Prunus spinosa*). The sloe stones may be from a burnt down shrub of blackthorn, hinting at the possibility of scrub regeneration after the abandonment of the site.

Penannular gully 4 and associated features
Two samples from the southern terminal were analysed. Cereal remains were represented by finds of emmer (*Triticum dicoccum*) wheat grains from section C along with emmer wheat chaff in the form of glume bases and rachis fragments. Indeterminate grains of wheat along with spikelet forks and glume bases were also recovered. Non-economic plant remains included two seeds of *Melilotus* sp. and one fragment of a false oat-grass rootlet (*Arrhenatherum elatius*). The dominant remains, however, were sclerotia of the soil fungus *Cenococcum geophilum*.

Gully section 67 also contained indeterminate wheat. The wheat chaff suggested that it could be either spelt wheat (*Triticum spelta*) as glume bases of this wheat were identified, or of emmer wheat as spikelet forks, glume bases and rachis fragments of this wheat

Table 44: Long Range, charred plant remains from penannular gullies 4 and 269, and associated features

	4			269			Pit
Feature group	4			269			
Feature type	Penannular gully			Penannular gully			Pit
Feature / section	C	67	D	A	174	171	180
Context	60	68	151	162	172	170	181
Sample	3	5	38	45	49	63	53
Flot size (ml)	15	30	230*	10	110**	2	140
Cereal remains and other crops							
Triticum spelta glume bases	–	2	40	1	–	–	–
T. dicoccum grain	7	–	–	2	–	1	–
spikelet forks	–	1	–	–	4	–	–
glume bases	3	6	10	4	–	1	1
rachis fragments	3	3	–	–	4	–	–
Triticum sp. grain	2	4	10	–	8	–	–
spikelet forks	2	–	–	1	–	2	–
glume bases	2	6	30	3	4	–	–
Cerealia indet.	50f	16f	30f	10f	–	–	1f
Cerealia sprout	1	–	–	–	–	–	–
Pisum sativum	–	–	–	–	–	1	–
Weeds							
Corylus avellana nutshell	–	1f	–	1f	–	–	–
Chenopodium sp.	–	–	–	–	4f	–	–
Stellaria media	–	1	–	–	–	–	–
Persicaria maculosa	–	–	–	1	–	1	1
P. lapathifolia	–	–	–	–	–	–	1
Rubus fruticosus	–	–	–	–	1	–	2
Prunus spinosa	–	–	–	–	–	–	3+8f
Melilotus sp.	2	–	–	–	–	–	–
Conopodium majus	–	1f	–	–	–	–	–
Veronica agrestris	–	–	–	1	–	–	–
V. hederifolia	–	–	–	–	–	1	–
Poa type	–	1	–	–	–	–	–
Arrhenatherum elatius culm bases	–	–	–	–	–	–	–
rootlets/internodes	1	9	–	–	–	1	–
A. elatius var. *bulbosum* tubers	–	–	–	1f	–	–	–
Avena sp.	–	–	–	–	4	–	–
Phleum type	–	–	–	1	–	–	–
Bromus hordeaceus ssp. *hordeaceus*	–	–	–	–	–	–	–
Bromus sp.	–	6f	–	–	–	–	–
Poaceae stems	2	–	–	2	–	–	–
Leaf frags.	–	–	–	1f	–	–	–
Unident.	1	–	–	–	–	–	1
Cenococcum geophilum	x100s	x100s	–	32	x10s	21	x100s
Bud scales	–	–	–	–	4	–	–

* = sample split (x10); ** = sample split (x4); f = fragment

Table 45: Long Range, charred plant remains from post-hole/pit group 273; three-/four-post structure 27, pit 26, and four-post structure 270

	Feature group	*273*			*275*		*270*
	Feature type	*Post-holes/pits*			*Post-hole*	*Pit*	*Post-hole*
	Feature	*91*	*95*	*120*	*99*	*26*	*252*
	Context	*92*	*96*	*119*	*100*	*27*	*251*
	Sample	*11*	*13*	*26*	*15*	*8*	*71*
	Flot size (ml)	*10*	*2*	*15*	*13*	*16*	*54*
Cereal remains							
Triticum spelta grain		2	–	–	2	–	–
glume bases		3	–	–	22	–	–
T. dicoccum spikelet forks		2	–	–	–	–	–
glume bases		17	–	3	4	–	1
rachis fragments		4	–	1	9	–	–
Triticum sp. grain		3	1	2	1f	–	–
spikelet forks		2	–	1	4	–	–
glume bases		15	–	2	24	–	–
Hordeum sp. rachis frags		1	–	–	–	–	–
Avena sp. awn fragments		–	–	2	7	–	–
Cerealia indet.		65f	1f	7f	18f	–	–
Cerealia sprout		–	–	–	1	–	–
Weeds							
Ranunculus ficaria tuber		–	1	–	–	–	–
Corylus avellana nutshell		1	–	–	–	–	–
Chenopodium album		–	–	–	1+2f	–	–
Persicaria maculosa		–	–	–	–	–	1
P. lapathifolia		1	–	–	–	–	–
Polygonum aviculare		–	1	–	–	–	–
Vicia/Lathyrus sp.		1	–	–	–	–	–
Tripleurospermum inodorum		–	–	–	1f	–	–
Arrhenatherum elatius rootlets/internodes		1	–	–	4	–	–
Avena sp.		–	–	1	–	–	–
Bromus sp.		1	–	–	1f	–	–
Poa type		–	–	–	–	1	–
Poaceae stems		–	–	3	–	–	–
Culm nodes		1	–	–	–	–	–
Small Poaceae		–	–	–	1	–	1
Large Poaceae		1	–	–	–	–	–
Leaf fragments		–	–	–	1	–	–
Cyperaceae tuber		–	–	–	–	–	1
Unident.		1	–	–	–	–	–
Cenococcum geophilum		x100s	x100s	37	x100s	–	–

were retrieved. Non-cereals included single finds of a hazel nutshell fragment, chickweed (*Stellaria media*), pignut, and a *Poa* type grass caryopsis. Finds of rootlets of false oat-grass and caryopses of Brome (*Bromus* sp.) were more common. Again the sample was dominated by the numerous finds of the sclerotia of *Cenococcum geophilum*.

As little in the way of grain is recorded, it is suggested that these remains are from crop processing and the weed seeds present may have been associated with the grain. The presence of this processing waste again suggests that the crops were cultivated in the local area. The fragments of hazel nutshell and pignut tuber suggest that there may have been an element of wild food gathering in the diet.

Three/four-post structure 275
A sample from post-hole 120 contained very few remains (Table 45) but cereal chaff in the form of emmer wheat glume bases, rachis fragments, and indeterminate

wheat grains and chaff fragments were identified. The only weed taxa were oats (*Avena* sp.), and grass internodes, while the dominant remain was again the sclerotia of *Cenococcum geophilum*.

Four-post structure 270
A sample from the lower fill of post-hole (252) was analysed (Table 45). It contained very few charred plant remains apart from single finds of an emmer wheat glume base, redshank, a small grass caryopsis, and a fragment of a Cyperaceae (sedge) tuber.

Post-hole/pit group 273
Three samples from this group were analysed (Table 45). The samples from post-holes 91 and 99 were the richest, with very few remains being recovered from 95. The cereals identified from post-holes 91 and 99 include spelt wheat grains and glume bases, and emmer wheat chaff in the form of spikelet forks, glume bases, and rachis fragments. A single barley rachis fragment was also found in post-hole 91. Weed seeds were not common, generally being represented by single finds, but they all represent arable or disturbed habitats. The dominant taxa were that of sclerotia of *Cenococcum geophilum*. The remains represent crop processing waste.

Pit 26
This pit contained only a single identifiable find of a *Poa* type grass caryopsis.

Conclusions
The low numbers of remains present make it difficult to reconstruct the activities undertaken on the settlement. The tubers of lesser celandine from Neolithic pit 241 may at first suggest some deliberate collecting but there is no nutritional value to these tubers and they probably simply represent the local environment of damp grassland. The presence of a grain of barley may suggest that it was cultivated at that time.

The Middle–Late Iron Age samples were, overall, poor in the number of plant remains present. The crops grown were the glume wheats, emmer and spelt, along with some barley; other crops included peas. The majority of the cereal remains were of chaff, such as spikelet forks, glume bases, and rachis fragments of the glume wheats; a few grains of each were also found. The weed seeds are also generally indicative of arable and waste land, and this suggests that the remains are from crop processing waste, which further suggests that the crops being grown locally. The finds of pignut and hazel nutshell suggest that some foodstuffs were gathered. However, the lack of weed species and other plants hinders the determination of the local environments at the time that the settlement was occupied. The finds of sloe stones in pit 180, if it did cut penannular gully 269, may represent the re-establishment of scrub after the abandonment of the site.

Charcoal, by Rowena Gale

Charcoal was identified from one sample of Neolithic date and 16 of Middle–Late Iron Age date. The charcoal was mainly rather poorly preserved. Large quantities of charcoal were sub-sampled as follows: sample from penannular gully 4 section 172 (sample 49), 20% and post-hole 197 (sample 61), 50%. The results are summarised in Table 46. The anatomical structure of the charcoal was consistent with the taxa or groups of taxa given below.

Aceraceae. *Acer* sp., maple
Aquifoliaceae. *Ilex* sp., holly
Betulaceae. *Alnus* sp., alder; *Betula* sp., birch
Corylaceae. *Corylus* sp., hazel
Fagaceae. *Quercus* sp., oak
Leguminosae. *Ulex* sp., gorse and/or *Cytisus* sp., broom
Oleaceae. *Fraxinus* sp., ash
Rosaceae. Subfamily Pomoideae which includes *Crataegus* sp., hawthorn; *Malus* sp., apple; *Pyrus* sp., pear; *Sorbus* sp., rowan, service tree and whitebeam; *Prunus spinosa*, blackthorn
Salicaceae. *Salix* sp., willow and/or *Populus* sp., poplar

Neolithic

Pit 241
Charcoal from the shallow pit 241 was sparse and included oak sapwood and heartwood (some heartwood included very wide growth rings), and narrow diameter roundwood (2–3 mm) from ash.

Middle–Late Iron Age

Penannular gully 269
Five samples from the gully and associated features were examined. The sample from the lower fill of the southern terminal (section D, context 152) may have been burnt in the gully. The charcoal consisted of short lengths of narrow roundwood mostly measuring 5–10 mm in diameter, and included gorse/broom, oak, hazel, willow/poplar, blackthorn, and member/s of the hawthorn group. The growth rates were varied but only willow/poplar and some pieces of oak included wide growth rings. The sample from the secondary fill (159) of the inner side of the southern terminal section 161, was similar in character to that from the lower fill (context 152). The sample consisted mainly of roundwood measuring 7.5–40 mm in diameter. Taxa identified included predominantly gorse/broom, oak, and blackthorn. Other taxa present included willow/poplar, ash, maple, and member/s of the hawthorn group. The oak consisted of fast-grown roundwood ranging between 5 mm and 40 mm. A second sample (context 172) also from the secondary fill of the southern terminal section 174, was extremely rich in charcoal and a 20% sub-sample was examined. In common with the two previous samples, this sample consisted almost entirely of roundwood. Oak roundwood predominated but also included narrow twiggy material (diam. 2 mm) and some heartwood. Other taxa identified included hazel (diam. up to 20 mm), gorse/broom (diam. up to 20 mm), willow/poplar (diam. 5 mm) and ash.

Post-hole/pit 180 cut the gully and there was some evidence of burning or scorching of the soil, suggesting either that hot ashes had been deposited or that the feature was used as a fire pit. As well as sloe stones, the

Table 46: Long Range, charcoal (no. fragments identified)

Feature	Context	Sample	Acer	Alnus	Betula	Cory	Frax	Ilex	Pom	Prun	Quer	Salic	Ul/Cyt
Neolithic													
Pit 241	240	69	–	–	–	–	3r	–	–	–	12s,h	–	–
Middle–Late Iron Age													
Penannular gully 269 and associated features													
269/D	152	39	–	–	–	10r	–	–	4r	6r	26r	2	25
269/161	159	42	1	–	–	–	–	–	2	23r	56r,h	6	62r
269/174	172	49	–	–	–	4r	1	–	–	–	87r,s	1r	8r
Pit 180	181	53	–	–	–	–	–	25	2	30	2h	–	–
?hearth 196	197	61	–	–	–	–	–	–	–	–	58s,h	–	10
Penannular gully 4													
C	60	3	–	–	32	1	–	–	4	41	4r	–	6
A	55	7	–	–	–	8	–	–	2r	10	31r,h	6	–
Post-hole/pit group 273													
91	92	11	1	(1)	–	(1)	–	2	–	12	14r,h	–	2
99	100	15	–	–	2	4	–	–	–	–	3s,h	–	2
Three-post structure 274													
138	137	32	–	–	2	–	–	–	–	2	3s,h	–	–
Three-/four-post structure 275													
118	117	25	2	–	–	–	2	–	–	–	10h	–	–
Three-post structure 276													
145	146	36	–	–	–	–	–	–	–	–	30r,h	–	–
Pits													
206	207	68	1	–	–	4	–	–	–	1	11s,h	–	7
26	27	8	–	–	–	–	–	–	–	–	108,s,h	–	–
Hearths/pits													
52	51	2	–	–	–	1	–	–	–	–	57h	–	–
1182	1181	10021	–	–	–	–	–	–	–	–	129r,s,h	–	1

Key: Cory = Corylus; Frax = Fraxinus; Pom = Pomoideae; Prun = Prunus; Quer = Quercus; Salic = Salicaceae; Ul/Cyt = Ulex/Cytisus
r = roundwood (diam. <20 mm); s = sapwood; h = heartwood; ( ) = unverified identification

charcoal included mostly blackthorn and holly but also small quantities of oak heartwood, and a member of the hawthorn group.

Post-hole or hearth 196 was the only feature within the gully to contain charcoal but a large quantity was present and a 50% subsample was examined, mostly as oak sapwood and heartwood, but also gorse/broom.

Penannular gully 4
Charcoal was examined from both terminals of this gully. The southern terminal (section C) included a large amount of charcoal, including a high proportion of roundwood, with some fragments measuring up to 10 mm^3. Birch and blackthorn were most frequent, but oak, hazel, gorse/broom, and member/s of the hawthorn group were also present. The sample from the northern terminal (section A), was particularly rich in charcoal and pottery, suggesting that the area was used for the disposal of refuse. In common with the southern terminal the charcoal was mainly composed of large pieces of roundwood which included blackthorn, willow/poplar, hazel, oak roundwood and heartwood and member/s of the hawthorn group. Estimated diameters of roundwood from blackthorn, oak, and willow/poplar ranged between 10 mm and 15 mm. Stems of both blackthorn and oak included wide growth rings, e.g. three growth rings in oak, diameter 15 mm, and four growth rings in blackthorn, diameter 10 mm.

Post-hole/pit group 273
Charcoal from post-hole 91, included oak fast-grown roundwood (e.g. diam. 10 mm, 2 growth rings) and heartwood, blackthorn, gorse/broom, holly, maple, hazel/alder, and a piece of unidentified monocotyledonous stem (diam. 4 mm). Post-hole 99 included poorly preserved charcoal from which oak sapwood and heartwood, hazel, birch, blackthorn, and gorse/broom were identified.

Three-post structures 274–6
Charcoal from the fill of post-hole 138 in group 274 included oak sapwood and heartwood, birch, and

blackthorn. The charcoal from post-hole 118 of group 275 was mostly too poorly preserved to identify, but oak heartwood, ash, and maple were recorded. Post-hole 145 in group 276 mostly consisted of compacted charcoal, possibly the remains of either the post burnt in situ or fuel debris. The identification of a single species, oak, could be consistent with this but a narrow piece of twiggy/stem material (diam. 5 mm) amongst the heartwood which made up the remainder of the sample casts doubt on this possibility, unless the post still retained some vestiges of lateral growth.

Pits 206 and 26

Charcoal from the fill of 206 was frequent and included oak sapwood and heartwood, gorse/broom, blackthorn, maple, and hazel. Charcoal was abundant from the sample of the upper fill of feature 26 which is either a hearth or a large post-hole within which the post was burnt in situ. The charcoal consisted of slivers of oak, mostly heartwood but also some sapwood that had probably originated from a fairly wide pole, suggesting that the charcoal may be from a burnt post.

Hearths 52 and 1182

Hearth 52 produced quite large (up to 10 mm^3) but poorly preserved fragments of charcoal, mainly consisting of oak heartwood, though a small amount of hazel was also present. Hearth 1182 yielded evidence of burning in situ and charcoal from its base included rather comminuted fragments composed almost entirely of oak, mostly heartwood but also a few pieces of sapwood and twiggy pieces, and a small quantity of gorse/broom. Fuel residues from this hearth and pit/hearth 52 were comparable.

Discussion

The contextual evidence suggested that the majority of the samples originated from fuel debris although in two instances a structural origin seems a strong possibility.

Neolithic

The charcoal from pit 241 was oak and ash, probably from fuel residues.

Middle–Late Iron Age

Charcoal was usually very abundant in the terminals of the penannular gullies where it was associated with relatively large quantities of pottery – indicating the use of a convenient disposal area without having to venture too far from the home. Oak, blackthorn, willow/poplar, hazel, hawthorn group, and gorse/broom were common to most contexts, whereas maple, birch, and ash were rarely present. A high proportion of this material consisted of narrow roundwood measuring up to 20 mm in diameter (when charred). Growth rates varied from slow to moderate to fast; the latter seen in stems from oak, blackthorn, and willow/poplar. Pit 180 cut gully 269, and as its sides bore signs of scorching is interpreted as either a fire pit or a rubbish pit into which burning ashes had been deposited. Charcoal from this feature included mainly holly and blackthorn with small deposits of oak and hawthorn type. A truncated post-hole, 196 within gully 269 included a large quantity of oak sapwood and heartwood, and gorse/broom.

Charcoal from the fills of the post-built structures was sparser and less well preserved but with the exception of post-hole 145, comprised diverse taxa that included a range similar to that from the penannular gullies (Table 46). This charcoal almost certainly originated from fuel debris. The compacted fill of post-hole 145 was interpreted as the possible burnt remains of the post. The identification of a large quantity of oak, mainly heartwood, tends to endorse this, but the presence of a small piece of twiggy material was problematical – could this be attributed to the remnants of thin lateral growth persisting on the post following its conversion?

The charcoal from an isolated hearth or truncated pit 52, included oak heartwood and hazel. Burnt soil in the base of pit 26 also suggested a period of use as a hearth, but the feature may have been used later as a post-hole. A large quantity of charred oak slivers (mainly heartwood) may have originated from the base of the post burnt in situ. A similar preference for oak heartwood as hearth fuel is seen in hearth 1182. These residues differed markedly from those identified from the round houses, which were predominately roundwood, and may be indicative of some specific activity or function of these hearths or fire-pits.

Use of woodland resources

Most of the charcoal derived from fuel residues and the bulk of this consisted of roundwood from a range of trees and shrubs including oak, gorse/broom, blackthorn, hawthorn type, hazel and, less frequently, maple, birch, ash, holly, and willow/poplar. Most of the wood showed only moderate growth rates suggesting that wood was cut or scavenged from unmanaged woodlands or hedges. Some samples, however, included fast-grown oak, blackthorn, and willow/poplar which may imply that managed or coppiced/pollarded woodland was available. The charcoal-rich contexts associated with the round-houses testified to the almost consistent use of roundwood for domestic purposes; this equates with the traditional use of faggots for domestic hearths prevalent in Britain until the present century (Edlin 1949). This common use of roundwood in the round-houses, however, contrasts with residues from hearths or firepits 52 and 1182, for which oak heartwood was evidently the preferred fuel.

Charcoal from features 26 and 146 was credited as the residue from burnt posts associated with post built structures. If correctly assigned, oak was used in both instances and the posts were converted from trees mature enough to have developed heartwood.

Environmental evidence

The Iron Age settlement at Long Range was sited on a ridge to the west of the River Otter where the local soils varied between clay with pebbles, and sand. The charcoals indicated that a wide range of trees and shrubs was present in the Iron Age landscape. The abundance of oak in the charcoal suggested that oak woodlands were probably common. Oak grows on both clay and sandy soil usually in association with other woodland species. On clay such woodlands often includes hazel, ash, maple, and members of the Pomoideae. On sand, oak woodlands are generally more open and may include

M. Stuiver and R.S. Kra eds. 1986 Radiocarbon 28(2B): 805-1030; OxCal v2.15 cub r:4 sd:12 prob(chron)

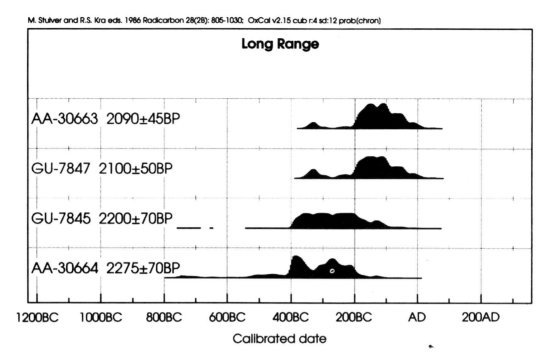

Figure 80   Long Range: probability distributions of radiocarbon dates

birch and gorse/broom. Blackthorn forms dense thickets that rapidly colonise open areas; associated shrubs include hawthorn and hazel. Holly tolerates both clay and sand, and also dense shade.

The results of the charcoal study suggest that unmanaged woodland areas persisted at the site, although there was also some evidence to suggest that coppiced or pollarded trees may have been available for cropping.

Conclusion

Charcoal deposits, probably mostly from fuel debris, identified from post-holes associated with structures across the site, indicated the use of a wide range of taxa. Particularly large deposits from contexts in gullies 4 and 269 indicated a preference for narrow roundwood for domestic use. The use of oak heartwood in fire pits from elsewhere on the site may suggest industrial or some other local activity. Evidence from oak charcoal from the pit 26 and post-hole 145 suggested the probable use of this wood for structural elements. Environmental evidence suggested that fuel was gathered from unmanaged wooded areas and possibly also from managed woodland.

The Radiocarbon Dates,
by Michael J. Allen

Four radiocarbon determinations were obtained from Long Range (Table 47; Fig. 80). The dates span about 400 years (400–1 cal. BC) of the Mid to Late Iron Age. Determinations from the mixed charcoal species in penannular gully 4 are statistically indistinguishable (at the 95% confidence level; Ward and Wilson 1987), from that from pit 26 (range c. 350–1 cal. BC). Their highest probability is in the later part of their calibrated

range (i.e. 200–1 cal. BC). The probability distributions of the results from gully 269 and the oak timber in post-hole 118 from the three-post structure 275 have a considerable overlap (range c. 400–50 cal. BC). Their highest probability ranges between 400 and 200 cal. BC. Although the probabilities of the two pairs of dates do overlap, they seem to represent two distinct episodes of activity. The dated events from the unenclosed site at Long Range are contemporary with those from Blackhorse (Fig. 93).

Discussion, by A.P. Fitzpatrick

The isolated pit 241 represents the earliest activity in the excavated areas. Its shallow bowl shape and the range of material from it – parts of three pots and three pieces of flaked stone – is consistent with the pit having been dug specially for their burial or deposition, a practice which is well known throughout the Neolithic in Britain (e.g. Thomas 1991, 59–64), although the fragmentary finds could still represent the discard of refuse. A flint ovate from Iron Age pit 26 was made in the Neolithic but appears to have been brought to the site from some distance after it had been buried in antiquity. The charcoal in pit 26 is thought to be from an oak post which may have been burnt *in situ*. Other evidence for activity in the Neolithic was rare, with only 12 pieces of flaked stone being recovered from the whole site.

Three, perhaps four, penannular gullies were identified in the Iron Age open settlement. Although the evidence is limited, it seems unlikely that all the round-houses were contemporary.

Penannular gully 4 and the three-post structure 274 immediately outside its entrance, seem likely to be of different dates. The radiocarbon dates for two of the

Table 47: Long Range, radiocarbon dates

Context	Material	Lab. no.	Result BP	$\delta^{13}C‰$	Calibration BC/AD (2σ)
N terminal penannular gully 4, secondary fill	Mixed charcoal*	AA-30663	2090±45	-25.1	350 cal. BC–cal. AD 10
Pit 26, top fill	*Quercus* sap-/ roundwood	GU-7847	2100±50	-25.8	360–0
S terminal penannular gully 269, top fill	Mixed charcoal**	GU-7845	2220±70	-24.8	400–100
Three-post structure 275, PH 118, single fill	*Quercus* charcoal	AA-30664	2275±45	-25.8	410–200

* = Pomoideae, *Prunus*, *Quercus*, Salicaceae charcoal
** = *Corylus*, *Fraxinus*, *Quercus*, *Ulex*/*Cytisus* charcoal

gullies, 4 and 269 are slightly different in date, although there is some overlap. The same is true of the dates from post-built structure 275 and pit 26. Although a few pots (IA4) which might be considered typologically early are present, elsewhere such vessels occur with more developed vessels and with which they are presumably contemporary. Apart from to the south, the full extent of the settlement is unknown, but on this basis only one round-house and associated its post-built structures may have stood at any one time within the 4th–1st centuries BC.

Few features survived within the penannular gullies; even the post-holes of the porches, which might have been expected to be more substantial features, were absent. Those features that did survive may have been heavily truncated pits rather than post-holes. However, the almost central position of post-hole 177 in 269 may indicate that it was a support. Unlike pit/post-hole 199, 4 m to the west, it did not contain significant quantities of charcoal and so seems unlikely to be a hearth. A few fragments of fired clay from features near to the round-houses may be from daub. The terminals of penannular gullies contained most of the pottery from the site, as well as significant quantities of charred plant remains and charcoal, which appear to represent the deliberate deposition or dumping of material in these locations. Otherwise, finds were scarce, comprising of a few fragments of querns.

Several post-built structures were identified, including either two or four-five-post structures (23), what may be three-post structures (274–6), and four-post structures (270). Post-hole group 273 is likely to incorporate the remains of a variety of structures of this sort. The charred plant remains suggest that cereals were stored on site, and it is possible that some of these post-built structures were granaries. A number of possible hearths were identified elsewhere, one of which (58) lay just outside round-house 4, but at the back of it, so it is uncertain whether it (like post-built structure 274) is contemporary. Hearths 1182, 52, and 26 were isolated features, the last containing the Neolithic ovate and a single sherd of Iron Age pottery. Although called a hearth here, the charcoal from 26 is from a single species, which raises the possibility that it derives from a post that was burnt *in situ*.

The charcoal from the features indicates an abundant supply of wood for fuel from both managed and natural woodlands in which oak was probably the most common tree and the favoured source of building timber and fuel. Charred plant remains were generally scarce, but they do indicate that cereals were processed on site and it might therefore be thought likely that they were grown locally. The absence of large pits suggests that cereals were stored above ground, most likely in some of the three–five post structures.

8. Blackhorse

by C.A. Butterworth

Introduction

This ditched enclosure *c*. 50 m square was identified as a cropmark during aerial reconnaissance carried out by F.M. Griffith of Devon County Council in 1984 (Chapter 1; Pl. 16). The evaluation which was undertaken when it became apparent that the site would be destroyed by the road improvement was summarised in *Schedule 4: Construction and Handback Requirements, Part 1, Annex 4A, Appendix 1, section 2.4.1* as follows:

> Evaluation excavations were undertaken by Exeter Museums Archaeological Field Unit in November 1994; seven trenches were opened up at this time. The enclosure ditch was sampled at the entrance and on the northern side. The western circuit was located and plotted within one trench but the ditch was not excavated. Pottery recovered from the ditch fills and from the other features suggests an Iron Age date for the enclosure.
>
> The excavations suggested the possibility of an earlier enclosure ditch of smaller size and encompassing a reduced area. Because of the limited time available for the evaluation excavation, it was not possible to define the extent of this feature. So far it has only been recorded in the western side of the enclosure.

A number of features were recorded within the limits of the main enclosure ditch including possible rectangular timber structures. The interrelationship and functions of these are unknown as yet. None of these features produced cropmarks in 1984.

Immediately to the east (i.e. outside) of the entrance a narrow curvilinear ditch was located for a short distance. Its function is unknown; it may be an entirely separate and unrelated feature, such as a ring-ditch. Two of the long, curving linear features recorded as cropmarks were demonstrated to be of post-medieval origin. The most easterly ditch was located but not excavated.

Topography, Geology and Land-use

The site, centred on SX 9782 9336, lay immediately south of the existing A30 road, towards the eastern end of a ridge running east from the edge of Exeter, some 900 m to the west of and overlooking the River Clyst (Figs 65 and 81). The ground fell from *c*. 33 m AOD at the west to *c*. 31 m at the east.

The underlying geology of the site is Dawlish Sandstone, with pockets of river terrace deposits to the south and clay to the north (Geological Survey of Great

Plate 16   Blackhorse: the enclosure as discovered from the air on 27 June 1984. Photograph DAP/AG2 by Frances Griffith, Devon County Council. Copyright reserved

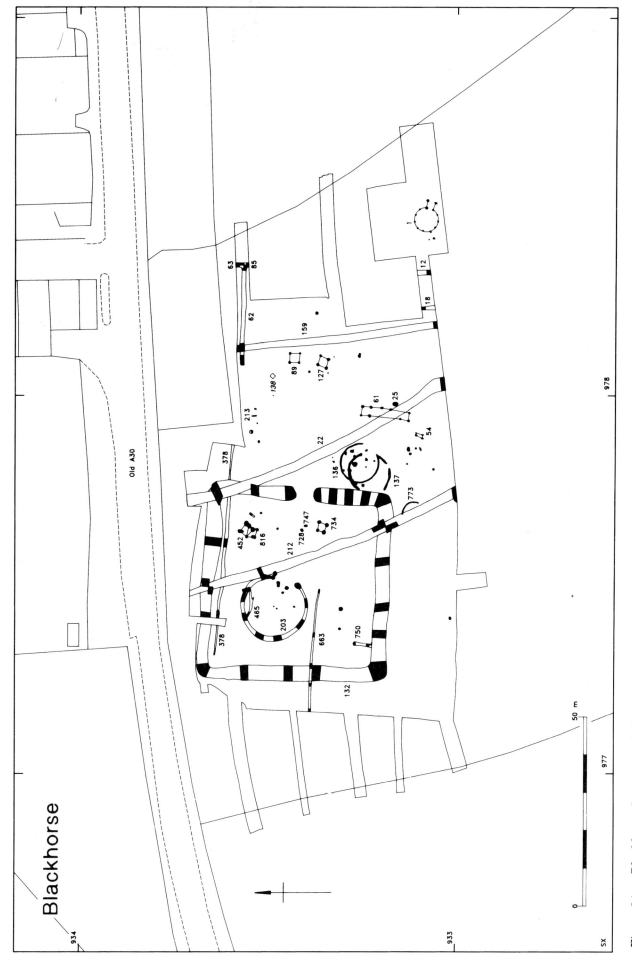

Figure 81   Blackhorse: location and plan of excavations

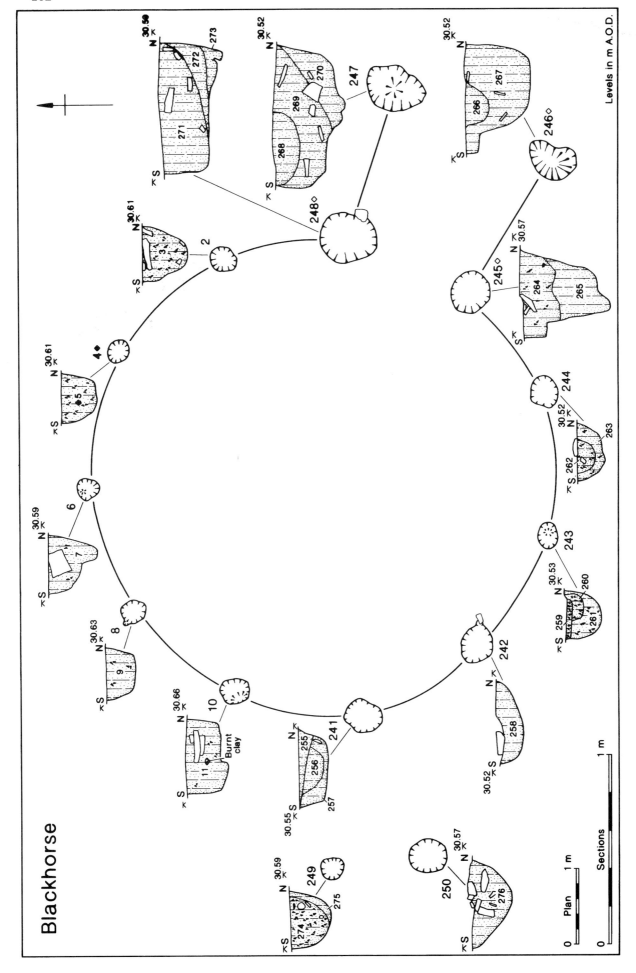

Figure 82   Blackhorse: plan and sections of round-house 1

Britain, Solid and Drift, Sheet 325, Exeter). The bedrock was predominantly sand with occasional spreads of loose, tabular sandstone, areas of clay and/or gravel, and irregular, linear, periglacial features. Some of these resembled archaeological features for short lengths and were interpreted as such during the evaluation, but could be seen in their true nature in the larger area exposed for excavation. There was much localised variation in texture and compaction (Pl. 17). The site was under grass at the time of the excavation but had previously been in cultivation. A considerable depth of sandy overburden was removed and the subsoil proved to be very mobile, causing both sand blows and the slumping of the sides of features under excavations.

Excavation Area

The excavation area (W2414.1) encompassed the full extent of the enclosure together with areas to its west and south and a larger one to the east (Fig. 81). The proximity of the A30 at the north and the need to maintain an access route meant investigation was limited in that area. Additional trenches, either 2 m or 4 m wide, were extended from the main excavation area, five at the west and three at the east. A further extension was opened off the southern trench at the eastern side. The area excavated between March and April 1997 was 7962 m². A number of features of natural origin were investigated but are not described further here; details can be found in the project archive.

Plate 17   Blackhorse: at the close of the excavation, viewed from the north-west. The old A30 in on the left of the photograph.Photograph DAP/ABI (1 May 1997) by Bill Horner, Devon County Council. Copyright reserved

Results

The earliest building on the site is a post-built round-house, 1, which is dated by radiocarbon to the Early–Middle Iron Age. It is considered likely, but cannot be proven, that a small group of other features are later in date, but also pre-date the building of the enclosure which represents the latest phase of activity in the Iron Age. This evidence appears to represent open and enclosed phases of settlement but the radiocarbon determinations from them provide considerable overlap.

Early–Middle Iron Age

Post-built round-house 1
The earliest activity is represented by round-house 1 (Figs 81 and 82) for which a radiocarbon date of 770–70 cal. BC (GU-7840; 2370±60 BP) was obtained; there were no finds, datable or otherwise, associated with the structure. This post-built building was apparently isolated, but as it was only just within the southern edge of the landtake, the possibility of other contemporary buildings to the south cannot be discounted. The building was supported by 15 posts and was c. 6.5 m in diameter; two outer post-holes marked the south-east facing entrance and there was another pair to the west. The post-holes of the main circle, 2, 4, 6, 8, 10, and 241–244, were at intervals of c. 1.7–1.9 m. The distance between the two pairs of post-holes at the entrance, 245 and 248 (inner), 246 and 247 (outer), was c. 2 m, and the post-holes of each pair were c. 1.8 m and c. 2.3 m apart. The two post-holes at the west, 249 and 250, were 2.1 m and 2.2 m from post-hole 241 and 0.8 m apart.

The post-holes of the porch were the largest, with diameters of between 0.47 m and 0.76 m and depths of 0.32–0.48 m. The other post-holes ranged between 0.26 m and 0.5 m in width and 0.14 m and 0.27 m in depth. They were predominantly filled with reddish–brown or yellowish–red sand or loamy sand, but some contained varying amounts of charcoal and were consequently darker. Some, but not all, of the charcoal may have been from structural timbers. No datable finds were recovered from the post-holes, but small pieces of fired clay were found in post-hole 10, and in 247–8 at the entrance.

Middle–Late Iron Age Features Outside Enclosure 132

Penannular gullies 136 and 137 and associated features
Immediately outside the south-eastern corner of the enclosure were two incomplete, overlapping, penannular gullies, 136 and 137, of a rebuilt round-house (Figs 81 and 83; Pl. 18). The relationship between the western gully, 137, and the enclosure ditch is unknown, the gully petering out before it reached the ditch. The gully may, however, have been the earlier feature, as when complete it would have extended across the infilled enclosure ditch and this was not seen to be the case. This should be set against the radiocarbon date of

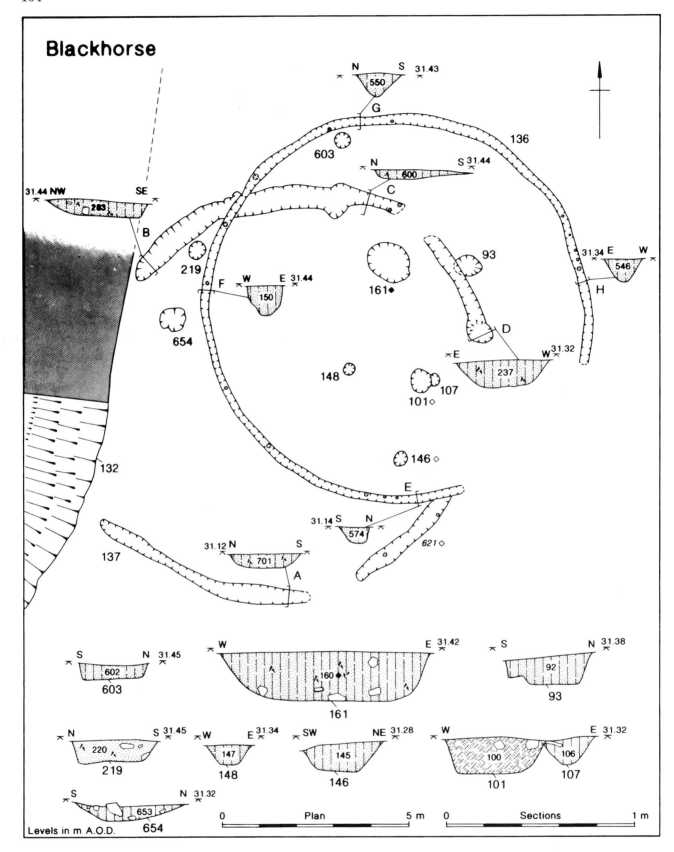

Figure 83   Blackhorse: plans and sections of penannular ditches 136 and 137

Plate 18   Blackhorse: penannular gully 136 and the more shallow and diffuse gully 137, viewed from the south-east. Enclosure ditch 132 is beyond. Note also the generator used to power the compressed air for cleaning parts of the site

200 cal. BC–cal. AD 20 (AA-30659; 2065±45 BP) obtained from pit 161, a feature near the centre of gully 136. Gully 137 was thought to be cut by 136 but the relationship between them was not determined with certainty.

Gully 137 was the less complete – being in four parts – but larger of the two gullies. It had an overall diameter of 11.4 m and internal diameter of 10.7 m; gaps of *c.* 1 m, 4 m, 1.5 m, and 6.8 m occurred at the north-east, east, south-east, and west respectively, the last and largest in the area of the enclosure ditch. The short south-eastern arc was thought to have been cut by gully 136, and did not continue to its north. The next section to the north started with a depression slightly broader and deeper than the rest of that part of the gully, which may have marked the northern side of a south-east-facing entrance. The gully was nowhere more than 0.17 m deep and was generally less than 0.1 m, with the shallowest section being only 0.05 m; its maximum width was 0.52 m. The feature showed a generally symmetrical, broad, shallow-curved profile, with only occasional irregularities. It was filled with reddish–brown to pale greyish–brown slightly loamy sand. Four possible stake-holes, ranging in depth between 0.06 m and 0.19 m, were recorded in the base of the gully (details in archive). Two of these were close together in the northern arc but the other two were more widely spaced in the south-eastern arc (Fig. 83).

Gully 136 was offset slightly to the north and east of 137. It had an overall diameter of 10.3 m and an internal diameter of 9.8 m, with a single break of *c.* 5 m at the south-east again perhaps marking an entrance. The gully was narrower than 137, with a maximum width of only 0.19 m, but was of comparable depth at between 0.08 m and 0.16 m; the profile was thus much more steep-sided. It was filled with reddish brown loamy sand. Seventeen possible stake-holes were recorded set irregularly around the base of 136 (details are held in the project archive). They varied in depth between 0.04 m and 0.14 m.

A small number of internal features was recorded, some of which were poorly defined and/or irregular and were almost certainly the result of root or animal disturbance; details of these are held in archive. One certain post-hole, 93, which was 0.64 m wide and 0.16 m deep, was thought to be cut by and therefore to pre-date gully 137. Pit 161 and post-holes 101, 107, and 148 were in the 'shared' interior of both gullies, with 161 almost central to 136; post-hole 146 was to the south of this trio. Post-hole 603 was inside 136 but outside 137; post-holes 219 and 654 were outside 136 but inside 137. Post-holes 101, 107, and 146 could have been components of an entrance to 137.

Pit 161 was roughly circular, 1.12 m wide and 0.27 m deep. It was filled with charcoal-flecked, dark greyish–brown loamy sand but showed no sign of *in situ* burning and so is not interpreted as a hearth, though it remains possible that it was. Pottery, grain, and chaff were found in the pit, as was charcoal from which a radiocarbon date of 200 cal. BC–cal. AD 20 (AA-30659;

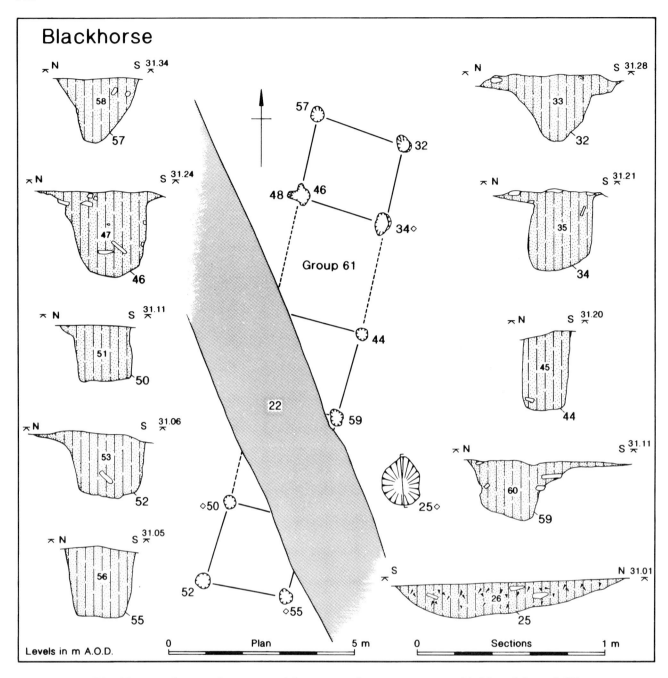

Figure 84 *Blackhorse: plans and sections of four- or twelve-post structure(s) 61 and hearth 25*

2065±45 BP) was obtained. Post-hole 107, 0.28 m in diameter and 0.12 m deep, was cut by a much larger post-hole 101, 0.52 m by 0.2 m; 107 was filled with reddish–brown loamy sand, 101 by similarly coloured clay. The other post-holes ranged between 0.23 m and 0.65 m in diameter and 0.1 m and 0.16 m in depth, and were filled with reddish–brown loamy sand.

Post-hole structure 61; hearth 25

Approximately 8 m east of gully 137, group 61 consisted of nine principal and one ancillary post-holes (Figs 81 and 84). These were the surviving components of either one twelve-post or three contiguous four-post structure/s which had been damaged by the digging of post-medieval ditch 22. The post-holes were in two parallel rows set c. 2 m apart, each row having an overall length of 13 m. The western row consisted of four principal post-holes, from south to north 52, 50, 46, and 57; 46 was abutted at its outer (western) side by post-hole 48. The eastern row comprised five post-holes, 55, 59, 44, 34 and 32. Three post-holes – two in the western row and one in the east – are assumed to have been destroyed by the later ditch. The nine main post-holes had an average diameter of 0.39 m and the average depth was 0.35 m. Post-hole 48 had a diameter of 0.2 m diameter and was 0.3 m deep. A quern fragment was found in post-hole 34, together with chaff; chaff and some spelt and emmer grains was present in larger quantities in post-hole 55.

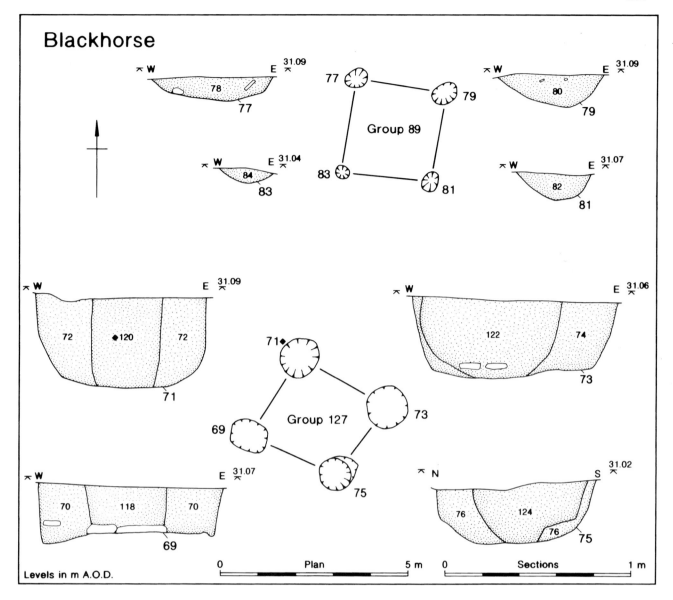

Figure 85   Blackhorse: plans and sections of four-post structures 89 and 127

Hearth 25 was less than 1 m east of group 61 and may have been associated with it. It was 1.2 m wide and 0.18 m deep. The single fill, a very dark brown loamy sand, contained much charcoal and chaff.

Four-post structures 89, 127 and 54

Two four-post structures, 89 and 127, were respectively 14 m and 20 m north-east of 61 (Figs 81, 84, and 85). Both were *c.* 3 m square. The post-holes of 89 (77, 79, 81, 83) were between 0.3 m and 0.6 m in diameter but none was deeper than 0.15 m. The post-holes of 127 (69, 71, 73, 75) were larger at up to 1.1 m wide and 0.47 m deep (Pl. 19). Post-holes 69 and 71 showed central post-pipes, 0.41 m and 0.37 m wide respectively, filled with greyish–brown rather than reddish–brown sand with which the features were otherwise filled. Pieces of flat sandstone at the bottom of post-hole 69 may have provided a firm base in an area of soft sand. Post-pipes were not noted in 73 or 75 but both showed evidence of disturbance, perhaps resulting from the removal of

Plate 19   Blackhorse: four-post structure 127 viewed from the south-east

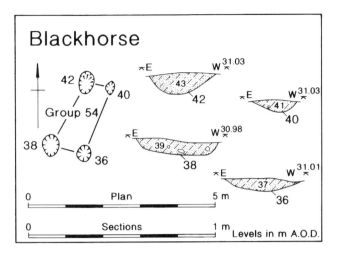

Figure 86   *Blackhorse: plans and sections of four-post structure 54*

posts. A radiocarbon date 390–100 cal. BC (AA-30662; 2175±50 BP) was obtained for 71.

A third four-post structure, 54 measuring *c.* 2.2 m by *c.* 1.2 m, lay within 4 m of the south-western end of group 61 (Figs 81 and 86). The post-holes (36, 38, 40, 42) were up to 0.6 m wide but none was more than 0.11 m deep.

Other features

A number of isolated, ill-defined or possible features were recorded to the east and south of the enclosure (Fig. 81). It is possible that several of these features, which did not contain any finds, are natural in origin. They are summarised here; further details are held in the project archive.

There were six post-holes in the vicinity of four-post structures 89 and 127: one to the west, two not far to the south-east and west of 127, two, possibly intercut, further to the south, and an isolated post-hole or pit base to the east (beyond ditch 159).

Ditch 159 crossed the eastern part of the site from north to south, cutting ditch 62. Ditch 18 was seen only in the south-eastern extension trench. It was on a similar alignment to and *c.* 3 m east of ditch 159.

A group of ill-defined features was recorded between four-post structure 54 and circular gully 137. This comprised two much truncated possible pit bases and five possible post-holes.

Gully 773 was *c.* 2.5 m from the south-eastern corner of enclosure 132 and was cut by post-medieval ditch 212. There was one post-hole or small pit south of gully 636.

Feature 138, sited towards the eastern edge of the site may have been a burnt-out tree-throw.

Ditches 378, 62 and 63/85/12

One of a number of features cut by and thus pre-dating the enclosure, ditch 378 ran on an approximate west to east alignment just within the northern enclosure ditch (Fig. 81). The ditch petered out, probably as a result of deeper machining, *c.* 3.5 m short of the north-western corner of the enclosure but continued out of the excavation trench to the east. Ditch 62 ran on a similar alignment from a terminal *c.* 21 m east of where 378 left the trench (only one terminal was seen, the other being presumed to lie beneath an unexcavated access route

Plate 20   *Blackhorse: the south-facing section of the south-west corner of enclosure ditch 132 (section K/451)*

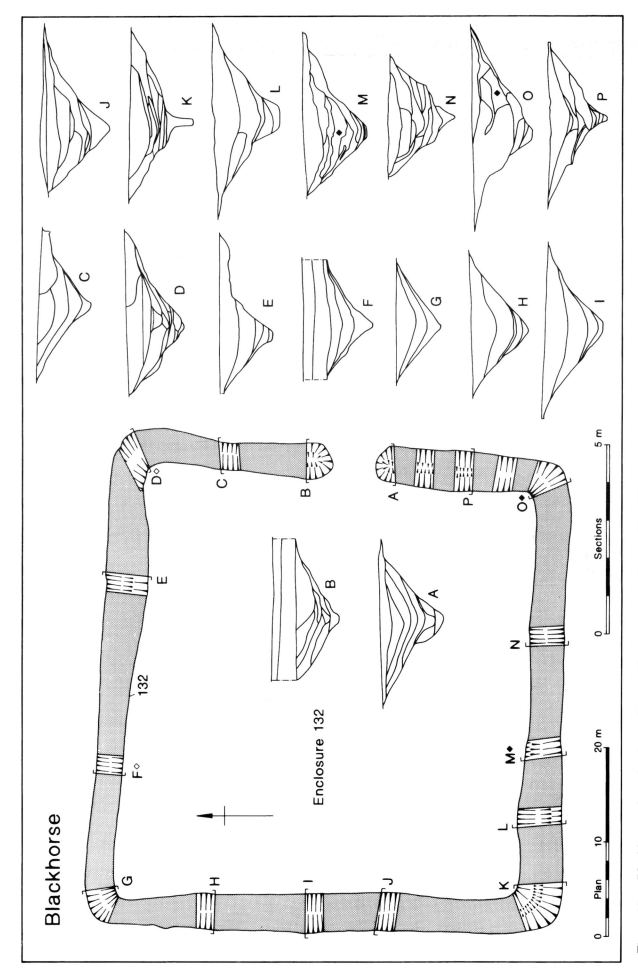

Figure 87   Blackhorse: plan of and simplified sections through enclosure ditch 132

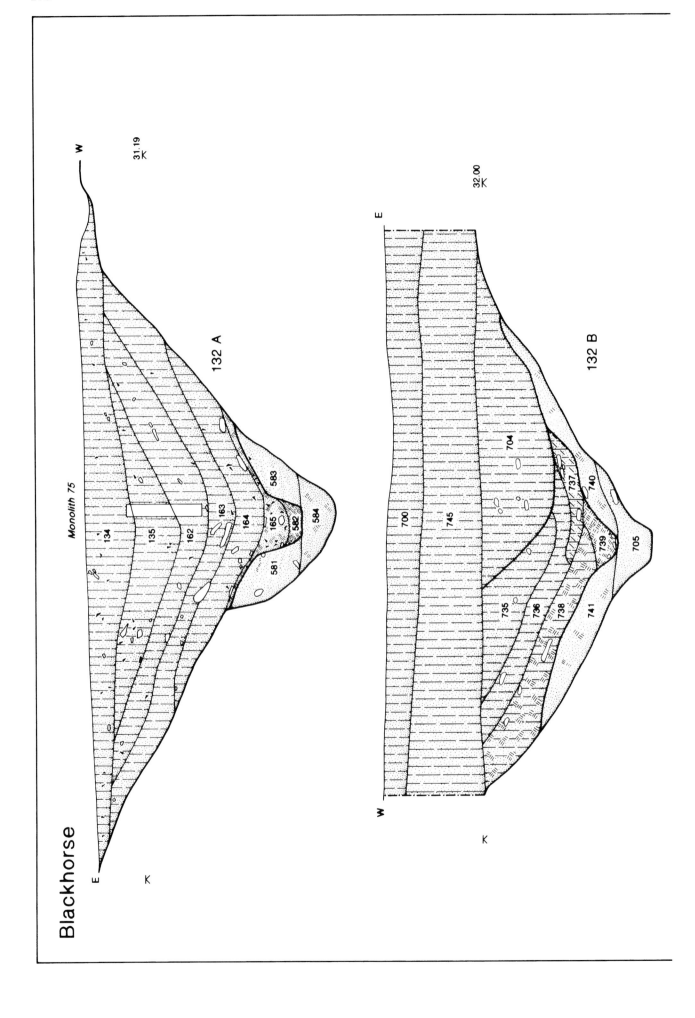

Blackhorse

Monolith 75

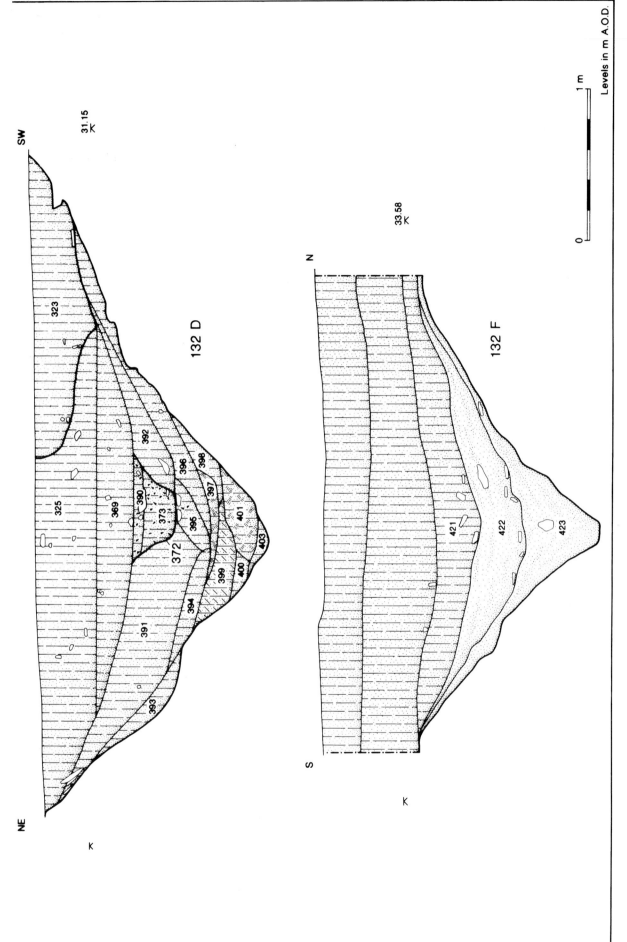

Figure 88   Blackhorse: sections A, B, D, and F through enclosure ditch 132

Plate 21   Blackhorse: the north-facing section of enclosure ditch 132 (section H/587)

along the north side of the trench). Ditch 62 joined north to south ditches 63 and 85 at a T-junction *c.* 26 m east of the terminal. Ditch 12, at the south of the site, may have been a continuation of 85.

Ditch 378 had a maximum width of 1 m in section at the eastern side of the excavation trench; its greatest depth was 0.27 m. In profile the ditch was variable, usually shallow and rounded but occasionally V-shaped. One section appeared to show a recut but this may have been the result of animal disturbance. The ditch was filled with strong brown loamy sand or silty sand.

Ditch 62 was larger, having a maximum width of 1.32 m and maximum depth of 0.23 m. It was rounded in profile and was filled with dark reddish–brown sandy loam. Many fragments of sandstone were noted in the terminal. A later north to south ditch, 159 (see below), cut ditch 62 *c.* 3.5 m east of the latter's terminal.

Ditch 85, which ran southwards, had a rounded profile with a maximum width of 1.25 m and maximum depth of 0.23 m. The ditch was not seen in the middle extension trench, but ditch 12 followed the same alignment across and out of the southern extension trench. It was filled with dark reddish brown sandy loam, as was ditch 63 which ran out of the trench to the north. This ditch, however, although of much the same width as 85, was deeper at 0.47 m and had a V-shaped profile.

Ditch 750

Only one other feature was certainly cut by the enclosure ditch, a short north to south ditch, 750, near the south-western corner (Fig. 81). It had irregular, undulating sides but a flat base, and was up to 1.15 m wide 0.26 m deep. It was filled with reddish–brown clayey sand.

The Enclosure and Features Within it

Enclosure 132: the ditch

The overall dimensions of the enclosure were 50 m north–south by 50 m to 52 m west–east (the greater width at the north) (Figs 81 and 87). There was a single entrance 4.7 m wide near the centre of the eastern side. A concentration of stones, perhaps representing the metalling of the entrance way was noted when the area was examined in the evaluation. There is no certain evidence for an entrance structure or gateway, unless post-holes 728 and 747 set some way inside the enclosure, were associated with one.

Twenty sections were excavated through the ditch, all but two of which are shown on Figure 87. The other two sections, one each on the northern and southern sides, are shown on Figure 81. The lengths excavated included both terminals (the northern one was excavated during the evaluation), intersections with other features and the corners. Complete profiles from the modern ground surface to the bottom of the ditch were recorded at the northern side of the enclosure (Figs 87; 88, F) and at the northern terminal (Figs 87; 88, B). The ditch was at least 3 m wide, the maximum width being 5.8 m at the south-east corner (Fig. 87, O); maximum depth was 1.85 m at the west side (Fig. 87, J). Because of the changeable and often unstable bedrock the ditch profile varied, sometimes even in opposite faces of the same cutting. Although usually symmetrical and quite steep-sided (e.g. Fig. 87, F–I; Pl. 20), the ditch was sometimes more open, stepped and/or asymmetrical (e.g. Fig. 87, L, N, O). As a consequence, the base of the ditch ranged from narrow (e.g. Fig. 87, N, P), to broad and flat (e.g. Fig. 87, L). A deep, narrow slot (0.5 m deep, 0.18 m wide) was recorded below otherwise open, shallow sides at the south-western corner (Fig. 87, K; Pl. 21) but was seen nowhere else in such an extreme form.

As with the profiles, the ditch fills reflected the variable natural deposits through which each section was cut (and in some sections led to difficulty in distinguishing fill from natural). 'Clean' redeposited sand and/or clayey sand predominated, with clays a lesser component. Inclusions, sandstone and gravel pebbles, were not generally common but echoed natural concentrations where these occurred. Occasional nodular mineral concretions were encountered in some eastern and southern sections.

It was clear that erosion could have affected the ditch soon after its initial excavation, for, during very wet weather, some emptied sections were both heavily scoured and held water. This combination resulted in slumping and/or undercutting and, in some instances, led to further collapse not only of vertical sections but of the ditch sides. Wind played a lesser but significant part, blowing dry, exposed sand into open features; c. 0.15 m of blown sand accumulated against the eastern edge of the trench during the two months of the excavation. The ditch would thus have started to fill quickly with soil from the sides, the surrounding area, and excavated during the ditch's construction. Several sections accordingly showed deep primary fills (e.g. Figs 87, F, J, N; 88, F). Others had interleaved layers and lenses indicative of more episodic, intermittent infilling (e.g. Figs 87, D, M, P; 88, D). Some of these sections were where the ditch was cut through clay or clayey sand, and this appears to have limited the effect of weathering, reducing the speed and quantity of soil entering the ditch. The rate of infilling slowed after the rapid early accumulation, the partly-filled ditch settling into a more gradual cumulative pattern. Radiocarbon determinations were obtained for charcoal from layers near the middle of two sections, one of 370–40 cal. BC (AA-30660; 2125±45 BP) from the south-east corner, and the other of 360–30 cal. BC (AA-30661; 2120±45 BP) from the southern side.

The slower infilling of the upper part of the ditch was punctuated by periods of stabilisation, marked in some but not all sections by darker humic horizons. Evidence of activity during such periods was rare, but two pits, 344 and 372, were recorded approximately half way up the ditch at the north-east corner of the enclosure (Fig. 88, D). Pit 344 was the later of the two, cut from c. 0.5 m below the (machined) top of the infilled ditch, and was 1 m in diameter and 0.3 m deep. It was slightly to the south of and cut a smaller feature, 372, 0.28 m deep and with a maximum width of 0.71 m (344 was in the centre of the cutting and therefore not drawn on section 324). The fills of both pits contained much charcoal and were thus easily visible, but, although occasional lenses of charcoal were recorded elsewhere, no other such features were recognised. Although some material would undoubtedly have been dumped into the ditch

there was no indication that it was deliberately infilled on a large scale.

The terminals were not markedly different in size or contents from the rest of the ditch, but one significant difference was recorded in the southern terminal, which had apparently been recut or cleaned out; this was seen nowhere else. The terminal was up to 4.45 m wide and 1.66 m deep, the sides steeply angled, straight on the west (inner) side, the lower half at the east dropping away sharply to a rounded base (Fig. 88, A). The recut was shallower, showing as a 0.25 m deep and 0.19 m wide clay-filled slot 0.23 m above the base (and primary fill) of the earlier ditch. The northern terminal was 3.65 m wide and 1.15 m deep, the sides sloping less steeply than those of the southern terminal, and the inner (western) side concave (Fig. 88, B). The flat base was again 0.19 m wide. There was no evidence that the base of this terminal had been recut.

Features inside the enclosure: penannular gully 203

A penannular gully, 203, and associated post-holes were located towards the north-western corner of the enclosure (Figs 81, 89). Part of the north-eastern arc of the ditch leading to the terminal was truncated by post-medieval ditch 212, and it was also cut further to the west by gully 465 but was otherwise complete. Gully 203 had an internal diameter of almost 16 m and an overall diameter of c. 17.5 m. An entrance c. 5.8 m wide at the east faced the entrance of the enclosure, almost 20 m away.

Nine sections were excavated, at least five of which showed that the ditch had been recut (indicated more clearly by stepped profiles than by the distinct cut of one ditch through the fill of the other). Although the later ditch was slightly offset to the south and west of the earlier one for much of its course, the ditches merged near the southern terminal. The southern terminal itself, however, was recut as a discrete pit-like feature, 227, 1.45 m long but no deeper, at 0.25 m, than the ditch itself. The northern terminal was slightly smaller than the southern one and appeared not to be constructed in the same manner. The eastern edge of gully 203 was truncated by post-medieval ditch 212 near the northern terminal, however, and the profile and dimensions of both features in this area are uncertain. Figure 89, F shows an intermediate cut, 223, which appears not to be part of 212 nor of the recut 203, which is represented by the stepped profile at the western end of the section. There was no discernible distinction between fills which might have helped to resolve the difficulty. The earlier ditch was generally broad, rounded and shallow, with a maximum surviving width of 0.8 m and maximum depth of 0.35 m. The recut ditch had a maximum width of 1.05 m and was up to 0.56 m deep, usually steep-sided and with a flat base. Both versions were filled with yellowish–red to reddish–brown loamy or silty sand. Substantial pieces of charcoal from a variety of woods, principally oak, gorse/broom, and hazel, were recovered from the recut ditch. A radiocarbon date of 160 cal. BC–cal. AD 90 (GU-7227; 2000±50 BP) was obtained for charcoal from the recut ditch. The upper fill of the southern terminal was dark with charcoal and contained charred cereal remains.

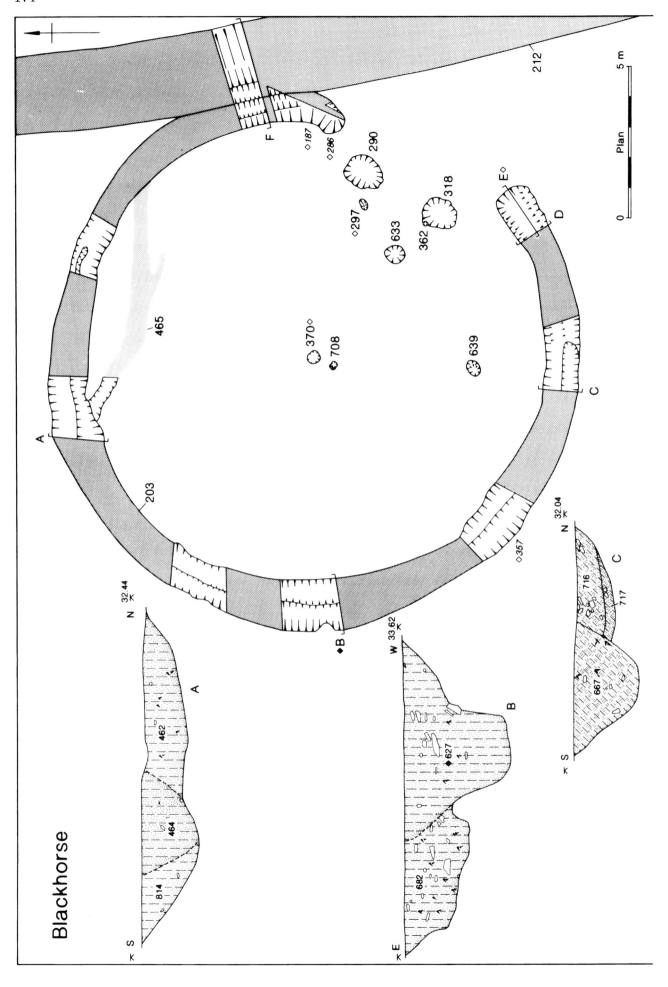

Blackhorse

Plan

5 m

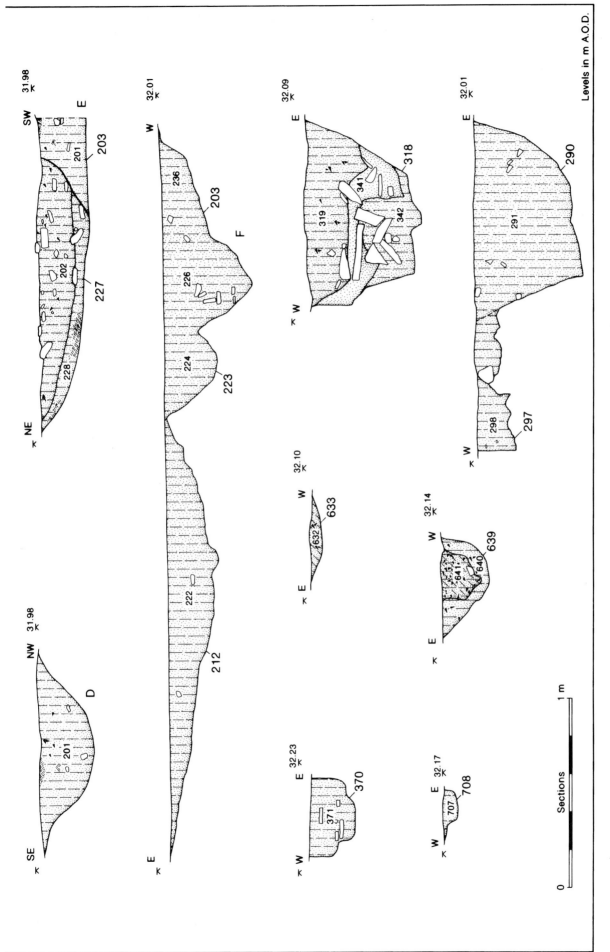

Figure 89   Blackhorse: plans and sections of penannular gully 203

Levels in m A.O.D.

Sections

0   1 m

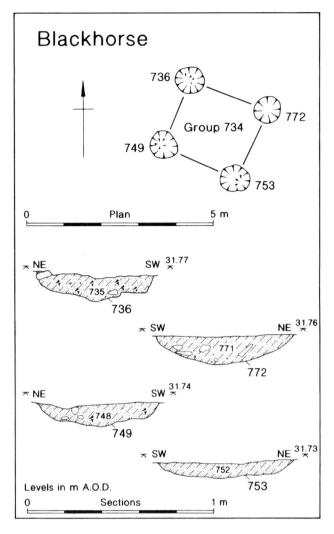

Figure 90   Blackhorse: plans and sections of
four-post structure 734

Four-post structures 734, 452 and 816

Three four-post structures, 734, 452 and 816 were
recorded within the enclosure (Figs 81, 90, and 91): 734
was some 5 m west of the southern entrance terminal;
452 and its probable replacement 816 were a similar
distance from the north-eastern corner. These structures have been attributed to the occupation of the
enclosure, though it is quite possible that they should be
associated with the earlier activity.

The post-holes of structure 734, although severely
truncated, were more clearly defined than those of 452
(Fig. 90). Three post-holes (736, 753, 772) were 0.72 m
in diameter and the fourth (749) was slightly smaller at
0.64 m; none was deeper than 0.15 m. They were filled
with yellowish–red to brown silty sand with occasional
large nodular mineral concretions. The structure was c.
2.75 m square.

Not only were the post-holes of four-post structures
452 generally larger than those of 734, but the overall
structure was larger, at c. 3.5 m square (Fig. 91). The
post-holes (292, 314, 382, 384) were between 1.1 m and
0.8 m in diameter and 0.15 m and 0.68 m deep. They
were filled with reddish–brown or dark reddish–grey
sand. Possible packing stones were noted in post-holes
292 and 384.

Structure 816, which measured c. 2.75 m by 3 m, was
set at an angle to and overlapped the southern half of
452; post-holes 320 and 383 replaced 314 and clipped
the south-western edge of 384 of the earlier structure
(Fig. 91). The northern edge of one of the other two
post-holes, 353, was cut or replaced by a later feature,
343. Post-hole 418 stood alone. The post-holes generally
were slightly smaller than those of the earlier structure,
being between 1.1 m and 0.6 m in diameter and 0.23 m
and 0.39 m in depth. They were filled with red to
yellowish–red sand, with 418 and 353 containing
possible packing in the form of sandstone fragments (not
in section for 353).

Other features inside the enclosure

Post-holes 728 and 747 may represent a two-post
structure located not far to the north of 734 and some
6.5 m from the entrance of the enclosure (Fig. 81). The
larger post-hole, 747, was 1.1 m wide and had a maximum depth of 0.3 m; 728 was slightly smaller. Both were
filled with strong brown sandy loam. Only two other
post-holes were recorded inside the enclosure, both
towards the south-west corner.

Features Later than Enclosure 132

Neither of these features was dated but their similarity
in form and fill to other Iron Age features suggests that
both may be of late prehistoric date. Gully 663 (Fig. 81)
ran from an eastern terminal across the enclosure ditch
(section J) and out of the trench to the west. It was at its
most substantial at the terminal where it was 0.73 m
wide and 0.28 m deep, and was filled with brown sandy
silt loam to reddish–brown or pale grey sand. Gully 465
(Fig. 81) was seen only where it curved from east to west
inside penannular gully 203. The gully was 0.5 m wide
and had a maximum depth of 0.3 m where it cut 203. It
was filled with strong brown sandy loam.

Just within the entrance were two large post-holes
or pits, 290 and 318, c. 1.4 m and 1.7 m respectively from
the north and south terminals of gully 203. They
presumably represent part of the porch of the house. The
broader of these, 290, was up to 1.32 m wide and 0.56 m
deep, and was filled with charcoal-flecked, dark
reddish–brown loamy sand; 318 had a maximum width
of 1.15 m but was 0.62 m deep. Within 318, the primary
fill, stony dark reddish–brown sandy loam, was overlain
by clean but similarly stony reddish–brown sand, which
was in turn beneath a stone-free sandy loam upper fill;
both the primary and upper fills contained much
charcoal. Two other post-holes, 297 and 633, were
located nearby; 297 was close to 290, and 633 was
further from, but may have been paired with 318. Post-
hole 297 was 0.35 m wide and 0.25 m deep, and 633 was
0.6 m in diameter but only 0.07 m deep. A possible fifth
post-hole, 362, 0.15 m in diameter and 0.34 m deep, was
contiguous with the north-western edge of 318. A central
post-hole, 370, 0.41m in diameter and 0.22 m deep, and
second, smaller one, 708, c. 0.35 m south-west of 370, 0.3
m in diameter and 0.08 m deep, were also recorded. The
only other feature within the ditch was another
post-hole, 639, 0.36 m wide, 0.26 m deep, at the south.

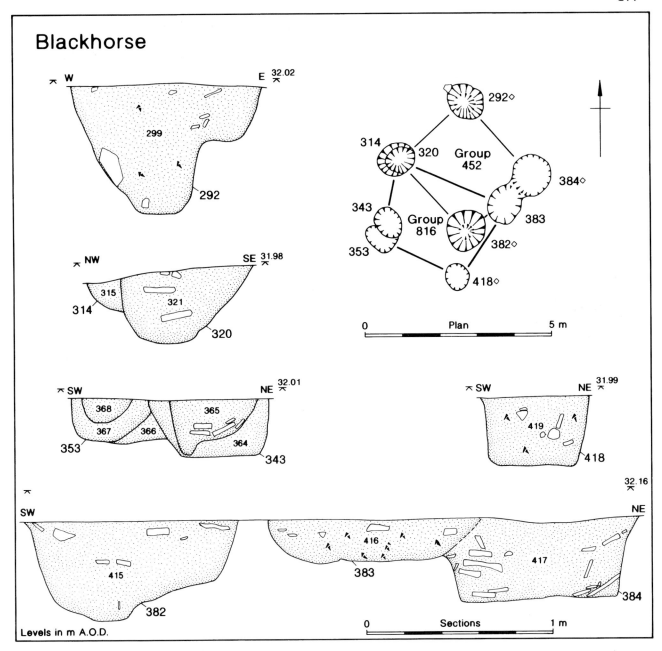

Figure 91   Blackhorse: plans and sections of four-post structures 452 and 816

Post-medieval ditches 21 and 212

Two post-medieval ditches, 22 and 212 ran across the site on slightly convergent, curved, south-east to north-west alignments (similar in orientation to the (removed) hedgebank on the site). Ditch 22 cut the north-eastern corner of the enclosure ditch; 212 cut the enclosure ditch just west of the south-eastern corner and approximately halfway along the northern side. Both ditches were wide but shallow, the northern sections through 212 showing undulating profiles, suggestive of divergent or misaligned recuts. A narrow slot containing a field drain was recorded cut immediately beneath ditch 212 in two of the three excavated sections.

Finds

Flaked Stone, by Peter S. Bellamy

Just 19 pieces (65 g) of flaked stone were recovered from stratified contexts together with six (34 g) unstratified pieces (Table 48). The methods used are those set out in Appendix 2. The raw material used is exclusively flint – mainly gravel flint with two pieces of chalk flint. It includes lustrous dark brown flint with a thin white cortex, a range of mottled grey brown and grey flints with coarse inclusions to pale grey opaque flint. The chalk flint is similar to that found at Beer, while the

Table 48: Blackhorse, flaked stone by type (no./wt (g))

Context	Flakes	Broken flakes	Burnt flakes	Blades	Broken blades	Tools	Chips	Total	Tool type
E enclosure ditch	2/5	6/19	2/17	1/3	–	–	1/0	12/44	
N enclosure ditch	2/4	1/1	–	–	–	–	–	3/5	
Penannnular gully 203	–	–	–	–	–	–	1/0	1/0	
Ditch 212	1/9	–	–	–	–	–	–	1/9	
Ditch 22	1/6	–	–	–	1/1	–	–	2/7	
Unstrat.	1/4	1/7	–	–	–	3/23	1/0	6/34	scraper, util. flake, burnt ret. flake
Total	7/28	8/27	2/17	1/3	1/1	3/23	3/0	25/99	

gravel flint is similar to material which occurs in the soils in the locality.

The assemblage comprises almost exclusively small flakes of undiagnostic character. The presence of two blades and one broken flake bearing traces of narrow parallel flake scars suggests that, in part, this material may be derived from a small blade industry and, therefore, could be Mesolithic or Early Neolithic in date. The tools and utilised pieces (one scraper; one utilised flake and one burnt retouched piece too fragmentary to characterise) were all unstratified and are not chronologically diagnostic but would fit comfortably within a Mesolithic or Early Neolithic context.

The pieces of worked flint are all in a sharp or slightly rolled condition indicating that they had not moved very far. They were recovered from the area of the Iron Age enclosure, with the majority of pieces found along the length of the eastern enclosure ditch. The presence of the flint artefacts on this site indicates that there was earlier prehistoric activity in the vicinity, but the small quantity of material recovered suggests that either the activity was very ephemeral or that the focus was outside the excavated area.

Other Objects of Worked Stone, by M. Laidlaw, with stone identifications by D.F. Williams

Other worked stone comprises fragments of four quernstones, two whetstones, one unfinished spindle whorl, one rubber and two possibly utilised pebbles. All are from contexts of Iron Age date.

The quern fragments comprise part of two rotary querns and two small fragments which could not be assigned with certainty to a specific type. The larger rotary fragment is possibly an upper stone, recovered from post-hole 34 in structure 61; this fragment is in a Permian lava, possibly rhyolite. The smaller fragment, from the south-east corner of enclosure ditch 132 (segment 151), is in quartz porphyry, deposits of which occur within the Permian Breccia. The two smaller quern fragments, both Permian lava, each have at least one worn surface surviving. These were found respectively in penannular gully 203 and enclosure ditch 132 (segment 453).

The two whetstone fragments, although fragmentary, are both in fine-grained sandstones, probably local Permian, with smooth worn surfaces; one is burnt. Both objects came from the south-east corner of enclosure ditch 132 (segment 151).

Part of a bun-shaped rubber, worn around the outer edge, was found in post-hole 654 (associated with gullies 136 and 137). Two sandstone pebbles, one from pit 318, associated with penannular gully 203, and the other from post-hole 4 within round-house 1, are not obviously worked but may also have been utilised as rubbers. The unfinished spindle whorl, recovered from enclosure ditch 132 (segment 457), has been trimmed to a disc shape but has only slight traces of perforations on either side.

Pottery, by M. Laidlaw and Lorraine Mepham

The pottery assemblage from Blackhorse, a total of 565 sherds weighing 5303 g, dates mainly to the Iron Age. Of this total 44 sherds (one medieval and 43 post-medieval) were recovered but are not discussed further here. The Iron Age assemblage includes a significant proportion of diagnostic rim forms and decorative motifs deriving from South-Western or Glastonbury-style decorated wares. The pottery is in a rather poor condition with laminated surfaces and abraded edges (mean sherd weight 9 g), and some sherds have a hard, natural sandy concretion adhering to surfaces. However, evidence of use survives as traces of burnt food residues and sooting on a number of sherds.

Fabrics

The 14 fabrics represented at Blackhorse consist of five sandy fabrics (Group Q), one grog-tempered (Group G), one with iron oxides (Group I), and seven with rock inclusions (Group R). The fabrics range from fine to moderately coarse. Within the four broad fabric groups, a variety of inclusion types are represented. Several fabrics cover a wide range of variation and some fabrics are visually very similar. Fabrics are described in full in Appendix 3, and fabric totals are presented in Table 49. Nine of the 14 fabrics also occurred on the Middle–Late Iron Age site at Long Range (see pp. 148–9, Chapter 7, and Appendix 3).

Samples of five fabrics (R9, R10, R12, R13, and R14) were selected for petrological analysis. The full petrological report is presented in Appendix 4, and a summary of the conclusions is included here. The five fabrics sampled were found to fall into three groups based on the principal inclusions present in the clay matrix of each sherd: volcanic (R9, R10, R14), gabbro (R12) and sanidine (R13).

David Williams writes:

> The most prominent non-plastic inclusions in the samples of fabrics R9, R10, and R14 are fragments of volcanic rock, composed principally of felspar microlites set in an altered dark brown matrix. The condition and composition of these inclusions suggest an origin in the Permian rocks of Devon, in particular those found in the district around Exeter (Tidmarsh 1932). Similar volcanic inclusions have been found by Peacock in group 6 of his Iron Age Glastonbury Ware study (Peacock 1969), and the writer has also noted them in Bronze Age pottery from two sites in Devon, Hayes Farm, close to Exeter (Woodward and Williams 1989), and Heatree, Manaton (Quinnell 1991).
>
> The inclusions within the clay matrix of fabric R12 (plagioclase felspar, amphibole and pyroxene) closely match Peacock's description of the gabbroic pottery from the Lizard Head, Cornwall (*ibid.*, group 1).
>
> Fabric R13 contains grains of potash felspar, in particular sanidine, as well as a wide range of small rock fragments, including volcanic material, sandstone, siltstone, shale, and quartzite. The fabric is similar to Peacock's description of his group 5 Glastonbury Ware Iron Age pottery (*ibid.*). He suggested that the source for the raw materials was derived from the Permian of the south-west, in particular the area north of Watcombe to Exeter and along the Crediton Valley as far as Colebrook.

In other words, two of the three groups identified petrologically, although constituting 'regionally produced' wares, could have been made within the local area; only the gabbroic ware (R12), represented by three sherds, has an origin further afield.

On the basis of macroscopic comparison with the sampled sherds, two further fabrics (Q1, R15) were identified as containing inclusions of volcanic origin, and one fabric (R8) as comparable with the sample containing sanidine. One of the sandy fabrics (Q17) can be identified as Durotrigian ware with a probable source in the Wareham-Poole Harbour area of Dorset.

The five remaining fabrics (G7, Q2, Q4, Q5 and I1) contain no geologically distinctive inclusions, and cannot therefore be tied to source(s), but there is no reason to suggest that these do not have an origin local to the site.

Forms

Diagnostic rim sherds have been used to construct a vessel type series, although the range of forms present

Table 49: Blackhorse, pottery fabric totals

Fabric	No. sherds	Weight (g)	% of period by wt
Grog-tempered fabrics			
G7	2	8	0.2
Sandy fabrics			
Q2	158	1808	37.8
Q4	4	43	0.9
Q5	46	490	10.2
Q17	7	48	1.0
Fabric with iron oxides			
I1	3	65	1.3
Volcanic fabrics			
Q1	9	61	1.3
R9	29	427	8.9
R10	42	474	9.9
R14	18	235	4.9
R15	1	15	0.3
Gabbroic fabric			
R12	3	46	1.0
Fabric containing sanidine			
R8	71	497	10.4
R13	128	571	11.9
Sub-total	521	4788	
Later pottery			
Medieval	1	2	
Post-med	43	513	
Total	565	5303	

is rather restricted. Of the 41 rims recovered, ten were too small to assign to form. Due to the lack of complete vessel profiles it was difficult in some cases to distinguish between jar and bowl forms; all forms have rim constrictions, but the height:rim diameter ratio is unknown. The vessel forms are fully described in Appendix 3 and briefly noted below. The correlation of fabric types for each vessel form is listed in Table 50.

IA1: Globular jars/bowls with plain inturned rims (Fig. 92, 2).
IA2: Ovoid or round-bodied jars/bowls with short necks, rounded or bead rims (Fig. 92, 1, 3–12).
IA3: Jars/bowls with longer necks, upright or curved with plain or rounded rims (Fig. 92, 13–15).
IA4: Jars with slight neck constriction, upright plain rims (Fig. 92, 16).

Vessel forms occur in a range of fabrics, and no form is restricted to a specific fabric, or even a fabric group. Forms IA2 and IA3 occur in almost equal quantities, with smaller (but again almost equal) numbers of forms IA1 and IA4.

Rim diameters are fairly consistent within forms IA2 and IA3 (IA1 and IA4 forms are too scarce for this aspect to be examined usefully). The beaded rim form IA2 tends to be slightly smaller than IA3; nine of the 11 measurable rims fall between 100 mm and 120 mm

Table 50: Blackhorse, Iron Age pottery, vessel forms by fabric type (no. of occurrences)

| Vessel form | Sandy | | | Fe Ox. | | | Volcanic | | | Sanidine | | |
	Q2	Q4	Q5	Q17	I1	Q1	R9	R10	R14	R8	R13	Total
IA1	1	–	–	–	–	–	–	–	–	–	–	1
IA2	5	–	–	1	1	1	1	4	1	–	–	14
IA3	2	–	1	–	–	–	3	2	1	–	5	14
IA4	–	–	–	–	–	–	–	1	1	–	–	2
Unident.	1	1	2	–	–	1	–	1	2	1	1	10
Total	9	1	3	1	1	2	4	8	5	1	6	41

diameter, with one example each of 80 mm and 160 mm. The necked form IA3 has a wider range between 120 mm and 180 mm; the 12 measurable rims are distributed fairly evenly within this range. The sample is too small to examine possible correlation between fabric/fabric group and size, but preliminary observation suggests that there is no such correlation. The size ranges observed for IA2 and IA3 forms, particularly the IA2 forms, are limited; there does not seem to be here the three-fold division recorded, for example, for the Late Iron Age phase at Cadbury Castle, Somerset (Woodward 1997, fig. 4.1). The IA2 forms from Blackhorse fall at the 'small' end of this spectrum, with IA3 forms covering the 'small to medium' range. The explanation for this variation could be activity-related; alternatively, functional variation in the social sense could be a factor, size variation being used to express social identity (*ibid.*, 33).

Forms IA2 and IA3 are well paralleled within Glastonbury or South-Western style assemblages from Somerset, such as Ham Hill (Morris 1987), Meare Village West (Orme *et al.* 1981; Rouillard 1987) and in phase 8 at Cadbury Castle (Alcock 1980), although all these sites have produced a wider range of forms. The

association, or rather the chronological overlap, of these forms with the less diagnostic (plain) forms of which IA1 and IA4 are examples has now been demonstrated with varying degrees of confidence at several sites, such as Meare Village West (Orme *et al.* 1981, 54–5) and Kent's Cavern, Torquay in Devon (Silvester 1986), and the significance of this will be explored further below.

One example of an IA2 jar occurs in the Durotrigian fabric Q17 (Fig. 92, 1); bead rim vessel forms are particularly common in Durotrigian assemblages from south Dorset, such as Hengistbury Head and Maiden Castle (eg. Cunliffe and Brown 1987; Brown 1991).

Decoration and surface treatments

A large proportion of sherds are decorated (24% of the total Iron Age assemblage by number of sherds). Decoration consists of incised, shallow-tooled or rouletted motifs around the shoulder or girth of the vessel, typical of South-Western or Glastonbury styles (Peacock 1969).

The range of decorative motifs represented here is fairly limited; the breakdown of motif by fabric type is given in Table 51. The most common motifs are geometric, and this group is dominated by chevron

Table 51: Blackhorse, Iron Age pottery, decorative motifs by fabric type (no. sherds)

| | Sandy | | | Volcanic | | | | Gab. | Sanidine | | |
	Q2	Q4	Q5	Q1	R9	R10	R14	R12	R8	R13	Total
Geometric											
Chevrons	18	–	–	1	10	5	2	–	7	1	44
Cross-hatch	–	2	3	3	–	–	–	–	–	–	8
Misc. diags	7	–	–	–	2	–	–	–	–	–	9
Notches	–	–	–	–	–	–	–	2	–	–	2
Curvilinear											
Arcs	4	–	–	–	–	–	–	–	–	17	21
Circles	1	–	–	–	–	2	–	–	–	–	3
Complex	2	–	1	–	–	–	–	–	8	–	11
Miscellaneous											
Misc. lines	7	1	–	–	2	1	1	–	3	12	27
Total	39	3	4	4	14	8	3	2	18	30	125

Table 52: Blackhorse, pottery by feature

Feature	Sandy	Iron Oxides	Volcanic	Gabbroic	Sanidine	Durotrig.	Later	Total
Ditch 132	2/26	–	1/4	1/4	9/39	1/7	–	14/80
Section A	15/63	–	5/61	–	10/39	–	–	30/163
Section B	1/7	–	–	–	8/36	–	–	9/43
Section C	1/2	–	–	–	–	–	–	1/2
Section D	6/21	–	–	–	–	–	–	6/21
Section H	3/34	–	–	–	1/7	–	–	4/41
Section J	17/332	–	11/178	–	24/174	–	–	52/684
Section K	2/12	–	–	–	–	–	–	2/12
Section L	17/115	–	14/216	–	21/144	–	2/8	54/483
Section M	37/264	–	10/74	–	1/10	–	–	48/348
Section O	48/992	3/65	30/421	–	23/187	–	–	104/1665
Section P	7/75	–	–	–	–	1/13	–	8/88
Section [189]	3/38	–	11/99	–	2/16	–	–	16/153
Section [480]	23/240	–	6/108	2/42	14/91	–	–	45/481
Section [498]	6/65	–	–	–	2/19	–	–	8/84
Structure 61	2/30	–	2/7	–	2/11	–	–	6/48
Structure 127	2/2	–	1/1	–	–	–	–	3/3
Pit 161	–	–	–	–	5/11	–	–	5/11
Penannular gully 203	3/7	–	3/26	–	72/263	1/3	–	79/299
Gully 636	1/6	–	–	–	–	–	–	1/6
Ditch 750	3/17	–	–	–	–	–	–	3/17
Total	199/2348	3/65	94/1195	3/46	194/1057	3/23	2/8	498/4742

designs, usually bounded by horizontal lines (Fig. 92, 3, 5–7, 13). The lines are mostly incised or tooled, although a small number of lines are formed by rouletting (Fig. 92, 9). A slight variation on the band of chevrons is a band of two-directional diagonal hatching (Fig. 92, 4). Sherds with miscellaneous diagonal lines, incised, tooled or rouletted, probably also derive from chevron designs. Other motifs, also found in horizontal bands, include short 'notches' (Fig. 92, 21) and bands of cross-hatching which varies from very close-set to quite 'loose' (Fig. 92, 14, 18).

Curvilinear motifs are rare. The most common are arcs (but note that 17 of the 21 sherds recorded are probably from a single vessel). There is one example of ring-and-dot stamps (two joining sherds: Fig. 92, 22), and one sherd with small concentric circles (not illustrated). Three vessels have more complex curvilinear designs incorporating tooled lines, rouletted 'notches' and cross-hatched infilling (two illustrated: Fig. 92, 19–20).

Decoration is found on sherds in a range of fabrics, although only on vessels of forms IA2 and IA3. Decorated vessels occur in all of the petrologically identified groups as well as the miscellaneous sandy fabrics, and it is interesting to note that one of the three examples of more complex curvilinear designs occurs in a 'local' sandy fabric (Q2); the other two are in sanidine fabrics R8 and R13. The evidence clearly points to local copies of regionally produced decorated wares. The presence of rouletting confirms that this technique is not, as has previously been affirmed, uncharacteristic of

South-Western style decorated wares in Devon. Other rouletted sherds are known from the County at Berry Down, Newton Abbot (Gallant and Silvester 1985, 43, fig. 3) and Honeyditches, Seaton (Silvester 1981, fig. 11, 19).

Significant quantities of sherds are smoothed and/or burnished on their external surfaces with concentrations in fabrics Q2 and R13, although such surface treatments occur in a range of fabric types.

Residues

Traces of residues, most likely from a domestic source such as burnt food and sooting are present on a large percentage of sherds. The residues are most common on the internal surface of sherds, often around the upper part of the body below the rim and in a small number of cases around the base. A significant proportion of sherds in fabric Q2 and R8 have residues surviving. The majority of the sherds with residues are body sherds; only three rims attributable to form types are recorded (two IA2 forms and one IA1 form). Residues occur on both decorated and undecorated vessels.

Distribution

All but 21 of the 519 Iron Age sherds recovered came from stratified Iron Age contexts. Of these only 14 sherds came from features outside the enclosure: one from gully 636 (fabric Q2), five from pit 161 (fabric R13), six from structure 61 (fabrics Q2, R9, R10, R13), and two from four-post structure 127 (fabrics Q5, R10) (Table 52). None of these sherds are in diagnostic forms, and the only decoration consists of miscellaneous lines on sherds from pit 161, from an unknown decorative scheme. Pit 161 has produced a radiocarbon date of 200 cal. BC–cal. AD 20 (AA-30659; 2065±45 BP).

The overwhelming majority of sherds came from the enclosure ditch and features within it. Of these 401 sherds (77% of the total Iron Age assemblage by number) were recovered from a number of sections through the enclosure ditch 132 (Fig. 103, below), particularly the south-eastern sector, from the terminals round to the southern side (nine sections: 327 sherds in total), the largest concentration within the south-east corner (section O: 104 sherds). There is a smaller concentration in the south-west corner (52 sherds). Very small quantities were recovered from sections on the western and northern sides of the enclosure ditch, and five sections produced no pottery at all. Partly due to this and the low absolute numbers, there is insufficient data to meaningfully assess the vertical distribution of sherds within individual sections of the enclosure ditch. Radiocarbon dates of 370–40 cal. BC (AA-30660; 2125±45 BP) and 360–30 cal. BC (AA-30661; 2120±45 BP) were obtained respectively from central ditch fills in the south-east corner and the southern side.

The concentration noted in the south-eastern sector could be partly, but not wholly explained by the greater number of sections excavated in this area as the volume of soil excavated in individual sections is broadly comparable across the enclosure. Such spatial variation in the quantities of pottery within the enclosure ditch might be due to the redeposition of material from a midden located within the south-eastern corner of the enclosure, or more complex factors could be at work, reflecting a symbolic emphasis on certain areas of the enclosure through structured deposition (Hill 1995).

The emphasis on the south-east is echoed within the internal penannular gully 203. This structure produced a relatively small quantity of pottery (79 sherds), of which 72 came from the southern terminal. A radiocarbon date of 160 cal. BC–cal AD 90 (GU-7227; 2000±50 BP) came from the recut of the ditch.

Discussion

The Iron Age assemblage from Blackhorse, together with that from Long Range (see above), has provided a valuable addition to Glastonbury or South-Western style ceramics in the region. Although not a particularly large assemblage, Blackhorse is now the largest group of this date in the county. Also of note here is the presence of a small quantity of Durotrigian ware likely to originate from south Dorset.

The Glastonbury style assemblage contains a range of fabric types, most of which can be tied to a source area local to the site, although it is apparent that several different sources are represented, three of which can be correlated with the regionalised production centres identified by Peacock (1969, groups 1, 5, and 6). The identification of groups 5 and 6 is perhaps not surprising, given their likely source within the Permian rocks of south Devon; the relative rarity hitherto of identified group 6 sherds has most probably been due to lack of known assemblages in the area (see, for example, Silvester 1986, 14). The presence of a small proportion of a non-local gabbroic fabric, with a source on the Lizard peninsula in Cornwall, is interesting although not unusual; this petrological group has a wide distribution outside its area of manufacture (Peacock 1969, fig. 2).

In contrast to the range of fabrics, both vessel forms and decorative motifs, perhaps surprisingly, demonstrate a limited repertoire. Only four vessel forms were identified, of which only two appear to have been decorated. These are jars or bowls (the distinction is not always apparent), necked or with beaded rims, most commonly decorated with geometric designs. The assemblage from Kent's Cavern, at 417 sherds previously the largest assemblage of this date from Devon, contains a much wider range of forms and decorative styles, despite a lower proportion (15%) of decorated sherds (Silvester 1986). The geometric designs found on the Blackhorse vessels find perhaps their closest parallel at other sites in Devon, at Milber Down, which produced a similarly restricted range (Fox et al. 1949–50), Blackbury Castle (Young and Richardson 1955, figs 10, 11) and at Hembury (Liddell 1930, pl.xxvii). What is interesting, however, is the evidence that South-Western styles were being copied in fabrics other than Peacock's petrologically distinct groups, fabrics which are presumed to be of local origin, a situation observed elsewhere in south Devon, for example at Honeyditches, Seaton (Silvester 1981, 63).

With the four radiocarbon determinations obtained from pit 161, enclosure ditch 132 and penannular gully 203, this assemblage has some contribution to make to the debate on the currency of plain wares at this period. It is of interest to note here the presence, albeit scarce, of the plain forms IA1 and IA4, found here in association with, and in comparable fabrics to the decorated wares. These plain forms are usually dated to the 5th–3rd centuries BC. Similar forms to IA4, for example, are recorded in phase 7 at Cadbury Castle (Alcock 1980). The apparent association of plain and decorated wares has also been recorded at Blackbury Castle (Young and Richardson 1955), Meare Village West (Orme et al. 1981), Honeyditches, Seaton (Silvester 1981), and Kent's Cavern, Torquay (Silvester 1986), and has led to the postulation that plain forms continued in use later than was previously thought. An alternative view has been put forward by Quinnell, who argues for an earlier introduction of decorated wares, perhaps as early as the 5th century BC (Miles 1977, 106), but this applies only to those wares of Cornish type, and has not yet been demonstrated for other varieties. Certainly the evidence from Blackhorse demonstrates conclusively the association between plain and decorated wares, within a date range of the 4th–1st centuries BC, a date range comparable to Long Range.

The presence of Durotrigian ware, albeit in very small quantities, merits further comment. These sherds do have an implication for dating – Durotrigian wares appear in Dorset only from the mid 1st century BC – but, given their provenance, their significance appears to relate more to the last use of the site than to the main period of activity. Seven sherds were recovered altogether, six from the enclosure ditch and one from penannular gully 203; in every case these sherds came from upper fills – from tertiary fills of the enclosure ditch, and from the recut of gully 203. The illustrated

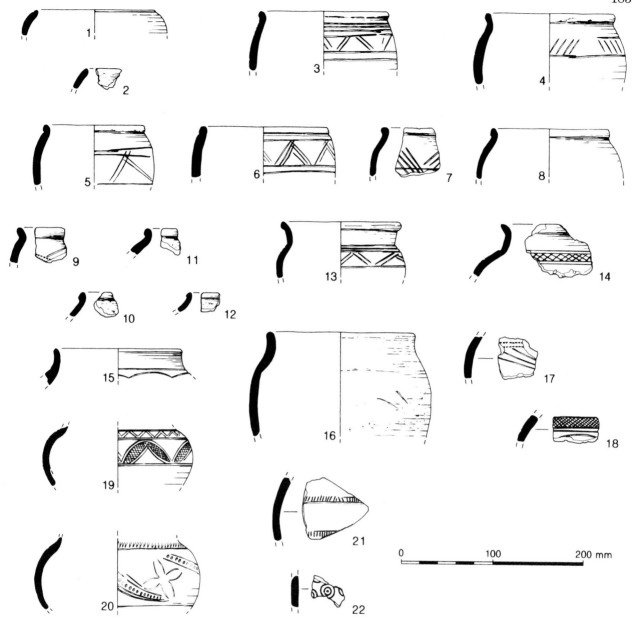

Figure 92   *Blackhorse: Middle–Late Iron Age pottery. Scale 1:4*

vessel from the enclosure ditch (Fig. 92, 1) came from the same context as the two grog-tempered sherds (section 457). It appears, therefore, that these sherds were arriving at the site immediately prior to its abandonment, and conveniently date this abandonment to the later 1st century BC.

List of illustrated vessels
(Fig. 92)

1. Plain rounded jar (form IA1), fabric Q4. PRN 202, context 556, enclosure ditch 132 (section 457).
2. Plain rounded jar (form IA1), fabric Q2. PRN 159, context 156, enclosure ditch 132 (section 151).
3. Ovoid jar with beaded rim (form IA2), fabric R14; horizontal/chevron motifs around shoulder. PRNs 135/136/142, context 194, enclosure ditch 132 (section 189).
4. Rounded jar with short everted, rounded rim (form IA2), fabric Q2; chevron hatching around shoulder.

PRN 122, context 155, enclosure ditch 132 (section 151).

5. Rounded jar with beaded rim (form IA2), fabric Q2; band of chevrons around girth. PRN 131, context 155, enclosure ditch 132 (section 151).
6. Ovoid jar with beaded rim (form IA2), fabric R10; horizontal/chevron motifs around shoulder. PRN 132, context 155, enclosure ditch 132 (section 151).
7. Rounded jar with slight shoulder and short everted, rounded rim (form IA2), fabric R9; band of chevron hatching around shoulder. PRN 150, context 156, enclosure ditch 132 (section 151).
8. Plain, rounded jar with short everted, rounded rim (form IA2), fabric R10. PRN 207. Context 558, enclosure ditch 132 (section 457).
9. Rounded jar with short everted, rounded rim (form IA2), fabric Q2; ?rouletted and tooled decoration around shoulder. PRN 67, context 477, enclosure ditch 132 (section 478).

10. Rounded jar with beaded rim (form IA2), fabric Q2. PRN 74, context 482, enclosure ditch 132 (section 480).
11. Rounded jar with beaded rim (form IA2), fabric R10. PRN 168, context 201, penannular gully 203 (southern terminal).
12. Rounded jar with beaded rim (form IA2), fabric Q1. PRN 35, context 134, enclosure ditch 132 (section 133).
13. Necked, rounded jar (form IA3), fabric R9; band of chevrons around shoulder. PRN 151, context 156, enclosure ditch 132 (section 151).
14. Necked, rounded jar (form IA3), fabric Q5; narrow lattice band around shoulder. PRN 172, context 427, enclosure ditch 132 (section 439/451).
15. Necked, rounded jar (form IA3), fabric Q2; incised arcs around shoulder. PRN 192, context 483, enclosure ditch 132 (section 480).
16. Plain. shouldered jar (form IA4), fabric R14. PRN 178, context 427, enclosure ditch 132 (section 439/451).
17. Decorated body sherd, form unknown, fabric R9; rouletted and incised decoration. PRN 87, context 508, enclosure ditch 132 (section 476).
18. Decorated body sherd, form unknown, fabric Q4; band of cross-hatching above ?arcs. PRN 90, context 511, enclosure ditch 132 (section 476).
19. Decorated body sherd, probably form IA3, fabric R8; complex curvilinear and chevron motifs. PRN 154, context 156, enclosure ditch 132 (section 151).
20. Decorated sherd, probably form IA3, fabric R13; complex curvilinear motifs. PRN 182, context 432, enclosure ditch 132 (section 439/451).
21. Decorated body sherd, form unknown, fabric R12; incised 'notched' motifs. PRN 68, context 481, enclosure ditch 132 (section 480).
22. Decorated body sherd, form unknown, fabric R10; ring-and-dot motifs. PRN 144, context 194, enclosure ditch 132 (section 189).

Environmental Analyses

Charred Plant Remains,
by Alan J. Clapham

Twenty-two samples were analysed, the majority of which were well preserved permitting identification to species (Tables 53–6).

Round-house 1
Samples from two of the post-holes of this building were analysed but there were few charred plant remains (Table 53). Spelt wheat (*Triticum spelta*) was represented by a single grain and a glume base, while a grain of emmer wheat (*T. dicoccum*) was also recovered. Non-economic species identified include a single radish (*Raphanus raphanistrum*) pod fragment in 245 and rootlet fragments of false oat-grass (*Arrhenatherum elatius*).

Penannular gullies 136 and 137
Two samples each from gullies 136 and 137 were analysed (Table 54). The sample from gully 137 (section C) contained few plant remains; single finds of oats (*Avena* sp.) and blinks (*Montia fontana* ssp *chondro-*

sperma). Only a few remains were recovered from section 621 of the same gully; indeterminate wheat glume bases, fragments of indeterminate cereal grains, and two rootlets of false oat-grass. Post-hole 146 only contained single finds of an emmer wheat glume base and a sclerotia of *Cenococcum geophilum*.

Pit 161 was, however, very rich in remains and was dominated by cereals; grains of bread and spelt wheats (*Triticum aestivum* and *T. spelta*) were recovered. Other cereal remains included chaff fragments, including spikelet forks, glume bases, and rachis fragments of emmer and spelt wheat as well as spikelet forks and glume bases of an indeterminate wheat species. Of the glume bases that could be identified to species, those of spelt wheat were the more common. In relation to the chaff remains there were few fragments of indeterminate cereal grains.

Weed species recovered from include fat-hen (*Chenopodium album*), knotgrass (*Polygonum aviculare*), black bindweed (*Fallopia convolvulus*), sheep's sorrel (*Rumex acetosella*), clover (*Trifolium* sp.), ribwort plantain (*Plantago lanceolata*), oat awn fragments (*Avena* sp.), and brome grass (*Bromus* sp.). All of these species are indicative of arable cultivation. The charred plant remains from this pit represent the remains of crop processing. The general lack of cereal grains suggests that the chaff was used as tinder after the grains had been released from the enclosing glumes and the pit, which may of course have been a hearth, may therefore contain clearings or sweepings from hearths.

Post-hole structure 61; hearth 25
Samples from two post-holes from the eastern row of this structure(s) were analysed, as was one from the nearby hearth, 25 (Table 54). Post-hole 34 contained

Table 53: Blackhorse, charred plant remains from round-house 1

	Feature type	Post-hole	Post-hole
	Feature	4	245
	Context	5	264, 265
	Sample	2	33
	Flot size (ml)	40	58
Cereal remains			
Triticum spelta grain		–	1
glume base		1	–
T. dicoccum grain		–	1
Triticum sp glume bases		1	5
Cerealia indet.		2f	2f
Weeds			
Raphanus raphanistrum capsule		–	1
Arrhenatherum elatius rootlets		2	7
Poaceae internodes		–	2

f = fragment

Table 54: Blackhorse, charred plant remains from gullies 136–7 and associated features, post-hole structure 61 and associated features, and post-hole structure 127

	137	137	136	136	61	61		127
Feature group	137	137	136	136	61	61		127
Feature type	Gully	Gully	Pit	Post-holes			Hearth	Post-hole
Feature / section	621	C	161	146	34	55	25	71
Context	620	600	160	145	35	56	26	120
Sample	59	60	25	23	8	13	6	19
Flot size (ml)	17	14	110(30)	6	16	80	90(22)	35
Cereal remains and other crops								
Triticum aestivum grain	–	–	4	–	–	–	–	1
T. spelta grain	–	–	12	–	–	2	–	–
tail grain	–	–	–	–	–	1	–	–
spikelet forks	–	–	4	–	–	1	–	–
glume base	–	–	100	–	–	21	116	–
rachis fragments	–	–	12	–	–	4	–	–
T. dicoccum spikelet forks	–	–	16	–	–	8	–	–
glume bases	–	–	52	1	3	28	104	2
rachis fragments	–	–	16	–	1	12	12	–
Triticum sp. grain	–	–	4	–	1	1	48	–
spikelet forks	–	–	12	–	1	3	32	–
glume bases	2	–	380	–	2	109	1416	2
rachis fragments	–	–	–	–	–	–	64	–
Hordeum vulgare grain	–	–	–	–	–	–	–	1
Secale sp rachis fragments	–	–	–	–	1	–	–	–
Avena sp.	–	1	–	–	–	–	–	–
Vicia faba cotyledon	–	–	–	–	–	1	–	–
Cerealia indet.	4f	–	36f	–	3f	42f	220	12f
Embryos	–	–	–	–	–	–	4	–
Rachilla	–	–	–	–	–	1	–	1
Weeds								
Corylus avellana nutshell	–	–	–	–	–	1f	–	–
Chenopodium album	–	–	4+8f	–	1	3	–	–
Chenopodium sp.	–	–	–	–	–	–	4+28f	1
Montia fontana ssp *chondrosperma*	–	1	–	–	–	–	–	–
Spergula arvenis	–	–	–	–	–	2	–	–
Persicaria maculosa	–	–	–	–	1	–	–	–
P. lapathifolia	–	–	–	–	–	1f	–	–
Polygonum aviculare	–	–	4	–	1f	3	–	–
Fallopia convolvulus	–	–	4f	–	1	2f	12+24f	–
Rumex acetosella	–	–	4	–	1	1	12	–
Brassicaceae indet.	–	–	–	–	–	–	4	–
Aphanes arvensis	–	–	–	–	1	–	–	–
Vicia / Lathyrus sp.	–	–	–	–	–	4	–	–
Trifolium sp.	–	–	4	–	–	1	–	–
Plantago lanceolata	–	–	4	–	–	–	4f	–
Carex sp. (biconvex)	–	–	–	–	–	–	4	–
Arrhenatherum elatius rootlets	2	–	–	–	3	–	20	3
Lolium sp.	–	–	–	–	–	1	–	–
Avena sp. awn frags	–	–	28	–	–	3	88	–
Bromus sp.	–	–	4	–	–	–	–	–
Bromus / Avena sp.	–	–	–	–	–	3f	–	–
Small Poaceae	–	–	–	–	–	3	–	–
Poaceae internodes	–	–	12	–	–	8	–	–
Leaf fragments	–	–	–	–	1	–	–	–
Unident.	–	–	–	–	–	–	4	–
Cenococcum geophilum	–	–	–	1	–	–	–	–

Table 55: Blackhorse, charred plant remains from penannular gully 203 and associated features

	Feature group	203			Post-hole	Post-hole	Shallow feature
	Feature type	Penannular gully					
	Feature	187	E	357	370	297	286
	Context	188	202	356	371	298	287
	Sample	27	28	44	47	40	39
	Flot size (ml)	150(18)	50	30	18	60	41
Cereal remains							
Triticum spelta grain		–	–	–	–	–	1
glume base		8	5	2	–	25	6
rachis fragments		–	–	–	–	1	–
T. dicoccum spikelet forks		–	1	–	–	–	–
glume bases		–	15	–	–	1	14
rachis fragments		–	3	–	–	–	2
Triticum sp. grain		–	2+2f	–	–	2	–
spikelet forks		–	–	1	–	4	3
glume bases		16	25	–	–	29	40
basal rachis fragments		8	–	–	–	–	1
Cerealia indet.		8f	8f	3f	1f	8f	16f
Embryos		–	1	–	–	–	–
Weeds							
Corylus avellana nutshell		–	1f	–	–	–	–
Chenopodium album		–	6f	–	–	1	1
Persicaria maculosa		–	–	–	–	–	1
P. lapathifolia		–	–	–	1	1	–
Fallopia concolvulus		8	3f	–	–	–	1
Rumex acetosella		–	1	–	–	1	2
Vicia / Lathyrus sp.		–	–	–	–	2	–
Melilotus sp.		–	–	–	1	–	–
Trifolium sp.		–	–	–	–	1	–
Origanum vulgare		–	–	–	–	1	–
cf *Euphrasia* sp.		–	–	–	20	–	–
Galium aparine		–	–	–	1	–	–
Luzula sp.		–	–	–	–	–	1
Arrhenatherum elatius var *bulbosum* tuber		8	–	–	–	–	–
A. elatius rootlets		–	7	4	4	7	6
Avena sp. awn fragments		8	–	1	–	5	–
Phleum sp.		–	–	1	–	–	–
Danthonia decumbens		–	–	1	–	–	–
Small Poaceae		–	1	1	–	1	–
Poaceae internodes		–	–	–	1	1	–
Unident.		–	1	1	–	1	–
Buds		8	–	–	–	–	–
Pteridium aquilinum pinnule		–	–	–	–	1	–

Table 56: Blackhorse, charred plant remains from enclosure ditch 112 and features associated with enclosure 132 (four-post structure 452)

Feature group		132			452	
Feature type		Enclosure ditch			Post-holes	
Feature/section	O	M	F	382	384	292
Context	156	561	422	415	417	299
Sample	20	71	72	52	54	41
Flot size (ml)	23	11	8	30	33	35
Cereal remains						
Triticum aestivum grain	–	–	–	–	–	1
rachis fragments	–	–	–	–	–	2
T. spelta glume base	–	–	1	–	1	3
T. dicoccum spikelet forks	–	–	–	1	–	–
glume bases	5	2	–	1	1	10
rachis fragments	–	1	–	–	1	4
Triticum sp. grain	–	–	–	3	–	–
glume bases	2	4	2	2	–	36
Avena sp.	–	–	–	–	–	1
Cerealia indet.	1f	1f	1f	3f	2f	15f
Weeds						
Corylus avellana nutshell	–	1f	–	–	–	–
Chenopodium sp.	–	–	1	–	–	–
Persicaria maculosa	–	–	–	–	–	1
Rumex acetosella	1	–	–	–	–	1
Plantago lanceolata	–	–	–	–	–	1
Arrhenatherum elatius rootlets	3	–	4	8f	10	4
Lolium sp.	–	–	–	–	–	1
Avena sp. awn fragments	1	1	–	–	–	5
Bromus sp.	–	–	–	–	–	1f
Danthonia decumbens	–	–	–	–	–	1
Small Poaceae	–	–	–	1	–	–
Poaceae internodes	3	–	–	6	–	–
Leaf fragments	–	–	–	–	1	–
Unident.	–	–	1	–	–	–

some cereal chaff and indeterminate wheat grains. Weed species recovered included fat-hen, redshank (*Persicaria maculosa*), knotgrass, black bindweed, sheep's sorrel, and parsley-piert (*Aphanes arvensis*), all of which are indicative of arable cultivation or disturbed ground. Post-hole 55 was richer in charred plant remains and was dominated by cereal remains. Grains of spelt and indeterminate wheat were identified but the majority of the cereal remains were of chaff remains amongst which emmer and spelt wheat were identified in similar quantities. A cotyledon of field bean (*Vicia faba*) was also identified. The non-economic species recovered were those associated with arable cultivation but were present in small quantities in comparison those of cereals. The charred plant remains are again indicative of crop processing. The lack of grain suggests that the cereal chaff was deposited after processing.

The charred plant remains from hearth 25 were again very rich, the majority consisting of cereal chaff,

with both spelt and emmer present. The non-economic species were again indicative of cultivation and not as frequent as the cereal remains.

From this evidence it is possible to deduce that crop processing activities were carried out in the vicinity.

Four-post structure 127

In contrast, the number of charred plant remains recovered from this structure was very small (Table 54). A single grain of bread wheat, two glume bases of emmer, and a grain of barley (*Hordeum vulgare*) were identified. Weed species are represented by an indeterminate chenopod and fragments of false oat-grass.

Enclosure ditch 132

Samples from ditch sections O, M, and F were analysed (Table 56). The flot sizes of these samples were small and this is reflected in the charred plant content of the samples. Remains of cereals and non-economic species alike were rarely recorded, though the latter were again representative of arable field conditions.

Penannular gully 203 and associated features

Three samples were analysed but the number of charred plant remains was low (Table 55). Spelt and emmer wheats were present and the non-economic species are indicative of arable conditions. There is no evidence for burning *in situ* in the southern terminal and it is suggested that the charred remains represent debris from crop-processing which has been redeposited.

A shallow feature 286 within the northern terminal of the gully was dominated by cereal remains, though the number of plant remains was small. Spelt and emmer wheat were present and though few weed species were present, they were indicative of an arable environment. These remains could all have blown in to the feature from from other sources.

Post-hole 297 produced the remains of cereals – spelt and emmer – and weeds. The weed species were, in general, indicative of arable conditions, though the presence of a single find of wild marjoram (*Origanum vulgare*) may be indicative of dry grassland, hedge bank, or scrub. The post-hole in the centre of the structure (370) contained few charred remains; only a single fragment of cereal grain with the other remains indicative of arable or disturbed environments.

Four-post structure 452

The number of remains was low (Table 56). A single bread wheat grain was recovered from post-hole 292 and this was associated with a partially articulated rachis fragment consisting of two rachii fused together. The size of the rachis suggests that the bread wheat was of a dense-headed variety. Spelt wheat was represented by glume bases and emmer by glume bases and rachis fragments. The non-economic species are again indicative of arable conditions. These charred plant remains again derive from represent crop-processing.

Discussion

A total of 53 plant categories was identified, but only three samples could be considered rich; hearth 25, post-hole 55, and pit 161, all of which lie outside of the enclosure and were dominated by cereal chaff remains. There is, however, little difference between the remains from features inside and outside of the enclosure. Few cereal grains and weed seeds were recovered, suggesting that the remains represent the final stages of crop-processing. Bread, spelt, and emmer wheat were represented by grains and chaff. In some cases, especially in the richer samples, the chaff remains were very well preserved, and in some cases whole spikelet forks of emmer with the rachis still attached were recovered. Barley was represented by a single grain and rye (*Secale cereale*) was represented by a single rachis fragment, although the presence of rye may be in the capacity as a weed as is the most likely case with the oats present in the samples.

It can be suggested that the crops grown in the locality included bread, spelt, and emmer wheat. The presence of the chaff remains of these species suggest that the crops were processed either on the site or within the vicinity. If the crops were stored on site it may be that they were stored in a clean state, i.e. as grain, not as spikelets and the rarity of weed seeds may support this, although it is more likely that the remains represent the final stages of crop-processing. The lack of weed seeds also prevents the determination of other habitats present around the site. The crop-processing product was probably used as a tinder and deposited in the pits while the remains in many of the other features, especially in the enclosure ditch, may be redeposited material.

Charcoal, by Rowena Gale

The preservation of the charcoal varied from excellent (in round-house 1, post-hole 4) to degraded and friable, e.g. post-hole 55 from the four-post structure group 61. It should be noted that when discussing possible structural timbers, the stem measurements are from charred material. When living these stems may have been up to 40% wider. The results are summarised in Table 57 and described in full below. The following taxa or groups of taxa were identified:

Aceraceae. *Acer* sp., maple
Aquifoliaceae. *Ilex* sp., holly
Betulaceae. *Alnus* sp., alder; *Betula* sp., birch
Corylaceae. *Corylus* sp., hazel
Fagaceae. *Quercus* sp., oak
Leguminosae. *Ulex* sp., gorse and/ or *Cytisus* sp., broom
Oleaceae. *Fraxinus* sp., ash
Rhamnaceae. *Frangula alnus*, alder buckthorn
Rosaceae. Subfamily Pomoideae which includes *Crataegus* sp., hawthorn; *Malus* sp., apple; *Pyrus* sp.,pear; and *Sorbus* spp, rowan, service tree and whitebeam. *Prunus spinosa*, blackthorn.
Salicaceae. *Salix* sp., willow and/ or *Populus* sp., poplar

Round-house 1

This building may have been destroyed by fire. Charcoal from three post-holes was examined. Charcoal from post-hole 4 was composed of a large quantity of well preserved material which included a high proportion of roundwood and slivers from much wider wood, e.g. planks or posts. This was identified as oak, stem diameter 10 mm; gorse/broom, stem diameter 5 mm; holly, stem diameter 10 mm; blackthorn, stem diameter 10 mm; hazel, stem diameter 5 mm. A large piece of oak stem which measured 30 mm in length, 10 mm in diameter, and included three wide growth rings, was almost certainly from coppiced growth. Oak sapwood and heartwood was also present. Stem fragments (diam. up to 5 mm) from unidentified monocotyledonous material (e.g. grasses, reeds, cereals) were also recorded.

Conflagration of the building would have resulted in the massed debris from its burnt components settling into gullies and post-holes – perhaps the excellent condition of the charcoal in these contexts can be attributed to conditions pertaining to the fire; following this the charcoal may have lain undisturbed. Although the character of the charcoal (roundwood and posts/planks) suggested a possible origin from structural components (e.g. wattle and posts), the taxa

Table 57: Blackhorse, charcoal (no. fragments identified)

Feature	Context	Sample	Acer	Alnus	Betula	Cory	Fran	Frax	Ilex	Pom	Pru	Quer	Sal	U/C
Round-house 1, post-holes														
4	5	2	–	–	–	3r	–	–	4r	–	3r	91r,s,h	–	2
246	266-7	34	–	–	–	1	–	–	–	–	1	36s,h	–	–
248	271-3	36	–	–	–	6	–	–	–	–	–	22s,h	–	1
Features within penannular gullies 136 and 137														
PH 101	100	21	–	2	–	–	–	–	–	–	–	26s,h	2	2
Pit 161	160	25	1	–	–	–	–	–	–	2	4	10s	–	6r
Post-structure 61, post-holes														
50	51	11	–	–	1	2	–	–	–	1	1	20r,s	–	5
55	56	13	1	1	–	–	–	–	–	–	–	28s,h	–	10r
Hearth 25	26	6	–	–	1	–	–	1	–	–	3r	16r		10r
Four-post structure 127														
PH 71	120	19	–	–	–	2	–	–	–	–	–	21s,h	–	2
Feature														
138	140	17	–	–	–	–	–	–	–	–	–	76s,h	–	–
Enclosure ditch 132														
O	156	20	–	(2)	–	(2)	–	–	–	–	(1)	8s,h	(1)	(1)
M	561	71	–	–	–	–	–	–	–	–	–	6	–	–
F	422	72	–	–	2	–	–	–	–	1	1	8r,h	–	–
Pit within 132														
372	373	50	32	–	–	–	–	–	–	–	12	10r	8	1
Penannular gully 203														
187	188	27	–	–	–	1	–	–	–	–	–	50r,h	–	9
E	202	28	–	–	–	–	–	–	–	2	1	16r,s,h	–	1
357	356	44	–	1	3	1	–	1	–	–	3	53r,h	1	1
286	287	39	–	2	1	5r	–	–	–	–	–	14r,h	–	3
Post-holes within penannular gully 203														
370	371	47	–	–	–	–	–	–	–	1	1	5	–	1
297	298	40	–	4	3	–	–	–	–	–	1	54r,h	–	12r
Group 452, post-holes														
382	415	52	–	–	–	1	1	–	–	1	1	7s,h	–	7
292	299	41	–	–	2	–	2	–	–	–	–	9r	–	5
Group 816, post-holes														
418	419	55	–	–	1	–	–	–	–	–	1	14s,h	–	1

Key: *Cory = Corylus*; *Fran = Frangula*; *Frax = Fraxinus*; Pom = Pomoideae; *Pru = Prunus*; *Quer = Quercus*; *U/C = Ulex/Cytisus*
r = roundwood (diam. < 20 mm); s = sapwood; h = heartwood; ( ) = unverified identification

identified were not wholly consistent with typical hurdle-making. Oak, hazel, and blackthorn have traditional associations with the craft but holly, gorse and broom would be unusual in this context. Gorse and holly are far better used as firewood. It is feasible that charcoal from this feature was either fuel debris or a mixture of fuel debris and burnt structural materials. The charred monocot material could relate to either fuel or thatch.

Post-holes 246 and 248 were part of the porch and both included hazel, and oak sapwood and heartwood. The sample from post-hole 246 also included gorse/broom and some cokey or slightly vitrified material, and, in addition, blackthorn was present in the sample from post-hole 248.

Penannular gullies 136 and 137
Post-hole 101 may have been part of the entrance to round-house 137. Charcoal from the fill of the post-hole included oak sapwood and heartwood, alder, gorse/broom and willow/poplar. The charcoal from shallow pit 161 which lay within both 136 and 137, but was perhaps a central feature within gully 136, consisted of oak sapwood, maple, blackthorn, gorse/broom, and the hawthorn group.

Post-hole structure 61; hearth 25

Charcoal from post-hole 50, included oak roundwood and sapwood, blackthorn, gorse/broom, the hawthorn group, hazel, and birch. Charcoal from post-hole 55 was fairly abundant but poorly preserved. Taxa identified included oak sapwood, maple, blackthorn, gorse/broom, and alder.

Hearth 25 was relatively charcoal-rich, (sample 6), and contained oak roundwood, blackthorn roundwood, gorse/broom roundwood, ash, and birch.

Four-post structure 127

Post-hole 71, contained oak sapwood and heartwood, gorse/broom, and hazel.

Feature 138

Feature 138, which is undated, sited towards the eastern edge of the site, is interpreted as a burnt out tree-throw. The abundant charcoal was 25% subsampled and consisted of large fragments (up to 20 mm in length) of fast-grown oak sapwood and heartwood. The identification of a single taxon supports the interpretation of this feature.

Enclosure ditch 132 and internal features

The poor preservation of charcoal in ditch sections O, M, and F may have been due to the general erosion and waterlogging of the ditch. The fills of the ditch suggested a gradual natural silting and much of the charcoal probably accumulated through windblow or disturbance, rather than by deliberate dumping. In some places, however, it is likely that material was deliberately deposited. For example, the south-eastern corner of the ditch, section O, contained rather friable charcoal that was heavily infiltrated with ?iron deposits. Its poor condition hampered identification. Oak sap- wood and heartwood was recorded. Unverified taxa included blackthorn, gorse/ broom, hazel or alder, and willow/poplar. The charcoal from section M in the south of the ditch was in similarly poor condition but identified as oak. Charcoal from the northern arm of the ditch in section F included Oak roundwood and heartwood, blackthorn, hawthorn type, and birch.

Pit 372 was one of two in the secondary fill of ditch section D in the north-eastern corner of enclosure 132. A 25% sub-sample of the large quantity of charcoal (sample 50) from this pit was examined and identified as maple, blackthorn, oak roundwood, gorse/broom, and willow/poplar.

Penannular gully 203, and associated features

Charcoal was identified from both the terminals and the southern arc of the gully. A 50% subsample of the large volume of charcoal from the northern terminal of ditch section 187 (context 188) was examined. This consisted of oak roundwood and heartwood, gorse/ broom, and hazel. The oak roundwood was from fast-grown stems of various widths up to 20 mm. The latter characteristically included three growth rings. Some fragments still retained bark and it was evident that the wood was felled during the dormant period.

Charcoal from the sample of the shallow feature 286 immediately adjacent to the outer side of the northern terminal consisted of oak roundwood and heartwood, gorse/broom, alder, birch, and hazel. The hazel consisted of short lengths of roundwood measuring up to 12 mm in diameter which included moderate growth rates and up to nine growth rings.

The southern terminal had been recut as a discrete pit-like feature, in which the blackened fill suggested the deposition of burnt material, if not burning *in situ*. The sample (28) included oak roundwood, sapwood and heartwood, gorse/broom, blackthorn and the hawthorn group.

A wide range of taxa was identified from the sample from section 357 in the southern arc of the gully, including oak roundwood and heartwood, blackthorn, gorse/broom, hazel, birch, alder, ash, and willow/poplar.

The central post-hole 370 contained oak, blackthorn, gorse/broom, and hawthorn type. A small piece of ?coal was also noted.

Charcoal was relatively frequent particularly towards the base of post-hole 297 (sample 40), one of a number near the entrance. Oak roundwood predominated, although a few fragments of heartwood were also noted, together with blackthorn roundwood, gorse/broom, alder, and birch.

Four-post structures 452 and 816

Samples from two unusually large post-holes 382 and 292 in four-post structure 452 both contained oak sapwood, blackthorn, gorse/broom; in addition post-hole 382 included hazel, hawthorn type, and alder buckthorn, and post-hole 292 included birch. Charcoal from post-hole 418 in structure 816 also contained oak sapwood, gorse/broom, birch, and alder buckthorn. It may be significant that alder buckthorn was identified at the site only from these post-holes.

Discussion

Most of the charcoal probably represents fuel debris that either accumulated in or was dumped into hollows, pits or ditches. Where features were associated with the round-houses, the fuel is likely to be from domestic use whereas the origin of deposits from four-post structures (function unknown) is less certain and could implicate other activities. Fuel consisted largely of roundwood from a wide range of trees and shrubs, although oak appears to have been the preferred wood, often with the use of wider roundwood or billets including heartwood. There was some evidence to suggest the occasional use of coppice wood, particularly oak. The type and character of the fuel appears to have changed little throughout the occupation.

Round-houses 1 and 136–7
Round-house 1 appeared to have had single phase of use and was possibly destroyed by fire. It would be fair to assume that if the house had burnt down a large quantity of burnt and charred material from the wooden components would have settled in and around the site. Larger pieces may have been recycled as firewood. With this knowledge, the interpretation of the charcoal from the three post-holes analysed is difficult. The range of taxa identified included oak, gorse/broom, holly, blackthorn, and hazel. A high proportion of roundwood was present (probably including coppiced oak) and, in

addition, oak from wider stems/poles. By implication this material could have originated from wattle hurdles and posts however, while oak, hazel, and blackthorn have traditionally been used for such work, it would be unusual, although not impossible, to use gorse, broom and holly. Gorse, broom, and holly do, however, provide excellent firewood (Edlin 1949; Lucas 1960) and it seems more likely that this material (and possibly all the charcoal from this sample) may have originated from a hearth. The preference for narrow roundwood for domestic hearths was demonstrated from fuel deposits from the Iron Age round-houses at Long Range (Chapter 7).

Charcoal from pit 161 and post-hole 101, both enclosed within penannular gullies 136 and 137, probably derived from fuel. The taxa identified included oak, alder, gorse/broom, willow/poplar, maple, blackthorn, and the hawthorn group. There is a strong similarity between the fuel debris from these features and that identified from round-house 1.

Environmental evidence
The settlement at Blackhorse was sited on high ground overlooking the River Clyst. Soils were sandy with areas of clay and/or gravel. Oak was evidently widely available and although some of the charcoal suggested the use of coppiced wood, much of the fuel appeared to have been gathered from trees of slower growth and probably, therefore, from unmanaged woodland. Oak heartwood was common indicating the use of wood from trees attaining a degree of maturity. The composition of the local woodland, therefore probably consisted mainly of oak with ash, maple, and hazel on the heavier soils, with heath or more open woodland on the sandier ground with oak, birch, and gorse/broom. Blackthorn, hawthorn, and gorse probably formed marginal woodland or scrubland, while damper patches on lower levels and areas around the river supported wetland species such as alder, alder buckthorn, willow, and poplar.

Conclusion
The charcoal was probably mostly from fuel debris – there was no clear evidence to suggest that it derived from structural elements. A wide range of wood species was used with emphasis on oak, and there appeared to be little differentiation between samples from the various features. Much of the fuel was probably from domestic hearths although that associated with post-hole structures may have derived from other activities.

The landscape included a wide variety of trees and shrubs characteristic of sandy/clay soils. Oak woodland probably dominated, possibly with some areas more typical of heathland, with birch and gorse, or scrub consisting of blackthorn, hawthorn, and gorse. The nearby River Clyst would probably have provided a suitable habitat for wetland species. The evidence suggested that some areas of oak were probably coppiced.

The Radiocarbon Dates,
by Michael J. Allen

Six radiocarbon determinations of charcoal recovered from a range of different features and structures provide a series of Iron Age dates (Table 58; Fig. 93).

The determination from post built round-house 1 falls within a radiocarbon plateau resulting in a calibrated range of 400 years (770–370 cal. BC). The date is, however, undoubtedly earlier than all the others from the site.

The other results provide a coherent group with determinations from the main fill of the enclosure ditch (132) and from a four-post structure (127) well outside the enclosure to the east, all being statistically indistinguishable at the 95% confidence level (Ward and Wilson 1978). These range between 390 and 30 cal. BC, but the highest probability (of the ditch samples at least) fall between 200 and 100 cal. BC. Thus some structures and activity inside and outside the enclosure were contemporary. The probability distributions of determinations from penannular gully 203 within the enclosure, and from pit 161 within pennannular gullies 136–7 both overlap, providing dates of about 160 cal. BC–cal AD 90. Although these distributions provide considerable overlap with those from the enclosure ditch 132, they suggest a activity at a slightly later date.

These dates compare well with those from Langland Lane and Long Range and indicate that the settlements are broadly contemporary (Table 67).

Table 58: Blackhorse, radiocarbon dates

Context	Material	Lab. no.	Result BP	$\delta^{13}C‰$	Calibration BC (2σ)
Recut penannular gully 203, single fill	*Quercus* charcoal	GU-7227	2000±50	-24.1	160 cal. BC–cal. AD 90
Pit 161, inside penannular gullies 136-7, single fill	*Prunus* charcoal	AA-30659	2065±45	-26.6	200 cal. BC–cal. AD 20
Enclosure ditch 132, S side, central fill	*Quercus* charcoal	AA-30661	2120±45	-23.3	360–30
Enclosure ditch 132, SE corner, central fill	*Prunus* charcoal	AA-30660	2125±45	-26.4	370–40
Four-post structure 127, post-hole 71, single fill	*Quercus* sapwood charcoal	AA-30662	2175±50	-24.7	390–100
Round-house 1, post-hole 4, single fill	*Quercus* sapwood/ roundwood charcoal	GU-7840	2370±60	-24.9	770–370

192

M. Stuiver and R.S. Kra eds. 1986 Radiocarbon 28(2B): 805-1030; OxCal v2.15 cub r:4 sd:12 prob(chron)

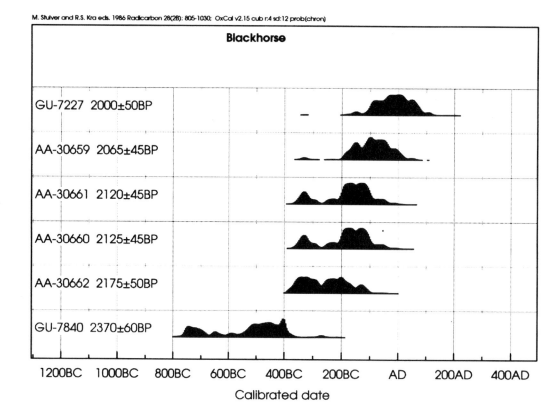

Figure 93   Blackhorse: probability distributions of radiocarbon dates

Discussion, by C.A. Butterworth and A.P. Fitzpatrick

The small quantity of flaked stone from the site (17 pieces) hints at early prehistoric activity but no datable features earlier than the Iron Age were encountered. The earliest settlement activity is represented by round-house 1 which is of Early/Mid Iron Age date, yielding a date of 770–370 cal. BC (GU-7840; 2370±60 BP). It is possible that this building was burnt down, but the charcoals also include species more commonly used in domestic hearths, which could, of course, represent the cause of any fire. There were no finds and few charred plant remains were present, so it is not possible to suggest the use(s) of the round-house. It is possible that field boundaries 378 (which was cut by enclosure 132), 62 and 63/85/12, which are not otherwise dated, could be contemporary with this round-house.

There is no certain evidence to establish any sequence between those features inside and outside of enclosure 132, but it is possible that there was an earlier, unenclosed, phase which was supseded by an enclosed one. Gully 137 may be suspected to have been earlier than the ditch as it was not seen to cut the infilled enclosure ditch. If this round-house and 136 also are indeed earlier then, as with round-house 1, they too could have lain within the area demarcated by ditches 378, 62, and 63/85/12. The gullies of both buildings are noticeably slighter than the penannular gullies from the other Iron Age sites examined in the project, and this is not due to plough damage. A number of possible stake-holes were also identified within gullies 136–7, suggesting that they were ring-groove houses.

Post-holes 146 and 107/101 may represent part a porch of house 137. Pit 161, which yielded a radiocarbon date of 200 cal. BC–cal. AD 20 (AA-30659; 2065±45 BP) may represent a central hearth within 136. This date is later than that of 370–40 cal. BC (AA-30660; 2125±45 BP) from the secondary fills of the south-east corner of enclosure 132, but there is a considerable overlap. The truncation of gully 137 is probably due in part to the succeeding occupation of round-house 136. Otherwise few features can certainly be attributed to the houses.

It is possible that a further round-house was present. Amongst a number of irregular linear features of natural origin recorded on the site, details of which are held in archive, was a semi-circular gully, 773. This gully did not contain any finds and was truncated by post-medieval ditch 212. Although the radius of the arc suggests that it would have been appreciably smaller than those of gullies 136–7, it is possible that this feature was a round-house. A short length of an undated straight, shallow, gully (750) which was cut by the southern arm of enclosure 132 had a flat base, which may suggest that it too was not of natural origin.

A number of the post-built structures which lie outside of enclosure 132 may be contemporary with round-houses 136–7. Group 61 is considered more likely to represent three separate four-post buildings than one long one, and they and also four-post structure 89 share a common alignment. Four-post structure 127 which yielded a radiocarbon date of 390–100 cal. BC (AA-30662; 2715±50 BP) is aligned more closely with the four-post structures within enclosure 132 and may be contemporary with them. The post-holes of structure 127 are also noticeably deeper than those of the adjacent four-post structure 89, although the same distinction may be made between the shallowness of four-post structure 734 in relation to the depth of four-post structures 452 and 816, all of which lie within enclosure 132. Four-post structure 127 may not have been visible from inside round-house 203. In contrast the slight nature of four-post structure 54 is quite marked in relation to the other well-defined groups, and it may be that these posts represent two two-post structures, perhaps drying racks.

Hearth 25 which is situated immediately adjacent to the three four-post structures in group 61 and close to group 54, yielded abundant charred plant remains including quantities of chaff which suggest on-site cereal processing.

The period, if any, between an open settlement and an enclosed one is unknown. The radiocarbon dates from features inside and outside of the enclosure overlap, and the pottery from these features is similar. Enclosure 132 appears to have had four post-structure either side of the entrance, and a single large round-house sited slightly off-centre. The orientation of the entrances of the enclosure and the round-house are slightly different. This sort of simple square enclosure containing round-houses and four-post structures is widely attested throughout the British Iron Age.

The limited evidence of recutting or clearance of the enclosure ditch, the scarcity of internal features and limited evidence of their replacement or repair suggest that the enclosure was short-lived. Within it, only penannular gully 203 and four-post groups 452 and 816 showed signs of recutting and replacement. If the gully not only defined a round-house but acted as a drain, it might well have needed clearing in only a short time, observation during the excavation showing how quickly cut features could become infilled. The two post-holes of the porch which survive are very substantial features, and could also represent replacements, although no evidence for this was observed.

The radiocarbon date of 160 cal. BC–cal. AD 90 (GU-7227; 2000±50 BP) from 203 is slightly later than those from the secondary fills of the enclosure ditch of 370–40 cal. BC (AA-30660; 2125±45 BP) from the south-east corner and 360–30 cal. BC (AA-30661; 2120±45 BP) from section M in the centre of the southern arm. In view of the overlap between the dates this should not be seen as indicating that round-house 203 continued in use after the enclosure ditch was infilled.

The rapid infilling of the enclosure ditch due to the very mobile sandy subsoil may have contributed to the demise of the enclosure, although heavy erosion from bare subsoil would probably have been less during the lifetime of the enclosure than during the excavation. The effort of recutting the enclosure ditch seems not to have been considered worth repeating; the only certain evidence of this was at the southern entrance terminal. That activity continued while the enclosure ditch was filling was shown by the presence of two undated pits or hearths cut into the partly-filled ditch at the north-east corner.

Of the few features demonstrably later than the enclosure, gully 663 crossed the wholly infilled enclosure ditch and is otherwise undated but it may be suspected that it relates to the pair of curvilinear post-medieval field boundary ditches, 22 and 212.

The finds from the enclosure and related features constitute a modest assemblage; principally pottery with a few querns, rubbers, and an unfinished stone spindle whorl. Many of these were concentrated in the south-eastern part of the enclosure ditch. In order to make the distribution comparable more readily, only sections A, P, and O in the south-eastern arm of the ditch have been considered. The other two sections have not been included (Fig. 102, below). A similar distribution of finds is apparent in gully 203.

The charcoals are mostly from fuel debris and indicate that oak woodland, areas of heathland, wetland, and scrub all lay nearby. Although there is some evidence for coppicing, most of the wood comes from unmanaged woodland. The charred plant remains are very similar to those from the other sites of Iron Age date, indicating the final processing of bread, spelt, and emmer wheat, which were probably grown locally, and presumably stored on site. Large quantities of chaff which indicate threshing and winnowing were only found in features outside the enclosure.

9. Studies of the Sites of Prehistoric Date

This chapter presents six studies that review the materials from the sites of prehistoric date, before we turn, in Volume 2, to the sites of Roman date and the abrupt cultural changes that the Conquest brought. The finds of prehistoric date from Pomeroy Wood are not included in these analyses as it is possible that a considerable quantity of them were introduced to the site in the Roman period amongst the turf for the rampart facings of the early Roman military base.

The opportunity of review is particularly important for the environmental evidence, as it comprises the first large and relatively well dated group of assemblages recovered from later prehistoric settlements in east Devon. It also provides the opportunity for a preliminary attempt to characterise the farming practices of the area in this period. The environmental data is considered by types of material; firstly charcoal, followed by the charred plant remains, then drawing on these studies a crop-processing model for the Bronze and Iron Ages is presented. Following a review of the radiocarbon dates for the prehistoric sites, certain aspects of the material culture are reviewed. Finally, a brief synthesis is presented.

The Charcoal: Environmental and Artefactual Evidence, by Rowena Gale

The quality and quantity of the charcoal naturally varied from site to site (Table 59). At the three enclosed sites of Castle Hill, Hayne Lane, and Blackhorse, charcoal was relatively abundant, whereas at Patteson's Cross, Langland Lane, and Long Range, charcoal tended to be sparse and poorly preserved. The taxa identified from each site are summarised in Table 60, which also indicates the number of contexts in which each taxon was identified. Provisional identifications and contexts where dating was ambiguous or insecure have not been included here.

Environmental Evidence

Although the topographical features of each site differed, the underlying soils mostly consisted of sands

Table 59: charcoal samples from prehistoric sites by period

Site	Period	No. samples
Castle Hill	Neo, M–LBA	29
Patteson's Cross	E–MBA	23
Hayne Lane	M–LBA	17
Langland Lane	M–LIA	8
Long Range	Neo, M–LIA	16
Blackhorse	E–LIA	8
Total		101

with clay and gravel. Blackhorse, Long Range, Castle Hill, and Hayne Lane were in fairly close proximity to streams or rivers. The tree flora appears to have been more or less similar throughout the region and heathland species were common at most sites. The high frequency of oak charcoal at all six sites suggests that oak formed the major component of the woodland environment.

Only a small number of contexts of Neolithic date were examined and consequently the environmental evidence from this period was sparse, although charcoal from Castle Hill identified oak (*Quercus*), hazel (*Corylus*), blackthorn (*P. spinosa*), hawthorn type (Pomoideae) and willow/poplar (Salicaceae). A greater volume of charcoal was available from Middle Bronze Age horizons at Castle Hill, and suggested that the environment was characterised by heathland, supporting ericaceous shrubs, birch (*Betula*), gorse (*Ulex*), oak, and pine (*Pinus*). The status of pine in southern Britain at this period is uncertain and its distribution may have been patchy. Although pine was common throughout Britain in the Postglacial and Mesolithic periods, it appeared to have been restricted to northern regions in subsequent periods (Rackham 1990). Its presence at Castle Hill, combined with other recent evidence, e.g., in the Late Iron Age at Wytch Farm, Dorset (Gale 1991), testifies to its survival in the south into the late prehistoric era, although perhaps in isolated local habitats.

The remaining woodland taxa identified were similar to those from Castle Hill, typified by acid-loving species, suggesting a landscape of similar character. The frequency of blackthorn and hawthorn in the charcoal tends to endorse the suggestion of marginal woodland, heathland or scrubland. The fruits of both (sloes and hawthorn fruits were identified at Castle Hill) are devoured by birds, thus aiding seed dispersal. Once established these spiny, shrubby species rapidly colonise cleared or open land and form dense thickets. They also provide effective hedging against livestock. Holly (*Ilex*) occurred at all sites except the two adjacent sites of Patteson's Cross and Langland Lane, but since charcoal was generally sparse at both sites, the absence may not be significant. Holly tolerates most soils and conditions but, despite its excellent qualities as fuel, it is rarely identified from archaeological sites. This may be indicative of distribution patterns, difficulty in cutting or working the extremely hard timber, or reverence for the mystic associations of the tree (Grigson 1958). Both ash (*Fraxinus*) and maple (*Acer*) occur in oak woodland and in more open sites but neither may have been particularly common in the region since they were generally poorly represented in the charcoal. Alder (*Alnus*), willow (*Salix*) and/or poplar (*Populus*) and alder buckthorn (*Frangula alnus*) were only identified from sites within striking distance of rivers or streams where suitable wetland conditions would have existed.

Table 60: Overview of identified charcoal from prehistoric sites by no. of contexts sampled

Period	Site	No. contexts sampled	Acer	Alnus	Betula	Corylus	Frangula	Fraxinus	Ilex	Pom	Prunus	Quercus	Salic	Ul/Cyt	Pinus
Neo	Castle Hill	3	–	–	–	1	–	–	–	1	2	1	1	–	–
Neo	Long Range	1	–	–	–	–	–	1	–	–	–	1	–	–	–
MBA	Castle Hill	22	–	13	1	7	–	2	2	6	10	21	1	7	2*
E–MBA	Patteson's Cross	8	1	–	–	1	–	1	–	–	5	8	–	2	–
M–LBA	Hayne Lane	17	–	10	4	12	–	6	2	10	12	16	5	4	–
M–LIA	Long Range	15	4	–	3	7	–	2	2	5	8	17	4	8	–
E–MIA	Langland Lane	8	–	–	1	1	–	–	–	–	4	8	–	5	–
M–LIA	Blackhorse	23	3	5	8	9	2	2	1	6	13	23	3	18	–
	Total	96	8	28	17	38	2	14	7	28	54	92	14	44	2

Pom = Pomoideae; Salic = Salicaceae; Ul/Cyt = Ulex/Cytisus; * = identified by A. Clapham

Woodland Management

Although some charcoal exhibited fast-grown wood there was little conclusive evidence of coppicing or woodland management. Oak may have been coppiced at or near to the Iron Age settlement at Blackhorse, and possibly during the Bronze Age at Castle Hill, and Hayne Lane, and also at Long Range, though the evidence from the last three was very tenuous. If the population density was low, the natural woodland reserves may have sustained the requirements of the settlements.

The Use of the Woodlands

With the exception of the Neolithic enclosures at Castle Hill, all the sites of prehistoric date are settlements, often with post-built round-houses and a range of other post-built structures. The charcoal from these settlements was often associated with domestic refuse, suggesting that much of it was fuel debris. In some contexts, however, single taxon deposits suggested either selective use of fuel woods or independent artefactual origins, such as posts or structural components.

The fuel used at these settlements would most likely have consisted of wood and any other combustible material that was readily available, such as crop processing waste, herbaceous material, and low shrubs. Leaf fragments of ling and heather (*Calluna vulgaris* and *Erica tetralix*) were identified at Castle Hill and both have traditional uses as fuel (Edlin 1949). Coal may also have been used, as fragments of coal were found at Castle Hill and Hayne Lane. The use of charcoal for domestic purposes in the prehistoric era is probably unlikely and the type and character of firewood appears to have remained much the same from the Middle Bronze Age to the Late Iron Age.

Although most of the samples came from contexts where spent fuel (charcoal) had been tipped or had aggregated, direct evidence of fuel residues *in situ* after burning may be present at Long Range (hearth 52). Large quantities of charcoal, and possible traces of scorched earth in some other features at this site, such as penannular gully 269, may also have been caused by small fires but this is consistent with the dumping of hot ashes.

It was evident that although fuel usually consisted of roundwood from a wide range of trees and shrubs, oak was used most frequently and often included heartwood. When used in combination, this mixture would have provided a long-lasting, energy efficient heat source. Narrow roundwood (or faggots) produces a hot, although relatively short-lived fire, whereas oak billets or logs which include heartwood sustain high temperatures for a longer period. In contrast, at Hayne Lane, one of the samples from the enclosure ditch (138) and that from a pit in round-house 458 (pit 54), consisted of charcoal from a single taxon (blackthorn in the ditch and oak in the pit), and may implicate a more specific use fuel. There was no direct evidence for the industrial use of fuel from any of the sites.

The most energy efficient firewood is obtained from dense woods, such as oak (with heartwood), blackthorn, gorse, ash, hawthorn type, and holly. Oils present in ash and holly allow green wood to burn well, and fresh evergreen holly leaves burn fiercely. Maple, hazel, and resinous birch also make excellent firewood (Edlin 1949; Lines 1984), and pine is good but tends to spit. Alder, willow, and poplar, however, are less efficient since their high moisture contents adversely effect the quality; to some extent this can be countered by adequate seasoning, although the woods are light in weight and quickly burn away. Although a strong element of selection was evident from the fuel residues (e.g., the preference for oak), fuel gathering would have been dependent on species growing in the immediate environment. The bulk of the fuel was probably taken randomly from unmanaged woodland or hedgerows, although some of the oak was characteristic of coppice wood, for example that from Blackhorse.

In some contexts the associated evidence suggested the burnt remains of structural components as the more likely origin for the charcoal. At Blackhorse, round-house 1 may have burnt down after only a short period of use and the charcoal from the post-holes was anticipated to be from the charred structure. However, the wide range of taxa from these contexts suggested that while some of the charcoal might have been structural in origin (i.e., species commonly used for hurdles and posts, etc), other species such as gorse/broom and holly were more likely to represent fuel. At Patteson's Cross, Hayne Lane, and Long Range there was also evidence to suggest the use of oak posts, although it was not possible to estimate the dimensions of the posts from the fragmented material. The presence of heartwood indicated that the posts were made from stems or poles that were probably at least 20 years of age, and possibly considerably more. Oak heartwood provides strong, durable posts with a potential working life of many centuries; it has formed the framework of major structures for millennia and it was probably used for this purpose at the prehistoric settlements.

The Charred Plant Remains: Environmental and Economic Evidence, by Alan J. Clapham and C.J. Stevens

Introduction

The first part of this section (A.J.C.) follows the changes in land-use and agricultural activity use between the six sites of prehistoric date. The second part (C.J.S) models the storage practices evidenced by the samples, and how these practices changed through time.

A lack of opportunity has meant that there have been relatively few archaeobotanical and palaeoecological studies of the landscapes of lowland Devon. Amongst the older excavations in this area, that at Hembury produced spelt wheat, but it is uncertain whether the material is Neolithic, Iron Age, or even Roman in date

(Helbaek 1952; Bell 1984; Moffett *et al*. 1989). The only published material from modern excavations is from the Bronze Age ring ditches at Hayes Farm, Clyst Honiton but, as with many samples from ditches, these contained few charred plant remains: cereals such as indeterminate wheat and chaff, and weeds such as black bindweed, brome grass, and campion (Pearson 1989). In consequence the data recorded from the settlements of prehistoric date in the present project cannot be placed readily within an existing interpretative framework.

Instead most palaeo-environmental work on sites of prehistoric date in Devon has been in the upland regions of Dartmoor and Exmoor (Bell 1984). Even so, the evidence from Exmoor remains sparse, although it may at least be said that the dominant vegetation from the Neolithic onwards was moorland, with some pastoral grazing. In contrast, the importance of Dartmoor in this type of study has long been recognised (Bell 1984), with pollen being the principal category of evidence (Caseldine and Hatton 1984), and plant macrofossils appearing only rarely. The pollen data that are currently available suggest that, during the Neolithic, there were small scale woodland clearances and, at Shaugh Moor, a pattern of small scale clearance and regeneration appears to have continued until the beginning of the 2nd millennium BC (Beckett 1981; Bell 1984). In other places this pattern seems to have ceased much earlier.

In the Bronze Age there is a significant increase in the amount of woodland clearance with little apparent regeneration, emphasising the importance of pastoralism (Beckett 1981). Charred plant remains are, however, rare. A few remains of barley, wheat, and *Vicia* sp. were recovered from a hut circle on Holne Moor (Bell 1984), as was also the case in the extensive sampling of the houses and deposits within the Shaugh Moor enclosure (Smith *et al*. 1981; Bell 1984).

According to Simmons (1969), the Iron Age indicates a change in subsistence pattern with a shift from the uplands to the lower ground (Bell 1984). Some settlement still continued into the Iron Age, though, and at Shaugh Moor there are cultivation terraces (Smith *et al*. 1981), cereal grains and weed pollen.

The patterns that emerge from the analyses discussed here therefore form what is, in effect, a preliminary statement on the prehistoric 'economies' of lowland Devon. The following summary attempts to provide a framework for future research, although it is recognised clearly that, in order to support or refute the conclusions it reaches, more work on a range of sites using all types of environmental evidence is necessary.

The Plant Remains

Some 115 samples of charred plant remains were analysed. As with the charcoal, most of the samples came from ditches and post-holes and are subject to related taphonomic processes. In general though, the plant remains were well preserved allowing the identification of 109 charred taxa (Table 61), of which 24 belonged to crop categories and 86 were of non-cultivated taxa. The botanical and ecological evidence for each of these categories is reviewed below.

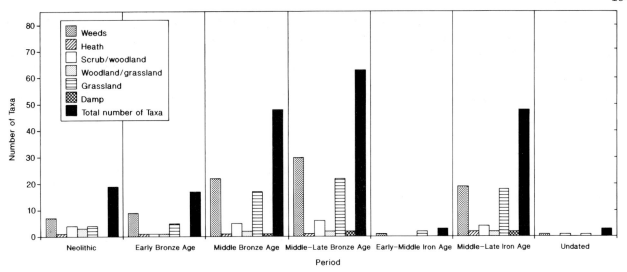

Figure 94   Number of taxa by habitat represented in the charred plant remains from prehistoric sites, by period

Crops

The majority of the crop remains are cereal chaff, such as wheat spikelet forks, glume bases, and rachis fragments. In general, few grains of cereals were recorded and those that were come from pits. Even allowing for the relatively large data-set, when assessed chronologically, the numbers of samples from each period remain small. Accordingly the chronological trends recorded must still be regarded as being very much preliminary observations.

Neolithic

For this period the dominant cereal remains are spikelet forks of emmer wheat (*Triticum dicoccum*) (Table 61a) from the Neolithic enclosure ditches at Castle Hill. As spikelet forks are present, it can be assumed that this particular crop was either stored on site or at least processed in the vicinity of it. Although it is not possible to be sure that the crop was cultivated in the locality, it is assumed that this was the case.

Early–Middle Bronze Age

A far larger number of samples from a greater variety of features was analysed from this period at Patteson's Cross and Castle Hill, the majority from post-holes (66% of dated contexts sampled). The increase in the sample size obviously increases the chance of recovering a larger number of crop types and 17 crop categories representing nine species were identified. Three types of wheat were found, which include one free-threshing hexaploid, bread wheat (*Triticum aestivum*) and two glume wheats, one of which was tetraploid, emmer, (*T. dicoccum*) and one hexaploid, spelt wheat (*T. spelta*). In all casees wheat grains of these types were identified . Chaff remains in the form of spikelet forks and glume bases were also recovered for emmer wheat and glume bases for spelt wheat (Table 61a).

Barley was identified as the hulled variety; both full and tail grains were identified, as well as rachis fragments. Other cultigens identified include pea

(*Pisum sativum*) and flax (*Linum usitatissimum*), although these crops were not as common as the cereals.

It may be assumed that in this area of lowland Devon, there was an increase in the crop resources in the Early/Middle Bronze Age that was maintained until the Roman Conquest.

Middle–Late Bronze Age

Despite the smaller number of sites, effectively just Hayne Lane, the wider range of archaeological features again results in the recording of what may be thought to be a more representative number of crop taxa (Table 61a). The wheats include; bread, spelt, and emmer, with grains of all bread types present and with chaff remains of the glume wheats, emmer and spelt.

Barley was represented by hulled (including tail) and naked grains (although only in small numbers) and chaff, in the form of rachis fragments, was also recovered. It was not possible to determine whether the barley grains were of the two- or six-row varieties, although some of the grains were twisted, suggesting that six-row barley was present.

Other crops present include the field bean (*Vicia faba*) and peas and flax. It was not possible to determine whether the flax represented a crop used for oil or fibre; or indeed both.

The greater presence of cereal remains, of both grains and chaff, suggests that crop-processing was taking place within the vicinity of the settlements. The discovery of grain in some of the small pits/large post-holes may suggest that some of these features were used for storage, although this was clearly not a widespread practice. In general the greater presence of cereal remains and crop remains suggests that they were being cultivated locally.

Middle–Late Iron Age

Thirty-nine samples were analysed from this phase (Table 61a). Bread, spelt, and emmer wheat were again identified, represented by both grain and chaff. In the case of bread wheat, an articulated rachis was found consisting of two nodes. The small size of the individual rachii suggests that this wheat was of a dense-headed variety. Other cereals identified included hulled barley; chaff remains of this crop were also recovered. A rachis fragment of rye (*Secale cereale*) (Table 61a) was identified but the small number of finds suggests that rye was present as a weed of the other cereal crops and not as crop in its own right. Other cultigens identified again include field bean and pea and once again it can be suggested that the crops were grown and processed locally.

The non-cultivated plant species

Thirty-nine of the 86 identified non-cultivated plant categories were considered to be weeds of crops, 4 represent heathland, 6 scrub/woodland, 3 woodland/ grassland, 30 grassland, and 4 species indicate damp conditions (Table 62b). Although most species are specific to a certain type of habitat some have the ability to grow in widely varying conditions. The distribution of taxa and habitat types by period are shown in Table 62 and Figure 94, although it must be emphasised that one of the main reasons for the variation in the number of taxa and habitats represented through time may simply be the wide variation in the number of samples analysed from each period. It is also often the case that samples from the earliest contexts are under-represented and linked to this is the taphonomic

problem in which earlier contexts are subject to reworking or biological and physical destruction for a longer period.

As might be expected, the commonest habitat represented by the plant species is that of weeds. It is assumed that the majority of this category was growing with the crops and that they form part of the crop-processing residues. The other categories present, especially those of scrub/woodland and woodland/grass-land may indicate the presence of field-edge species such as greater stitchwort (*Stellaria holostea*), bramble (*Rubus fruticosus*), sloe (blackthorn: *Prunus spinosa*) and lesser celandine (*Ranunculus ficaria*).

The other major habitat type represented within the samples was grassland. Some of these taxa such as the vetches (*Vicia* spp.), clover (*Trifolium* sp.) and the grasses (e.g., *Arrhenatherum elatius* – false oat-grass) can be found in, and may be indicative of, arable cultivation. However, the high number of species present which tend to be found only in grasslands, for example ox-eye daisy (*Leucanthemum vulgare*), suggests that here they represent a grassland habitat.

Weeds

The largest habitat type recorded was weeds of cultivation, which can also include disturbed ground. The largest number of the weed taxa is found at the sites

Table 61: a) Identified cereals and other crops from prehistoric sites by period

Period / Crops	Neo	EBA	MBA	M–LBA	E–MIA	M–LIA	Undated
Triticum aestivum grain		■	■	■		■	
rachis frags			■	■		■	
T. spelta grain			■	■			
tail grain			■	■		■	
glume bases			■	■		■	
spikelet forks			■	■		■	
rachis fragments			■	■			
T. dicoccum grain		■	■	■		■	
tail grain			■	■		■	
spikelet forks	■		■	■		■	
glume bases			■	■			
rachis frags			■	■			
Triticum sp. grain			■	■			
spikelet forks			■	■			
glume bases			■	■			
rachis frags			■	■			
Hordeum vulgare hulled grain	■	■	■	■		■	
tail grain		■	■	■			
naked grain				■			
Hordeum sp. rachis frag.			■	■		■	
Secale cereale rachis frags			■	■		■	
Vicia faba			■	■		■	
Pisum sativum			■	■			
Linum usitatissimum			■				
Number of sites	2	2	2	2	1	3	1
Number of samples	7	5	33	29	2	39	1

Table 61: b) Identified non-cultivated plant species from prehistoric sites by period

Period	Neo	EBA	MBA	M–LBA	E–MIA	M–LIA	Undated
Weeds							
Ranunculus subgenus Ranunculus			■				
Papaver rhoeas				■			
Papaver sp.				■			
Chenopodium polyspermum				■			
C. album		■				■	
Chenopodium sp.	■		■			■	
Atriplex sp.	■					■	
Stellaria media			■	■		■	
Spergula arvensis		■	■	■		■	
Silene sp.		■	■	■		■	
Persicaria maculosa	■	■				■	
P. lapathifolia		■				■	
Polygonum aviculare		■	■			■	
Fallopia convolvulus		■	■			■	
Rumex acetosella						■	
Rumex sp.	■					■	
Malva sylvestris				■			
Viola sp.	■		■	■			
Lepidium sativum				■			
Sinapis sp.				■			
Raphanus raphanistrum			■		■		
Brassicaceae indet.						■	
Anagallis arvensis			■				
Aphanes arvensis						■	
Hyoscyamus niger			■				
Solanum nigrum		■		■			
Veronica arvensis				■			
V. agrestris						■	
V. hederifolia				■		■	
Veronica sp.				■			
Galium aparine	■		■			■	
Lapsana communis			■				
Anthemis cotula			■	■			
Chrysanthemum segetum	■						■
Tripleurospermum inodorum			■			■	
Avena sp.	■			■		■	
Bromus sp.				■			
Bromus/Avena sp.				■			
cf Elytrigia repens				■			
Heath							
Pteridium aquilinum						■	
Calluna vulgaris	■						
Erica tetralix		■	■	■		■	
Danthonia decumbens						■	
Scrub/Woodland							
Corylus avellana nutshell	■	■	■	■		■	
Stellaria holostea				■			

200

Table 61: (continued)

Period	Neo	EBA	MBA	M–LBA	E–MIA	M–LIA	Undated
Rubus fruticosus	■		■	■		■	
Prunus spinosa	■		■	■		■	
Crataegus sp.			■	■		■	
Sambucus nigra	■						
Woodland/Grassland							
Ranunculus ficaria	■	■				■	
Conopodium majus	■						
Ajuga reptans	■						
Grassland							
Stellaria graminea			■	■			
Vicia cracca			■	■			
V. hirsuta			■	■			
V. tetrasperma		■	■	■		■	
Vicia/Lathyrus sp.	■	■	■	■		■	
Lathyrus pratensis			■				
Melilotus sp.		■		■		■	
Medicago sp.			■				
Trifolium sp.			■	■		■	
Linum catharticum			■			■	
Prunella vulgaris			■	■		■	
Origanum vulgare						■	
Mentha sp.			■				
Euphrasia sp.			■			■	
Odontites vernus			■				
Plantago lanceolata			■	■		■	
Leucanthemum vulgare			■				
Luzula campestris							
Luzula sp.						■	
Festuca type		■				■	
Lolium type				■	■	■	
Poa type	■			■		■	
Arrhenatherum elatius culm bases			■	■		■	
A. elatius rootlets/internodes	■		■	■		■	
A. elatius var bulbosum tubers			■	■	■	■	
Bromus hordeaceus ssp. hordeaceus			■	■		■	
Phleum type				■		■	
Poaceae stems				■		■	
Culm node			■	■		■	■
Small Poaceae	■		■			■	
Damp							
Montia fontana ssp. chondrosperma						■	
M. fontana				■			
Cladium mariscus			■				
Carex sp.				■		■	
Number of sites	2	2	2	2	1	3	1
Number of samples	7	5	33	29	2	39	1

Table 62: Number of identified plant taxa per habitat type for each period

Habitat	Neo	EBA	MBA	M–LBA	E–MIA	M–LIA	Undated
Weeds	7	9	22	30	1	19	1
Heath	1	1	1	1	0	2	0
Scrub/woodland	4	1	5	6	0	4	1
Woodland/grassland	3	1	2	2	0	2	0
Grassland	4	5	17	22	2	18	1
Damp	0	0	1	2	0	2	0
Total taxa	19	17	48	63	3	48	3

of later prehistoric date, with the Middle–Late Bronze Age producing the largest assemblage (Table 62).

Table 63 shows the habit and height range that the weed taxa can attain. Most are either erect, trailing, climbing, or scrambling. The trailers, climbers, and scramblers were most likely to have been using the crop stems as support, whilst the tall erect species could have been growing at the height of the crop. This suggests that the crops were not harvested by ear-plucking but either by uprooting or cutting near to the culm base. This is supported by the presence of less tall weeds that would have been left in the field if harvesting had taken place any higher up the stem. The lack of culm bases within the samples also suggests that the latter scenario was the case. The presence of rootlets of the false oat-grass suggests that some uprooting did take place, as these rootlets would only have been removed in the final stages of crop-processing (Hillman 1981; 1984).

In general, the weeds are of a cosmopolitan nature, being able to grow in a variety of soil types and conditions. The presence of stinking mayweed (*Anthemis cotula*) suggests that during the Middle–Late Bronze Ages heavier clay soils were being exploited as well as the more acidic sandy soils which are indicated by the presence of corn marigold (*Chrysanthemum segetum*).

The presence of wild radish (*Raphanus raphanistrum*) at Castle Hill during the Middle Bronze Age (albeit only one capsule) can be considered as an early record as Greig (1991) suggests that it is not until the Iron Age that this weed species becomes prominent; wild radish is also present in this region in the Middle–Late Iron Age. Henbane (*Hyoscyamus niger*) is a thermophilous weed and this may suggest that either shallow soils were being utilised or that it is indicative of the presence of manure heaps or even of manuring, although, again, only one example was recovered from a post-hole.

Overall the weed seeds apparently indicate no change in the pattern of land-use nor changes in the harvesting practices throughout the occupation of the area.

Heathland
Only four taxa indicative of heathland were identified from the samples, these species were bracken (*Pteridium aquilinum*), heather (*Calluna vulgaris*), cross-leaved heath (*Erica tetralix*) found as leaf and pinnule fragments, and caryopses of heath-grass (*Danthonia decumbens*) (Table 62). This latter species which

Table 63: Habits and height ranges of the identified weed taxa

	Height range (cm)	Habit
Ranunculus subgen. *Ranunculus*	10–100	cre/e
Papaver Rhoeas	60–80	e
Chenopodium polyspermum	<100	e
C. album	<1500	e
Stellaria media	<50	e
Spergula arvensis	<60	e
Persicaria maculosa	<80	d/e
P. lapathifolia	<100	d/e
Polygonum aviculare	<200	pro/scr
Fallopia convolvulus	<1500	tr/cl
Rumex acetosella	10–30	e
Malva sylvestris	<100	spr
Lepidium sp.	<60	d/e
Sinapsis sp.	<100	e
Raphanus raphanistrum	<75	e
Anagallis arvensis	<20	pro
Aphanes arvensis	<10	d/e
Hyoscyamus niger	<80	e
Solanum nigrum	<70	d/e
Veronica arvensis	<30	d/e
V. agrestis	<30	pro/as
V. hederifolia	<60	pro/scr
Galium aparine	300	pro-scr
Lapsana communis	<100	e
Anthemis cotula	<50	e
Chrysanthemum segatum	<60	d/e
Tripleurospermum inodorum	<60	e/as
cf *Elytrigia repens*	<1500	e

Key: e = erect; pro/scr = procumbent/scrambling; tr/cl = trailing/climbing; d/e = decumbent/erect; spr = spreading; pro = procumbent; pro/as = procumbent/ascending; e/as = erect/ascending; cre/e = creeping/erect

is now found only on heathlands has, in the past, been thought to have been an arable weed (Greig 1981).

The use of heathland is indicated from the Neolithic to the Middle–Late Iron Age, and may have been for the provision of bedding for animals, for thatching for dwellings, or for use as fuel (see Gale, above). However, this habitat component was very small with only single or a few finds being identified. The heathland is most likely to have existed on the shallow sandy soils in lowland east Devon.

Scrub / woodland

The scrub/woodland habitat type forms only a small proportion of the remains (Table 62) and was represented by six species, four of which were woody including hazel (*Corylus avellana*), sloe, hawthorn (*Crataegus* sp.) and elder (*Sambucus nigra*). The other two species were greater stitchwort and bramble. The only species to be found throughout was hazel, in the form of nutshell fragments. Although hazel charcoal was recorded, it was not present at all of the settlements and no elder charcoal was recorded.

These remains suggest the presence of woodland or scrub, most likely as scrub around the edges of cultivation. Five of the species (hazel, bramble, sloe, hawthorn, and elder) produce edible nuts, fruits, or berries that may have been collected from the wild to supplement the diet. The presence of greater stitchwort suggests that the areas of scrub could have been quite dense, as this species prefers shady habitats.

Woodland / grassland

Three taxa represent a woodland/grassland component (Table 62). These were lesser celandine, pignut (*Conopodium majus*) and bugle (*Ajuga reptans*). The remains of lesser celandine and pignut were of tubers, whilst bugle was represented by nutlets. All three species can occur in both woodlands and grasslands and it may be suggested that they represent the clearing of the former and development of the latter. Lesser celandine and bugle prefer damper conditions, while the edible tubers of pignut have also been used as a wild food resource. These species appear to occur throughout and it is possible that this may represent woodland clearance.

Grassland

Some 34 taxa can be considered to represent grassland, with the largest assemblage again occurring in the Middle–Late Bronze Age (Table 62). No taxa occurred throughout, though both clover (*Trifolium* sp.) and false oat-grass are found from the Middle Bronze Age onwards.

One of the commonest finds was that of rootlets and internodes of false oat-grass, but unlike most records for Britain (Greig 1991), very few tubers were recorded. There are two forms of false oat-grass: one which produces swollen basal internodes (often called tubers), and one that does not. The tuberous onion couch grass (*Arrhenatherum elatius* var *bulbosum*) can be a pernicious weed of arable land, spread by the breaking-up of the tubers by ploughing. Once it becomes established it is a very difficult weed to eradicate (Robinson 1988). In

non-arable situations, such as rough grassland, far fewer tubers are produced and reproduction is by seed.

False oat-grass is commonly found on well-aerated, moderately deep, neutral or near neutral soils (pH 5.0–8.0) of high to moderate fertility. According to Pfitzenmeyer (1962), false oat-grass can be abundant in lightly grazed or mown grasslands but is intolerant of heavy grazing or close mowing and is therefore much rarer in heavily grazed pasture (although some types have developed which are more resistant). It is also intolerant of shade and is usually absent from mature woodland, although it may occur in regeneration glades and open scrub. It can also be widespread in long-established hay-meadows where it is often found with ox-eye daisy and sheep's sorrel (*Rumex acetosella*) which have also been recorded here.

Table 64 shows (after Pfitzenmeyer 1962) the species that can be found with false oat-grass in a variety of habitats. The 20 species that are asterisked indicate those taxa that have been recorded in the current project. The presence of rootlets and internodes within the samples along with the other indicators of grassland (Table 62) suggests two possibilities.

The first is hay-making. As the number of tubers is low, the possibility that they come from abandoned fields is not a strong one (*cf.* Robinson 1988) and, as false oat-grass is intolerant of heavy grazing, a pastoral use can also be dismissed as being unlikely. Light grazing, as can happen with a hay meadow, causes little damage and when this added to the fact that false oat-grass responds well to manuring (provided by the grazing animals), it suggests that the grassland species could be the remains of hay, which would be an early identification of this crop.

The second possible activity is the ploughing up of grassland followed by cultivation. Some taxa, such as hairy tare (*Vicia hirsuta*) and smooth tare (*V. tetrasperma*), clover, red bartsia (*Odontites vernus*), and ribwort plantain (*Plantago lanceolata*) can survive in arable conditions. This, linked to their association with the cereal and chaff remains as well as the more obligate segetals, suggests this as a possibility. However, the presence of grassland species such as wild marjoram (*Origanum vulgare*), ox-eye daisy, meadow vetchling (*Lathyrus pratensis*), ribwort plantain, medick (*Medicago* sp.) and field woodrush (*Luzula campestris*) point more towards hay-making as the dominant practice. The presence of hairy and smooth tare can be considered to be early records as these species are usually found in Iron Age contexts (Greig 1991).

It is difficult to determine which practice is prominent and most of the species could survive in disturbed habitats for several years before being eradicated. Many of the species present are indicative of dry grassland, some of which prefer base-rich soils (ie fairy flax (*Linum catharticum*) and wild marjoram) as well as rich soils, i.e., ox-eye daisy. Therefore it is possible that the grassland has been ploughed up to provide more arable land, in which some of the grassland species survived for a few years. In order to determine which of these activities is the more likely, it would be necessary to analyse more samples from these sites and carry out pollen analyses from suitable lowland deposits.

Table 64: Plant specied associated with *Arrhenatherum elatius* in grassland habitats

Achillea millefolium	*H. perforatum*
Anthoxanthum odoratum	*Juncus articulatus*
Anthriscus sylvestris	*Lamium purpureum*
Bellis perennis	*Lathyris pratensis**
Betula pendula	*Leucanthemum vulgare**
Brachypodium sylvaticum	*Linaria vulgaris*
Campanula rotundifolia	*L. catharticum**
*Carex flacca**	*Lolium sp.**
*C. sylvatica**	*Lotus pedunculatus*
Carlina vulgaris	*Mercuralis perennis*
Centaurea nigra	*Myosotis arvensis*
Cerastium fontanum	*Origanum vulgare**
Cirsium palustre	*Plantago lanceolata**
C. vulgare	*Poa media*
Clinopodium vulgare	*P. nemoralis*
Cornus sanguinea	*P. pratensis*
Dactylis glomerata	*Potentilla reptans*
Deschampsia spitosa	*Prunella vulgaris**
Equisetum palustre	*Ranunculus subgenus Ranunculus**
Festuca spp.* (includes *F. ovina, F. rubra, F. tenuifolia*)	*Rubus fruticosus*
Galeopsis tetrahit	*Salix aurita*
*Galium aparine**	*Silene sp.**
G. verum	*Stachys sylvatica*
Geum urbanum	*Stellaria media**
Glechoma hederacea	*Taraxacum sect. Ruderalia*
Helianthemum nummularium	*Teucrium scorodonia*
Heracieum sphondylium	*Thelypteris palustris*
Hieracieum sp.	*Trisetum florescens*
Hippocrepis comosa	*Tussilago farfara*
Holcus lanatus	*Urtica dioica*
H. mollis	*Veronica spp.**
Hyacinthoides non-scripta	*Vicia cracca**
Hypericum hirsutum	*Viola sp.**

After Pftizenmeyer 1962. * = species identified in samples from the current project

Damp

Three taxa can be said to be indicative of damp ground: blinks (*Montia fontana* including *M. fontana* ssp. *chrondrosperma*), fen sedge (*Cladium mariscus*) and indeterminate sedges (*Carex* sp.). Blinks can be found in most damp, bare, patches and often in muddy trampled areas. The sedges (both fen and *Carex* sp.) prefer areas of higher water-table and are often found on fens, streams, river, and pond banks, with fen sedge preferring base rich conditions. The finds of indicators of damp ground were not common in the samples, being recorded from the Middle Bronze Age to the Middle–Late Iron Age and probably represent a casual part of the assemblages.

Summary

The commonest habitat type was arable, followed by grassland. The greater majority of the taxa occur in the Middle and Late Bronze Age and the Middle–Late Iron Age, though this is largely a product of the chronological distribution of the samples. Two possible scenarios exist for the presence of these two habitats. One is that they represent two separate activities, one where crops are cultivated and the other is used for light grazing and the production of hay. The other scenario is that the grassland component represents the ploughing up of grassland, in order to produce more arable land. Most of the grassland species are capable of surviving in arable conditions or they may represent the field edge, which was once part of the grassland.

The other habitats include heathland, scrub/woodland, and woodland/grassland, as well as damp ground, all of which could have been present around the settlements. The presence of the woodland/grassland component in the Neolithic may be the precursor to the ploughing up of the grassland. It may also signify the continuing change in the landscape whereby the Neolithic/Early Bronze Age represents woodland clearance for both arable and grassland, with the grassland being converted to arable in the Middle and Late Bronze Age as part of a process which continued into the Middle–Late Iron Age.

The Application of a Crop-processing Model

The investigation of charred assemblages from a wide range of sites of prehistoric and Romano-British date in central and southern England has revealed two distinct methods of crop storage. One in which crops are stored relatively unprocessed, the other in which crops are stored as semi-cleaned spikelets. These different storage methods have been related to differences in the social organisation of agricultural communities (Stevens 1996). The techniques used in that research to investigate at which stage in their processing crops were stored have also been applied to the sites examined by the current project, in order to determine if any regional differences or changes through time are apparent.

Background

The analysis of assemblages in the Upper Thames Valley suggested that most charred assemblages result from a single taphonomic event (Stevens 1996). This is the charring of waste from the daily processing of cereals taken from storage. Hillman (1981; 1984) stated that the traditional communities inhabiting the wet regions of modern Turkey stored their cereals as spikelets that were taken and processed piecemeal, on a day-by-day basis, with the waste often thrown straight onto the fire.

The sequence of processing events outlined by both Hillman (1981; 1984) and Jones (1984; 1987) can be divided into:

- those which take place before storage. For a few weeks after harvest, in bulk, i.e., the whole crop is processed as one unit, possibly in the fields away from the settlement.

- those which take place after storage: On a day-by-day basis, piecemeal, i.e., as much grain is taken and prepared as is needed for that day, and taking place within the settlement, if not around the hearth itself.

The waste from the former (pre-storage) sequence is highly unlikely to survive in the archaeological record. In part, as both Hillman and Jones state, this is because its components are often light and fragile, and unlikely to survive charring. More importantly, however, unless the waste from these stages is kept as fuel it is highly unlikely to ever be charred, and even in these cases the number of charring events compared to those which take place on a daily basis are largely insignificant.

If assemblages of charred plant remains mainly represent the charring of waste from the daily processing of crops taken from storage, then such waste can tell us at what processing-stage the crops were stored. For example, as sheaves, in an unprocessed state; as unclean spikelets, threshed and winnowed, but unsieved; as semi-clean spikelets, sieved, but unpounded; or lastly, as cleaned grain, pounded with the removal of the glumes.

The application of models from Hillman (1981; 1984), van der Veen (1992), and Jones (1984; 1987) to assemblages from the Upper Thames Valley allowed the development of a taphonomic model (Stevens 1996). The model suggests that two different storage practices were commonly practised during prehistoric and Romano-British periods in central and southern England:

- storage probably as sheaves but possibly as uncleaned spikelets
- storage as semi-cleaned spikelets

Such storage practices have been attributed to differences in the social organisation between sites, related to the amount of bulk processing carried out during a short period in late summer prior to storage. This conclusion was reached because sites frequently contained evidence for only one practice, and also because such practices and differences between sites continued for hundreds of years (Stevens 1996). The patterns can be summarised thus:

- storage in an unprocessed state, as sheaves or uncleaned spikelets, indicative of lower levels of social organisation involved in agriculture; i.e. harvesting, any bulk processing prior to storage, and field preparation are carried out at the family level.
- storage as semi-cleaned spikelets, indicative of higher levels of social organisation involved in agriculture. Harvesting, bulk processing, and field preparation are carried out by either large households, or possibly between multiple households

Methods

For the application of this model to the current sites, certain key elements within each sample were quantified, then the ratios between them calculated.

The ratio of glume bases to estimated grains of emmer/spelt wheat

The ratio of glume bases to hulled wheat grains has been used by van der Veen (1992) to demonstrate that most of the assemblages from the north-east of England would seem to result from the charring of waste from pounding and fine sieving. As most prehistoric communities in Britain are likely to have stored crops as spikelets (van der Veen 1992; Hillman 1981; 1984), a high ratio of glume bases to grain must be indicative of the charring of waste from the pounding of cereals after they have been taken from storage.

For the current project the numbers of glume bases in each sample were added together and the number of spikelet forks doubled and added in. The probable number of hulled wheat grains in the samples was then estimated by first calculating the ratio of glume wheats to free-threshing wheats, then by dividing the unidentified wheat grains by this ratio. If no free-threshing wheats were present in the sample, all wheat grains were assumed to belong to glume wheats. Next the ratio of barley grains to this first estimate of hulled wheat grains was calculated. The unidentified cereal grains were then further divided by this ratio.

In the event of only unidentified cereal grains being present in the sample they were then assumed to all belong to hulled wheats. In this way the number of grains probably represents an over-estimation rather than an under-estimation of the actual number of grains of glume wheats present. The number of grains to glumes on average is 1:1 (cf. van der Veen 1992, 81), so that grains divided by glumes for unpounded spikelets prior to or during storage is equal to 1 (logged (10) = 0). Glume rich samples, derived from processing waste after the wheat spikelets have been pounded and sieved are therefore less than 1 (negative logged (10) values). Cleaned cereal grains that have been pounded and the glumes removed in theory contain almost no glumes so that the number of grains is much greater than glumes.

Given the bias in preservation against glume bases in favour of grains (Boardman and Jones 1990), pre-charred assemblages which were originally glume rich are likely to have contained maybe hundreds (logged (10) c. >2) or possibly even thousands (logged (10) c. >3) of glumes to every grain found (cf. Robinson and Straker 1991). From the examination of spikelet assemblages, which were almost certainly burnt *in situ*, from storage pits upon archaeological sites, the maximum preserved ratio to be expected is 1 glume to every 2–3 grains (logged (10) c. 0.4).

The ratio of weed seeds to grain

It has been suggested that the ratio of all weed seeds to grain can be used to differentiate between processing waste (high in weed seeds) and crop product (high in grain). However, accidental loss of grain during 'daily processing', may lead to grains outnumbering weed seeds, but still being outnumbered by glume bases (Stevens 1996). In cases where crops were believed to have been stored as semi-cleaned spikelets and/or grain, grains predominated over weed seeds (which were dominated by large weed seeds). In cases where crops are stored as uncleaned spikelets, then under good

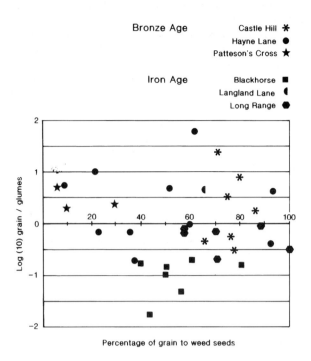

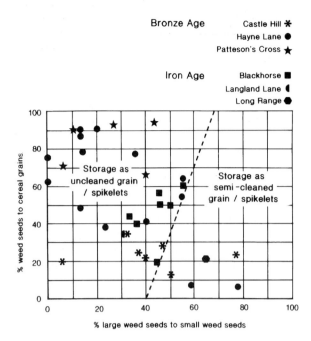

Figure 95   Percentage of grain to weed seeds in samples plotted against the logged ratio of estimated glume wheat grains divided by total glume bases for samples and amalgamated samples from each site of prehistoric date

Figure 96   Percentage of weeds seeds to cereal grains in samples from prehistoric sites plotted against the percentage of large to small weed seeds. The dotted line shows the division as seen from Upper Thames Valley sites between the two different crop storage practices

preservation conditions, the number of weed seeds far outnumbers the numbers of grains.

The results of the first two ratios are shown in Figure 95, with the percentage of grain to weed seeds shown along the X axis and the logged value of grains/glumes shown on the Y axis. Some of the plots result from amalgamated samples, where the number of grains, glumes and weed seeds for individual samples numbered less than 30.

The ratio of small weed seeds to large weed seeds
The last stage of the examination was to calculate the percentage of small weed seeds to large (grain sized) weed seeds. Many of the larger weed seeds are of a similar size to the grain or spikelets and are subsequently only removed either in the final sievings, after pounding or through hand-sorting, and are therefore almost always present in assemblages, but in greatest quantity in grain stored as semi-cleaned spikelets (Hillman 1981; 1984; Jones 1984; 1987). The smaller weed seeds are, conversely, removed through fine sieving, which is one of the earlier stages (*cf.* Hillman 1981), and so are less abundant in waste from crops stored as semi-cleaned spikelets/grain and more abundant in those stored as semi-cleaned spikelets/ grain.

The percentage is taken from the total of all weed seeds which could be ascribed to one of three categories, small seeded (< 2.5 mm), intermediate (those with seeds falling between 2 mm and 3.5 mm. Species which were longer than 3 mm, but frequently less than 2 mm wide; for example, *Lolium perenne*, were also ascribed to this

category) and large seeded, grain sized weed seeds (>2.5). Intermediate species seeds tend to be more common in assemblages dominated by small seeds (Stevens 1996) and therefore only large weed seeds are used to distinguish between storage patterns on sites.

The results are shown in Figure 96, with only individual samples containing more than 15 weed seeds and amalgamated samples plotted. The dotted line shows the division of the two storage patterns as seen for sites in the Upper Thames Valley (*ibid.*).

Preliminary conclusions
With respect to the ratio of grain to glume bases, almost all the samples from the Iron Age sites can be seen to be generally glume rich, indicative of waste from the last processing stages (Fig. 95). The Bronze Age sites are more mixed, with many containing higher proportions of estimated hulled wheat grains than glume bases. In spite of this higher ratio of grains to glumes in the Bronze Age, it is still believed that the majority of samples result from the charring of pounding and sieving waste of crops taken from storage, rather than from the burning of the crop product resulting from, for example, parching accidents or the cleaning of storage pits.

One possible reason is that differences in preservation conditions between the Bronze Age and Iron Age sites led to an even greater bias towards the destruction of glume bases on the Bronze Age sites leading to even greater ratios of grains to glumes.

A second possibility for the differences revolve around a possible greater proportion of barley grains seen in some Bronze Age samples. The technique described above is generally more likely to over-estimate the number of hulled wheat grains. Therefore, if barley is quite dominant then the number of wrongly ascribed grains from the unidentified cereal category as hulled wheats that are in fact barley may be quite high.

Lastly, if barley was the more dominant crop on the Bronze Age sites then, prior to the dehusking of such grains, spikelets of hulled wheats (if growing as weeds) may be removed through the use of the wheat sieve prior to dehusking (cf. Hillman 1981, figs 5–6) or through hand sorting. Such a differential removal of hulled wheat spikelets from barley grain (or free-threshing wheat grains), and their subsequent burning with other cereal processing waste, would lead to higher ratios of hulled wheat grains to glumes and could therefore also be used to further support the patterns seen.

Storage patterns as seen on the excavated sites

Many of the samples contained very few weed seeds, grain and/or chaff, often indicative of poor preservation conditions. This is further emphasised by the low number of identifiable cereal grains. The problems of the over representation of both grains over weed seeds and chaff, and to a lesser extent of large weed seeds over smaller weed seeds must therefore be taken into account.

Bronze Age

For the Bronze Age sites, Patteson's Cross was dominated mainly by small weed seeds, which out numbered both larger weed seeds and grain. The site appears to have been storing its grain in a relatively unprocessed state, possibly even as sheaves. Such a pattern is indicative of low levels of social organisation during, and straight after, harvest. The samples had very few glume bases compared to estimated glume wheats, although most cereal grains were not identifiable and so may have been of barley rather than glume wheats.

Smaller weed seeds, as opposed to larger weed seeds, generally dominated the samples from Castle Hill, although all contained more grain. The samples were also all grain rich as opposed to glume rich, with the exception of three samples from four-post structure 1754. The results for most of the samples may indicate similar patterns to that seen for Patteson's Cross, especially if poor preservation is responsible for the high proportion of grains. The samples from four-post structure 1754 also contained very high ratios of glume bases to weed seeds, however, indicating that a taphonomic bias may not be entirely the cause. This high ratio of grain and in some cases glume bases as seen for many of the assemblages is discussed below.

Similarly the samples from Hayne Lane are mainly dominated by small weed seeds. The samples are on the whole, therefore, of similar arable storage and processing practices to those described for Patteson's Cross. Several samples, however (four from the post-holes of round-house 458), contained high ratios of grains to weed seeds and two of these had mainly large weed seeds, although the number of weed seeds in these samples was very low. The ratio of grains to glumes was also very high, so it is possible that these samples may represent the charring of semi-cleaned grain. However, it is equally possible that the samples may represent material that came into the post-holes from trampled hearth material, which would strongly favour the preservation of cereal grains as opposed to glume bases and weed seeds. Samples from round-house 459 also contained a high proportion of barley and slightly higher amounts of large weed seeds. The ratio of glumes to grain was, however, higher. The possibility that this sample represents the mixing of processing waste with semi-cleaned barley cannot be ruled out, although the problems are similar to those outlined above.

Iron Age

Blackhorse shows a similar pattern to the Bronze Age sites, again mainly dominated by smaller weed seeds, with the proportion of grain to weed seeds being approximately equal. Again several of the samples were quite low in weed seeds, and possibly the pattern is somewhat distorted by preservation conditions. Generally, the pattern is similar to Patteson's Cross.

From Langland Lane the samples were generally very poor, so the domination of grain is perhaps unsurprising. However, small weed seeds dominate over larger ones, perhaps indicating a similar pattern to the other sites. The samples from Long Range were dominated by grain over weed seeds, and small weed seeds over large weed seeds. However, several of the samples were also fairly glume rich so that the differences may not entirely be due to preservation, but may indicate storage as semi-cleaned spikelets. However, in light of the small amount of material and number of samples, it is difficult to state this with any certainty.

General conclusions

With the exception of Long Range, the results as plotted in Figure 96 seem to indicate that most samples probably result from storage in an uncleaned form. This further suggests that agricultural activities were organised on the basis of individual family groups (Stevens 1996). Similar patterns can be seen at the Bronze Age settlement at Trethellan Farm, Newquay, in Cornwall, where the ratio of small weed seeds was generally higher than those of large seeds, but many samples were also dominated by grain (Straker 1991). The Iron Age pattern also compares well with the sites lying in the west of the Upper Thames Valley (Stevens 1996; forthcoming). However, the amount of grain in the samples from the current project is generally much higher. In part this may be due to poor preservation conditions, however, the number of rootlets present may, as suggested by Clapham, indicate some uprooting of crops, though the presence of non-twining species, also indicates some cutting low down on the culm (cf. Hillman 1984). Crops harvested by uprooting naturally contain fewer seeds of weed species, and it is possible that some of the results seen indicate a mixture of harvesting methods, by uprooting and sickle, which would in turn explain some of the higher proportions of grain.

Summary

As we have seen, most of the palaeo-environmental evidence for modern Devon in the prehistoric period is palynological with few analyses of plant macrofossils. Although that evidence suggests that there was small scale woodland clearance and regeneration during the Neolithic, the Bronze Age saw a reduction in woodland regeneration with pastoralism becoming the main farming practice. As has often been discussed, the economic activity that can be inferred from pollen studies is rather limited in certain regards, and is often regional rather than local. The evidence gleaned from the analyses of the plant macrofossil of the settlements studied here suggests a far more complicated picture. The charcoals and macrofossils suggest that woodland clearance occurred in the lowlands during the Neolithic and that emmer wheat was being cultivated. In the Bronze Age there may well have been increased agricultural activity with the clearing of grasslands in order to cultivate more crops, such as emmer, spelt, and bread wheats along with others such as barley, and also the celtic bean, peas, and flax. It appears that a similar suite of crops was cultivated in the Iron Age in contrast to Wessex where emmer had practically disappeared by the Iron Age (Table 62). Other habitats may have been exploited such as the moorlands, which may well have been present in patches on the lowlands. In general, arable cultivation appears to have been the main agricultural activity in the lowland region.

The crop-processing model suggests that the crops may have been harvested by a combination of cutting low down on the stem, most likely with a sickle, and uprooting. Unlike the pattern seen at Iron Age hillforts in Wessex and beyond (for example, Maiden Castle, Dorset, Danebury, Hampshire, and Wandlebury in Cambridgeshire (Stevens 1996)), the crops appear to have been stored with a minimal amount or possibly even no processing, as either sheaves or threshed and winnowed crops. These crops were then stored (possibly in three- or four-post granaries) and small quantities taken out and processed piecemeal as and when they were needed. This small scale year round processing consisted at least of coarse sieving to remove remaining straw and grass stems (i.e., false-oat grass and rootlets), fine sieving to remove small and intermediate size weed seeds, hand sorting to remove grain sized (large) weed seeds, and, lastly, the pounding and removal of glumes or husks. The waste from this processing was subsequently use or accidentally became incorporated into domestic fires and finally into the archaeological features from which they were recovered.

The amount of processing carried out before storage is largely influenced by either climatic factors (*cf.* Hillman 1981) or the amount of available labour around harvest. It is possible that some of the patterning seen may result from the somewhat wetter climate in the south-west than further east and north. However, only the analysis of more sites in the region can determine the cause of such differences. In the Upper Thames Valley differences between contemporary sites in the same climatic region were interpreted as being due to differences in the social organisation of agricultural labour. At present then, all the sites in the region display patterns that are associated with smaller levels of social interaction for agricultural activities, with at least harvesting and initial mass processing carried out by individual families or small households.

The Radiocarbon Dates,
by Michael J. Allen

The series of 28 determinations obtained from the six sites of prehistoric date has been discussed on a site by site basis above. It is helpful to review briefly the evidence for these absolute determinations for the relative chronology as it is the first time that a sequence of absolute determinations has become available for east Devon. The results are presented in Table 65 and in a single figure containing all the probability histograms (Fig. 97).

The radiocarbon dates span the Neolithic at Castle Hill (AA-30670, 4630±50 BP, 3610–3140 cal. BC) to the Late Iron Age at Blackhorse (GU-7227, 2000±50 BP, 160 cal. BC–cal. AD 90). The probability distributions enable some intra-site comparison from which a crude chronological framework for the radiocarbon dated archaeological activity can be provided (Table 65). This data can be used to model phases for the series of dated events and six dated episodes of activity emerge. This sequence is, however, only of radiocarbon dated events; other activity for which there is archaeological or artefactual evidence cannot be accounted for within this model and it is for this reason that the pottery has been the principal material used for dating. The dated phase events modelled here are radiocarbon date ranges.

The dated events ascribed to the Neolithic at Castle Hill are spread over nearly a millennia. In the wider context of the suite of dates, this is an isolated dated episode and there is a short gap before the next dated events (the Early Bronze Age dates from pits at Castle Hill and Patteson's Cross). However, from the Middle Bronze Age to the Late Iron Age a series of phases can be modelled which prescribe discrete, rather than overlapping, groups of dated events or phases. A continual sequence is not present but a series of discrete 'phase events', which are set out below (Tables 66 and 67).

A series of dated events occurs between 1500 and 1000 cal. BC and includes the use of the enclosure and the setting out of the field system at Castle Hill, the building of the enclosure or compound and the round-houses at Patteson's Cross, and the farm compound and round-houses at Hayne Lane. It may be noted that the longevity of occupation at Hayne Lane attested by the radiocarbon dates is difficult to reconcile with the other categories of evidence (Chapter 5). The phase event ends by *c.* 1000 cal. BC and although the radiocarbon probability distributions for the next phase event (1000–800 cal. BC; Middle–Late Bronze Age) overlap the previous; the highest probability is that together they represent a discrete and subsequent event. Only one determination at Blackhorse occurs between this phase (Middle–Late Bronze Age) event and the last prehistoric phase, though many of the dated events in this last phase (400–1 cal. BC; Middle–Late Iron Age) may have had their undated origins in the

Table 65: Radiocarbon results from prehistoric sites (all based on charcoal)

Site and Context	Species	Lab. No.	Result BP	$\delta^{13}C‰$	Calibration BC (2σ)
Blackhorse					
Recut penannular gully 203, single fill	*Quercus*	Gu-7227	2000±50	-24.1	160 cal. BC–cal. AD 90
Pit 161, inside penannular gullies 136-7, single fill	*Prunus*	AA-30659	2065±45	-26.6	200 cal. BC–cal. AD 20
Enclosure ditch 132, S side, central fill	*Quercus*	AA-30661	2120±45	-23.3	360–30
Enclosure ditch 132, SE corner, central fill	*Prunus*	AA-30660	2125±45	-26.4	370–40
Four-post structure 127, post-hole 71, single fill	*Quercus* sapwood	AA-30662	2175±50	-24.7	390–100
Round-house 1, post-hole 4, single fill	*Quercus* sapwood/ roundwood	GU-7840	2370±60	-24.9	770–370
Long Range					
N terminal penannular gully 4, 2ndry fill	Pomoideae, *Prunus*, *Quercus*, Salicaceae	AA-30663	2090±45	-25.1	350 cal. BC–cal. AD 10
Pit 26, top fill	*Quercus* sap/ round-wood	GU-7847	2100±50	-25.8	360–0
S terminal penannular gully 269, top fill	*Corylus, Fraxinus, Quercus, Ulex/Cytisus*	GU-7845	2220±70	-24.8	400–100
Three-post structure 275, PH 118, single fill	*Quercus*	AA-30664	2275±45	-25.8	410–200
Langland Lane					
N. terminal, penannular gully 76, single fill	*Prunus, Quercus, Ulex/Cytisus*	AA-30665	2295±45	-23.9	410–240
Hayne Lane					
Round-house 458, post-hole 44, single fill	*Alnus, Corylus* roundwood, Pomoideae, *Prunus, Quercus* sapwood, Salicaceae, *Ulex/Cytisus*	AA-30679	2715±50	-26.7	900–800
Pit 113, SW of round-house 458, single fill	*Corylus, Fraxinus,* Pomoideae, *Prunus, Quercus* roundwood, Salicaceae	AA-30680	2730±55	-25.0	1000–800
Enclosure ditch 19, E side, dumped burnt material	*Alnus*, Pomoideae, *Prunus, Quercus* sapwood, Salicaceae	AA-30676	2725±50	-25.6	1000–810
N terminal, enclosure ditch 19, secondary fill	*Prunus*	AA-30677	2980±50	-28.9	1400–1040
Round-house 459, post-hole 287, single fill	*Corylus* l	AA-30678	3125±50	-28.2	1520–1260
Patteson's Cross					
S terminal ditch 4066, enclosure 4068, secondary fill	*Prunus, Quercus, Ulex/Cytisus*	AA-30668	3040±45	-25.5	1430–1160
Round-house 2357, post-hole 4060, single fill	*Quercus* sap/hearthwood	AA-30667	3120±50	-26.1	1510–1260
Round-house 1705, post-hole 1735, single fill	*Quercus* sapwood	AA-30666	3280±45	-25.1	1690–1440
Pit 1788, single fill	*Quercus* sapwood	AA-30669	3630±45	-27.7	2140–1880
Castle Hill					
4-post group 1812, single fill PH 1745	*Quercus* heartwood	AA-30672	2765±50	-25.9	1080–820
W terminal enclosure ditch 5026, primary fill	*Prunus*	AA-30673	2985±50	-26.6	1400–1050
Enclosure ditch 5026, top fill	*Prunus*	AA-30674	3035±50	-24.7	1420–1130
Field system ditch 107, single fill	*Corylus*, Pomoideae, *Prunus, Quercus* sapwood, Salicaceae, *Ulex/Cytisus*	AA-30671	3060±55	-24.6	1440–1150
Enclosure ditch 5026, primary fill	*Quercus* sapwood	AA-30675	3115±50	-23.7	1510–1260
Pit 1130	*Corylus* charcoal	AA-32605	3850±60	-23.7	2470–2130
Enclosure 219, terminal N side	charcoal	Beta78183	4220±60	–	2920–2600
Enclosure 219, terminal S, side, single fill	*Prunus*	AA-30670	4630±50	-25.0	3610–3140

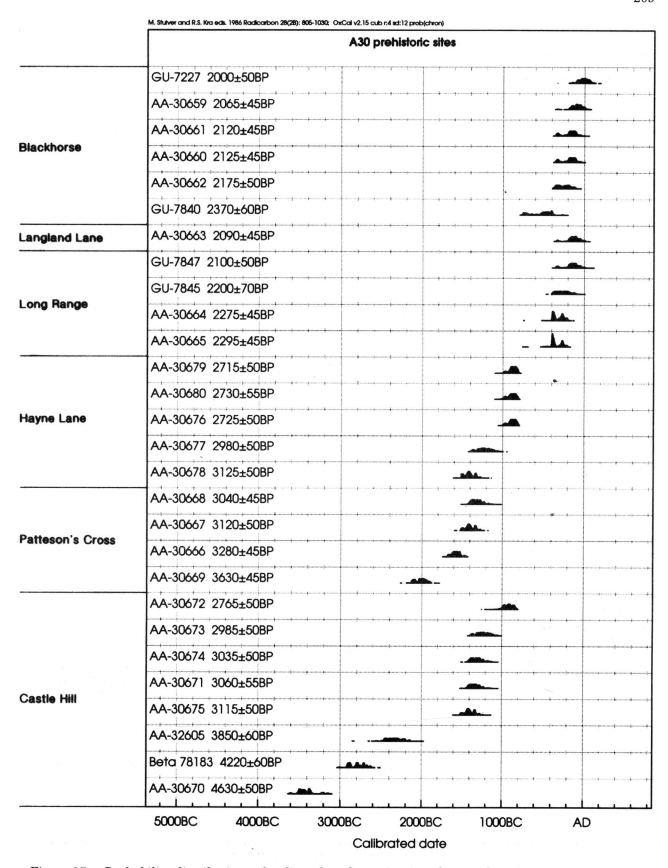

Figure 97   Probability distributions of radiocarbon determinations from prehistoric sites

Table 66: Radiocarbon phases for the prehistoric sites

Neolithic	Early Bronze Age	Middle Bronze Age	Mid–Late Bronze Age	Early Iron Age	Mid–Late Iron Age
3600–2600 cal. BC	2400–1990 cal. BC	1500–1100 cal. BC	1000–800 cal. BC	750–400 cal. BC	400–1 cal. BC
Castle Hill					
	Castle Hill				
	Patteson's Cross				
		Hayne Lane			
		Castle Hill			
			Hayne Lane		
			Castle Hill		
				Blackhorse	
					Blackhorse
					Langland Lane
					Long Range

Table 67: Occurrences of radiocarbon dated events by dated phase period

Phase	Period	Date (cal. BC)	Determinations
6	M–LIA	400–1	Blackhorse: GU-7227 AA-30659–62
			Langland Lane: AA-30665
			Long Range: AA-30663–4, GU-7847, GU-7847
5	EIA	750–400	Blackhorse: GU-7840
4	M–LBA	1000–800	Hayne Lane: AA-30677, AA-30679, AA-30680
			Castle Hill: AA-30672
3	MBA	1500–1100	Hayne Lane: AA-30677–8
			Patteson's Cross: AA-30666–8,
			Castle Hill: AA-30671, AA-30673–5
2	EBA	2400–1990	Castle Hill: AA-32605 Patteson's Cross: AA-30669
1	Neo	3600–2600	Castle Hill: AA-30670, Beta-78183

Early Iron Age phase. This is particularly true of the activity at Blackhorse.

The final prehistoric dated phase (400–1 cal. BC), like that of the Middle–Late Bronze Age occurs as a discrete episode, and includes penannular gullies, four-post structures and pits at Blackhorse, a penannular gully at Langland Lane and penannular gullies and pits at Long Range.

Material Culture, by Lorraine Mepham

The artefactual assemblages recovered from the six sites of prehistoric date combine to form a valuable data-set which provides an opportunity, currently unparalleled in Devon, to examine aspects of material culture from a chronological sequence extending from the Mesolithic period through to the Late Iron Age. This section aims to present an overview of the combined artefactual assemblage from the six excavations. As noted above,

the finds of prehistoric date from Pomeroy Wood are not included here as it is possible that a considerable quantity of them were introduced to the site in the Roman period amongst the turf used in the rampart of the early Roman military base.

It must be admitted straight away, however, that the artefacts are limited in terms of material types represented; pottery and flaked stone make up the bulk of the combined assemblage. Other material types – other worked/utilised stone, fired clay – are present in much smaller quantities, and not on every site. This places a limit on the functional and economic aspects that can be explored; there is scant evidence, for example, of craft activities such as textile production (limited to five loomweights and one spindle whorl from Hayne Lane, and a possible spindle whorl from Blackhorse). Nevertheless, the assemblages enable two main themes to be pursued:

- the exploitation of raw materials on a local and regional basis, as exemplified by the flaked stone assemblages and, to a lesser extent, the other worked stone objects;
- ceramic production and distribution from the earlier Neolithic to the Late Iron Age.

A third theme, intra-site spatial patterning in artefacts for various sites has been presented within the individual site reports, and is summarised below.

Exploitation of Raw Materials

The assemblages of flaked stone (1100 pieces in total were recovered) provide evidence for the use at various times of Greensand chert, Portland chert, chalk flint, gravel flint, and flint from clay-with-flints. Of these, Greensand chert, gravel flint, and flint from clay-with-flints deposits may be regarded as locally accessible raw materials, while Portland chert, Beer flint, and chalk flint would have been brought in from further afield.

The evidence from these has to a large extent confirmed the patterns of raw material exploitation already observed for the county for the early prehistoric period, in which Mesolithic assemblages are characterised by a diverse use of localised raw materials (e.g., Greensand chert in east Devon), while Neolithic assemblages are typified by a pronounced use of good quality flint, predominantly non-local, mainly from chalk or clay-with-flints, with little from beach deposits or river gravels (Norman 1975; Silvester *et al.* 1987; Berridge and Simpson 1992). The pattern is, however, perhaps not so clear-cut. While present at many of the sites there is insufficient material of Mesolithic date to allow comment, but the early Neolithic blade industry at Castle Hill utilised both flint and chert, although it is difficult to be certain what proportion of each raw material was used. There is evidence for chert knapping on site at Castle Hill in the form of refitting flakes and cores from enclosure ditch 218; the evidence for on-site flint knapping is more ambiguous.

Exploitation patterns for the Bronze Age in Devon have not as yet been established, but evidence from the current project do not suggest a preference for a particular type of raw material. The identifiable Bronze Age industries from Castle Hill, Patteson's Cross and Hayne Lane indicate the use of both chert and flint. Chert was again being knapped on site at Castle Hill, where refitting cores and flakes were found in the features to the west of the Middle Bronze Age enclosure, and also at Hayne Lane, where refitting material came from the enclosure ditch. This seems to mark a return to the pattern observed for the Mesolithic period in earlier work, with an emphasis on the use of locally available raw materials, although chalk flint is still in use at this time. The expedient use of local raw materials is characteristic of Bronze Age flint assemblages throughout lowland England (e.g., Ford *et al.* 1984; Young and Humphrey in press). In all three of the Bronze Age industries, however, there does appears to be a preference for flint to be used for tool manufacture.

Alongside the flint and chert can be set the small amount of other worked stone, which occurs on four sites (Castle Hill, Hayne Lane, Long Range, and Blackhorse) as portable objects (quernstones, whetstones, rubbers, and two spindle whorls). In nearly every case the stone types utilised can be found within the local Permian series, and this includes lavas (quernstones), quartz porphyry (one quern fragment), and fine-grained sandstones (whetstones, rubbers, and spindle whorls). This pattern obtains on both Bronze Age and Iron Age sites (there are no stone artefacts earlier than Bronze Age). The only exception is a single Middle Bronze Age greenstone whetstone from Castle Hill.

Ceramic Production and Distribution

The total prehistoric assemblage from the six sites amounts to 2903 sherds weighing 27,137 g, and covers a chronological sequence, albeit intermittent, from the Early Neolithic through to the Late Iron Age. For the early prehistoric period (early Neolithic to Early Bronze Age) the evidence is sparse, but three sites (Castle Hill, Hayne Lane, and Patteson's Cross) produced good Middle or Middle–Late Bronze Age groups, and significant Middle–Late Iron Age groups came from Blackhorse and Long Range.

The Early Neolithic period is represented by the three vessels from Long Range, all in locally produced (sandy or chert-tempered) fabrics. The occurrence of locally manufactured wares alongside imported Cornish gabbroic ware pots is well known (Whittle 1977, 77–82), and the use of Greensand chert as a temper has been recorded elsewhere (Liddell 1931, 92; Smith 1981). Other early Neolithic groups have been recorded in Devon from Hazard Hill (Houlder 1963), Membury (Tingle 1999), and Haldon, Nymet Barton, and Raddon (H. Quinnell pers. comm.), and serve to demonstrate a range of fabric types representing a variety of local sources, which are as yet poorly understood. There is little more that this small group can add to the ceramic sequence for Devon beyond the confirmation that Early Neolithic ceramics do occur outside the major sites such as Hembury, although their discovery is likely to be a matter of chance, as in this instance. In this respect the excavation here of a single isolated pit can be compared with the discovery of a similarly isolated pit group at Nymet Barton (Quinnell unpubl. b).

If the evidence for the early Neolithic is sparse, the Late Neolithic is practically non-existent in Devon. Apart from two very tentatively identified sherds from Beer Head (Cleal 1998a), only one other group is published, comprising eight sherds (three Fengate style and five Grooved Ware) from Topsham (Smith 1975), and the addition of at least three, and possibly four Peterborough ware vessels from Castle Hill is therefore something of a windfall. Interestingly two (possibly three) of these are in non-local granitic fabrics with a potential source south of Dartmoor, indicating a regional production centre further to the west, although this area is as yet devoid of Late Neolithic ceramics (Quinnell 1994a, 51). It may be worth noting here the use of granitic clays in early Neolithic ceramics from assemblages around Dartmoor, e.g., Nymet Barton (Quinnell unpubl. b), suggesting that the exploitation of these sources marks a continuation from an earlier period. In addition to the granitic wares, the single chert-tempered rim sherd suggests production more local to Castle Hill.

Bronze Age ceramics are rather better understood, thanks to recent synthetic work by Parker Pearson (1990; 1995), although the emphasis here has tended towards Cornwall rather than Devon. The current sites can add very little to the Early Bronze Age ceramic sequence in the south-west. Beaker sherds were found in small quantities at Castle Hill, all apparently residual, while Collared Urns and Food Vessels are notable by their absence. The presence of the Beaker sherds does, however, serve to indicate some continuity in ceramic production from Beakers to Trevisker and other Middle Bronze Age styles, in the use of grog tempering which dominates the assemblages from Castle Hill and Hayne Lane. Parker Pearson's conclusion from his study of Beaker fabrics in the south-west was that most represent local manufacture (1990, 12), and there is no reason to assume otherwise here.

There is certainly an emphasis on local production on all three Bronze Age sites, but with an increasing range of fabric types through time. At Patteson's Cross, the earliest of the three on the basis of radiocarbon dates, the earliest feature (2140–1880 cal. BC (AA-30669; 3630±45 BP)) contained only chert-tempered fabrics; in other features (one dated 1430–1160 cal. BC (AA-30668; 3040±45 BP) chert temper was supplemented by grog temper. Fabrics containing volcanic inclusions were found at Castle Hill (broadly contemporary with the later activity at Patteson's Cross), and these are augmented by granitic and sanidine fabrics at Hayne Lane (dates ranging between 1400–800 cal. BC). The evidence here accords with that found on other sites – the small Trevisker assemblage from Heatree, Manaton, includes granitic and volcanic fabrics (Quinnell 1991), and a volcanic fabric was recorded at Clyst Honiton (Woodward and Williams 1989). Overall it is becoming apparent that east Devon is characterised by a greater variety of fabrics in the Middle Bronze Age than was recognised by Parker Pearson (1990; 1995), whose two main groups, both containing greenstone, are largely confined to the west of the county.

In terms of 'cultural influences', Trevisker style is much in evidence at Castle Hill, exemplified by a range of forms and decorative traits which can be widely paralleled across the south-west. The geographical location of the sites examined in the current project, however, places them at a cultural cross-roads in terms of ceramic styles. Other influences, less apparent than Trevisker, include Deverel-Rimbury style vessel forms at Patteson's Cross and Castle Hill. In all cases, however, this is a movement of ideas, not a movement of pots; both Trevisker and Deverel-Rimbury styles occur almost exclusively in locally produced fabrics, which fits Parker Pearson's notion of a 'frontier zone' in Devon, through which Trevisker influences, but not the pots themselves, permeated eastwards, while other influences were spreading westwards from Wessex (Parker Pearson 1990; 1995). It may be more appropriate, indeed, to see these assemblages, particularly Castle Hill, as showing a mixture of traits from the two ceramic traditions rather than as an association of vessels from both styles; this point has also been made for the recently excavated assemblage from Chard Junction Quarry, 20 km to the north-east in Dorset (Quinnell unpubl. a). The latter site provides perhaps the closest parallels for the assemblages from the current project, and emphasises the fact that much still needs to be explored in the interaction between the two ceramic styles. Beyond this the affinities of the sites from the current project appear much closer to assemblages further east and north in Somerset, than to the south-west – close comparisons can be made, for example with the Trevisker-related assemblages from Brean Down and Norton Fitzwarren (Woodward 1989; 1990), and this affinity continues into the later Bronze Age.

Elsewhere in Devon the later Bronze Age ceramics mark a discontinuity with Trevisker styles, in that there appears to be a new emphasis on local, as opposed to regional sources (Parker Pearson 1995, 97). This, however, is based on sparse evidence, since very few ceramic assemblages of this date are known (Silvester 1980). In this instance the discontinuity is not apparent, since those local sources were already in operation in the Middle Bronze Age. Evidence from the current sites tends to confirm the suggestion, based on the Dainton assemblage, that plainer wares were replacing

Trevisker styles in Devon by the end of the Middle Bronze Age (p. 112). Again, close parallels can be drawn with the Somerset sites. This replicates the situation elsewhere in southern England where Deverel-Rimbury ceramics are replaced by plainware (and subsequently decorated) 'post-Deverel-Rimbury' assemblages; the term 'post-Trevisker' has been suggested as more appropriate to the Late Bronze Age/Early Iron Age assemblages of the south-west (Quinnell 1994b, 77).

There is an apparent hiatus in the ceramic sequence in the first half of the 1st millennium BC, between the Late Bronze Age plainwares from Castle Hill and Hayne Lane to the Middle–Late Iron Age assemblages of Blackhorse and Long Range, despite the recognition of a phase of Early Iron Age activity at Blackhorse (radiocarbon dated to 770–370 cal. BC (GU-7840; 2370±60 BP). Whether this is representative of a real hiatus cannot be determined on present evidence. Other assemblages within this date range are even more elusive than for the Late Bronze Age, but the county was not completely aceramic at this period. Assemblages dated to the Early Iron Age, characterised by a range of shouldered jars and bowls, have been recorded at Mount Batten, Plymouth (Cunliffe 1988, fig. 26), Dainton (Willis and Rogers 1951, fig. 6) and Blackbury Castle (Young and Richardson 1955, fig. 10).

For the Middle–Late Iron Age, the two sites at Blackhorse and Long Range have produced pottery assemblages which are essentially comparable, comprising a range of simply decorated South-Western style wares, including fabrics from three of the regional production centres identified by Peacock (1969), but also including similar decorated wares in local fabrics, and accompanied by plain wares in similar fabrics. The identification here of Peacock's group 6 (volcanic) fabrics is interesting, given their relative scarcity up to now, but this has almost certainly been due to a lack of fieldwork in this area rather than to a real absence. Radiocarbon dates place the Blackhorse settlement in the 2nd –1st century BC, while Long Range has a wider potential date range, from 4th–1st century BC. Close similarities between the pottery assemblages suggest that there is at least some period of overlap if not total contemporaneity, with the Blackhorse settlement being occupied later. Together these assemblages confirm the association of plain wares with decorated wares, and suggest a sequence in which regionally produced decorated wares are introduced from at least the 4th century BC, to be copied by local potters, the local wares gradually becoming plainer. Cultural influences here may be regional, but seem to be limited to east Devon and south Somerset; the only long-distance imports are occasional sherds of gabbroic and Durotrigian ware. Decorative traits match those of other assemblages in the area, such as Blackbury Castle (Young and Richardson 1951, pl. xiv, figs 10–11) and Milber Down (Fox et al. 1949–50, figs 8–9), with an emphasis on simple geometric rather than complex curvilinear designs. Quinnell suggests that Devon could have been aceramic during the last century before the Roman conquest (1994b, 78), although the radiocarbon dates from both Blackhorse and Long Range could extend the ceramic sequence into the 1st century BC, and possibly as late as the first decades of the 1st century AD.

A Summary, by A.P. Fitzpatrick

This section briefly reviews in chronological order the local and regional setting of the sites and finds of prehistoric date before touching lightly on the broader theme of landscape. The Neolithic monuments at Castle Hill are, however, treated in more detail, as there is rather more uncertainty as to their exact nature than those of the other sites.

While the current project has delivered a valuable set of excavations that cover much of the later prehistoric period, the sequences they provide do not span the whole of that period. Nor, despite being found in the same project, do they necessarily possess any intrinsic unity, nor can they automatically lay claim to being representative of the area. In consequence the opportunity to write a prehistory of east Devon here, tempting though it may seem, has been eschewed. The importance of the excavations very much lies in the fact that many of the sites are the first of their kind to be excavated and published in the South-West.

Palaeolithic and Mesolithic

The earliest evidence recovered in the course of the project is represented by the Lower Palaeolithic handaxe found at Gittisham Forge. With the example found in a watching brief at Hayne Farm in 1993, they are the most northerly handaxes yet found in the Otter valley. The fact that two recent Watching Briefs within 700 m of each other have both recovered handaxes may simply be coincidental, but the topography of the two findspots is very similar which suggests that other finds are likely to be made on these gravels, recalling the concentration of finds in the Axe valley 15 km to the east (Todd 1987, 40–1; Wessex Archaeology 1993). In the meantime it may be said the two handaxes demonstrate for the first time that Lower Palaeolithic hunters had penetrated to the foothills of the Blackdown Hills.

There is little doubt that the recurrent discovery of Mesolithic–Bronze Age flaked stone at the sites excavated in the current project indicates that these places had been used for activities, and perhaps settlement, long before permanent settlements were established. This evidence is consistent with the recognition of extensive multi-period flint scatters in several parts of Devon (e.g. Berridge 1985; Miles 1976; Silvester *et al.* 1987), and the results of the watching brief at Hayne Farm which also recorded a scatter largely of Mesolithic date, even though there was relatively little evidence for this in the area before the current project (*cf.* Miles 1976, fig. 1).

Neolithic

Neolithic activity was identified in two of the excavations, at Long Range and Castle Hill. The two Neolithic monuments at Castle Hill fall within an extensive, but in many ways poorly understood, group of monuments. After briefly setting the scene, those monuments and their affinities are examined in their wider, and also local, contexts.

The Neolithic in east Devon

At Long Range it is clear that pit 241 was a single, isolated, feature within the excavated area. Its shallow bowl shape and the range of material from it – parts of three pots and three pieces of flaked stone – are consistent with the pit having been dug specially for their burial or deposition. This practice is well known throughout the Neolithic in Britain (Thomas 1991, 59–64; Tingle 1999, 12).

In general sites of Neolithic date, whether settlements or other monuments, remain rare in east Devon; the best known is the causewayed enclosure at Hembury (Liddell 1930; 1931; 1932; 1935; Todd 1984; 1987, 67–106). The flaked stone and the possible reused macehead from Castle Hill may be compared with the material from Hembury, although the small amount of Peterborough Ware from Castle Hill is later than the plain wares found at Hembury, and the radiocarbon dating is consistent with this (Fig. 98). Elsewhere, another causewayed enclosure has been discovered at Raddon, west of the River Exe (Griffith 1994, 88, fig. 1; Tingle 1998, 95). The case for the site at High Peak on the south coast at Sidmouth (Pollard 1966; 1967a) being a causewayed enclosure, or a hilltop settlement of a type increasingly well known in the south-west (*cf.* Griffith 1994, 88; Tingle 1998, 94–5), remains open.

Other ritual and funerary monuments are discussed further below, but as is the case elsewhere in Britain, other types of Neolithic settlements are rare in east Devon. The Late Neolithic one at Topsham is perhaps the best known (Jarvis and Maxfield 1975, 257–8, fig. 14) but the character of other sites, for example Salcombe Hill, Sidmouth (Pollard and Luxton 1978) is simply unknown. Other 'sites' are represented either by scatters of flaked stone which include material of Neolithic date (Miles 1976, 5), or by small quantities of pottery alone (Silvester 1981, 57–9, 78–9). However, as the find from Long Range reminds us, small quantities of pottery need not indicate the existence of settlements.

Turning to the monuments at Castle Hill it is apparent that they fall within a widely distributed group of monuments, and it is necessary to view them in this wider context. It is suggested here that enclosure 219 at Castle Hill represents the heavily denuded and truncated remains of a long mortuary enclosure. Enclosure 218 may be the terminal of either a cursus, or a long mortuary enclosure.

Long mortuary enclosures and related monuments

Although long mortuary enclosures are an increasingly well-known and widely distributed type of monument there is continuing uncertainty over their precise definition and nomenclature (Loveday and Petchey 1982, 17–20, fig. 33; Buckley *et al.* 1988; Kinnes 1992, 19, 90; D. Jones 1998), let alone their purposes. Loveday has classified long enclosures, which are largely known from air photographs rather than excavation, as being between 20–80 m long and 15–25 m wide, and forming part of what he called a 'cursus continuum' (*ibid.,* 18). The more neutral term 'oblong ditches' has also been preferred for monuments that are known only from the evidence of air photographs and could be of later date (*ibid.,* 17; Williamson and Loveday 1988).

214

M. Stuiver and R.S. Kra eds. 1986 Radiocarbon 28(2B): 805-1030; OxCal v2.15 cub r:4 sd:12 prob(chron)

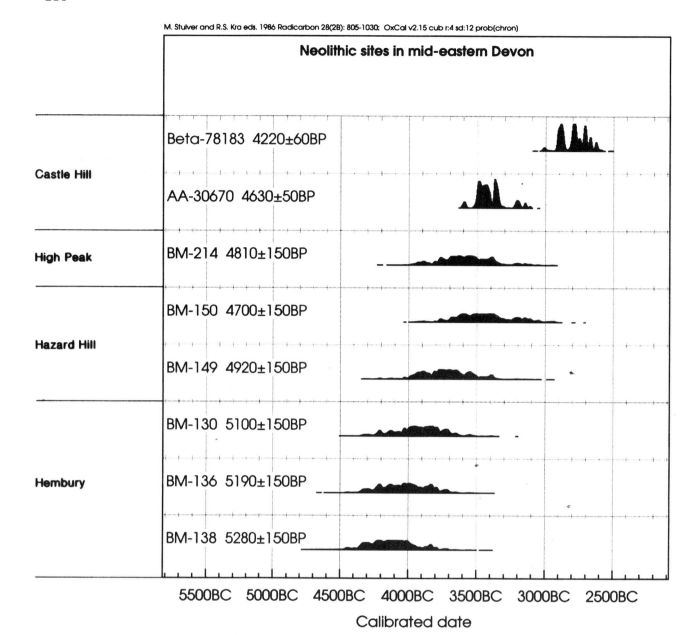

Figure 98   *Probability distributions of radiocarbon determinations from Neolithic sites in mid-eastern Devon. Sources: Fox 1963; Houlder 1963; Pollard 1967a*

Excavated examples of this group have been called variously 'long mortuary enclosures' (Vatcher 1961) or more cautiously 'long enclosures' (Whittle *et al.* 1992, 148), in distinction from the free standing mortuary houses which sometimes represent the first phase of activity at long barrow sites. The description 'long mortuary enclosure' is used here while accepting that clear evidence from the small number of excavated sites for their having played a role in mortuary practices is slight indeed (e.g., Barrett *et al.* 1991, 54; Kinnes 1992, 19). In essence the appellation relies on two strands of evidence; the first is that the excavator of the Dorchester-on-Thames monument recovered part of a human jaw within the enclosure at surface level after mechanical excavation. The second strand of evidence is the way in which the shape of the enclosure is presumed to echo those of long barrows. However, the

rarity of finds which might suggest domestic occupation, strongly supports the interpretation of these monuments as being associated with mortuary rites that involved secondary burial.

The shapes of those monuments that have been excavated ranges from the rectangular to the oval, and display considerable variety in detail (Loveday 1989, fig. 4:9). At least two enclosures are, like those at Castle Hill, open at one end but at Barford, Warwickshire (*ibid.*) and North Stoke, Oxfordshire (Case 1982) the opposing end is curved rather than right-angled. The Castle Hill enclosure is best paralleled by sites in central southern England, at Dorchester-on-Thames (Whittle *et al.* 1992) and Yarnton (Hey 1997, 106, fig. 10.5 and pers. comm.) in Oxfordshire, and Normanton Down in Wiltshire (Vatcher 1961), which is the most similar in size (Fig. 99).

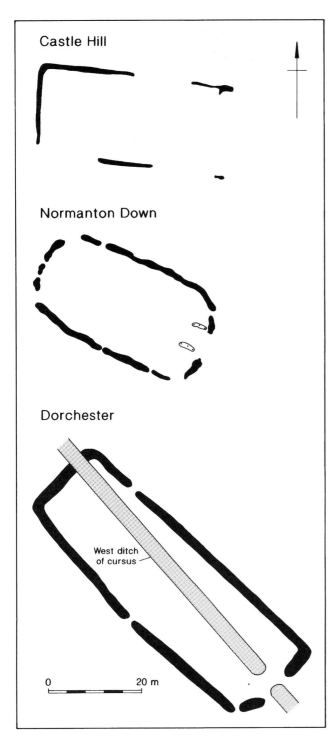

Figure 99   Comparative plans of Neolithic long mortuary enclosures

The ditches of these sites have causeways and at Normanton Down an internal bank survived as an earthwork until shortly before excavation. The slight evidence for hurdling in the ditches of enclosure 218 at Castle Hill recalls the fence in the ditch of enclosure at Inchtuthil, Perth and Kinross (Barclay and Maxwell 1991; 1998, 2).

None of the features recorded within the Castle Hill enclosures can be shown to be contemporary with them, but in enclosure 219 the shallow and undated pit 139 lies centrally and is oriented along the axis of the enclosure. It recalls the larger and deeper pits known at the Barford and North Stoke enclosures (Loveday 1989, 60, 66–7) and the axial pits beneath some long barrows, such as at Horslip, Windmill Hill, Wiltshire (Ashbee *et al.* 1979, 212, fig. 2).

The dating evidence from the Dorchester-on-Thames, Normanton Down and Yarnton enclosures is consistent, though none have yielded large assemblages of finds. The pottery from the upper fills of the ditches at all of them includes Peterborough ware and it is also recorded as having been found in the secondary fills of the long mortuary enclosure at Charlecotte, Warwickshire (Loveday and Petchey 1982, 18).

The stratigraphic position of these sherds suggests that the monuments date to the earlier Neolithic, and this echoes the sequence recorded at long barrows. Pottery from the primary fills of the ditches of long barrows is rare, and is almost invariably from plain bowls, apparently sometimes occurring even when decorated styles were current. However, the continuing deposition of Peterborough and Beaker wares in the secondary fills of these ditches is widely attested in southern England (Kinnes 1992, 109–11, 117–20, fig. 2.7.1–2; Thomas 1991, 70, 92, fig. 5.9).

The earlier Neolithic date from enclosure 219 also accords well with the radiocarbon dates from other long mortuary enclosures in England. Antler from the base of one of the bedding trenches for the 'chamber' at Normanton Down yielded a radiocarbon date of 3510–2920 cal. BC (BM-505; 4510±103 BP; BM-505). Although no radiocarbon dates are available for the Dorchester-on-Thames monument, it was cut by a cursus which elsewhere along its length yielded a radiocarbon date of 3510–2920 cal. BC (BM-2433; 4510±100 BP; Whittle *et al.* 1992, 152, tab. 12). The bank barrow adjacent to the North Stoke enclosure has a determination of 3640–3370 cal. BC (BM 1405; 4672±49 BP).

Regionality
Although only a small number of long mortuary enclosures have been excavated, there are, as might be anticipated, hints of regional variation. The sites in Scotland are distinctive (Barclay and Maxwell 1991; Barclay and Russell-White 1993), while Whittle has suggested that the enclosure at Dorchester, Oxfordshire has strong similarities with local tombs and other monuments. It is less easy to establish if this is the case with the Castle Hill enclosures, or indeed the other related, but unexcavated sites in Devon.

Those sites include the three oblong ditch sites at Nether Exe and North Tawton (Loveday and Petchey 1982, 18; Griffith 1985, fig. 1, x; pl. 10, b; 1990, 24, fig. 6; 1994, 88–9, pl. 2). The relationship of these sites to other types of monuments is uncertain. East Devon lies between two well-known traditions of megalithic tombs, in Cornwall and in the Cotswold-Severn region. The number of certain long barrows known on Dartmoor is small (e.g., Quinnell 1994a, 51–2; Todd 1987, 86–7; Fleming 1987, 112) and the nearest well-examined grouping of non-megalithic monuments is to the east in Cranborne Chase. It is with these monuments that the long barrow from Tiverton, which appears to have a U-shaped ditch, finds its closest analogies (Smith 1990, 24).

The Cranborne Chase long barrows are sufficiently distinctive for Ashbee to have distinguished them as his 'Cranborne Chase' type (Ashbee 1984, 15; Barrett *et al.* 1991, 36–43, fig. 2.17). Kinnes (1992) has classified these and related monuments in a rather different fashion but the presence of a 'U'-shaped ditch (Kinnes's type B) remains characteristic. The ditches around long barrows in Cranborne Chase are often open at the eastern end, and there is a clear preference for them being aligned to the east, and especially the south-east (Kinnes 1992, fig. 2.2.8; 2.2.11.A5). It is possible therefore that enclosure 219 at Castle Hill echoes the shape of the enclosing ditches of these long barrows. Certainly the length of enclosure 219 at *c.* 43 m falls within the median distribution of the lengths of long barrow mounds in the south-west, and the preferred location for these sites is generally on riverine gravel terraces, as at Castle Hill (Pl. 27).

Long enclosures and other monuments

While the other enclosure at Castle Hill, 218, could also be a long mortuary enclosure, it is perhaps more likely that it is the terminal of cursus, or bank barrow, or other type of monument within the closely related sites which comprise the 'cursus continuum.' These monuments regularly occur in close proximity to each other (Kinnes 1992, 65, 71, fig. 2.2.2–3; D. Jones 1998, 92). Distinguishing one type of monument from the others in the 'cursus continuum' on the limited amount of enclosure 218 that has been revealed is not possible. It is helpful, however, to recall Richard Bradley's comments 'that bank barrows are elongated mounds, whilst cursus monuments are particularly long rectangular enclosures' (1983, 15). The shallowness of the ditches of enclosure 218 at Castle Hill makes it hard to envisage any substantial co-axial mound, but the western end is certainly not enclosed.

As we have seen, a few other long enclosures are known in Devon. At Nether Exe there are two, one of which may in fact be a cursus, as well as numerous barrows and ring ditches. A large collection of flaked stone of Neolithic date has also been recovered by fieldwalking (Griffith 1990, 24, fig. 6). There are also two long enclosures from North Tawton further to the west. As recorded all these monuments are *c.* 75 m long (Loveday and Petchey 1982, fig. 32; Griffith 1985, fig. 1, x, pl. 10, b; 1994, 88–9, pl. 2). As a number of ring ditches immediately to the north of the Neolithic monuments at Castle Hill are known from aerial photographs (Pl. 22), it seems likely that other monuments of earlier Neolithic and also Bronze Age date remain to be discovered in the vicinity of Castle Hill.

The local setting

Monuments make and are part of their landscapes and it is appropriate to conclude with a brief examination of the local setting of the monuments at Castle Hill. The two monuments also need to be seen in relation to each other as the recurrent physical juxtaposition of related monuments in the Neolithic emphasises their association in the rituals enacted at them and also the importance of those places over many centuries (Bradley 1993). The evidence of the Peterborough Ware from the ditches, at what would have been the eastern end of the

monument and in the secondary fills, is entirely consistent with the evidence from related sites. As Thomas has suggested (1991, 70, 92), this may reflect a change in the association of the monuments from one with a concern with the recently deceased, to one with the ancestral dead.

The monuments at Castle Hill, both of which were apparently open at their opposed terminals, and both possibly with some form of setting in the centre, form part of this wider pattern of association and juxtaposition. Despite the damage caused to it by the Middle Bronze Age field system, there is little doubt that enclosure 218 was originally open at its western end. If the western segments of the enclosure were an extension, the monument would originally have terminated, facing west, at approximately the same point as the eastern facing enclosure 219. The location of the amorphous and undated pit 685 centrally within what might have been the original end of enclosure 218 can hardly have been fortuitous. Some of the local meanings of the monuments are surely reflected in the way that both lie above the floodplain and the orientation of enclosure 219 to the east means that it faces along the valley of the westward flowing River Otter. Enclosure 218 faces the rising sun as it appears over the southern side of the valley.

Bronze Age

The Bronze Age in Devon

In contrast to the Neolithic, the evidence of Bronze Age date from the project is more abundant and superficially at least, less problematic. The Bronze Age settlements which were examined, particularly Castle Hill and Hayne Lane, also provide valuable additions to the archaeology of this period in south-western England as whole where few lowland settlements have been examined extensively (Pearce 1983). To the south-west those lowland settlements which have been excavated on any scale – Trethellan Farm, Newquay (Nowakowksi 1991), Trevisker, St Eval (Apsimon and Greenfield 1972), and Gwithian (Megaw 1976) – are all on or close to the north Cornish coast. To the north-east the unpublished Middle Bronze Age settlement at Chard Junction Quarry, 20 km to the north-east of Hayne Lane, completely excavated in 1997 (J.W. Hawkes pers. comm.), with Shearplace Hill north of Dorchester (Rahtz and Apsimon 1962) one of the few well-explored sites in Dorset outwith Cranborne Chase.

The study of Bronze Age Devon has been dominated by Dartmoor in recent years (Fleming 1987; 1994), yet when compared with the evidence for the extensive intake of land there, there is little sign of pressure on the land in the particular area of the lowlands of east Devon examined by the project. Although parts of the uplands of Dartmoor were cultivated (Maguire *et al.* 1983), arable appears, as might be expected, to have been less important than the rearing of cattle and sheep.

Indeed, despite the appearance of an Early Bronze Age boundary at Patteson's Cross and the laying out and, perhaps piecemeal, development of a field system at Castle Hill during the Middle Bronze Age, there are comparatively few referents with the intake of the upland fringes of Dartmoor. While there may be a common idea of definition and enclosure, there is nothing from the lowlands of east Devon – or elsewhere in Devon (Silvester 1979, 43–4) – which bears comparison with the reave systems which regularly encompass areas of many hundreds of hectares or more (Fleming 1983, 220). In view of the extensive occupation of the land and the diversity of the landscape in the lowlands this should not be surprising.

The Bronze Age settlements

The impression which emerges from those sites examined in the current project and one that is supported by the recurrent discovery of earlier flaked stone at all the sites excavated and the evidence of the charred plant remains, is of the gradual establishment of long-lived settlements in areas which had been exploited for millennia before. The charred plant remains suggest a gradual, though perhaps episodic, sequence of woodland clearance, creation of pasture, and conversion to arable. The evidence of the buildings and fields at both Patteson's Cross and in particular Castle Hill, which spans much of the Bronze Age, also suggests the gradual shifting of settlements within a small area. Much the same impression is given by the Iron Age settlement at Blackhorse.

The cultivation of cereals as well as other crops in fields of the sorts that have been identified at Castle Hill clearly played a significant part in the lives of the inhabitants of the Castle Hill and Hayne Lane settlements. Gathered resources; nuts, berries, and the like, were also used. In the absence of evidence from animal bone and pollen, the balance between those resources and livestock and also hunted animals and fish remains unknown. One of the interpretations, to which the evidence of the charred plant remains is susceptible, is that some of the remains may be from hay, which was presumably used for the overwintering of cattle in or close to the settlement.

At Castle Hill only a part of the settlement enclosure, presumably a farmyard, could be examined and it was not possible to identify any buildings with certainty. This suggests that, in common with Middle Bronze Age farms elsewhere in southern England, including Shearplace Hill in west Dorset, the buildings were sited towards the rear of the compound. The deposition of what may be midden material in the enclosure ditch as Castle Hill is also similar to that at South Lodge in Cranborne Chase. Around the farmyard and also outside it were a range of post-built buildings, some of which are of four posts, with others likely to be of two posts.

In contrast, the lack of finds and charred plant remains from the Middle Bronze Age post-built buildings at Patteson's Cross suggests that they may not be dwellings or, at least, not ones which were occupied permanently. It does not appear that the two buildings were in use at the same time even though one of them (round-house 2357) may have been built with a double ring of posts which might suggest that the two buildings comprised the residential module seen at the Middle/Late Bronze Age settlement at Hayne Lane.

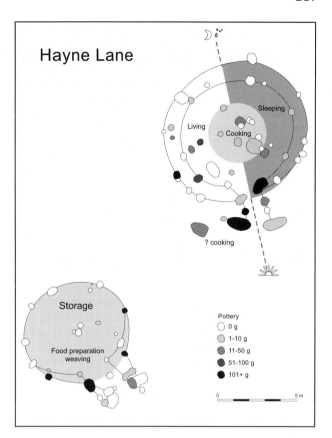

Figure 100   Interpretation of Bronze Age buildings at Hayne Lane

This familiar and widely found settlement module of a major house and an ancillary hut with a range of ancillary storage buildings and other structures appears to have been rebuilt at least once at Hayne Lane. The difficulties in interpreting the mass of post-holes should not be underplayed and are considered in Chapter 5 but the distribution of finds within the buildings (Fig. 100) shows that most of the pottery and flaked stone is found at the front and right hand side of the major residential house when viewed looking out of the porch. At least one cooking trough was sited outside the porch. The smaller building contained much less pottery and flaked stone but did contain small fragments of quern, a spindle whorl and a number of loomweights which were probably placed as foundation deposits. This may be interpreted as showing that the building was used for food preparation, textile working, and perhaps storage. The residential house has higher magnetic susceptibility readings confirming that different activities took place within the two buildings. Scattered around the site were a range of three-and four post buildings, some of which may be storage structures and a number of two post structures may have been used as drying racks, perhaps for hay.

This settlement module is thought occur widely within the Bronze Age of southern England. As well as the Shearplace Hill, Dorset settlement, there are strong similarities between the organisation of the Hayne Lane and those at Trevikser and with the recently excavated Middle Bronze Age farm at Chard Junction Quarry.

218

*Plate 22   Castle Hill: ring ditch and length of
ditch north of the excavation. The railway line is
at top right. Photograph DAP/XE6 (25 July 1994)
by Frances Griffith, Devon County Council.*

Comparisons can also be made with some aspects of
these settlements with those to the west on Dartmoor.
While stone built and also timber buildings on Dartmoor
are numerous (Fleming 1988, 78–9, 87, 92), whether
within enclosures or in the fields, they are frequently
small. On occasions, however, the style of stone
buildings compares directly with the lowland timber
buildings. This is best shown at Dean Moor where living
and cooking areas, and sleeping quarters could all be
suggested from the internal division of the buildings and
the distribution of finds. Those finds also show that
grain-processing and weaving, and perhaps pottery
manufacture were all practised (Fox 1957; Fleming
1979, 125).

Other Bronze Age sites
The evidence from the Bronze Age from the current
project is almost exclusively from settlements, but the
dead may not have been buried far from them. An
increasing number of ploughed-out ring ditches are
known from aerial photography in Devon though few
have yet been sampled by excavation (Jarvis 1976, 62–7;
Griffith 1994, 91–2; Simpson *et al*. 1989). It is not known
what date are the ring ditches immediately to the north
of Castle Hill (Pl. 22), though the presumption is that
they are Bronze Age. Most, but not all, of the dated
barrows in Devon are Early Bronze Age, but barrows
and cairns are not the only types of Bronze Age funerary
monuments. Many burials elsewhere, notably to the
east in Dorset, occur in flat cemeteries and it is perhaps

in this context that some of the charcoal filled pits
recorded in the Watching Brief to the east of the settlement (Fig. 5) might be seen.
    To the south of the current project on the heath lands
which form the eastern edge of the Otter Valley and the
head of the Sid Valley a range of well-preserved Early
Bronze Age cairns and barrows stand on the hilltops and
ridges of the Greensand plateau of Broad Down and
Farway. In their design many of the monuments have
distinct regional characteristics (Pollard 1967b; 1971),
but in other regards, particularly in the types of goods
selected for burial, they share characteristics with
burials in Wessex (Fox 1948; 1969, 39–40, fig. 2; Grinsell
1983, 14, fig.2) and beyond. Fox suggested that, as in
many other regions of Britain, the people buried there
lived on the valley floor before being brought to the high
ground to be cremated and buried (*cf*. Pearce 1983, 146,
fig. 4.11).

Conclusion
All of this suggests, that while much of the evidence from
east Devon may be compared with the well known remains on Cranborne Chase and in Wessex as a whole
(*cf*. Fleming 1994, 64–5), and the pottery with that from
Somerset as well as Cornwall, these regions all form
regional variations on well-established themes in the
British Bronze Age (*cf*. Quinnell 1988, 10; Johnson
1980).

Iron Age

As with the Bronze Age settlements, the three Iron Age
sites at Langland Lane, Long Range, and Blackhorse
make a valuable addition to the knowledge of the Iron
Age in the region. For while the well-preserved
monuments on Dartmoor may have overshadowed the
Bronze Age of Devon, this has also tended to obscure
how little is known of the Iron Age in Devon as a whole
(Silvester 1979). Apart from the site at Kestor, which
probably dates to the earlier Iron Age (Fox 1954), the
first securely dated Iron Age settlement on Dartmoor
was in fact only excavated as recently as the 1980s
(Gibson 1992). This point should not be over-
emphasised, however, as little work has been undertaken on non-hillfort settlement in western Dorset or,
the Lake Villages of Glastonbury and Meare apart, in
much of Somerset (*cf*. Cunliffe 1982).

The Iron Age in east Devon
In common with much of Britain early work on the Iron
Age focused on hillforts and they were a major concern
of the Devon Archaeological Exploration Society.
However, while the distribution of hillforts is well
known in east Devon, the quantity and quality of the
information on them recovered by excavation is limited.
Only three hillforts have seen recent excavation;
Dumpdon, Hembury, and Woodbury Castle. Slightly
further to the south, Blackbury Castle was examined
under the aegis of the Exploration Society in the early
1950s. Hembury lies 5 km north-west of Honiton,
overlooking the Otter Valley and commanding the
Blackdown Hills to the north. Dumpdon lies in a similar
position further to the east (Todd 1992), while Woodbury

Castle lies further to the south on a ridge between the valleys of the Rivers Exe and Otter (Miles 1975).

Little is known of either Dumpdon or Woodbury Castle and at Hembury, despite the excavation of more substantial areas in the 1980s relative to the work of Liddell in the 1930s, only a few fragmentary traces of circular buildings have been recorded (Todd 1984, 26). It may at least be said that the defences of both Woodbury Castle and Hembury display the sort of long and complicated sequences familiar elsewhere in Britain. In this regard, as Quinnell (as Miles 1975, 185) has noted previously, both sites have more in common with the hillforts of Wessex than the multiple enclosure sites characteristic of the remainder of the south-west (Fox 1952; 1960).

Chronology

Accordingly the relative chronology of the Iron Age in Devon as a whole is not well-defined and the uncertainties of radiocarbon dating due to the plateau in calibration do not assist. The determinations from Woodbury Castle 1930±200 BP (HAR-235(S) 400 cal. BC–540 cal. AD) (Jordan *et al.* 1994, 233–4) (cited as bc rather than BP in the excavation report) and the group from Gold Park on Dartmoor are associated with only small quantities of material. In this respect the 10 determinations from the current project are particularly useful in providing a sequence through much of the Iron Age.

These dates also introduce some new uncertainties. There is an apparent gap in the ceramic sequence from the current project between the Late Bronze Age plainwares at Hayne Lane, which are not abundant, and the Middle–Late Iron Age assemblages of Long Range and Blackhorse. This is most likely to reflect the date of the sites excavated but a general decline in the manufacture of pottery is also plausible (Todd 1987, 156). It may also be significant that the small and undiagnostic group of pottery from Langland Lane superficially shares as many similarities with pottery of Middle–Late Bronze Age date as with the other Middle–Late Iron Age sites. However, the date from Langland Lane is consistent with those from Blackhorse and Long Range where the pottery assemblages with their range of decorated South-Western style wares from local and non-local sources accompanied by local plainwares are very similar. As with much of the Bronze Age pottery, many of the stylistic affinities of the Iron Age vessels lie to the north and east in Somerset rather than further to the south-west.

None of the Iron Age sites appears to have been occupied at the Roman conquest, or more precisely at the time that Roman material began to appear on rural settlements. The hillfort at Hembury may not have been occupied in the last century or so before the Roman Conquest (Todd 1984, 261). It has been suggested that Devon could have been aceramic during the last century before the Roman conquest (Quinnell 1994b, 78). It is possible that a similar situation may have existed elsewhere in England at this time, for example in parts of East Anglia. However, as with the Early Iron Age, it is difficult to distinguish between this and other possibilities, such as a widespread shift in the pattern of settlement pattern, or simply a lack of evidence.

The settlements

With the exception of the single Early Iron Age round-house at Blackhorse which, like the Middle Bronze Age ones at Patteson's Cross, did not contain any pottery, the three settlements are dated broadly to the Middle–Late Iron Age. It appears that the enclosure of settlements occurs late in the sequence. At Langland Lane, Long Range, and in perhaps two of the three phases of building at Blackhorse, the settlements were unenclosed. The enclosure at Blackhorse appears to represent the last phase of building at the site. Similarly, the enclosed settlement at Holcombe to the south-east was established even later in the Iron Age; perhaps even in the early Roman period (Pollard 1974, 76–7).

The three Iron Age settlements were built in quite different positions, though all appear to be on slightly higher ground than those of Bronze Age date. Blackhorse occupies a low, but at *c.* 30 m AOD, locally prominent ridge overlooking the River Clyst and on the edge of the Exe valley in an area with very sandy soils. Long Range straddles the crest of a ridge at *c.* 160 m AOD on the high ground between the valleys of the Rivers Exe and Otter. The soils are heavy clays. Langland Lane lies on a clay and gravel terrace of the River Otter at *c.* 70 m AOD.

Despite their diverse locations, the evidence for farming from these sites is generally consistent. In contrast to the Bronze Age sites, the charred plant remains from Langland Lane and Long Range were generally poorly preserved, and this is also true of the samples from the ditches and gullies at Blackhorse. However, all three sites yielded evidence for bread, spelt, and emmer wheat, and small quantities of barley, and field beans and peas were also recognised. Most of these remains were found in deposits of material, often including pottery, which may have been deliberately placed in specific locations, such as the terminals of ditches and gullies (*cf.* Hill 1995).

At Long Range the evidence for crop-processing includes a barley crop and also some indication of the gathering of a wild harvest in the form of pignuts and hazel nuts. As with the sites of Bronze Age date there is the suggestion that the some of the crops were harvested by a combination of cutting low down on the stem, and by uprooting. They were then stored uncleaned. There is little reason to suggest that Long Range was significantly different from the slightly later settlement(s) at Blackhorse so the apparently higher proportion of grain that was stored as semi-cleaned spikelets at Long Range may be due to the small size of the sample. It is also possible, though, that there was a period of greater social hierarchisation at the time that the hillforts in east Devon were built and that this was reflected in the organisation of agricultural labour. The data are, however, too small to allow further these matters to be explored further.

At Blackhorse the best evidence for crop processing in the form of chaff from cereals and species characteristic of cultivated fields comes from the round-houses 136–7 and the range of four-post buildings outside the enclosure. These buildings may be earlier than the enclosure but due to the poor preservation of the samples from the enclosed settlement it is difficult to assess if there were any changes through time.

Architecture

The change during the course of the Iron Age from smaller post-built houses, which sometimes occur in pairs as a major house and an ancillary hut, to a single larger residential building, is emphatic (Figs 101 and 102). The demarcation of the Iron Age houses by the digging of boundary ditches that encircle them also clearly distinguishes the houses of Middle–Late Iron Age date from those of Bronze Age–Early Iron Age date. This emphasis on the definition of space is a recurrent feature of the Iron Age settlements over much of southern England.

In some regions this definition occurs intermittently, suggesting that it was not necessarily functional. Accordingly, it remains uncertain if the penannular gullies at Langland Lane, Long Range, and Blackhorse were circular drainage gullies or held the timbers of 'ring groove' or trench built houses. In the case of Langland Lane it is important to remember that the site was identified as the topsoil over it was being stripped by box scrapers and it is likely that smaller post-holes were destroyed (*cf.* Guilbert 1975). However, in view of the range of building techniques known in the Iron Age (e.g., Allen *et al.* 1984), evidence that the trenches held timbers is required to demonstrate convincingly that the gullies are foundation trenches. This may be evident within only two of the gullies, both at Blackhorse. Here a number of possible stake-holes were found in gullies 136 and 137 and on this basis it may be suggested that these buildings were stake built with the entrances being braced by timber sills. There is no evidence for any porch. It is noticeable that these gullies are rather smaller than the other wider, and deeper, gullies of Iron Age date (Fig. 102).

No evidence for stakes or other timbers was recorded in the other five complete penannular gullies or the fragmentary one(s) at Long Range. All of these gullies are appreciably wider than gullies 136–7 at Blackhorse, and post-holes which would have supported the substantial timbers of the porch were encompassed by gullies 203 at Blackhorse and 76 at Langland Lane. As all four of the posts of the porch were identified at Langland Lane, it must be regarded as probable that all five of the complete gullies represent 'eaves drip' gullies and that all evidence for the foundations of the house proper had been destroyed by cultivation. It is note-worthy that gully 203 is sited at the highest point of the low hill on which the Blackhorse settlements were built, and the Langland Lane and Long Range settlements were also on the highest points in their environs.

This location and the use of a different building technique, may account for the preservation of the earlier post built round-house 1 at Blackhorse, as it is sited slightly off the crest of the hill. It may be noted in parentheses here that this suggests that house 5 at Gold Park, Dartmoor is less likely to have been trench built than was claimed (Gibson 1992). No certain packing stones or postholes were recovered from the penannular gully, which again encompasses the porch. In contrast packing stones and post-holes were identified at structure 1, only *c.* 50 m away, but there was no evidence for an internal ring of substantial timbers. Nonetheless, it is salutary to recall that with the addition of the building(s) from Berry Down hillfort near Newton Abbot

in the south-west (Gallant and Silvester 1985, 48) these are almost all of the Iron Age timber buildings known in Devon.

Social Space

The setting of the Neolithic monuments at Castle Hill in their landscape has been considered above. The settlements examined by the current project have yielded valuable spatial information which inform a wider context. The organisation of the Bronze Age settlement at Hayne Lane has been summarised above and discussed more fully in Chapter 5 above where it has been argued that the houses comprise a 'module' of a major residential house and an ancillary building. The distribution of the finds within them also allows an interpretation of the way the buildings were used to be advanced (Fig. 100).

A series of studies on the Iron Age of Britain have shown that the uses, and social construction of space, were often clearly prescribed (e.g., Fitzpatrick 1997, Gwilt 1997; Hill 1995; Parker Pearson 1996). The entrances to the Bronze and Iron Age houses from the current project face to the east or south-east (Figs 101 and 102) (Oswald 1997), as do the entrances to the enclosures at Castle Hill and Blackhorse, and in this they form part of a now well-defined tradition. This order is also reflected in the discard and deposition of material culture although the only category of data which is sufficiently numerous to provide reliable information is the pottery.

The sample is, however, too small, and generally fragmented, to explore any correlations between form, fabric, and decoration in a meaningful way. Despite some of the pottery coming from features with clear stratigraphic sequences, the material was not deposited consistently through those sequences. Instead, much of it was found in relatively large deposits, either in the terminals of penannular ditches or in the south eastern corner of the enclosure ditch at Blackhorse. At present, it can only be said that little variation or correlation is apparent between form, fabric, decoration and sequence.

All the pottery from Langland Lane came from the northern terminal of the penannular gully. At Long Range 137 of the 146 sherds in gully 4 came from the terminals, with most in the northern terminal. Seventy-one of the 81 sherds found in gully 269 also came from the terminals, with most found in the southern terminal. At Blackhorse 72 of 79 sherds in gully 203 came from the southern terminal. No pottery was found in gullies 136–7 at Blackhorse which are likely to represent foundation trenches.

This may also be expressed as if viewed from the inside of the houses looking out.

Left	*Right*
Langland Lane (76)	
Long Range (4)	
	Long Range (269)
	Blackhorse (203)

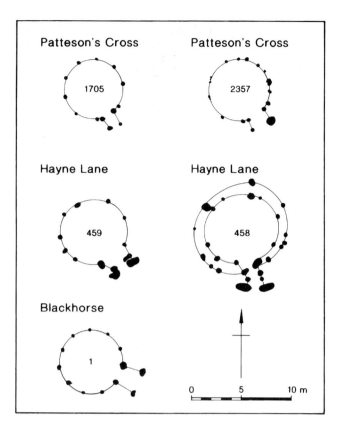

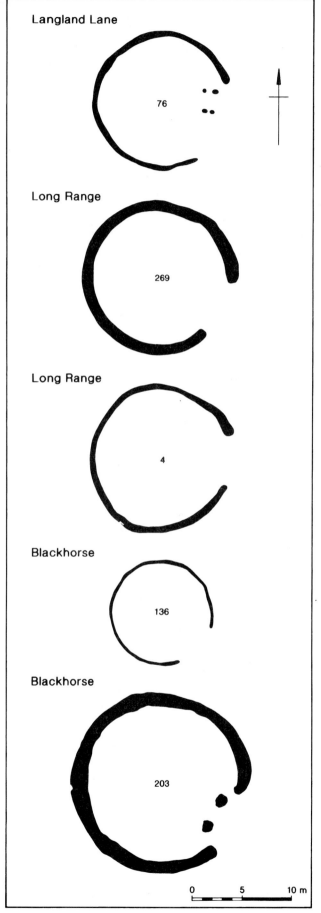

Figures 101 (above) and 102 (opposite) Bronze Age and Iron Age round-houses (post-hole and gully structures) from the prehistoric sites

This 'pattern' is not necessarily of chronological significance as at Long Range both the radiocarbon dates and the pottery agree that gully 269 is earlier than gully 4.

The importance of these distributions is underscored by the distribution of material within the enclosure ditch at Blackhorse (Fig. 103). Here the pottery, but also the objects of stone are clearly found principally in the southern half (or right hand side) of the enclosure. The distribution of the objects of stone is also shown in Figure 103. Of these, two of the three quern fragments, one of the two rubbers and the piece of unworked granite all come from the southern half of the enclosure ditch and the penannular gully, a type of distribution which is becoming increasingly well known on sites of Iron Age date throughout the British mainland.

The other objects of stone from Blackhorse were a fragments of quern in post-hole 4 of Early Iron Age house 1 and in post-hole 34 of structure 6, a rubber which was found in pit 318 which lay within gully 203, and an unidentified object was found in post-hole 654 (associated with gullies 136 and 137). The two quern fragments may have been reused as packing for posts, but the other two objects occur in post-holes or pits sited centrally within houses and may represent accidental breakages or losses.

At Long Range only the charcoal from southern terminal of gully 269 was suitable for analysis, which in itself echoes the distribution of the pottery. The charred plant remains from both terminals were sufficiently well-preserved to merit analysis but there were no

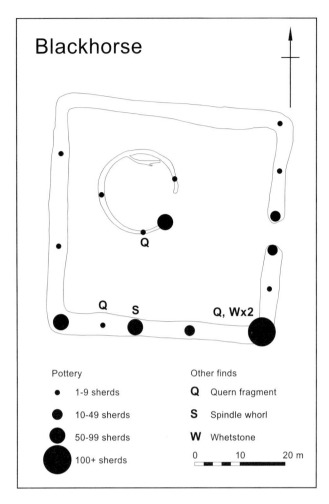

Blackhorse

Pottery
- 1-9 sherds
- 10-49 sherds
- 50-99 sherds
- 100+ sherds

Other finds
- **Q** Quern fragment
- **S** Spindle whorl
- **W** Whetstone

0   10   20 m

Figure 103   Blackhorse: distribution of finds in enclosure ditch 132 and gully 203

significant differences between the samples. Charcoal was sufficiently well preserved in both the terminals of gully 4 for the samples to be analysed and this shows that, like the pottery, there was more material in the northern terminal and that some of this material may have been burnt *in situ*. At Blackhorse only one sample from the enclosure ditch and penannular gully 203 contained significant quantities of charred plant remains and charcoal, the southern terminal of the gully. It is possible that, once again, this material was deliberately burnt *in situ*.

These patterns of deposition are characteristic of much of the Iron Age in southern England but the excavation of the settlements of Blackhorse, Langland Lane, and Long Range provides the first opportunity to examine them in Devon. It is clear, though, that these settlements have more affinities with those of Dorset and Somerset than with the emerging pattern of settlement types in Cornwall.

Landscape

Although it is commonplace for archaeologists to talk of continuity in settlement or in the landscape, it should be recognised there is little evidence for this on the sites of prehistoric date. Castle Hill provides the longest sequence, which might span the later Neolithic and much of the Bronze Age, but there is little evidence for Early and Late Bronze Age activity within the excavated area. The Middle Bronze Age field system was laid out across the largely infilled Neolithic monuments whose meanings, if they had not been forgotten, seem likely to have changed.

Instead most of the excavated areas have some evidence for the episodic use and reoccupation of particular areas and settlements. At Patteson's Cross the two round-houses may be separated by several generations, and the land boundary and compound may be similarly different in date. The same may also be true of Hayne Lane where one possibility among several is that the settlement was reoccupied or rebuilt after several generations had passed. Only at the latest of the sites, Blackhorse, is more intense and perhaps continuous activity seen over a shorter period. Here it seems likely that there was an open settlement in which there were at least two phases of building before it was eventually enclosed. It is not known with any certainty which of these phases, if any, the land boundaries should be associated.

The environmental evidence allows the inference that there was a general sequence in which woodland was cleared and set to pasture, before that in turn became arable land. There is also some evidence for episodes of regeneration and clearance within this broader pattern. The general impression from the structural remains and the finds is consistent with this in suggesting the repeated use of locales that were often used first in the Mesolithic. This is not the longevity or continuity of individual settlements rather than the gradual development of the landscape. The settlement pattern in the Roman period shows scant regard for this history.